MAKING WONDERFUL

MAKING WONDERFUL
Ideological Roots of Our Eco-Catastrophe

MARTIN M. TWEEDALE

UNIVERSITY of ALBERTA PRESS

Published by

University of Alberta Press
1–16 Rutherford Library South
11204 89 Avenue NW
Edmonton, Alberta, Canada T6G 2J4
amiskwaciwâskahikan | Treaty 6 | Métis Territory
uap.ualberta.ca | uapress@ualberta.ca

Copyright © 2023 Martin M. Tweedale

Library and Archives Canada Cataloguing in Publication
Title: Making wonderful : ideological roots of our eco-catastrophe / Martin M. Tweedale.
Names: Tweedale, Martin M., 1937– author.
Description: Includes bibliographical references and index.
Identifiers: Canadiana (print) 20220419582 | Canadiana (ebook) 20220419604
   | ISBN 9781772126242 (softcover) | ISBN 9781772126587 (EPUB)
   | ISBN 9781772126594 (PDF)
Subjects: LCSH: Ecology—Philosophy. | LCSH: Human ecology. | LCSH: Religion and
   science. | LCSH: Environmental disasters.
Classification: LCC QH540.5 .T84 2023 | DDC 577.01—dc23

First edition, first printing, 2023.
First printed and bound in Canada by Blitzprint, Calgary, Alberta.
Copyediting by Matthew Kudelka.
Proofreading by Tania Therien.
Indexing by Adrian Mather.

All rights reserved. No part of this publication may be reproduced, stored in a retrieval system, or transmitted in any form or by any means (electronic, mechanical, photocopying, recording, or otherwise) without prior written consent. Contact University of Alberta Press for further details.

University of Alberta Press supports copyright. Copyright fuels creativity, encourages diverse voices, promotes free speech, and creates a vibrant culture. Thank you for buying an authorized edition of this book and for complying with the copyright laws by not reproducing, scanning, or distributing any part of it in any form without permission. You are supporting writers and allowing University of Alberta Press to continue to publish books for every reader.

University of Alberta Press is committed to protecting our natural environment. As part of our efforts, this book is printed on Enviro Paper: it contains 100% post-consumer recycled fibres and is acid- and chlorine-free.

This book has been published with the help of a grant from the Canadian Federation for the Humanities and Social Sciences, through the Awards to Scholarly Publications Program, using funds provided by the Social Sciences and Humanities Research Council of Canada.

University of Alberta Press gratefully acknowledges the support received for its publishing program from the Government of Canada, the Canada Council for the Arts, and the Government of Alberta through the Alberta Media Fund.

*To all those who in the future will wonder
how they could have been left with such a world.*

CONTENTS

ACKNOWLEDGMENTS | IX
PREFACE | XI
INTRODUCTION | XVII

1 Human Life before There Were Cities | 1
2 The Trauma of Urban-Dominated Civilization | 19
3 Designers of the Inner Self | 39
4 From Zarathustra to Revolutionary Millennialism | 77
5 Apocalyptic Thought in the Medieval West | 139
6 Reformation and Utopia | 167
7 Secularizing the Millennium | 225
8 The Cult of Science | 277
9 The Vulgarization of the Millennium | 317

CONCLUSION   *Unleashing the Western* Gesellschaft | 359
NOTES | 381
WORKS CITED | 411
INDEX | 417

ACKNOWLEDGMENTS

*For helpful comments and criticism: Earle Waugh,
Charlie Schweger, and Charlie Richmond.*

*For steady encouragement and advice:
Maureen McGinley and Michelle Lobkowicz.*

*For reading a longer earlier version and
making many suggestions: David Millar.*

PREFACE

> Any effective teacher will have to try first of all to get his students to recognize uncomfortable facts—facts, I mean, that go against their own partisan opinions.
>
> —Max Weber, *The Scholar's Work*

This work is a response to my own increasingly firm conviction that Earth's ecological community consisting of the whole realm of living things, humans included, is headed for a catastrophe of immense proportions, although the exact shape it will take, the time it will take to occur, and the full extent it will attain cannot be reliably predicted. In the past few decades a huge number of written works have appeared which warn us that this is certainly a very real threat, if not a complete certainty. They also show that the catastrophe if it comes will be the result of the immense burden that the astounding growth of human economic activity coupled with exploding population has in recent times placed on the planet's natural resources and capacity to recycle the waste products that activity generates. In this book I assume that the reader has absorbed much of this literature and is by and large convinced of its message. What I go on to do is ask how this has come about. What follows is my very partial answer to that question.

Thoughtful people have very naturally focused on the very different questions of what is physically responsible for our predicament and how humanity can avoid, or at least mitigate, this catastrophe, and they have put forth some very astute and technically clever proposals. In fact, we now know the physical causes of the environmental collapse we face and, in general outline, the measures that need to be taken to ameliorate it. I do not at all mean to disparage the work that has been done to produce this knowledge, but in this work I am tackling a different question: What happened, or what did people do, that led us into this predicament in the first place? We now find ourselves destroying the natural cradle that holds and supports our civilization and way of life. How could it possibly have come about that we find ourselves in a situation in which we seem hell-bent on our own destruction? Is this not an equally urgent question to address?

Any full answer to the question, if such a thing is even possible, will have a multitude of facets. There will be a story about the development of modern science and technology, another story about politics, another about capitalist economics, another about education, and so on. I have limited myself here to ideology, and perhaps I should say exactly what I mean by that term. An ideology is a constellation of ideas and arguments, often drawn from philosophical and religious sources, which for those attracted to it serves as a justification of and motivation for some sort of program of action designed to promote societal change or preserve a certain societal order.[1] I do not use the term, or its adjectival form "ideological," pejoratively, as many nowadays frequently do. There is no implication from these terms themselves that what they label is false, misguided, biased, or subject to any of the commonly recognized intellectual faults, although these may in fact be present. Nor do I at all deny that ideological ideas have frequently been used as cover for purposes other than forwarding the ideals espoused by the ideology itself, purposes like getting rich and maintaining power and status, whether this is done by self-deception or with conscious intent. The whole popularity of an ideology may depend more on the ease with which it can serve these extrinsic purposes than on the intrinsic attractiveness of its ideals. Witness the way Christian doctrines were used as cover by the Spanish conquistadors in their pillaging of large sections of the Americas.

It is my contention in this book that the enormous economic and political expansion of Western civilization in the nineteenth and twentieth centuries that led to Western worldwide hegemony and to the very ecological destruction whose causes we seek to determine was promoted by an ideology peculiar to the West, one that had its beginnings in the ancient world but only reached full maturity in the second half of the nineteenth century. I do not maintain that this ideology is the key to the whole answer to our original question, but I do think it played a significant role. Against those who argue that ideology in general is at best a sort of epiphenomenon riding like foam on the waves of the real underlying determiners of history, I will not be arguing here. Instead I will be assuming that readers do not find this at all plausible, although neither do I suppose they think that ideology is anything like the whole story.

What follows, though, is not by any means a complete history of the ideological developments that led up to the economic expansion that has brought us to this fateful pass. What I mostly do is take the reader on a tour of a selection of texts that seem to me to express forcefully certain lines of thought that have proved significant. Out of the texts from modern Western sources arise a complex of ideas that have been taken by many to justify and inspire that expansion, and I hope to present those ideas in such a way that the reader can understand them and feel how attractive they can be. But I precede those texts with other ones mainly from ancient Greco-Roman culture, in which lines of thought were invented that were definitely not favourable to the kind of expansion the modern West has experienced and continues to promote. The aim in this case is to show that the course the West took was not an inevitable one for any technologically sophisticated civilization that had become urban-dominated. I have also included a few texts from sources in ancient and medieval India and China to show that similar tendencies were at work there, but, on account of the limits on what can be included in a single volume, my treatment of ideological developments in those cultures is far briefer than I would have liked. Using the work of a variety of scholars I have tried to place these extracts in their historical and cultural contexts. Very little of this book is based on my own original scholarly work; rather, it depends on the often groundbreaking research of others. I am particularly indebted to books by Norman Cohn and David F. Noble, but there are many other scholars whose work I have shamelessly borrowed from, while conscientiously crediting them in the notes.

Learned readers may want to challenge the choice of texts and authors I have made, and I welcome that. There may well be others that would have better illustrated the ideas I want to highlight. Also, it is not my contention that the texts and authors here presented were the most influential either in their own day or later, although some of them certainly did exercise great influence on people's ideas and even on the policies of the powers that be. Rather, I merely take them as illustrating with particular clarity and force certain ideas that became a significant part of an influential ideological complex. Sometimes the ideology illustrated is one that I claim constrained the sort of economic development we are trying to explain; in other cases it is part of what promoted and was seen to justify it.

Finally, I want to emphasize that my claim that some idea contributed to the ideological complex that has justified the kind of development that is leading to catastrophe in no way implies that I find that idea obnoxious or wrong-headed. Indeed, some ideas in that complex I am very attracted to. Likewise, where I claim that some idea contributed to a thought-system that constrained humans from taking the disastrous course they have, I am not implying that I find that idea attractive or clearly on the right track. In fact, a number of such ideas I find hopelessly unattractive. There are just a few occasions, however, where I have indulged my professional competence in philosophy to point out flaws in reasoning and other weaknesses. The reader should feel free to disagree with my assessments. What I warn the reader against, however, is the impulse to think that ideas that are so good could not possibly lead to something so bad, or that ideas that are so bad could not possibly lead to something so good. Learning to still that impulse in myself has been one of the chief benefits to me of this whole study, and I recommend it to my readers, whoever they may be.

Note to the Grammatically Sensitive Reader

At times I have used the pronoun "they" and its other cases, "them" and "their," as gender neutral and singular in number. On two occasions I have even used "themself" as a singular reflexive pronoun. I have tried to do this only where my intuitions found the practice fairly natural. In adopting this device, judged deviant by some, I draw encouragement from the fact that the great grammarian of the English language, Otto Jespersen, supported the practice with an example from Thackeray and another from Shakespeare. See his *Essentials of English Grammar* (University of Alabama Press, 1964), section 19.6_2, 193.

INTRODUCTION

*A man is the only kind of varmint, sets his
own trap, baits it and then steps in it.*
—John Steinbeck, *Sweet Thursday*

The "eco" in both "ecology" and "economics" comes from a Greek root meaning what belongs peculiarly to oneself, or more particularly to one's home. But the two words just mentioned have taken that meaning in virtually opposite directions. Ecology has assumed that our home was something we humans found ourselves in when we emerged from the last ice age and have gone on to modify in innumerable ways. That home had its own systematic order, its own *logos*, and our intrusion has meant the progressive dismantling of that order and the substitution of human-made arrangements. Economics, on the other hand, assumed at its start in Greek philosophy that our home was something we constructed and needed to govern according to certain rules we devised, its *nomoi*, although with the rise of classical economics in the late eighteenth and early nineteenth centuries the construction was thought to have rules of its own that humans violated at their peril. Human beings have always, then, lived to one degree or another in both of *two* homes; the one being "artificial" in the sense of a product of artful design, the other being something bequeathed to us by the evolution of life on Earth and "natural" in that sense.

We now know that the planet faces an *eco*-catastrophe, and the home that will be demolished is both of the above, both the tattered remnants of the one we humans found ourselves in at the beginning of the Holocene and the elaborate one we have constructed for ourselves in modern times. One recent writer, Elizabeth Kolbert, has spoken of, if not quite predicted, a "sixth great extinction" of the forms of life on Earth, an extinction brought about by the proliferation of our particular species of human, *Homo sapiens*, throughout the earth and the accompanying construction of a home totally unsuited to the home originally given us.[1] Our eco-catastrophe has seemed to Kolbert the outcome to be expected once we see how our species in its rampage across the continents has for thousands of years carelessly exterminated other life forms in its pursuit of its own prosperity and comfort. Some have proposed that this looming event is about to chime in a whole new geological period, the Anthropocene, in which the natural world will be dominated and transformed by the results of human activity. But whether it should be viewed as an extended period or just a boundary event between the Holocene and the next period remains to be seen. In either case, life on Earth is bound to change dramatically on account of the recent expansion of the elaborate "home" that humans have built for themselves, even if that home itself ends up being destroyed as a result.

I find myself in partial agreement with this view of the matter, but at the same time, I think there is another story to be told, a story in which the denouement of the career of *Homo sapiens* does not look nearly so inevitable. First of all, we need to recognize that the eco-catastrophe we now face is planetary rather than local, and multidimensional rather than limited to one aspect of the ecosystem. What we see happening is a collapse of the entire Holocene system of life on the whole of the planet. None of the previous human-induced environmental destructions compare in either extent or depth. Put simply, Spaceship Earth is in danger of becoming uninhabitable by most of the forms of life familiar to us, including our own, and this is a totally new threat.

Second, the enormous size of this catastrophe is not the result of the usual ways humans have arranged and expanded their artificial home; rather, it is the result of the recent explosion of one form of human culture, that of Western

Europe as it has achieved worldwide hegemony. It is the exponentially expanding power of the West's industrial economy, with its amazing scientific and technological advances and its goal of mass consumption, that has brought on this disaster. This is what made possible the stunning acceleration in human population growth after 1800, while at the same time enabling a large and ever-growing section of that population (although not by any means the majority) to live an incredibly affluent lifestyle that put unprecedented demands on natural resources. Any objective inquiry into the causes of our eco-catastrophe has to look carefully at why the West went in this direction and other advanced civilizations did not.

Instead of seeing the human race as akin to yeast blindly exploding in a vat of grape juice only to consume its own source of sustenance, we can, if I am right, see, on the one hand, one single cultural mode, the modern Western, as peculiarly oriented toward what led to this ecological disaster we now face, and, on the other hand, other cultural modes with ways of life developing that were compatible with a truce between the needs of our two homes, even though those ways were not mainly formed for that purpose. We can see traces of such ways in both peoples with Paleolithic and those with Neolithic technologies, but more to the point, we find them in the urban-centred civilizations of ancient India and China, where those ways persisted until very recently. The ancient Mediterranean world also saw the rise of an ethos that when adhered to lessened the stress that human life placed on its original inherited home. It was the surprisingly quick destruction of such traditions in the modern period that eliminated any possibility of developing them into fully practical ways in which humans could lay their constructed home peacefully within the nest that had been bequeathed to them 12,000 years ago. Not that this latter home was ever the same as it had been in the early Holocene—certainly humans had already affected it, even partly demolished it, in the course of their proliferation—but it was, at least until recently, not anything that humans had consciously constructed either, and it continued to provide cover for a multitude of life forms and their habitats that have astonished those with minds sufficiently open and observant to study them.

The question I want to raise, then, is why this fateful turn was taken in modern times. Why, that is, was there no process for enriching while modifying traditional ways so that humans could at least see out the remainder of the Holocene in a way that left both homes intact? The story to be told has to focus on Western civilization, for it is within that civilization that the ideas arose that were to lead to the demise of those conceptions of how life is to be lived that were the cornerstone of the traditions whose development might have saved us. In other words, until very recently in human history there were traditions regarding the direction human life should take that were taming the human animal into something compatible with its civilization's continued existence on Earth, even though that was not exactly their conscious aim. Such traditions could have been further nurtured and embellished so that civilization would be "sustainable" on Earth, at least until the great and ineluctable climatic cycle slowly plunged us into another ice age. There were paths—other than the one we have followed over the last three centuries—that might well have avoided today's eco-catastrophe. Why were they not followed in the West, as they were in India and China until the late eighteenth century, when those civilizations had to respond to Western hegemony? Why did the West reject those other paths for the path it did choose? Those are basically the questions I want to answer. Among the roots of that turn we will find the basic ideological sources of our eco-catastrophe.

The answer I present in the following chapters takes the form of a story that begins far back in prehistory and thus views human development in a context that spans the entire career of our species on Earth. It is particularly important to examine the momentous rise of urban civilizations some 5,000 years ago, for that turn in the way humans organized their communities was so opposed to the ways of humans in the preceding three hundred or so millennia that it could not but have had traumatic consequences for humanity as a whole. Out of that trauma eventually arose ways of thinking about the world, human beings' place in that world, and what a good life for a human being consisted in. My contention is that the resulting thought-systems had important long-run consequences for the societies in which people, particularly the elites, came to adopt them. I contend that we cannot fathom why the Chinese and Indian civilizations developed the way they did from ancient times up to the eighteenth century without understanding how people in those societies—often very powerful people—thought about themselves and their world. The same goes for late ancient and medieval Europe. Nor can we hope to pierce the mystery of why modern Europe took the drastically different turn it did unless we grasp that at work there was another ancient thought-system, fundamentally at odds with all the others, that in some measure, largely inadvertently, focused people on utopian hopes which opened the door to total disregard for the intrinsic value of the home given to us without our conscious design.

The need to keep this work to a manageable length has meant that I have no space to describe in detail developments in ancient India and China and must instead concentrate on the West, beginning with a tour of certain philosophical ideas in the Greco-Roman world that were very influential among the literate elite. But this emphasis on the West should not blind us to the fact that until modern times, India had a more advanced scientific and philosophic tradition than did the West and that China was ahead of the whole rest of the world in technology until the late eighteenth century. These historic realities are an obstacle to the facile explanation for why we now face ecological catastrophe, that is, the one that claims it is due simply to the ever increasing sophistication of science and technology coupled with a universal urge to see it used for endlessly augmenting comfort and convenience. Advances in science and technology have certainly been a prerequisite for falling into this predicament, but had they been sufficient, India and China would long ago have led the way.

Some will say that this cannot be right, because ideas, no matter how widely or deeply held, are not what determine the course of history. According to one school of thought it is developments in how society goes about materially maintaining itself—new "means of production," revolutions in the "relations of production"—that are crucial, and the ideologies that people invent are then fitted to these developments without having much of a causal impact upon them, and consequently have little independent influence upon the general course the society follows throughout its history. Without denying that technologies and the power structures that are put in place to direct those technologies are very important for understanding history, I will be assuming in this work that thought-systems, once adopted by the leading members of a society, have very significant independent effects on how that society responds to its various challenges, including effects on technological development and the distribution of power within the society.[2]

If thought-systems were merely carefully reasoned philosophical accounts of the world, then skepticism with regard to their influence would probably be justified. But such systems are often accompanied by *phantasy*, that is, by works of poetic imagination with an immense power to move the human spirit and entrance the mind. In later chapters I shall be using this word "phantasy" without any connotation of falsity or self-deception, although many phantasies do in fact contain much self-deception. I also ask the reader to allow me to use the alternative spelling, "fantasy," as a different word by which I will mean imaginative fictions motivated by a desire to escape from reality. All fantasies are phantasies, but not all phantasies are fantasies, if we adhere to this usage.[3] Aristotle's philosophy made little use of phantasy, whereas Plato employed it widely. I believe that as a consequence, despite its superior rational coherence, Aristotelianism never achieved the following that Platonism did in the ancient world. Nor, despite the poetic efforts of Lucretius, did the austere rationalism of Epicurus attain the influence of the Stoics, who were quite happy to make use of the phantastic resources of traditional Greek and Roman religion. Thought-systems sustained by elaborate phantasies continue in most religious traditions to the present day, and it is hardly to be denied that they exercise immense power over those who take them to heart. The poetry of such phantasies can be extremely moving even to non-believers—witness the poetry of the ancient Hebrew prophets and of Sufi saints. My contention is that once a thought-system enfolds within itself poetic phantasy, it can wield a huge influence over the course of the society that adopts it, and I am far from alone in believing this, although I shall not defend it here.

Consequently, many chapters of this book will engage enthusiastically with ideas that we would call philosophical or religious. In describing these I shall make no claim for originality; rather, I shall be relying heavily on the work of other scholars and limiting myself pretty much to points that are relatively uncontroversial in scholarly circles; where there is controversy, however, I shall certainly mention it. In general, what originality this work possesses is confined to the way it relates the results of scholarly research in the humanities to the question of how it is that we are now confronted with this eco-catastrophe, which we seem helpless to avoid. Much has been written about the science of climate change, ocean acidification, species extermination, and so on; and much has been written about the technologies that have contributed to the above as well as those that offer some hope of alleviating the problems. The physical sciences, the applied sciences, even the social sciences, have all chimed in on this topic, often in highly illuminating ways. I shall certainly not be totally neglecting them in what follows, but I have long thought that the humanities—the study of history, philosophy, religion, literature, and art—have a major contribution to make in this area, and this work testifies, I hope, to how true that is.

But I do not think that what scholarship in the humanities reveals presents us with "solutions" or "modes of adaptation" that are of significant practical use. Nor does it offer much in the way of predictions about the future. As much as I believe there is a story to be told about how humans have interacted with their given home, a story that makes sense of why we find ourselves in our present difficulties, I definitely do *not* believe that in some sense it was all determined from the beginning. History could have gone in radically different directions. Of course, there are very general predictions one can feel assured are correct, such as the prediction that shortages of food and water accompanied by an increasingly chaotic climate are going to wreak a great deal of havoc on all living beings, including the human community, over the remainder of the current century. But how exactly humans and life generally will react to all that is largely undetermined and unpredictable. Historians long ago rejected the idea that they must show how events were determined by what preceded them and would have been predictable had we knowledge of the laws that govern human affairs as well as detailed knowledge of the preceding situations. Explanations in the most rigorous of the physical sciences may fit that model, but it is not a template for explaining *all* subject-matters, especially not those in the human domain.

Yet I do find that the realization that some important roots of our eco-catastrophe lie in the ways we think about and imagine our lives in this world has had an effect on my own personal mental mode of coping with this crisis. Strangely enough, when I see that the roots lie in deeply held, rarely questioned, phantasies and ideals present in so much of humanity including myself, I find I grow more charitable toward the admittedly foolish ways of my fellow human beings and less self-righteous in my own supposed wisdom. I certainly do not expect this to be the reaction of most readers of this book, but I do hope that in one way or another, it will help them adjust their mental outlooks so that they can cope better with what lies ahead.

The chapters that follow fall basically into two sections. The first section turns on what I call the "trauma" of the transition to urban-dominated civilization and on ideological attempts to cope with that trauma in ancient civilizations. As I noted earlier, a full treatment of these attempts would take us deep into philosophical and religious ideas in India, China, and the Mediterranean world, but limitations on the length of this study have forced me to concentrate on the last. The point here is to show that the religious and philosophical ideologies developed in China, India, and the Greco-Roman world were significant in restraining those civilizations from progressing in a direction that would eventually have led to planetary eco-catastrophe. The second section traces the development of a very different line of thought in the West, which in the modern era succeeded in breaking down the ancient ideological barriers to the development of a culture that was capable of, and inherently disposed toward, creating eco-catastrophe, albeit unintentionally. This Western ideology was utopian and was convinced that humans could, by developing science and technology, bring about a wonderful world of mass consumption. To be sure, the ancient ideologies that the utopian one dismantled were not particularly concerned about protecting our naturally given home; it is just that they worked against the rise of a culture that would have been enormously destructive of that home, without that being their conscious aim. The ideology that arose in the modern West did not consciously and explicitly encourage the total destruction of that natural home, but it did justify and spur the development of a culture that in the end could not but bring about such a catastrophe. I try to present many of the elements of that ideology as highly seductive so that the reader can feel and understand their attraction. The second part of this book, then, is the story of how older ideological barriers were successively breached, but it does not claim that this process was inevitable. At many points the currents of thought could have gone in other directions, so that we in the West would now be living in a culture very different from the one we have. But the end of the story is that the culture we now have is in a trap of its own making that will inevitably lead to massive destruction of both our homes. And this is true even though the ideology that led us here is now being challenged from many directions and does not dominate people's minds nearly to the extent it once did.

When in chapters 4 through 9 I turn to ideological developments in the West, the story develops as a gradual replacement of outlooks and visions that constrained economic expansion with others that justified and encouraged it in its most ecologically destructive form. There was first of all (chapter 4) the rise of a phantastic ideology that replaced the almost universally dominant concern to protect the existing order against the perils of chaos with one that looked to the future, when, after many tribulations, the whole world, humans and their society included, would be transformed into something utterly blissful for its human inhabitants. It is my contention that this expectation provided the emotional energy needed to drive the sort of expansion of Western culture we are concerned with. In chapter 5 I posit that the Christian ideology of the West's medieval period was, in its mainstream, one that discouraged any utopian plans for this world, yet harboured a counter-movement grounded in the future-oriented expectations described in chapter 4. The breakdown of that mainstream ideology, particularly in the Protestant domain of the sixteenth and seventeenth centuries, is the topic of chapter 6. It was replaced with something still Christian but fascinated with the possibility of Christians greatly improving life through their own endeavours in this world.

It thus becomes a question of what that improvement consisted in, for if it was mainly religious and moral, or even just spiritual in the broad sense, then there was still no ideology that justified massive economic development and mass consumption of the sort capable of causing an ecological collapse. Chapter 7 shows how there arose in the West a vision of expected future improvement that would leave religion behind even while very much incorporating religion's intellectual and moral benefits in its conception of "progress." But that improvement would have to include gargantuan increases in physical power if it was to do the damage we see today. In the seventeenth century, Francis Bacon was already pointing to the union of theoretical science with technological arts as offering this sort of power, and in the nineteenth century this idea was taken up with a vengeance. Chapter 8 describes how this generated a cult of its own that justified the enormous cultural effort required to realize Bacon's vision. All that remained was to sideline entirely the intellectual and moral aspects of what was meant by "improvement" or "progress," and in this regard, chapter 9 shows how the philosophy of hedonism came to capture the nascent profession of economics, thus providing the justification for gauging "improvement" as increase in mass consumption. We in the West still largely live in the ideological world dominated by the results of the story that the final chapters of this work recount.

A warning, however, to the reader. The story just alluded to does not show that the ancient ideologies by exerting this restraining effect were thus admirable and worthy of revival. Nor does it show that the modern ideology of the West by removing those restraints was thus deplorable and worthless, fit only for the junk heap. The latter ideology was in many ways a great advance over what had gone before; it did much to ease the "trauma" that humanity had suffered when it adopted urban-dominated civilization. The former ideologies, by contrast, had left much of that trauma unattended to. Perhaps my judgment here is biased; I am, of course, a person educated in the Western tradition and so am imbued with some peculiarly Western values. But my contention is that the attractiveness of much of the ideology of the modern West is part of the reason it became so powerful and blinded so many to some of its very dangerous excesses. If readers find themselves repelled by many of the ideas that unintentionally constrained Greco-Roman civilization from perpetrating a world-circling, biologically disastrous economic explosion, and at the same time are deeply attracted to the ideas in the West that laid the foundation for precisely that explosion, then I have achieved most of what I intended; for then readers will experience in their own hearts what was motivating people to adopt the course that, so it turns out, has ended in catastrophe. In any event, the reader is welcome to draw his or her own conclusions as to what were mistakes and what were great insights in these various ideologies that have had such impact on people's thoughts and sentiments.

1

HUMAN LIFE BEFORE THERE WERE CITIES

> Know your brothers and sisters [nature]
> around you in all their forms.
> The secret of a good life is to live in
> harmony with them.
> —Gairemnog, in the epic of the Rongmei of Nagaland

It is now common knowledge that around 5,000 years ago in the land between the two great rivers of Mesopotamia there came to exist states centred on cities and that out of this mode of civilization[1] developed cultures making use of writing, highly specialized trades, long-distance commerce, sophisticated artistry, advanced metallurgy and technology, laws, and many other of the achievements we still take as marking the greatest advances human beings have made in their time on this earth. Less recognized perhaps are some cultural features that emerged from this form of civilization and that today have a less than glowing reputation; I mean the large-scale use of slaves, the imposition of oppressive rule by small elites, the training of professional military machines, highly destructive warfare, occasional genocide, the assignment of divine or near-divine status to autocrats commonly known as kings or emperors, massive public works often entailing much environmental destruction, violent changes in ruling regimes, and so forth. It is a central thesis of this book that the shift to this sort of civilization was a kind of collective trauma for the people who were touched by it, directly or indirectly, and that if we are to understand the ideologies that will be the topic of later chapters, we need to begin by developing some understanding of what was involved in this transition.

I call the type of civilization just mentioned "urban-dominated" because of the dominating role cities play in it. The earliest examples are the ones in Mesopotamia and the eastern Mediterranean (including Egypt), the Indus valley, and the Yellow River region of China. Later examples heavily influenced by these pioneers were the one on the Ganges plain of India and the Greco-Roman civilization, which was preceded in the Mediterranean region by the Mycenean, Minoan, and Etruscan.[2] But to grasp what the transition to urban-dominated civilization meant for people we first need to have some awareness of what came before it and, indeed, has persisted alongside it right through to the present day. This chapter is dedicated to that task, that is, a very brief look at how humans lived before there were cities.

Humans in the Paleolithic Era

Creatures of the genus *Homo* have been on this planet for at least 2 million years. One early species of this genus, *Homo erectus*, mastered fire, made tools, and managed to spread itself very widely in the Old World about 1.8 million years ago. These creatures originated in Africa but eventually spread to both Europe and Asia. The remarkable ability of humans to adapt themselves to various climes and environments was thus established long before the arrival of our own species, *Homo sapiens*. Our sort of human originated in east or south Africa at least 200,000 years ago and probably were around in Africa 100,000 years before that;[3] they too spread beyond Africa, with some members reaching the Middle East around 170,000 years ago. Then around 70,000 years ago something occurred that nearly exterminated *Homo sapiens*. Research into the DNA of existing humans shows that at some point in that time period there were at most just a few thousand, possibly a few hundred, of our species in existence, and all people now are descended from that small population.[4] The catastrophic event may well have been the massive eruption of Mount Toba, a volcano in Sumatra, at about this time, and the sudden cooling of the world's climate that followed.[5] Afterwards, the gradual migration out of Africa began again, and by no less than 40,000 and possibly 50,000 years ago humans had reached as far as Australia.

Like *Homo erectus*, and indeed like all species of *Homo*, *Homo sapiens* lived in small bands and survived by foraging, that is, hunting and gathering sustenance from the natural home.[6] The lives people lived in Paleolithic times were certainly very different from the way almost the whole of humanity lives now, but it is easy, I think, to overstate the differences between us and them. In particular, we should avoid ascribing to them certain mental deficiencies such as lack of language. My own inclination is to take language as basically a biological development, that is, the development of a mental organ with associated speech organs that occurs through natural evolution and not by human design. It would not surprise me to find that *Homo erectus*, indeed all the species of *Homo*, had some sort of linguistic capacity.[7] There is good reason to believe that our own species had language from the start. Of course, this does not rule out that humans invent words and grammatical constructions as they go along. The language capacity makes possible the refinement of the ways humans use that capacity and consequently the diversification of the languages of groups that have little or no contact with one another. All human languages, however, have syntax, and often quite complicated syntax, which makes possible the creation and expression of new thoughts, and thus a creativity both mental and social that is today unrivalled in the animal kingdom. The possession of language helps explain how early humans were able to adapt to so many different environments; it also enabled them to have cultures that could develop and change in countless ways. The day when we can rest assured that early tool-using humans were mentally and culturally deficient compared to modern humans is long gone. We do not know the specifics of what they thought about, what linguistic creations they brought forth, and how they designed their communal arrangements, but it now seems very likely that they were doing such things in complicated ways.

Language, of course, opens the door to all sorts of ways of understanding and imagining the world, as well as communicating those ways. No doubt these varied across the many widely scattered groups as they spread from Africa to all parts of Eurasia and on into the Americas. That said, observation of groups that have only recently emerged from a Paleolithic way of life reveals that there was a universal acceptance that most, if not all, of the phenomena in the world around them were to be understood as manifesting personalities that could be talked about in much the same way one talked about human personalities. It seems likely that the linguistic tools for explanation arose first in relation to the behaviour of humans themselves—talk of wanting, knowing, fearing, enjoying, and so on—and then got applied to animals, plants, and even what we think of as inanimate things like storms, rivers, and heavenly bodies. The reverse, where the characteristics of non-human denizens were applied back on humans to refine talk about them, would have followed. Or perhaps there was from the start a sort of dialectical interaction between the two realms of discourse.

We Westerners of the twenty-first century are the inheritors of centuries of development of ways of talking about the world around us that do not rely on this assumption of the ubiquity of personalities, so it seems nearly incomprehensible to us how people could be so convinced that these non-human personalities—that is, spirits—were the basic reality of what they experienced, in much the same way the human mind is viewed as the basic reality behind what we experience when we see and hear the physical actions of human beings.[8] But Paleolithic humans had little in the way of vocabulary to *explain* what they saw other than the vocabulary applicable to personalities. I do not mean they were unaware of the sensible characteristics of things; certainly they had a strongly honed empirical knowledge of their world and possessed sortal concepts that allowed for much categorization of that world without reliance on the language of personality. But when it came to *understanding* what was going on in this world of constant change and immense variety, the language they were equipped with was that of understanding persons, a language designed to make sense of and organize the chaos of overt behaviour.

Some recent philosophers have disparagingly called this the language of "folk psychology," which implicitly acknowledges that this is the language used by the unsophisticated—and by the sophisticated as well in their unsophisticated moments—across the entire human spectrum. I doubt that this language was "invented" by *Homo sapiens*; for reasons lost in the mists of evolutionary development, it was probably something that was gradually refined as the line of *Homo* evolved into our own species. Like language generally, it is something that has also been crafted through conscious thought and invention, but the basis is innate. Indeed, its evolution and that of the evolution of language itself, not to mention evolutionary changes in the brain, may all be closely associated.

The conception of the world as basically made up of interacting spirits with human-like personalities offers up immense room for human phantasy to go to work. The spirits have motives, emotions, purposes, whims, that is, all the sorts of things we find operating behind human behaviour. Here the storyteller can have a field day creating tales that literally make trees, mountains, storms, and the like come alive in ways that impress themselves on the listener and make him or her into a more alert and sensitive observer of the scene. They also render the surrounding chaos less utterly strange and alien, as it must have seemed when first encountered. The surroundings can thus become much more a "home," the primal nature-given home I spoke of in the introduction.

Once this spirit world is accepted, it naturally seems possible to influence it in much the same way one can influence other people; it may even be possible to communicate with the spirits, and doubtless persons will arise, perhaps endowed with what we call schizophrenia, who claim to be able to do just that.[9] Hence the universality of practices such as sacrifices, libations, and prayers among peoples whose connections with their prehistoric roots have not yet been entirely severed. Experiences of awe and fear in the face of natural phenomena like thunderstorms, mountains, winds can be accepted as revelatory of some basic spirit realities, as can experiences of calm and refreshment when encountering groves, oases, and gently gurgling streams.

The reader will no doubt have heard of many other manifestations of this outlook on the world. My only aim here is to engender a recognition that even though such an outlook does not produce any really effective way of controlling nature, nor even much in the way of predictive power, it does fulfil ably a deep psychic need: the human being need not be faced with the utterly absurd, to use Camus's term, when he or she looks around; the spirit world is different from the human world—its characters are not so easily comprehensible or predictable—but not utterly different. The same categories apply in both cases.

Within this general outlook there must have been a great variety of stories and practices among the various human groups. Expressing that outlook would have been various art forms like poetry, song, dance, instrumental music, and painting. We all know of the cave paintings found in France and Spain, some of which may date back 30,000 years or even further. But this is just a remnant that was lucky to survive into the present. The overwhelming majority of the art produced by Paleolithic humans did not survive more than a few years, or in some cases a few days, after its creation. Body art, for example. Dress for another. We must imagine that life among these people, when it was not disturbed by climatic crises or natural disasters, was largely spent creating artistic works of poetry, song, dance, painting, sculpture, apparel, and so on, and was not one of perpetual labour and anxiety.[10] Within communal gatherings stories would be told of the spirit world that gave meaning to the experiences of daily life and satisfied the need to understand what the world they lived in was all about. That world itself provided a rich variety of experiences as each individual came into contact with its various animal and plant denizens and learned their ways and uses. Meeting animals and watching them in their natural habitat can be an extremely moving, almost mystical, moment in a person's life. Paleolithic humans would have had such experiences to a far greater extent than urbanized modern people do.[11]

In sum, Paleolithic life, when it was functioning well, which would have been most of the time, provided lots of what human beings then enjoyed most and that even today are the areas where we most find creative human minds at work. We sometimes do these things in far more sophisticated ways (and sometimes in less), but as the role of so-called primitive art in our culture shows, there can be a freshness and honesty about the less sophisticated that goes missing in our own productions. The ancient myths passed down to us from time immemorial were transformed as they passed through a series of cultures, but in them there must be elements that survive from the Paleolithic world and give them an appeal that can only come from their resonance with something basic in our psyche even today.

Origins and Development of Settled Life

Fragments of civilization (i.e., settled life) must have appeared in Paleolithic times. Sometimes the foragers would have chanced on a location that provided a completely reliable and adequate source of food, an example being some peoples along the northwest coast of North America who feasted on abundant runs of salmon. James C. Scott in *Against the Grain* has laid out the case for settled life in wetlands and along rivers where people did not rely much on domestication of plants but instead depended on wild varieties, as well as on hunting, trapping, and fishing wild animals. This seems to have been the case in southern Mesopotamia thousands of years before the rise of city-states there.[12] Nevertheless, there is archaeological evidence of domestication of grains in the Levant as early as 19,400 years ago, although the Neolithic period is generally thought to have begun later at the start of the Holocene, some 12,000 years ago. The shaping of stone tools and the use of obsidian in knives was refined to a high degree during the upper Paleolithic. The most common evidence of the technology of early settled cultures, are the bountiful remnants of the ceramic containers they made. That said, the baking of clay to make ceramics goes back at least 20,000 years in China, and ceramic figurines were baked in Moravia as long as 24,000 years ago.[13] The craft was definitely known, then, to some Paleolithic peoples.

The transition to agricultural settlements developed around the domestication of plants and animals seems to have begun about 10,000 years ago in the Levant. From there it spread around the Fertile Crescent and into southern Turkey. By 7,000 years ago it had reached Egypt and extended itself into the Balkans and central Europe as well as deeper into the Middle East. Maize was farmed in Central America as long as 9,000 years ago, and rice in China 8,000 years ago.

The social ramifications of this transition to settled life were enormous. Permanent dwellings had to be established with long-term storage capacity. Pens might well have been needed for domestic animals. In some places irrigation channels had to be dug and maintained. A labour force had to be organized and deployed to do the work of tilling, planting, weeding, and harvesting, as well as tending the animals. As the quality of grains improved through breeding and more land was brought under cultivation, a larger population could be supported, and in more fortunate communities it was possible to dedicate part of the populace solely to the production of the baskets, pots, jars, and other accoutrements that the whole operation required. Thus a certain amount of division of labour into various crafts occurred, allowing for the refinement of skills in various aspects of manufacture and construction.[14]

In other words, we had in the early days the creation of pretty much self-sufficient villages, although it may well be that from the start trade with other settlements provided some of the requirements, as would often enough trade with non-settled foragers. Certainly, as time went on, trade would usually become more and more important to sustaining life in individual communities. The creation and maintenance of such a village called forth organizational skills well beyond those required of Paleolithic foragers, and handicraft skills were extended in quite new directions, such as carpentry, furniture-making, pottery, and weaving. The shift was essentially from basic reliance on the primal, natural home, to life that mainly relied on the second, artificial home that humans organized by and for themselves. This was a huge task, which at the beginning must have been carried out step by step as people curtailed their foraging in the natural habitat and spent more effort on creating a habitat they themselves had designed.

Life in such a farming community would have been a lot harder physically and more trying mentally than the way of the Paleolithic forager. So much field work, animal tending, and shelter constructing would have seemed horribly unpleasant and demeaning compared to foraging and hunting in the wild, given that the latter was still a real option.[15] The question naturally arises, then: Why *did* human beings ever take up farming? The transition must have occurred first in areas where the population had become so large that the natural home no longer provided a sufficient supply of what that population needed to survive and where migration to areas more amply endowed was simply not feasible. Paleolithic foragers would have had some experience of horticulture—that is, tending plants, whose fruits would have been almost immediately consumed once they ripened—and would have expanded that practice to grow quantities of grains that could be stored for future use, or for trading. A similar development would have occurred with a few animals. The transition to full agriculture may well have happened gradually in this way. Of course, once it was well developed, the farming way might well have been exported from its originators to other peoples who found foraging and mere horticulture insufficient for their needs.

Farming was not the only alternative to the foraging life. Some people became nomadic pastoralists, following herds of animals, culling what they needed as the animals made their annual migratory circuit. Indigenous people in Canada's North followed caribou herds in this way well into the twentieth century. Closer to settled life were people who engaged in transhumance, tending herds of animals and moving them over the course of the year from one grazing ground to another. This practice can, of course, be combined with fully settled life, as it is in a part of Italy to this day. Conflicts between agriculturalists and pastoralists certainly arose and could turn deadly. Recent DNA evidence indicates that the farming cultures in Neolithic Europe were largely wiped out in the mid-third millennium BCE as pastoralists from the Russian steppes asserted their presence. They may have brought with them a proto-Indo-European language.[16] It is likely, though, that symbiotic relations could at times develop, with the pastoralists providing the farmers with meat and hides and the farmers reciprocating with manufactured goods.

The Precariousness of Agricultural Communities
A successful farming community could support in a small region a much greater population than the foragers could have. There were, however, very significant downsides to this new way of life. First of all, storms, droughts, floods, torrential rains, and other severe weather anomalies could be disastrous for a farming community while posing only a major nuisance to foragers. The latter, with their minimal light-weight possessions, could fairly easily up and move to some other area where the damage was not so great. But, more importantly, the natural home they depended on was much less likely to be severely damaged than were the crops and structures the agricultural community relied on. By replacing their natural home with an artificial construction, the farmers, paradoxically enough, had made themselves more vulnerable to natural disasters; in fact, natural events that were not at all disasters for the foragers became disasters for them.

Another source of anxiety for farming villagers was the threat of insect and disease infestations that could devastate their crops. Of course, animals such as rodents and roaming herbivores posed a threat as well, but farmers would have quickly learned techniques to limit their depravations. Against hordes of locusts and grasshoppers, or invisible bacteria, mould, and viruses, they had no such recourse. Devoting large areas of tilled soil to one or just a few crops made their food supply much more vulnerable to these pests than was the natural environment on which foragers depended.

Even worse was the threat of diseases to the farmers themselves that came from keeping domesticated animals. We now know that the influenza virus made the transition from domesticated fowl to humans with devastating results. Such transitions were and are much more likely to occur when humans and animals share the same close quarters, as they would have in many farming communities.[17] Again, foragers were better positioned, since the only animals they were close to were the dogs that some of them kept as aids in hunting and protection. This kind of threat was exacerbated among the farmers by their diet, which was often much less varied and hence less healthy than that of foragers. Unless the farmers had access to wild-growing edible plants and fruits, they would have been less prepared to fight off diseases. Add to all this the threat that traders from distant communities would arrive carrying diseases to which local people had little or no natural immunity. It is very easy to underestimate the extent of trade routes in the Neolithic world even before the rise of cities.[18]

Furthermore, the very success of an agricultural community in creating for itself supplies of foodstuffs as well as manufactured goods led to another threat: bands of brigands might raid the village to take by force what they had no intention of producing themselves. Note too that, as trade developed, the goods the villagers possessed came to have exchange-value as well as use-value. Brigands, then, might raid a wealthy community not to supply their own needs but to gain purchasing power on some distant market. Indeed, it is possible that entire tribes made their living mainly in this way. Now communities had to consider how to defend themselves against such predators.

Wealth of the sort just mentioned led to the final peril the farmers had to face: inequality of wealth and power within their own ranks and a consequent burgeoning of resentments and feuds that could tear the community apart. Add to this the creation of a warrior class and a warrior leader to meet the threat of brigandage, and the rise of an oppressive elite becomes a real possibility. There is clear archaeological evidence that class divisions were present in some Neolithic villages and towns. These threatened the unity and solidarity of the community, and unity and solidarity were crucial to the community's continued existence. Again, foragers suffered very little from this pathology simply because they had almost no wealth.

Coping Strategies of Neolithic Farming Communities

The reader may now well wonder how the agricultural way of life of the Neolithic era managed to survive at all given the perils just described that it had brought upon itself. And yet it certainly did survive, and people have continued to live that way in many places right up to this day. How was that possible? What follows are my own conjectures as to an answer, but these are only reasonable speculations that concur with what we know of modern agricultural societies and of the history of peoples both ancient and modern.

To begin, the problem of organization and discipline was dealt with virtually everywhere through the development of customs that all members of the community were brought up to respect and rely on. As I said earlier, my guess is that settled life developed in the beginning only by incremental steps. People would make changes in how they did things; some of these changes would prove deleterious in the long run and be abandoned; but others would prove their worth so that people came to make it a rule to continue with them and not think about how they might be revised. In other words, large-scale planning was avoided in favour of solidifying a proven way of proceeding as beyond question, while welcoming incremental improvements. Even so, a certain amount of government was required to ensure that customs were inculcated and followed, to judge the advisability of proposals for improvements, and to arrange for defence against hostile neighbours.

The form that this government took would have varied widely, but the heavy reliance on elders that persists in village societies to this day suggests strongly that gerontocracy was very often preferred. This fit neatly with the reliance on custom, since who better than the elders would know what custom prescribed, given that there was as yet no writing and the past was preserved solely in the memories of living persons and the poetry they had committed to heart? The government of a sizeable population—and we are imagining here several hundred to several thousand persons—necessarily involves some inequality between rulers and ruled. Combine this with community wealth and the opportunity clearly arises for the emergence of a ruling class that appropriates more than its fair share of that wealth for its own use. I have already mentioned the dangers posed by class inequality. But we need not suppose that most settlements had much in the way of such arrangements. Probably the less wealthy and the less populous the community, the less inequality we would find.

Under the rule of custom, the day-to-day running and maintaining of the artificial home became to a large degree automatic, at least during good times.

The need for inventive, designing thought as regards these matters was minimized. So, just as Paleolithic foragers with their detailed knowledge of the natural environs did not have to do any planning of their primal, natural home but simply accepted it as it came, so in normal times the settled villagers accepted the structure and routines of their artificial home pretty much as they came. A way of life that would never have been imposed on them by the evolutionary forces of nature thus came to feel as natural as if it had been. At the same time, the real natural world outside the "pale" of the settlement tended to become the "wild," a region whose organization was obscure and not particularly friendly to human life as the villagers knew it. People who still lived in it became "savages," not to be trusted and definitely inferior in character and level of development. This is just a tendency, of course, and the degree to which it took root would not have been great at the beginning and would have always varied across contemporaneous communities. Many settled peoples would still have depended to some extent on hunting and foraging and would have maintained a fairly detailed knowledge of their natural surroundings. They might even have nurtured a symbiotic relation with non-settled people so that the latter gained useful tools from the villagers in exchange for meat or hides, for example. But the more extensive and complex settled life became, the stronger became the tendency to view the natural surroundings and the people who lived non-settled lives in them as alien. Here is the origin of the disrespect for, and even fear of, untamed nature that all settled peoples generally more or less exhibit the more settled they become.

The vulnerability of the settlement to climatic and other natural anomalies seems to have been universally handled not so much by government and custom but by another institution with its roots in Paleolithic foraging life, albeit one that acquires a whole different dimension among settled people: religion. In fact, it may be best not to treat the mere belief in a spirit world, which probably has been with *Homo sapiens* since the beginning, as religion at all, and instead reserve that term for something that had only a fragmentary existence before the rise of civilization. Religion is an institution that amply reveals its origins in the anxieties felt by settled people who were well aware of the precariousness of their way of life.

Common to all the most ancient mythologies of settled peoples is the creation of the world by the union of sky and earth. This is conceived as sexual;

sometimes rain is thought of as the semen of the sky fertilizing the earth. Some myths envision the natural world as developing only after sky and earth have been forced apart to allow space and light. But an additional creation is often added in which the original world is a chaos with no differentiation into permanent or semi-permanent entities. It takes a special deity, one who imposes order, to make a livable cosmos. But the forces of chaos remain in existence and need to be continually repelled.[19]

In ancient Egyptian myths there is a monster, Apophis, who threatens to destroy order and has to be beaten back by the god Seth. In the Indian *Rig Veda*, the god Indra is able to create an ordered world only after defeating the monster Vritra and his mother or mate Danu, who represent these forces of chaos. In Mesopotamian myths the gods who keep the world in order are themselves unreliable and require the assistance of humans by sacrificial rites in order to keep up their work. Some peoples were actually fearful that the sun would fail to appear the next day or would not return to its heights after its descent toward the winter solstice.[20] There is a widespread story about a god or gods causing a flood that virtually wipes out the human race. Such phantastic tales would not have survived long had they not given voice to real fears that haunted settled peoples, and I suggest those fears were rooted in a recognition of the real precariousness of their settled lives. There were occasional floods that destroyed everything; there were droughts that made growing crops impossible; there were windstorms that blew down both crops and shelters; there were in some places earthquakes and volcanic eruptions. All of these could annihilate whole communities or leave in their wake immense human suffering. Is it any wonder, then, that these mythologies are so concerned with the preservation of order and imagine deities whose primary task is just that?

Many peoples came to recognize the regularity of the movements of stars, sun, and moon, and they devised ways to carefully observe these cycles and bring their own routines into harmony with them. Hence the famous stone circles of prehistoric Europe. These practices would have occurred in the context of treating the heavenly bodies as governed by mostly benign spirits, the Sky Gods, whose regular habits engendered and maintained the cycles of seasons and tides on which many communities depended. Looking downward, settled peoples were keenly aware of their dependence on the fertility of the earth, which was itself the physical embodiment of a powerful spirit. The analogy of this soil fertility with female fertility must have been noticed long before civilization, but settled people embellished it into cults of a female spirit of the earth, an Earth Goddess, who needed to be honoured and propitiated with frequent sacrificial and other rituals.[21] The to them obvious affinity between female sexuality and the activity of the Earth Goddess gave a special place to women in the community who were past menarche. Often they were thought to possess power that rendered them dangerous during their menstrual flow. This no doubt also contributed to the practice of seeing women as analogous to soil and eventually as the property of men.

Another nearly universal aspect of ancient religions is the recognition that some things are clean and pure and others are unclean and impure and that washing with water can cleanse the latter. It comes to be felt that human beings themselves can by their activities or because of what they associate with become unclean and in need of cleansing. Water, already recognized as powerful in the process of generation and growth, is granted magical properties in this regard.[22] We see then that settled people are anxious not just about their surroundings but also about themselves; they frequently feel the need to wash away some of what they have become and make a fresh start on a cleaner slate. In some cases all of this interacted with some sort of belief in a spirit life for the individual after their physical death, a realm that provided further play for the anxious mind.

In sum, settled humans phantasizing within the framework of a spirit world, which had come down to them from the very origins of humanity, elaborated systems of beliefs and ways of viewing the world that allowed them to interact with the spirits or gods they believed had so much power over their way of life and their surroundings. They alleviated their sense of helplessness in the face of a precarious existence by investing what they observed with a meaning that, they thought, would allow them to deal with what was basically at work in those phenomena. Their own lives became objects of evaluation, and the subsequent anxiety was relieved by magical rites. The endless variety of myths and rituals that are attested in ancient literature and in the reports of travellers and anthropologists evidence the alacrity with which people entered into this enterprise and the opportunity it gave for creative phantasy.

What about the problem of securing the community and its wealth against raiders and brigands? Obviously this would have been a major concern in some areas, such as the Middle East, and hardly any problem at all in other regions, such as some communities in the New World. Where it was a problem it led to the compression of physical shelters into as small an area as possible in order to facilitate defence. Fortifications were erected. Weapons of war were developed. The men of the community may have been organized and trained for combat against other people. This may have led to an elite class of warriors, whose prestige gave them greater power and privilege in the community than what other people possessed. Fighting would usually have required a leader to provide unified command, and this could well have led to the establishment of a system of warrior-chiefs. Neighbouring communities might ally themselves in order to fend off raiders from more distant regions, and this in turn might have led to some overarching political structure encompassing those different communities. In general, the wealthier and more populous a community, or allied communities, became, the more concerns about security would increase and the more institutions such as those just mentioned would be established and elaborated on.

Where warfare called forth the responses just mentioned, the danger for the Neolithic settled life of class division would have been exacerbated—that is, there would have been a greater opportunity for some sort of elite to form who could appropriate to themselves much more wealth and social power than ordinary people had. The result could be class conflict leading to community disintegration. I don't want to emphasize this problem very much here, as I think it becomes crucial only when we get to urban civilization, which will be the subject of the next chapter. But I do think that pre-urban settlements came up with ways to handle this problem too. In large measure it would have been through instituting customs demanding that those better off share with those less fortunate and that everyone curtail their personal desires in order to advance the good of the whole community, the "common weal," as modern Westerners would call it. Intentionally misleading others to advance one's own fortunes at their expense—malicious lying, in other words—would be especially condemned. Violation of such customs would be deemed dishonourable, and this sort of "taboo" might well be supported by religious phantasies about what would displease the gods and perhaps provoke their anger. Also, the idea mentioned earlier that a person could become unclean because of how they conducted themselves led to self-examination and self-criticism and its attendant anxieties, and this could be adapted to an ethic calling for proper respect for others and concern for their well-being. In other words, a morality might well develop, inculcated through the education of the young so that they came to intuitively recognize some behaviour as "sinful." Such a cultural device could be used to curtail self-aggrandizing behaviour as well as regulate all sorts of areas of life like sex, family relations, and the exchange of goods. Penalties might be instituted for breaches of these regulations. Carried to an extreme, morality can attempt to totally control the lives of individuals and thereby eliminate any occasion for anxiety over interpersonal conflict. Total harmony would be purchased at the cost of all spontaneity and cleverness. Needless to say, human nature would not long tolerate such an extreme result, but various intermediate degrees of it are familiar enough in human community life.

Obviously, the origin of morality is a very complex and highly speculative topic. What I have said in the preceding paragraph should not be read as a claim that morality is simply an artificial creation responding to particular social needs. Certainly individuals in Paleolithic foraging bands would have to have exhibited a degree of respect and care for one another, and they would have appreciated common virtues such as courage, honesty, and fairness. The unity and success of the band required that. My view is that the feelings motivating such behaviours were innate and present in members of the genus *Homo* from the start. What, then, did civilization add to that entirely natural base? I think that wealth accumulation—and in some cases the resultant warfare—opened up what hitherto had been non-existent or very rare opportunities for individuals to gratify their desires for status and power. These desires are natural enough, but they vary greatly in intensity among different individuals. In most they are not strong enough to overcome innate feelings of the sort that maintained unity in foraging bands; in some people, however, the temptations overwhelm those feelings, and once such people find success in their self-aggrandizing ways, others feel compelled to compete with them. The result is the formation of power elites, competition among them for power, and, in the end, violent conflict among factions. All this is usually highly destructive of the unity of the community, and in Neolithic times, people soon became wise enough to see that special motivations had to be put in place to reinforce the feelings that counteracted the motivation for personal status and power. Hence the measures mentioned in the preceding paragraph. Once these practices were seen to have considerable success, they were often applied to other areas of life so as to make behaviour more reliable and regular and thus less prone to the sorts of conflicts that would have threatened the community's unity. To the extent that these admittedly artificial measures were put in place to reinforce the innate feelings that had already been at work in bonding together foraging bands, we arrive at what I would call "morality," but whether to so limit the extension of the term depends entirely on how significant you think the addition of these basically artificial elements is. My view is that they answer to deep anxieties fostered in people who have experienced how precarious life in civilization really is. Morality is part of the therapy for such anxieties, but that is quite compatible with its also being an enhancement of innate and hence perfectly natural inclinations.

The main point of the preceding discussion is this: The very success of early settled life produced a dynamic in which ever more elaborate devices were called upon to maintain the viability of the whole enterprise of carving an artificial home out of the natural one. No doubt this dynamic was stronger in some areas and barely noticeable in others, but over the millennia of the early Holocene it had an effect almost everywhere that settled life existed. To the modern observer it presents a picture of very slow progress in the technological, political, and cultural realms. But it is progress toward something that is increasingly removed from what people can comfortably exist in without a good deal of deliberate education and habituation from an early age. Fortunately for civilization, the human mind is extremely malleable, and with the right kind of upbringing it can adapt with alacrity to the devices I have described above. The cares and anxieties attendant on settled life could be managed and for the most part *were* managed successfully in the earliest village-type civilizations. By and large people could lead lives that, while having the usual mixture of happiness and tragedy, seemed meaningful and satisfying to most of them most of the time. It is doubtful that this can be said about the urban-dominated civilizations that eventually followed.

2

THE TRAUMA OF URBAN-DOMINATED CIVILIZATION

> Man has lost the capacity to foresee and to forestall.
> He will end by destroying the earth.
> —Albert Schweitzer, *The Words of Albert Schweitzer*

The Earliest Shift to Cities

The site of the present-day city of Jericho served as a gathering place for foraging people at least 10,000 years ago, and some sort of permanent settlement was established there around the middle of the tenth millennium BCE.[1] This settlement came to house several hundred people, who depended on farming cereals as well as hunting. It represented a very early stage of settled life, as no pottery has been found in its ruins. Yet this was no simple village. It had a massive stone wall, and inside the wall was an impressive tower 3.6 metres in height and equipped with a stone staircase. Perhaps the wall was simply a barrier against floods, but it might also have protected the residents from other humans keen to raid the settlement for its stored goods. It shows in any event that even in the earliest days of settled life some people felt the need for walls around their settlements, and also a tower, although it is not clear what function it served.

Another revealing site of early settled life is Çatal Höyük in what is now southern Turkey.[2] A town existed there from about 7500 to 5700 BCE. Its physical structure was quite remarkable: there were no pathways between dwellings; rather, people moved about on the rooftops and entered their homes through holes in the roof. This community survived by both agriculture and hunting and made extensive use of pottery. There is evidence of a vigorous religious cult with much emphasis on deities connected with the generative capacities of humans and the natural world.

The early dates of both the above settlements indicate that in the Fertile Crescent from the very beginnings of civilization people tended to congregate into very compact living arrangements rather than the free-standing residences we think of as typical of a village. These compact towns must have become very common in southern Mesopotamia sometime in the fourth millennium BCE, for we know that late in that millennium the area was divided into a number of city-states controlling regions with clear boundaries, sometimes marked by irrigation canals.[3] This was the beginning of the first really urban civilization, that of the Sumerians. It can be called "urban" not because most of the people lived in populous towns of some sort but because the town had become the political and religious centre of an agricultural area in which there might be many villages, all of which were largely under the governance of an elite who carried out their governing functions in the town. Such a town can now rightly be called a city (*urbs*). Its elite residents dominated the surrounding territory, and thus the terms "urban-dominated" and "urban-centred" can be applied to the society as a whole.

By the late fourth millennium a number of such city-states had been founded near what is now the Persian Gulf, each of which was dominated by a city that contained a temple and was ruled by some sort of autocrat who combined religious and political authority—a priest-king, if you will.[4] The area surrounding each city was its agricultural base, and its boundaries were carefully marked. Farming here was unusually dependent on irrigation via canals leading from the two great rivers that brought the water of life from the mountainous regions far to the north. Planning, constructing, and maintaining the canals, and allocating the water to its various users, would obviously have required a great deal of careful designing and central control. What in pre-urban farming communities had been left to nature—that is, to whatever rains might fall—was now something people themselves largely managed, although of course this was still dependent on cyclical increases and decreases in the flow of the rivers. This impressive engineering feat had the advantage of making crop failure much less likely, although in the long run the land became salinized and gradually much less fertile.[5]

It is not clear what factors brought about the shift from agricultural towns to urban-dominated societies. Perhaps it was competition between towns for water and territory; perhaps nomadic invaders imposed themselves on the agriculturalists. But it is clear that the transition was violent, for once formed, these early city-states were soon at war. We know from the Stele of the Vultures that in the mid-third millennium BCE the city of Lagash waged war on another city, Umma, and defeated it with a carefully disciplined phalanx of spearmen.[6] To appreciate what all this meant for the people involved I find it helpful to use a theoretical apparatus I have borrowed from Ferdinand Tönnies's great work *Gemeinschaft und Gesellschaft* (often translated as *Community and Association*),[7] a work in which he laid down basic general concepts for the study of society.

Using Tönnies's Basic Concepts to Understand the Urban Shift

The title of the work names two of these concepts. A *Gemeinschaft* is a community in which the members are united by forms of what Tönnies called *Wesenwille*,[8] that is, motivating feelings or thoughts that arise in a person more or less automatically as they confront life's situations. *Wesen* derives from the German for "being," and a person's *Wesenwille* reflects what they already *are* as opposed to some ideal they might want to be. Such motivations may arise from what is innate, but they also comprise what early upbringing has made into a "second nature." What unites a *Gemeinschaft* is not just the love of the surroundings and people one has grown up with but also the feeling that the customary ways of the community reflect the right and proper way of doing things, as well as the confidence that one's companions share these values and are thus people one understands and consequently can trust. In this way the members treat their *Gemeinschaft* as an end in itself.

A *Gesellschaft*, by contrast, is an association in which the members are united by a shared form of *Kürwille*[9]—that is, what motivates them is a shared goal of some sort, and they see the association as a fairly efficient or even necessary means of attaining that goal.[10] It is illustrated in modern life by "societies" for doing something, such as the Society for the Protection of Animals, and by profit-making societies such as business corporations.[11] In a *Gesellschaft* decisions are made on the basis of instrumental reasoning and invention, and the criterion for a good decision is entirely a matter of how well it forwards the goal of the *Gesellschaft*. Whereas organization in a *Gemeinschaft* is governed by what *feels* right because it aligns with traditional ways, in a *Gesellschaft* the organization is governed by what is judged to be most efficient in attaining a goal or set of goals.

Tönnies's analysis of the two kinds of will—that is, the psychology behind the two forms of human association—is worth examining in some detail here, as it will provide the basic theoretical framework for what follows in this book. *Wesenwille*, he says, takes three forms. Most basic is "delight,"[12] which consists in innate drives arising from a person's existence as a biological organism.[13] Prominent among these drives are those for self-preservation, nourishment, and sex. Layered on top of that is "habit," that is, desires arising from the pleasure one takes in activities one has practised and become familiar with, perhaps even expert in. It applies as well to things like a familiar environment or diet.[14] Finally, there is "memory." This is a knowledge of what is valuable, good, or right based on experience and teaching. This knowledge is conscious and finds articulation in language.[15] The traditional family unit exhibits most fully behaviour motivated by *Wesenwille*, and hence the family is the archetypical *Gemeinschaft*.

Kürwille operates entirely at the conscious level and presumes that the person's motivational structure is already well developed.[16] Here the establishment of an end or goal is all-important and actions are judged by their imagined efficiency in attaining that goal. *Kürwille* also has three forms layered one on the other, of which the first and most basic is "deliberation," in which short-term costs are weighed against longer-term benefits when considering whether to adopt some means (considered as costs) to attain some goal (considered as a benefit).[17] The second form is "discrimination," where the agent has a dominant goal, recognizes a variety of ways of achieving it, and must choose among them.[18] The third and last form of *Kürwille* is "concept," by which Tönnies means the motivation that arises from framing in language general concepts with which to evaluate ends and means. Its peculiar manifestation is the formation of general principles governing action undertaken via *Kürwille*.[19] One of the highest achievements of *Kürwille* thinking is the creation of laws, by which some of the intuitive motivational structure arising out of *Wesenwille* can be replaced with a totally conscious motivation to make one's behaviour accord with carefully crafted principles articulated in language deploying general concepts.

Although ends–means thinking ("instrumental reasoning" if you like) is central to *Kürwille*, Tönnies did not mean that *Wesenwille* has no use for goals. Rather, the difference lies in the relationship the goal has to the action aiming at it. In *Kürwille* the action is conceived as a mere means of no intrinsic value, but in *Wesenwille* the goal gives the action meaning and thus renders it valuable in itself. Consider this contrast: On the one hand, we have someone attending to a sick person, making sure they are comfortable, fed properly, getting their medications, and so on. The goal is the invalid's recovery, but even if they do not recover, the action may well have intrinsic value for the agent. On the other hand, we have the action of filling out a tax form in order to receive a rebate. Here the action is a worthless nuisance if it does not succeed in obtaining the rebate. In other words, in *Kürwille* success in achieving the goal is the only thing considered intrinsically worthwhile, while in *Wesenwille* the effort made to achieve the goal is worthwhile whether or not the goal is achieved, and this is the case even when the effort is painful or involves sacrifice.

The two types of will are associated with two types of human character and two types of goodness in humans, although in reality no one is purely of one type or the other. Instead, everyone displays both types of will; it is just that some lean more to the one than to the other, and this in varying degrees. Characters ruled by *Wesenwille* act on the basis of urges and intuitive feelings, whether these are innate or the results of habituation and training. These feelings are genuine and not concocted to serve some consciously imagined ideal. Such people evaluate situations in a gestalt-like way rather than by analyzing them into conceptually distinct aspects. These characters at their best have a built-in tendency toward friendliness and helpfulness, as well as a fully developed conscience—a "moral compass" as we now say.[20]

In contrast, the characters ruled by *Kürwille* operate in a much more conscious and self-conscious way. They are skeptical of intuitions and feelings whose sources remain in the obscurity of the unconscious.[21] They are given to calculation of the most efficient way of deploying available resources to obtain their ends. They delight in planning, especially when the goal is clearly defined, and this applies to the designing of their own life as well as the external environment.[22] At their best, *Kürwille* characters exhibit a capacity for self-criticism that is beyond the reach of the *Wesenwille* character. They see their own faults and strive to correct them. When feelings arise from obscure sources, they are able to step back and judge whether they are worth attending to or not. The *Gemeinschaften*, where *Wesenwille* dominates, can suffer from prejudices and superstitions that render those societies unable to meet new challenges. In particular, people from a foreign culture exhibiting different modes of behaviour may well appear obnoxious to the *Wesenwille* character living in a traditional *Gemeinschaft*. Hence arises xenophobia. Also, in the previous chapter we mentioned the role of morality in village communities and how this can be extended to the point that human spontaneity is drastically curtailed and a kind of stultifying moralizing comes to dominate social life. Here a person in that society acting on *Kürwille* may shine, for they will be capable of the self-criticism[23] that leads to reform.

Although combinable in the real activities of life, *Wesenwille* and *Kürwille* are opposed in the sense that the more action results from the one the less it results from the other, the more life is conducted in accord with the one the less it is with the other. Consequently, the more a social bond has a *Gemeinschaft* character the less it will have the character of a *Gesellschaft*, and conversely. There is, then, built into the fabric of both individual lives and social constructs a certain tension or opposition, which can be at times quite severe.[24] Tönnies was particularly alive to this conflict and saw it operating in modern Europe as traditional life in peasant villages and towns eroded in the face of the intrusion of the commercial economy dominated by the city. To him this meant the coming to power of the merchants and the need for people to adopt their *Kürwille* approach to life, an approach that devalues the "folkways and mores" of the common people and their whole *Wesenwille* way of acting.[25]

The great accomplishment of pre-urban civilization was to take the kind of *Gemeinschaft* that Paleolithic foraging bands must have had and elaborate and extend it so that settled life could be lived within it. This it accomplished mostly through the enlargement of the area ruled by custom and by intensifying the process of educating the young. All of this enabled people to navigate the much more artificial and technically sophisticated ways of a settled, agrarian community by relying for the most part on what felt natural and right, that is, on forms of *Wesenwille*. Of course, villagers had plenty of occasions to exercise *Kürwille* as well in the course of solving the various problems of social, economic, and political life as they came along. Human life is never run entirely on just one of these two sorts of will. Nor, it must be said, is a community ever entirely a *Gemeinschaft* or entirely a *Gesellschaft*, since the reasons for staying within the community will always involve some measure of both sorts of will. It is just that in some communities, like the pre-urban village, *Wesenwille* is overwhelmingly dominant, and in others, like a modern corporation, *Kürwille* is.

Within a *Gemeinschaft*, the means–ends thinking of *Kürwille* is mainly a servant of the *Gemeinschaft*, and the small *Gesellschaften* that form within the community are there to perform specific tasks such as preparing religious ceremonies or managing a harvest. The *Gemeinschaft* is the overarching unity; the other unities, including those organized for specific ends, function within it and serve it. Instrumental reasoning and inventiveness have a place, but that place is within an overall structure that does not rely on such thinking for its justification.

For a whole society to become dominated by *Kürwille*, and thus to become predominantly a *Gesellschaft*, is for its activities that were previously undertaken by people motivated by *Wesenwille* to be taken over by artificial institutions designed by people operating by *Kürwille*. Thus in our own modern, Western society, education of the young, care of the sick, elderly, and indigent, provision of the necessities of life, and so on, are now mostly run by carefully designed organizations created to fulfil set goals. In all these institutions calculations of costs and benefits are crucial in overseeing their operations. Modern Western society is unique in the history of humanity in how far this transition has been carried out, as well as in the high degree to which persons with expertise in calculation, planning, and design are esteemed. *Wesenwille* has been largely restricted to the realm of interpersonal relations, especially in modern urban life. Tönnies saw this transition taking place in his own day and realized that it would lead to the penetration of *Gesellschaft* into all aspects of social life within a city. He wrote as follows:

> However, both [the town and the village] possess many features of the family, the village more, the town fewer. Only if the town changes into a big city does it lose these features almost completely; the isolated persons or even families exist opposite to each other and have their common location only as a coincidental and deliberately chosen place to live. But as the town continues inside the big city (which they indicate by their names), so the *Gemeinschaft* way of life, as the only real way, lasts inside the *Gesellschaft* mode, even if it is also withering and in fact dying away.[26]

But then he goes on to predict *Gesellschaft* domination of the entire world and the resultant exclusion of common people from the "active" part of humanity:

> On the other hand, the more all pervasive the *Gesellschaft* condition comes to be in a nation or in a group of nations the more the entire "country," or the whole "world," comes to be similar to a single big city. However, in the big city, and thus within the *Gesellschaft* condition, only the elite, the rich, the cultured are really active and alive, and they set the standard to which the lower classes, out of a desire partly to supplant some particular one of them, partly to become like them, have to conform in order to achieve for themselves the arbitrary power typical of a *Gesellschaft*.[27]

My thesis in this chapter is that the earliest urban-dominated civilizations, those of Mesopotamia and Egypt, and to a lesser extent the later ones in India and China, reversed the old, traditional ordering whereby society was governed as a *Gemeinschaft* and *Gesellschaft* organizations operated in the service of that *Gemeinschaft*. Now *Gemeinschaften* operated in the context of a *Gesellschaft* and served the purposes of the *Gesellschaft*. Accordingly, whereas earlier communities were led by persons predominantly exhibiting a *Wesenwille* mentality and character, now the *Kürwille* types with their emphasis on planning and efficiency came to power. In applying Tönnies's concepts to the ancient and original creation of cities, I certainly go beyond anything he himself proposed, but it seems to me that the conflict Tönnies described between the two forms of social organization, as well as the tensions between their psychological bases, *Wesenwille* and *Kürwille*, may well help explain why that transition was on balance a disaster for humanity, a trauma not just for the peoples who fell within such civilizations but for many peoples who were merely in contact with them and not incorporated within them. The trauma was the result of dominance by an elite who functioned on entirely different motivational principles than what the common people deemed right and fair and whose thinking was dominated by abstract goals to the disregard of traditional modes of living. This enraged and frustrated the majority of people, who still operated within a *Gemeinschaft*, which now had to serve the ends of the elite. This was the core of the collective trauma that overtook a large part of humanity in the ancient world.

I suggest that already in this very early period a basically *Gesellschaft* organization had become dominant in these Sumerian states and was managing in a consciously goal-directed way the *Gemeinshaften* in which the farmers still lived. The religio-political autocracy was a consequence of the need for central planning and to justify ideologically the substitution of human will for the forces of nature, as well as the domination of rational planning over custom. The priest-king had some sort of special relationship to the gods, An and Enlil. Indeed, the accepted view was that it was the gods themselves, not humans, who had established the irrigation system, which made its maintenance a religious duty. In this way, ordinary farming folk could be brought to accept the domination of an urban elite over the basics of their economy. Each city's temple was on a raised platform, no doubt symbolizing its proximity to the gods who lived in the sky. Religion cast a veil of sacredness over the *Gesellschaft*; what was in fact a coup of *Kürwille* overthrowing *Wesenwille* in the affairs of the communities got dressed out as divine ordinances, communicated through a special person acting as their conduit. The power and prestige of the king, considered either as a vice-regent of the gods or as a god himself, became both the goal and *raison d'être* of the elite community immediately surrounding the king, and commitment to that goal bound that community together as a kind of *Gesellschaft* that ruled in a more or less *Kürwille* way the rest of the society. Variations on this sort of arrangement are what I believe we are looking at not only in ancient Sumer but in all the great kingdoms of the ancient Middle East.

How the Shift Played Out in the Middle East

The independence of the various Sumerian city-states must always have been tenuous. Once conflicts arose it was not easy to keep them from developing into serious wars. All sides would have viewed themselves as following divine directives, and any ruler's claim to divine favour would have been severely compromised had he been forced to capitulate to some other ruler's demands. Military forces would have developed, and quite likely these were professionalized from an early date. A *Kürwille* approach to warfare would soon have shown its advantages over the more chaotic, impulsive approach dominated by *Wesenwille*. From here on it was characteristic of urban-dominated civilizations to create trained military forces that used carefully designed tactics and technologies in order to intimidate, if not outright conquer, other peoples. Indeed, the military sphere became a paradigm of domination by *Kürwille* thinking and the cradle of many of the innovations that civilization was to adopt.

Another feature of the earliest Sumerian states was the growing importance they gave to slavery, something that had been of marginal usefulness in the pre-urban civilizations.[28] As Aristotle famously noted, a slave is a living tool, and tools—be they living or inanimate—are built into the *Kürwille* efficiency-oriented approach to life and hence crucial to a proper *Gesellschaft*. Most tools, especially carefully designed ones, are single purpose, and slaves had single purposes for the most part. Their lives were spent on specific tasks that few free persons would have devoted themselves to full time. No doubt many of these tasks involved hard physical labour (building and maintaining canals, for example), and the lives of such slaves would have been painful and short. But slaves were also used in crafts such as wood- and metalworking, and weaving and spinning, and were employed as scribes and musicians. Perhaps this was how the skills of such people came to be honed to such a marvellous degree of precision and efficiency, and why their craft products (clothing, jewellery, weapons, etc.) are so awe-inspiring even today for their beauty and sophistication.

It is easy to see how the city became a remarkably different place from the agricultural hinterland, where most of the populace continued to live in their traditional *Gemeinschaften*. In many ways, for an unbiased observer, urban life would have seemed much superior. What was available for purchase was clearly better than what was available in the hinterland. This was not entirely due to the superior work of professional artisans, for urban markets in the city attracted exotic goods brought in by long-distance traders. Those markets attained a prominence in economic life hitherto unknown to human communities, and with this came people who specialized in commerce and occasionally became very wealthy as a result. Commerce obviously lends itself to careful calculation and organization along *Gesellschaft* lines. Some traders by their dealings with foreign peoples would have risen above dependence on any one city-state and achieved a status where their loyalties were pretty much to themselves and their own organizations,[29] although, of course, they had to make sure they shared their wealth with the powers that existed in the various states where they did business.

Commerce may well have inspired the first systems of writing, for the earliest writing we know of records accounts of some sort. Record-keeping is the *sine qua non* for any sophisticated commercial operation or taxation system, but it needs to be accompanied by enumeration and basic arithmetic. And, indeed, this too seems to have originated in Sumeria. Their number system used place values much the way our own decimal system does, but the base was 60 rather than 10. The abacus was also developed quite early in Sumeria. Obviously, precise arithmetic calculations were highly valued in this civilization, and this contributed to the development of a sophisticated astronomy and the precise recording of the timing of events in the heavens.[30] These endeavours reached full fruition much later in Babylonian astronomy, whose extended records may have resulted in the discovery of the precession of the equinoxes.[31]

Writing and its close ally, arithmetic symbols, are, I believe, a sure sign of an elite at work with a basically *Kürwille* mentality. Ordinary spoken language depends heavily on the context surrounding speech to determine the meaning of the utterances a speaker makes in any given situation. These are usually filled with indexical words such as the personal pronouns, or words like "now," "here," "there," "today," and so on, whose reference is clear only to someone who knows the particular context in which they are uttered. What is meant by words implying comparison, like "large," old," "soft," and so on, can only be determined by knowing the intended comparison class, and this will be clear only by familiarity with the context. In addition, a written message does not carry with it any indication of the speaker's body language or tone of voice, aspects of spoken language that strongly indicate how the utterance is to be taken. Is it ironic, sarcastic, strongly felt or only mildly? In general, writing preserves utterances so that they occur apart from the whole original context of utterance and thus is most useful when the information being preserved and communicated is something that can be grasped without knowing anything about the particular context of the utterance. The meaning is now an abstract proposition, the basic tool of logical reasoning, and when arithmetic symbols are involved that meaning becomes the subject for calculation. Such thinking appeals to the *Kürwille* mentality; dealing with the vagaries of context introduces very troublesome complexities. People operating with *Wesenwille*, by contrast, are comfortable with grasping utterance meanings by situating them in the surrounding context, which the hearers more or less immediately fathom. This is all part of the *Wesenwille* holistic approach to thinking; it eschews splitting apart of a meaning that is independent of that context, and practical life in a *Gemeinschaft* usually has little need for such abstraction. It is not surprising, then, that writing arose very late in human history; there was no appreciable need for it until a *Gesellschaft* elite took on the task of organizing society.

Long-distance commerce may have been one factor that led to the next stage of urban-dominated civilization, its imperial era. The king of Uruk had united all the Sumerian cities under his rule, but not long after, another figure, speaking a different language, Akkadian, conquered not just the Sumerians but the whole of Mesopotamia and possibly all of the Fertile Crescent. This was Sargon the Great, who ruled from 2334 to 2279 BCE.[32] The urgent question here is why anyone would want to engage in such an outlandish enterprise. I doubt that the answer lies in attributing to Sargon some sort of psychopathic condition. More likely is that he could not secure his conquests in the south unless he extended his rule first to the north, and then to secure that he had to proceed even further, this time to the west, right out to the Mediterranean. This sort of progression has been a familiar feature of empires down through history. In modern times the British Empire provided numerous illustrations.

But what was the cause of the original insecurity? It seems unlikely that it was military threats that worried Sargon, for his conquests show that his own military machine was well able to handle any rivals in the region. More likely it was dependence on much needed goods from foreign sources, perhaps ores for the production of bronze. Not just the military but the whole urban economy may have become dependent on imports from foreign nations. Sargon and his homeland may have been put in the position of having to pay exorbitant prices for goods the luxurious lifestyle of Akkad could not do without. There is also the matter of slaves. Conquests of peoples often led to their being enslaved by the conqueror, with obvious benefits to the people of the conqueror's homeland, not to mention himself.[33] This is all speculation, of course; we simply do not know specifically what led Sargon to achieve his amazing imperial ambitions. But one can easily imagine that as different peoples became more and more economically dependent on trade, the opportunities for extortion, embargoes, and other human-produced distortions of the entire system grew. To a mind already well accustomed to practices of central control and rational planning, and imbued with the belief that the sky gods themselves were demanding an extension of these, the idea of imperial rule would be extremely natural, and its exercise all too feasible given the previous development of a highly disciplined professional military using the latest in metal weaponry and war chariots.

At any rate, with Sargon begins the nightmare of urban civilization in the Middle East. There were interludes of peace and prosperity, of course, and wonderful advances in the arts and sciences, but all this was deeply marred by the rise of empires and their catastrophic struggles for power. The imperial rule of the Akkadians managed to survive many rebellions by subject peoples and attempted coups by disaffected members of the elite. The resultant oppression could be fearful in its violence, and the king justified his rule by ever more exaggerated fantasies of divinity. The final king, Naram-Sin, proclaimed himself a god equal to any of those in the traditional pantheon of deities. He ruled from 2261 to 2224, when the empire suddenly collapsed under an onslaught by foreign invaders, leaving the city of Akkad in ruins and its population dying of famine.

This story could be carried on through the whole second millennium and into the first. Something similar could be told of the rise of the Mauryan Empire in India and the Han in China as responses to the conflicts that became more and more endemic to those cradles of civilization. But in the interest of keeping this work to a somewhat reasonable length, I am going to turn to some ancient literature that many of my readers will no doubt already be familiar with: the poetry of the ancient Hebrew prophets. Here we find accounts of how the rampaging imperial civilizations of the Middle East in the middle of the first millennium appeared to a relatively weak national group hard-pressed to stay in existence on its land in such a violent neighbourhood. We also see how this society's own transition to urban domination was viewed by people still wedded to their traditional *Gemeinschaft*.

Here is Isaiah[34] writing in the Northern Kingdom about its coming conquest by the Assyrians. From this passage we can garner some idea of the impression the disciplined Assyrian war machine made on the peoples it subjugated:

> He will raise a signal for a nation afar off,
>   And whistle for it from the ends of the earth;
> And lo, swiftly, speedily it comes!
>   None is weary, none stumbles,
>   None slumbers or sleeps,
>   Not a waistcloth is loose,
>   Not a sandal thong broken;
>   Their arrows are sharp.
>   And their bows bent,
>   Their horses' hooves seem like flint,
>   And their wheels like the whirlwind.
>   Their roaring is like a lion,
>   Like young lions they roar;
>   They growl and seize their prey,
>   They carry it off, and none can rescue. (5:26–29)

When the prophet Nahum describes the sack of the Assyrian capital of Nineveh, he portrays the horror in the following terms:

> The crack of whip, the rumble of wheel,
>> Galloping horse and bounding chariot!
> Horsemen charging,
>> Flashing sword and glittering spear,
> Host of slain,
>> Heaps of corpses,
> Dead bodies without end—
>> They stumble over the bodies! (3:2–3)

From these works of the Hebrew prophets we also get a view of the reaction, no doubt widespread, to the inequality that resulted from the adoption of the *Gesellschaft* rearranging of Hebrew society. Here is Isaiah again, excoriating the arrogance that has arisen with the new order's pride in its own achievements:

> Their land is filled with silver and gold.
>> And there is no end to their treasures;
> Their land is filled with horses,
>> And there is no end to their chariots.
> Their land is filled with idols;
>> They bow down to the work of their hands,
>> To what their own fingers have made.
> ...
> The haughty looks of man shall be brought low,
>> And the pride of men shall be humbled;
> And the Lord alone will be exalted in that day. (2:7–9, 11)

That last passage reeks of the resentment that people still living within the *Gemeinschaft* order must have felt toward the elite of the royal court and priesthood that since the time of Solomon had taken control of Israelite society as a whole. To the elite what was impressive was the "work of their own hands," that is, their consciously created affluence and military technology. The ordinary people, stuck in their *Gemeinschaft* ways, were viewed as hardly worth consideration, even though the whole society depended in the end on their toil in the fields and workshops of the land. A *Gemeinschaft* creates things too, but it does so on the basis of long-established customs and skills; innovation and inventiveness play minor roles and hence there is limited space for individuals to see themselves as something superior to the ordinary run of people. This blocks one serious pathway for class division to take hold and thus helps maintain a unity in that each member recognizes the importance of being part of the whole.

The Hebrew prophets were especially damning of the way the *Gesellschaft* mode of society led to the flaunting of ill-gotten luxury and disregard of the plight of the poor and the afflicted. Here are Jeremiah's sharp words protesting to the king the growing inequities in the land:

> Woe to him who builds his house by unrighteousness,
>   And his upper rooms by injustice;
> Who makes his neighbour serve him for nothing,
>   And does not give him his wages;
> Who says, "I will build myself a great house
>   With spacious upper rooms,"
> And cuts out windows for it,
>   Panelling it with cedar,
>   And painting it with vermilion.
> Do you think you are a king because you compete in cedar?
>   Did not your father eat and drink
>   And do justice and righteousness?
>   Then it was well with him.
> He judged the cause of the poor and the needy;
>   Then it was well.
> Is not this to know me?
>   Says the Lord.
> But you have eyes and heart
>   Only for your dishonest gain,
> For shedding innocent blood,
>   And for practicing oppression and violence. (22:13–17)

Or read these words of Amos on the subject:

> Hear this, you who trample upon the needy,
>   And bring the poor of the land to an end,
> Saying, "When will the new moon be over,
>   That we may sell grain?
> And the Sabbath,
>   That we may offer wheat for sale,
> That we may make the sphah small the shekel great,
>   And deal deceitfully with false balances,
> That we may buy the poor for silver
>   And the needy for a pair of sandals,
>   And sell the refuse of the wheat?" (8:4–6)

In Israel the rise to dominance of a *Gesellschaft* had led to a grievous class split, with concentration of wealth and power in an elite of royal retainers, priests, generals, and merchants, all of whom had mastered the *Kürwille* approach to life. The elite was then enticed into a disregard for the customary principles of fair play in their dealings with those still operating mostly in the *Wesenwille* way and thus unable to compete effectively for a share of the affluence. Even the king, whom the people trusted to enforce justice, had been corrupted, and no one was able to compel him to correct the wrongs.

This dynamic is a familiar one in modern times. No doubt it was at work even in pre-urbanized civilizations too, but there the *Gemeinschaft* reverence for custom and the priority given to the commonweal kept it in check in most places and times. Once a *Gesellschaft* comes to dominate, however, those restraints are largely removed, and rapacious individuals have their opportunity to gain individually while ignoring the needs and customary rights of the masses. The "nightmare," then, was not just a matter of imperialism and international war; it also was found right at home. The Hebrew prophets cast this disaster in terms of a people forgetting the demands of their God, Jehovah, and went on to view the catastrophic defeats at the hands of Assyria and Babylon as Jehovah's teaching the people a lesson. This phantasy, of course, was unreal; yet there may have been an element of truth in it. As Lincoln said, "A house divided against itself cannot stand." Israel had become a deeply divided society, and this would surely have weakened it in its conflicts with the Great Powers of the day. How much a similar story played out among the other smaller peoples of the region we cannot say for certain, but many of them must have adopted kingship and the other aspects of *Gesellschaft* in their efforts to maintain some measure of independence, and then some similar sort of division may well have afflicted them too.

That in brief is the trauma of civilization once it was centred on cities. The elite had become dominated by a *Kürwille* mentality that viewed society as a means to its own power and capacity to design the world. But *Kürwille* can be self-conscious; it can turn on itself if it feels the need. This is what happened in parts of the ancient world of the late first millennium BCE, and what resulted were ideologies that placed restraints on the very mentality that was driving humanity toward traumatic catastrophes. This development will be the subject of the next chapter.

Addendum

After I had finished writing and sent this work to the Press for publication, David Graeber and David Wengrow's book *The Dawn of Everything* appeared. It develops in detail the story of early human evolution that the two chapters above sketch only in rough outline. Among the many fascinating findings related in that book there is one that I want particularly to note here. According to Graeber and Wengrow, the earliest form of writing we know of, cuneiform script, first appears in the Sumerian city of Uruk around 3300 BCE and was originally used for recording transactions of goods and services.[35] A college of scribes developed, who administered "complicated relations between people, animals and things."[36] All this was in the service of activities carried on in the "houses of the gods," which Graeber and Wengrow say "resembled factories more than churches," and in which human labour was organized into standardized units. Here another Sumerian invention comes into play, the sexagesimal numerical system, which was used to precisely quantify time as well as quantities of goods. The authors claim that in Uruk's bookkeeping records "we find the ancient seedbeds of modern industrialism, finance and bureaucracy."[37]

Now it should be clear that these techniques—writing, mathematics, quantification, standardization—are achievements of what Tönnies called *Kürwille*, and, if Graeber and Wengrow are correct, their association with the central control of certain industrial processes means that we have here what amounts to the creation of a *Gesellschaft* that exists for certain definite purposes, namely the efficient completion of these industrial tasks. Before Uruk came under monarchical rule, this *Gesellschaft* served the purposes of an overarching *Gemeinshaft*, but the Kürwille mentality behind that *Gesellschaft* no doubt easily adapted to the expanded applications monarchy was eager to afford it in organizing the whole of society to serve that monarch. The two, then, *Kürwille* and domination, have a natural affinity for each other. Herein, I believe, lies the root of the trauma I described in chapter two.

3

DESIGNERS OF THE INNER SELF

> Human Kind is challenged, as it has never been
> challenged before, to prove its maturity, and its
> mastery—not of nature, but of itself.
>
> —Rachel Carson, *Silent Spring*

To some thoughtful people in the urban-dominated civilizations of the ancient world it became clear around the middle of the first millennium BCE that their human worlds were not functioning in a satisfactory way, and that, indeed, the lives of the people in their societies were deeply unsatisfying and flawed. In fact, although these thinkers came from the elite strata, they found their own lives unsatisfying. This happened in the civilization of the Ganges plain in India, culminating in the rise of Buddhism in the fifth century. It happened in China and is manifest in the teachings of Confucius and Lao Tzu around the same time. And it emerged in ancient Greece around roughly the same period. All these lines of thought exhibited the workings of *Kürwille* mentalities in that the thinkers stepped back from the world to critically examine it, only here they took psychological distance on themselves *and on their own Kürwille mindset*. The results were prescriptions for living that if adhered to would drastically curtail *Kürwille*'s obsession with power and planning. Evolving from these prescriptions were ideal ways of living that, at least among the educated elite, had immense attractiveness and directed adherents to goals very different from those people generally sought. Most notably, concerns for material prosperity, worldly success, magnificent undertakings, and physical comfort came to be seen as part of the problem, not part of the solution.

A full treatment of this topic should give roughly equal space to ideological developments in each of the three main civilizations involved: India, China, and the Greco-Roman world. That approach, however, would increase the length of this work well beyond the tolerance of most readers, so, consequently, I have decided to treat in detail only the last of the three mentioned above, while occasionally noting parallels in the other two. Since my treatment of ideas in India and China is so cursory, its aims are very limited. It does not show, for example, that those ideas had a profound influence on economic development in those societies, although in fact I think they did. My only goal is to show that some of the ideologies that developed in India and China were similar to the ones that became dominant among elites in the ancient Greco-Roman world with respect to their wariness of *Kürwille* thinking and disdain for material expansion. I think it is important to see that the reaction against *Kürwille* thinking and the *Gesellschaft* way of living was not limited to the West but arose fairly independently in all three of the great Eurasian civilizations. This, I think, constitutes evidence that the transition to urban-centred civilization had been traumatic. For our immediate purposes, however, it is crucial to address the ideas of philosophers in ancient Greece and Rome, since many of those ideas became incorporated into the Christian culture of the Western Middle Ages and thus formed part of the cultural milieu from which the modern West had to detach itself in order to proceed on its grandiose but perilous course, one that it persists in pursuing to the present day.

Ancient Greece and Its Discontents

The first urban-centred civilizations of the Mediterranean world north and west of Egypt and the Levant were the Minoan civilization in Crete and the Mycenaean in the Greek Peloponnesus, which were in place early in the second millennium BCE. For reasons not currently clear, they collapsed in the second half of that millennium.[1] Our attention here is instead on what developed in the Greek world in the first millennium BCE and how this influenced later developments in the Roman Empire, which by the end of the millennium controlled the entire Mediterranean littoral. In this period Greece was populated by people speaking a common language (an archaic form of Greek) but divided into various independent pockets whose rough boundaries largely followed the hilly terrain. Many of these pockets developed urban centres that dominated the surrounding agricultural land. Although all these groups recognized themselves as Greek and part of a common culture, they were frequently in conflict and rarely able to unite themselves even when threatened by the enormously powerful Achaemenid (i.e., Persian) Empire to the east. Nevertheless, the Greeks managed to defeat two Persian invasions in the early part of the fifth century and maintained their independence of foreign powers until conquered by the Macedonians in the late fourth century. They were the first people west of the Levant to break with traditional mythic thinking and explore new ways of imagining the role of humans in the cosmos and in society. Out of this ferment came the chief self-reflective perspectives of the elites in the Roman Empire.

Portions of the history of ancient Greece are familiar to just about everybody in the West, since so much of Western culture has its origins there. In particular, the achievements of fifth-century BCE Athens in so many fields of human endeavour continue to be lauded in schools and referenced in speeches. Athens was the Greek city that contributed most to the defeat of the Persian invasions; it was her fleet that won the crucial Battle of Salamis in 480. Afterwards, Athens used its sea power to dominate the other Greek cities of the Aegean and thereby exact the tribute that fuelled its affluence. Most of the citizens of the city could afford slaves, and there developed a sizeable leisure class whose main activities were politics and war. What most differentiated Athens from the earlier urban civilizations we have treated is its lasting attachment to "democracy." The leisured elite, in order to rule, had to please the mass of the citizenry and win votes in the assembly, in which all citizens were allowed a voice, at times even paid to participate.[2]

Affluence, it is often noted, has a tendency to undermine the traditional mores and values that were built up in earlier periods when scarcity was a continual threat. This happened in Athens of the fifth century BCE and led to people taking seriously new ideas about how life should be conducted, especially in the spheres of politics and education. In addition, there were challenges to traditional Greek religion with its pantheon of misbehaving deities. Cosmological ideas that rejected the role of personal gods in the formation of the universe and the creation of natural phenomena, in favour of non-teleological explanations, were launched in the Greek cities on the Aegean coast of Asia Minor. It is possible that contacts with Indian thought played some role in this. It is indisputable, though, that Indian ideas were introduced on the other side of the Greek world in Italy by the Pythagoreans, who believed in reincarnation and practised vegetarianism. These Pythagoreans also brought to the West a fascination with mathematics and a belief that the world generally admitted of being understood in mathematical terms.

On top of all this intellectual and spiritual ferment came the war in the fifth century BCE between Athens, mainly a sea power, and Sparta, a land power. The other Greek cities often had to ally themselves with one or the other of the parties to the dispute, and even the Persians were occasionally involved. Athens relied on the importing of supplies by ship from its satellites around the Aegean, while Sparta dominated on land. Two events in the end doomed Athens to defeat: first, an ill-advised attempt to seize Syracuse in Sicily, which ended in catastrophe, and second, a devastating plague. By the end of the fifth century Athens had to call it quits and submit to Spartan hegemony. This, however, did not last long, and early in the following century Athens was independent again, with a restored democracy. It became the intellectual centre of the Greek world, with Plato, Aristotle, Zeno the Stoic, and Epicurus all setting up schools there; but it never again achieved the economic and political power it once had.

Europeans from the Renaissance on often lauded the Greeks' achievements in art, architecture, drama, philosophy, and science, and sometimes even thought of the culture created in Athens in the fifth century BCE as the pinnacle of human development. But to most Greeks of the time it did not appear this way at all. Rather, to them, it was a period of chaos not only in politics but also in matters of mind and spirit. To many it seemed that the whole civilization was in a crisis that the political leaders were unable to manage and that the intellectuals were unable to fathom. One of these critics was Plato, whose writings have set the course for mainstream Western philosophy right up into modern times.

Plato and Socratic Ethics

Plato grew up in Athens during the war with Sparta as a young nobleman with aspirations to become a playwright. It is known that he entered a comedy into a competition, which he lost to Aristophanes. During the later part of the war he became involved with a group of young Athenians who regularly conversed with Socrates, an older man who was convinced of the need for ethical reform. Socrates left no writings of his own, and we know of him mostly through Plato's famous dialogues, in which he usually questions, with devastating effect, some person who is sure of his own wisdom about what constitutes excellent living. It is quite unclear how much these dialogues reflect the ideas and practices of the historical Socrates. Certainly the situations in which Plato places Socrates in these works are fictional, and scholars agree that some of the dialogues, like *Republic* and *Theaetetus*, go well beyond any ideas the historical Socrates would have entertained. In what follows I am going to assume that the Socrates of Plato's dialogues is mostly Plato's creation and that through this dramatic character Plato, writing in the early fourth century after Socrates's death, gives expression to his own deep misgivings about the politics and culture of his native city and Greece generally. Certainly, Plato, like a number of other followers of the historical Socrates, was deeply dismayed by Athens's execution of him in 399. Socrates's determination to live in accordance with his own teachings, even to the point of death, was impressive and made the moral inferiority of his accusers, and of the populace generally, all the more evident. His death turned Socrates into a moral hero for generations of intellectuals to come. It is this ethical teaching, associated with Plato's Socratic dialogues and so influential in later centuries, that we will be focusing on, since it, I claim, was an ideological force restrictive of the economic expansion and technological development of the ancient Mediterranean world and went on to infiltrate the Christian culture that emerged as the Roman Empire dissolved in the West.

Plato's *Apology*, which presents itself as an account of Socrates's defence of himself during the trial that ended in his sentence of execution, allows us to see what Plato took to be the chief motivations for Socrates's career as a verbal "gadfly" to the lifestyle and mores of his fellow Athenians. Here is what Socrates in *Apology* says he would say to Athenians if they allowed him to live on the condition that he give up his pestering interrogations:

> Men of Athens, I honour and love you; but I shall obey the god rather than you, and while I have life and strength I shall never cease from the practice and teaching of philosophy, exhorting anyone whom I meet and saying to him in that way I have: You, my friend, a citizen of the great and mighty and wise city of Athens, are you not ashamed of heaping up enormous amounts of money and honour and reputation, while caring so little about wisdom and truth and the great improvement of your soul, which you never regard or heed at all? And, if the person with whom I am arguing says: Yes, but I do care; then I do not immediately leave him or let him go, but rather I proceed to question and examine and cross-examine him, and, if I think he has no excellence in him but just says that he has, I criticize him for undervaluing the more important and overvaluing the less.[3]

His god-given mission, then, was to convince people that the improvement of the soul is much more important than amassing wealth and securing a good reputation. By "improvement of the soul" he meant, at least in part, a respect for truth and wisdom. He repeated the same theme, adding, as one of the less important goals, physical fitness, and emphasizing that what one should seek above all is "excellence" (*aretē*), that is, virtue of character:

> For all I do is go about persuading you all, old and young alike, not to take thought for your bodies and your wealth until you have first, and chiefly, cared about the great improvement of your soul. I tell you that excellence does not come from wealth, but that from excellence come wealth and every other of the things good for a man, public as well as private.[4]

Socrates conceives this mission as one given to him by the god Apollo and so equates abandoning it to disobedience to that highly esteemed deity. This justification emerges clearly in the following famous passage:

> Someone may say: "Yes, Socrates, but can't you just stay quiet and go off to some foreign city, and no one will interfere with you"? Now it is extremely difficult to make you understand why this is something I cannot do. For, if I tell you that to do what you suggest would be to disobey the god, and consequently I cannot stay quiet, you will not think I am serious. Or, if I say again that conversing daily about excellence, and about those other things which you have heard that I examine myself and others on, is the greatest of goods for a man, and that the unexamined life is not worth living, you are even less likely to believe me. Nevertheless, what I am saying is true, although it is something I have a hard time persuading you of.[5]

Issuing the demand to *examine* one's own life is Socrates's divinely given mission, and nothing could more clearly display the intent to turn one's own rational thinking, what we have called the *Kürwille* mentality, back onto oneself. The mainstream of ancient Western philosophy exemplifies this to the hilt.

It is important to note that Socrates always appeals to the self-interest of those whom he interrogates. His claim is not that they should stop seeking what is best for themselves and concentrate on what other people need, but that they are ignorant of what is genuinely in their own best interest, namely excellence of character. He claims too that his interrogation technique, which usually ends with using the person's own answers to demonstrate that their beliefs are inconsistent, is useful in putting the person on the path to reforming their life.

But what did Socrates have in mind by this "excellence" that makes a person's life good? Four excellences are frequently mentioned: courage, moderation, justice, and wisdom. In Plato's *Crito*, however, justice is treated as almost the whole of excellence:

> *Socrates*: ...Now see whether we agree on another proposition: that not living but living well is chiefly to be valued.
> *Crito*: Yes, we definitely hold to that.
> *Soc.*: And living well is equivalent to living honourably and justly; do we hold to that?
> *Cr.*: Yes we do.[6]

When Socrates in this same dialogue elaborates on what acting justly consists in, he emphasizes that it is always unjust to do something bad to another person, even in retaliation for their having done something bad to you. He recognizes that this goes against a widely accepted view, as the following passage shows:

> *Soc.*: And what of doing something bad in return for suffering something bad, which is what the many think, is that just or not?
> *Cr.*: Not just.
> *Soc.*: For doing something bad to a person is no different from acting unjustly?
> *Cr.*: Very true.
> *Soc.*: Then we ought not to retaliate or return what is bad for what is bad to anyone, whatever bad thing we may have suffered from him. But please consider, Crito, whether you really mean what you are saying; for this opinion has never been held, and never will be held, by any but a few people, and those who agree to this and those who do not, have no common ground and can only despise one another when they see how far apart they are.[7]

Fully understanding these passages requires acknowledging that the Greek word *dikaiosunē*, which is translated as "justice," really means what we would call being moral. Then read "just person" as "moral person" and "just act" as "moral act" and you will see the real significance of Plato's words: harming other people is always immoral.

But what does really harm a person? It is clear that the Socrates of *Apology* holds an unconventional answer to this question too. In the following passage he asserts that in doing an unjust act a person does far more harm to himself than he does to the sufferer of the injustice. Addressing the jury, he says:

> Please realize that if you kill somebody like me, you will harm yourselves more than you will harm me. Nothing will harm me, not Meletus nor Anytus,[8] they cannot, for a bad man is not allowed to

harm someone better than himself. I do not deny that Anytus may, perhaps, kill me, or drive me into exile, deprive me of my civil rights. And he may think, as others may think, that he is inflicting a great harm on me, but there I disagree. For the bad thing he is doing right now, unjustly taking away the life of another, is far, far worse.[9]

The theme is taken up at great length in Plato's *Gorgias*, where the following interaction occurs between Socrates and the sophist Gorgias's acolyte, Polus:

> *Pol.*: At any rate you will allow that he who is unjustly put to death is wretched, and to be pitied?
> *Soc.*: Not as much, Polus, as the person who kills him, and not so much as he who is justly put to death.
> *Pol.*: How can that be, Socrates?
> *Soc.*: This way: because doing injustice is the worst of bad things.
> *Pol.*: But is it the worst? Is not suffering injustice even worse?
> *Soc.*: Certainly not.
> *Pol.*: Then would you prefer to suffer rather than do injustice?
> *Soc.*: I wouldn't like to do either, but if I had to choose between them, I would prefer suffering to doing injustice.[10]

In the dialogue Polus tries to get Socrates to admit that a tyrant is happy as long as he is able to have everything that he thinks is best for him. But Socrates refuses to agree, and Polus brings up the case of the "Great King," that is, the Persian king:

> *Pol.*: Then clearly, Socrates, you would say that you did not know even whether the Great King was a happy man?
> *Soc.*: And I would be saying the truth, for I do not know how he is off for education and justice.
> *Pol.*: What! Is that all happiness amounts to?
> *Soc.*: Yes, that's right, Polus, that is what I teach: the men and women who are fine and good are also happy, as I maintain, and those who are unjust and depraved are wretched.[11]

The term "happy" translates *eudaimōn* and describes one who is living well. The meaning is less subjective than the English term "happy"; a person may not be *eudaimōn* even if they are enjoying their life, since the life they enjoy may be disgraceful.

Socrates's position can easily seem to involve an inconsistency, since if the only real harm that can be done to a person is to undermine their good character, persons who steal from others or even murder them would not seem to be harming their victims, and hence, if we follow the logic of the *Crito*, not really acting unjustly, that is, immorally, at all. Clearly Socrates would not accept this conclusion. It seems to me that the way to absolve him of this charge of inconsistency is to acknowledge that all that is required for an act to be unjust is for it to carry out an *intention* to harm another person; whether what is intended or inflicted is in reality harmful or not is irrelevant. As long as the malefactor thinks he is harming the victim he is acting unjustly. Meletus and Anytus think they are harming Socrates by bringing him to trial, but in fact Socrates is unscathed and his accusers are ruined beyond repair.

There are two other theses that Plato has Socrates espouse that are nearly as counter-intuitive as those just discussed. The first is that all the excellences—courage, moderation, justice, and wisdom—are essentially the same and that this is because the first three are all forms of the last, namely wisdom, where wisdom is knowledge of what is genuinely worth pursuing in life. Socrates is convinced that once a person knows what is really good for them, they will pursue it in the face of contrary impulses. In Plato's *Protagoras*, Socrates confronts a very popular professional teacher of the day, one of those whom Socrates's contemporaries referred to as a "sophist," that is, "wise one," often with a bit of sarcastic irony. Here is a passage from that dialogue that shows Socrates gaining Protagoras's acceptance of this controversial point:

> Uncover your mind to me, Protagoras, and reveal your opinion about knowledge, so I can know whether you agree with the rest of the world. Now the rest of the world think that knowledge is not anything powerful, or that it rules or commands us. Their idea is that a person may have knowledge, but nevertheless the knowledge in them may be overcome by anger, or pleasure, or pain,

or love, or perhaps by fear, just as if knowledge were a slave and could be pushed about by other things. Now is that your view? Or do you think that knowledge is a noble and commanding thing, which cannot be overcome, and will not allow a person, as long as they can distinguish between good and bad, to do anything which is contrary to knowledge, and that wisdom will provide all the strength they need.

"I agree with you, Socrates," said Protagoras; "and considering who I am I am bound to say that wisdom and knowledge are the most powerful things in human life."[12]

Again Plato has Socrates acknowledge that this is not the common view, and in what follows in the dialogue Socrates goes to great lengths to show how the common view can be countered. His argument here shows that Socrates adopts the position we can refer to as rational egoism, in both its descriptive and prescriptive senses: humans in their deliberate choices will always opt for what they firmly believe is best for them, and in fact they *should* deliberately choose what is best for them. Of course, the latter thesis means that they should choose what is *really* best for them, not necessarily what they deem best. This whole line of reasoning leads to the conclusion that people fall into immorality on account of their ignorance: they mistakenly believe that something in fact bad for them is good for them. The cure for immorality, if there is one, will then be some process of education.

In some of the "early" dialogues Plato has Socrates confess to puzzlement about what the knowledge that constitutes wisdom is knowledge *of*. It seems it must be knowledge of what constitutes the good life, *eudaimonia*, but Socrates's other statements indicate that it is the excellences that constitute a good life, and now we know that these all boil down to the very knowledge whose object of study we are seeking. The whole inquiry seems trapped in a circle. Nevertheless, even in *Apology* Socrates seems convinced of the second of the controversial theses I promised to bring up: the practice of examining by proposing answers to important questions and then finding flaws in those answers, what is called the *elenchus*, can lead to at least some of the knowledge that constitutes the excellence of wisdom. Pursuit of this method is crucial to what Plato calls *philosophia* and requires the cooperative effort of at least two people engaged in a serious conversation.

Plato's conception of how real knowledge is to be obtained relies heavily on being able to tease out the logical implications of views we already hold and then realizing that those implications contradict other views that we hold. The result is supposed to be that we are impelled to change our views in some way or other and in the end arrive at clearly defined concepts that allow for a quasi-mathematical elaboration of what we hold to be true. It is always in collaboration with other sincere inquirers after truth that, according to Plato, this process is to be carried out. In this respect, and in its reliance on intuitions about logical relationships, it differs markedly from methods that some Indian sages, for example, employed, which emphasized solitary meditation and ascetic practice as the way to enlightenment.[13] Plato's conception was to be the dominant one among Western philosophers up through the middle ages, and something the modern West had to overturn in order to make the advances in the physical sciences for which it is justly famous.

Notoriously, Plato has Socrates deny that he has yet attained the knowledge he seeks. Rather, he believes simply that by engaging in dialectical conversation he helps others see that they too do not have the answers as to how life should be led. Of course this is a step forward. Knowing that you are ignorant is at least better than being ignorant but not knowing it. In what scholars call the middle and later dialogues, however, Plato fashions something that goes well beyond the agnosticism of his early Socrates and certainly well beyond anything the historical Socrates might have thought.

First of all, Plato develops a theory of the human soul,[14] that is, the part of a person responsible for mental life and character development, by dividing it into three parts, each with a kind of life of its own. One part, often just called "appetite," subjects the person to cravings that arise automatically in various situations. Thirst, hunger, and sexual lust are the three cravings most frequently mentioned. A second part, called "spirit," is responsible for emotions like anger, indignation, resentment, pride, and so on. These are feelings that arise in response to perceived situations, such as insults, failures, and successes, and are, consequently, able to be modified through more extensive knowledge and reflection, in contrast to the cravings arising from appetite.

Finally, there is the part that through thought and reflection is able to pass judgment on the appropriateness or usefulness of the cravings and feelings emanating from the other two parts. This is generally called "reason" and was usually considered to be something possessed only by gods and humans. The excellence of character that had been the aim of Socrates's mission in Athens consists in reason being always able to enlist the aid of spirit in controlling the impulses arising from appetite.

But what would enable reason to have such dominating power? Plato's answer is knowledge—a knowledge, however, not of matters in the realm of ordinary experience, but of ideal *types*, which attract us by their clarity of form. Here Plato is enticed by the paradigm of mathematical knowledge made known to him by his Pythagorean associates, and in fact he comes to see the logical rigour of mathematics as a requirement for any genuine knowledge. All else is at best true belief. At least at one stage of his career he hoped that the practice of dialectical conversation would over time produce knowledge with the logically compelling force of mathematics in the minds of the participants, even about matters of ethics and politics. In his *Republic* an achievement of this sort is considered possible only for minds naturally suited to the rigours of abstract thought and specially educated for it. Plato lays out an elaborate plan of education in which mathematics plays an important role in accustoming students to abstract thinking. Those able to complete the full course—and this takes decades—attain real excellence of character; the rest can only hope that the amount of education they can persist through and their surrounding culture are able to instil in them true beliefs about what is correct behaviour. To this end Plato is happy to resort to the propagation of myths (he calls them "beneficial falsehoods") that provide motivation for the behaviour a well-ordered society requires.

What is important for the theme we are examining here is that Plato shifts totally what people should be aiming at in life (i.e., their conception of what constitutes a good life, *eudaimonia*) away from success in its usual terms (i.e. attainment of social power and wealth) toward the development of the individual's mind and character. He thinks this has important political implications, as emerges in the following passages from Plato's *Gorgias*, in which Socrates confronts Callicles, an ambitious young man who openly scoffs at Socrates's conception of the good life:

> *Soc.*: And now, my friend, since you are already starting on a career in public affairs, and are advising me to do so too and scolding me for not, suppose we ask a few questions of each other. Tell me, then, Callicles, how about making any of the citizens better? Was there ever anyone who was once depraved, or unjust, or immoderate, or foolish, and who became by the help of Callicles good and fine? Anyone, whether citizen or foreigner, slave or free? Tell me, Callicles, if a person were to ask these questions of you, what would you answer? Who would you say has been improved by association with you? There may have been good deeds of this sort which were done by you as a private person before you entered public life. Why will you not answer?
>
> *Cal.*: You're being contentious, Socrates.
>
> *Soc.*: No, I'm asking you this not because I love contending, but because I really want to know in what way you think that affairs of the city should be conducted. When you come to conducting them, do you have any other aim than the improvement of the citizens? Haven't we already admitted many times over that such is what the man engaged in public affairs is to do? Have we or haven't we? Answer. Well, I'll answer for you; we have. But if this is what the good man should do for the benefit of his own state, let me recall the names of those men whom you mentioned a little while back: Pericles,[15] Cimon,[16] Miltiades,[17] and Themistocles[18]; and ask whether you still think that they were good citizens.[19]

How little Socrates respects the supposed achievements of these heroes of classical Athens comes out a little later:

> *Soc.*: O, my dear friend, I say nothing against them regarded as servants of the state, and I do think that they were certainly more serviceable than those who are living now, and better able to gratify the cravings of the state; but as for transforming those

> cravings and not allowing them to have their way, and using the powers that they had, whether of persuasion or of force, for the improvement of their fellow citizens, which is the prime work of any good citizen, I do not see that in these respects they were at all superior to our present statesmen, although I do admit that they were more clever at providing ships and walls and docks, and all that.[20]

The true statesman, according to Socrates, is not primarily interested in developing the economic infrastructure that the affluence of the city requires but in improving the souls—that is, the characters—of the citizens, in other words, in doing just what Socrates claims he has been doing in his interrogatory examinations. Plato has made the moral improvement of the citizens the chief aim of politics, and in the phantastic utopia he constructs in *Republic* this is the aim of the ruling class (the "guardians"), who through their arduous education have achieved genuine knowledge of what the good life genuinely is. If statesmen follow Plato's advice, they will concern themselves much less with improvements to the state that merely increase the comfort of the citizens and much more with educating them into morally good citizens.

For Plato moral goodness is "concerned not with the outward behaviour, but with the inward, the true self, and with what concerns the inner governance of the self."[21] The truly moral person has been educated to know and love the "pattern...set up in the realm of what really is...of complete, divine happiness,"[22] which is the life of a soul whose parts function harmoniously. From this inner reformation flows the kind of behaviour that is characteristic of the moral person and of genuine *eudaimonia*, for in this person the parts of the soul will be ordered so as never to produce any immoral behaviour. Plato's *Kürwille* mentality has been deployed to design not the outward reality of a person's activities but the inner functioning of the human self.

Stoicism: Detachment and the Hegemony of Reason

The most influential school of thought in the late ancient Greco-Roman world, the Stoic school, largely perpetuated the focus on character development as the key to a good life, but it situated this within a distinctive cosmological theory.

The school was founded by Zeno of Citium, who came and taught in Athens in the late fourth century BCE. The next century saw the work of the most original of the Stoic philosophers, Cleanthes and Chrysippus, but almost all of their writings are lost, and we have to rely on later accounts for knowledge of their ideas. The Stoics carried the emphasis on excellent moral character (virtue) to the extreme of claiming that it was the only thing genuinely good for a person, and its loss the only evil. A major source for what we know of Stoic ethics is books 2 and 3 of Cicero's *De finibus bonorum et malorum* (*On the Ultimates in Goods and Evils*),[23] written at the time of Julius Caesar's rise to power. In it Cicero imagines a conversation between himself and several recently deceased eminent Romans, each of whom takes up a particular philosophic position as regards ethical questions. Among these is Marcus Porcius Cato (Cato the Younger),[24] who argues the Stoic position. Cicero has Cato begin his defense of Stoicism as follows: "In saying that anything except virtue is to be sought, or counted as good, you destroy morality itself, the very light of virtue, and you dismantle virtue completely."[25] "Virtue" here translates the Latin equivalent of what we have termed "excellence of character," and Cato's claim is that if you admit that anything other than virtue (*virtus* = *aretē*)—for example, health, wealth, or fame—is a good, you are undercutting your own possibility for virtue. By a good Cato means something that contributes to a person's own happiness (*felicitas* = *eudaimonia*), that is, having a good life. All things other than moral virtue are "indifferent" unless they amount to a corruption of a person's virtue. The question naturally arises as to why, given this view, a Stoic would prefer health to sickness, or prosperity to poverty; or does the Stoic in fact harbour no such preferences? In *De finibus* Cicero nicely puts this very question to Cato:

> Morality alone is the one thing which you call virtuous, right, praiseworthy and decent (its nature will be better understood if I refer to it by a variety of synonyms). So I ask you, if that is the only good, what else will there be to pursue? On the other side, if the only evil is what is base, vicious, indecent, corrupt and foul (here too a variety of terms will make things clear), what else will you say should be avoided?[26]

Cato's answer to this begins with the idea that some things are in accord with nature and others not, and that the former are "valuable" and worthy of selection:

> We begin with a classification: The Stoics call "valuable" (this, I think, is the term we should use) whatever is either itself in accordance with nature, or brings about something that is. Worthy of selection, therefore, is whatever has sufficient importance to be worthy of value (value the Stoics call *axia*). On the other hand, they call "non-valuable" what is contrary to the above. The starting-point, therefore, is that things in accordance with nature are to be adopted for their own sake, and their contraries are likewise to be rejected.[27]

"Accordance with nature" is sufficient to render something worthy of selection, but it is not sufficient to make it a "good," that is, something that contributes to the agent's *felicitas*; only what accords with the nature *of the agent* can be a good. However, once we see that a human agent's nature is rational, it is evident that selecting on the basis of rational consideration what is in accord with nature does accord with the agent's own rational nature, and is thus the very essence of being moral. It contributes, then, to that agent's *felicitas*, and hence is indeed a good. In other words, although what accords with nature in a given situation and is worthy of selection (hence valuable) may well be something that itself is neither good nor bad but rather, as the Stoics said, "indifferent," the act of selecting it on the basis of rational thought is indeed a good for the rational agent.

This line of thought is what leads Cato to say the following a little later in the dialogue:

> Here, though, one must immediately avoid the error of thinking that the theory is committed to there being two ultimate goods. Take the case of one whose task it is to shoot a spear or arrow straight at some target. One's ultimate aim is to do all in one's power to shoot straight, and the same applies with our ultimate

good. In this kind of example, it is to shoot straight that one must do all one can; none the less, it is to do all one can to accomplish the task that is really the ultimate aim. It is just the same with what we call the supreme good in life. To actually hit the target is, as we say, to be selected but not sought.[28]

Actually hitting the target, that is, success in one's endeavour, is to be selected, that is, it is what one tries to achieve, but shooting straight, that is, proceeding in one's endeavour in the best way possible, is the only thing that adds to the goodness of one's own life. Success, which may be thwarted by circumstances over which one has no control, adds nothing to one's own *felicitas*. Hence hitting the target, success, is not what one "seeks." The agent does not consider that his own *felicitas* is diminished by failure to hit the target; it is only diminished if his not hitting the target is due to some lapse or mistake of his in his effort to hit that target.

It is worth noting that this Stoic teaching accords nicely with something we find in the famous Indian text, the *Bhagavadgītā* (*Song of God*), which is included in the *Mahabharata*, the great work written down in the fourth or fifth centuries CE but which no doubt records stories composed orally much earlier and in many ways reflects life in the Ganges plain during the period of transition to urban civilization. In the *Bhagavadgītā*[29] the semi-divine figure Krishna advises the warrior (*Kshatriya*) Arjuna on the proper way for a member of that class to act in the world (among other things). In the passage below, Krishna is thinking of the performance of rituals, but clearly the message has a much more general significance.

> The man whose undertakings have lost
>   desire and calculation
> Is called educated by those with understanding.
>   His actions are consumed in the fire of wisdom.
> Not caring for the results of his work,
>   always content, not in need of support,
> Even when he becomes engaged in action,
>   he does not really do anything.

> Without wishes, with mind and body under control,
>> with no claim upon anything,
> Involved in no activity other than that
>> of the body alone, he cannot incur demerit.
> Pleased by whatever comes his way, outside the realm
>> of opposites, free from selfishness,
> Even-minded in success and failure,
>> even when he has acted his act does not imprison him.
> The actions of this man all vanish.
>> He has no attachment anymore. He is free.
> His mind is held steady in wisdom. He does
>> what should be done for the sacrifices. (4.19–23)[30]

Krishna is calling Arjuna away from acting in order to achieve some personally desired result. Although one aims at the goal of the action (in a ritual it would be the favour of the gods), success or failure in achieving it means nothing to the wise agent. What matters is correct performance. Nothing could be more opposed to the *Kürwille* thinking that leads to urban-dominated civilization, that is, to *Gesellschaft*, than this sort of advice. As noted earlier in chapter 2, *Kürwille* treats obtaining the goal as all that is valuable; the activity required to attain it is in itself either valueless or a cost of some sort. Here the exact reverse is proposed: the goal is of no account; the procedure taken to attain it is what matters to the agent.

But what, one might ask, is to motivate action if not a desire for results? The *Gītā* is not explicit about this, but the implicit message of it and of much of the *Mahabharata* is that one must rely on *dhamma*, the traditional ethic of the community, which in the Indian case calls on members of certain classes to fulfil the duties that particularly belong to that class. Arjuna is a *kshatriya*, a noble warrior, with all the demands on conduct that entails. Krishna is asking Arjuna to forget questions of whether the action is an efficient means of attaining some end, which is the *Kürwille* way of deliberating, and simply concentrate on what the *dhamma* demands of a true warrior, which is the *Wesenwille* approach. The original composer of this part of the *Gītā* has seen right to the heart of what is happening in the society around him or her and rebels against it in the most direct manner possible.

A variant on this theme is found in the thoughts attributed to Lao-tzu, presumed to be the ancient founder of Taoism in China. In the *Tao-te ching* (*The Way and Its Virtue*) he espoused the doctrine of "no action" (*wu wei*), that is, activity that has no "ulterior motive." Even the goal of achieving virtue constitutes such a motive and is not desired by the genuinely virtuous person, as the following passage maintains:

> The man of superior virtue is not (conscious of) his virtue,
> And in this way he really possesses virtue.
> The man of inferior virtue never loses (sight of) his virtue,
> And in this way he loses his virtue.
> The man of superior virtue takes no action, but has no ulterior motive to do so.
> The man of inferior virtue takes action, but has an ulterior motive to do so.[31]

This idea is the basis of the Taoist critique of the Confucian emphasis on disciplined striving for sagehood. Lao-tzu would have teachers discard talk of the typical Confucian virtues, for it only gets in the way of social peace and harmony:

> Abandon sageliness and discard wisdom;
> Then the people will benefit a hundredfold.
> Abandon humanity and discard righteousness;
> Then the people will return to filial piety and deep love.
> Abandon skill and discard profit;
> Then there will be no thieves or robbers.
> However, these three things are ornament and not adequate.
> Therefore let the people hold on to these:
> > Manifest plainness,
> > Embrace simplicity,
> > Reduce selfishness,
> > Have few desires.[32]

All this follows from the recommendation to take "no action," that is, not to pursue goals one has dreamed up for oneself:

> The sage manages affairs without action (*wu-wei*)
> And spreads doctrines without words.
> All things arise, and he does not turn away from them.
> He produces them, but does not take possession of them.[33]

Again, the question arises as to what then is directing the sage. In Taoism it is accord with the "Way," the *Tao*, that indescribable direction the cosmos is taking—a response that deserves a full treatment, but not here. I bring these Taoist teachings up only to note how completely they eliminate the basis of the *Kürwille* way of living. Enlightenment as to the *Tao* substitutes for adoption of goals to which the sage might apply some sort of instrumental rationality. In according with the *Tao* the activity itself is the only thing to be valued. In Taoism, *Kürwille* thinking has entirely undercut its own mode of action.

Returning to the Stoics, we find that their position requires that accord with nature, or disaccord, be an objective feature of things we might try to accomplish in the world and that we have the cognitive capacity needed to recognize such a feature. Stoic philosophers held that it was obvious that at a basic level, self-preservation and the nurture of offspring were natural to any animal, and that the naturalness here was evident. Cato puts it as follows:

> It should be immediately obvious from the shape and the parts of the human body that procreation is part of nature's plan. And it would hardly be consistent for nature to wish us to procreate yet be indifferent as to whether we love our offspring. Even among non-human animals the power of nature is evident. When we observe the effort they devote to breeding and rearing, it is as if we hear nature's very own voice. Thus our impulse to love what we have generated is given by nature herself as manifestly as our aversion to pain.[34]

Nevertheless, humans could come to recognize as natural for them a way of life that transcends what we know as natural by mere basic impulses. Here is Cato again expounding Stoic doctrine on this point:

> A human being's earliest concern is for what is in accordance with nature. But as soon as one has gained some understanding, or rather "conception" (what the Stoics call *ennoia*) and sees an order and, as it were, concordance in the things which one ought to do, one then values that concordance much more highly than those first objects of affection. Hence through learning and reason one concludes that this is the place to find the supreme human good, that good which is to be praised and sought on its own account.
>
> This good lies in what the Stoics call *homologia*. Let us use the term "consistency," if you approve. Herein lies that good, namely moral action and morality[35] itself, at which everything else ought to be directed. Though it is a later development, it is none the less the only thing to be sought in virtue of its own power and worth, whereas none of the primary objects of nature is to be sought on its own account.[36]

From the above we see that although certain basic impulses in humans are perfectly natural, life in accord with them is not the good for a human being; since humans are rational, their true good lies in something beyond that sort of life, in a sort of rational "consistency" that is equated with moral integrity. Loving one's offspring, for example, is in accord with nature and is, therefore, to be selected, but it is not something to be sought as an ultimate goal.

The Stoics reinforced their ideas about accordance with nature with a cosmology that saw the world as designed by an immaterial but active substance they called the "designing fire." This "fire" had as its purpose the life of rational beings (humans and gods), and it itself was supremely rational. The world was designed by this "fire" in such a way that the non-rational beings were there in order to facilitate the flourishing of the rational ones. Sheep, for example, were there to provide wool to clothe humans.[37] This rampant teleology grounds the objectivity of judgments about accordance with nature. The "fire" has not only designed creatures for certain ways of life and given them the faculties needed to carry out those ways of life, but also made certain creatures subservient to the needs of the rational ones.

Furthermore, the "fire" has designed and planned the whole world to be as rational an order as possible, given the limitations imposed by the material with which the "fire" has to work.[38] This means, first of all, that whatever occurs has a reason in what preceded it for why it rather than any alternative occurs. The principle immediately implies cosmic determinism, a doctrine the Stoics' philosophical rivals found deeply offensive. Second, it means that the world is in fact the best world possible. As much as things might seem to a human to be going badly, from the cosmic perspective of the "fire" everything is working out for the best. Clearly this idea reinforces the doctrine that success in our endeavours is not what is really important. Failure just as much as success is part of a predetermined course of events that leads to what is the best possible end result.

The upshot of this line of thought is a mental detachment of the rational agent from the outcomes of his chosen courses of action, an attitude the Stoics deemed necessary to living a genuinely good life. This conclusion is amply emphasized by Epictetus, a former slave turned Stoic teacher of male scions of the Roman elite. A student of his, Arrian, has left us what purports to be a *verbatim* rendering of Epictetus's classroom discussions as they took place in the late first or early second centuries CE, as well as a summary of his doctrines. From these works (the *Discourses* and the *Handbook*) we learn that Epictetus marks off what we do not have full control over from what we do, and that the latter consists entirely of our judgments about what we experience. Certainly things that are physically apart from us are not things we can entirely control, if we can control them at all. Moreover, the deliverances of our senses and the feelings and desires that arise spontaneously in us are also not things we can control. What we *can* control are our critical judgments about these; we can upon rational reflection sometimes correct what the senses are impelling us to believe, and we can reject as wrong the judgments about what is good or bad to pursue that our feelings and cravings drive us to adopt. For Epictetus this capacity is definitive of what the Stoics called "reason" and its status as "hegemonic."

Epictetus then concludes that the worthwhileness of our life depends entirely on whether we correctly go about using this faculty and not at all on anything else—that is, on any of the things over which we do not have total control. Adopting this point of view, we become detached from everything other than making correct critical judgments, that is, other than what gives precedence to the rational side of our nature and thus constitutes a moral life. But this does not mean we do nothing. We find in the *Discourses* the following interchange between Epictetus and one of his students asking questions:

> "*What then must we do?*" Make the best of what is in our power and use the rest according to its nature. "*And what is its nature?*" However god wishes it.[39]

This very briefly is the doctrine we noted earlier espoused by Cato. We make the best rational judgments we can and select what accords with nature, where nature is what the creator has designed a thing for.

The extent to which Epictetus thinks this leads to detachment from what happens to one in their interactions in the world can be judged by the following passages:

> And what was it Agrippinus[40] used to say? "I am not a hindrance to myself." Someone told him, "You are being tried in the Senate. Good luck." But it was eleven in the morning, and he was in the habit of taking a cold bath and exercising at that hour. "Let us be off and exercise." Someone told him as he was exercising that he had been condemned. "To exile," he said, "or death?" "To exile." "And my estate, what of that?" "It has not been confiscated." "Well, then, let us go to Aricia[41] and lunch there." This is what it means to have practiced what ought to be practiced, to render desire and aversion free from any injury or mishap. I must die. If now, then I die; if later, then now I will lunch, since the hour for lunch has arrived—and I will die later. How? As befits one who is returning what belongs to another.[42]

The last sentence reflects Epictetus's belief that the judging faculty that is under one's own control continues to exist after the destruction of one's body; it is the body that Agrippinus is saying "belongs to another"; in dying one leaves it to the material world to which it belongs. Anger at what happens to one is out of place, particularly when things are stolen from you.

> Why, then, are we angry? Because we attach such importance to the things that they take from us. So, don't attach importance to your clothes, and you are not angry with the thief. Don't attach importance to the beauty of your wife, and you are not angry with the adulterer. Know that the thief and the adulterer have no place in the things that are yours, but in those that belong to others and are not in your power. If you dismiss those things and set them at nought, with whom are you still angry? But as long as you set store by these things, be angry with yourself rather than with the thief and the adulterer.[43]

The basic point is nicely made in the following:

> I learned to see that everything that happens, if it is independent of my moral character, is nothing to me. Haven't you been benefitted in this respect? Why, then, do you seek advantage in anything other than that in which you have learned that the advantage resides?[44]

Detachment is also a pervasive theme in much of the thought of ancient India. In the *Bhagavadgītā*, from which we quoted earlier, Krishna advises Arjuna to give up desire entirely:

> A man is of firm judgment
>   when he has abandoned all inner desires
> And the self is content,
>   at peace with itself.
> When unpleasant things do not perturb him
>   nor pleasures beguile him,

> When longing, fear, and anger have left,
>> He is a sage of firm mind.
> That man has a firm judgment
>> who feels no desire toward anything.
> Whatever good or bad he incurs,
>> he never delights in it nor hates it. (2.55–57)[45]

Buddhism too, of course, warned against desires. The eighth-century Buddhist monk Śāntideva paints vividly the ethical implications of the philosophy of Nāgārjuna, the great Buddhist sage of the second century CE. Śāntideva emphasizes the development of what he calls the "Awakening Mind."[46] This requires bringing the mind under control, for a wandering mind can be a very destructive thing, like an elephant in rut.

> 5.1: One who wishes to guard his training must scrupulously guard his mind. It is impossible to guard one's training without guarding the wandering mind.
> 5.2: Rutting elephants roaming wild do not cause as much devastation in this world as the roaming elephant, the mind, let free, creates in Avīci and other hells.
> 5.3: But if the roaming elephant, the mind, is tethered on every side by the cord of mindfulness, every danger subsides, complete prosperity ensues.[47]

But this discipline requires renunciation of outward pleasures and rewards:

> 8.2: Distraction does not occur if body and mind are kept sequestered. Therefore, one should renounce the world and disregard distracting thoughts.
> 8.3: The world is not truly renounced because of attachment and the thirst for acquisitions and other rewards. Therefore, to renounce these, anyone with sense would reflect as follows:

> 8.4: Realizing that one well-attuned to insight through tranquility can destroy the defilements, one should firstly seek tranquility, and that by disregarding one's delight in the world.
>
> 8.5: For what person is it appropriate to be attached to impermanent beings, when that person is impermanent, when a loved one may not be seen again for thousands of lives?[48]

Śāntideva's emphasis on discipline finds a similar theme in Epictetus. Bringing oneself around to the desired level of detachment is not easy, and Epictetus emphasizes that it requires discipline and training. Often he compares the person on this path of character development to an athlete training for the Olympics. Here is a passage from the *Handbook*:

> In every undertaking, consider what comes first and what comes after, then proceed to the action itself. Otherwise you will begin with a rush of enthusiasm having failed to think through the consequences, only to find that later, when difficulties appear, you will give up in disgrace. Do you want to win at the Olympic Games? So do I, but for the gods! For that is a fine achievement. But consider what comes first and what comes after, and only then begin the task. You must be well-disciplined, submit to a diet, abstain from sweet things, follow a training schedule at the set times, in the heat, in the cold, no longer having cold drinks or wine just when you like. In a word, you must hand yourself over to your trainer, just as you would to a doctor. And then, when the contest comes, you may strain your wrist, twist your ankle, swallow lots of sand, sometimes be whipped, and after all that, suffer defeat. Think about all this, and if you still want to, then train for the games; otherwise you will behave like children, who first play at being wrestlers, then at being gladiators, then they blow trumpets, then act in a play.[49]

Chinese Confucian thinkers put great emphasis on discipline as well. To illustrate this, let me draw on a few passages from a twelfth-century anthology of Confucian philosophy prepared by two Confucian scholars of the day, Chu

Hsi (1130–1200) and Lü Tsu-Ch'ien (1137–1181).⁵⁰ The work gives texts by earlier thinkers followed by comments by the editors, most often Chu Hsi. The aim of this discipline or self-cultivation is described as follows. Here Master Ch'eng Hao is cited:

> The constant principle of Heaven and Earth is that their mind is in all things, and yet they have no mind of their own. The constant principle of the sage is that his feelings are in accord with all creation, and yet he has no feeling of his own. Therefore, for the training of the superior man there is nothing better than to become broad and extremely impartial and to respond spontaneously to all things as they come.⁵¹

Chu Hsi's response makes clear that impartiality is really just the same as the losing of self in an absorption into the whole of creation.

> To have the mind in all things and to be in accord with all creation is the same as to be extremely impartial, and to have no mind or feeling of one's own is the same as to respond spontaneously to all things as they come. (Chu Hsi, *Chu Tzu yü-lei*, 95:27a–b)⁵²

The opposite of the mind just described is the "selfish" mind, which Ch'eng I describes as follows:

> The sage feels the influences on the minds of all the people in the world. He is like heat or cold, or rain or shine, which penetrates everywhere and responds to all. This is firm correctness. It means that the mind is empty and free from selfishness. If one is hesitant in his movements and acts on things with a selfish mind, then he can only act on and activate those that he has thought of and cannot act on those that he has not thought of. Since a selfish mind that is attached to something is directed to a particular corner or a particular thing, how can it be broad and penetrate everything?⁵³

To achieve this state of "impartiality" is to possess the virtue of "humanity," a kind of love for all human beings. Let us conclude this short series of texts from the contents of the anthology with a kind of summation given by Master Chang Tsai:

> Earnestness, sincerity, vacuity, and tranquility are the foundations of humanity. Not to be flippant or faulty means to be earnest and sincere. When the mind is not obstructed or obscured, it will be vacuous and tranquil. It is difficult to understand humanity suddenly. In order to understand it, one must cultivate the Way for a long time and practice it concretely, and only then can he appreciate the meaning of humanity. For humanity must be well cultivated.[54]

"Humanity must be well cultivated." In other words, to achieve the chief virtue, humanity, the human being must cultivate their own self. That remark states the core of Confucianism. What is being cultivated here is the individual human mind, and the end result is the "sage," the "superior man," a moral exemplar who has eliminated his own self-centeredness and practises a sincere altruism. His example, especially if he is a ruler, has a beneficial effect on the morals of the citizens. Moral improvement is the key to both social and individual prosperity.

Confucians recommended the study of literary classics as part of the cultivation. Older Stoics had thought the education process involved the study of logic and the science of nature. It does not appear that these studies were important to Epictetus, although he was familiar with the basics. Rather, he thought mainly of practice in living by one's rational judgments even in the face of contrary emotions and feelings. The Confucians too would have approved that practice.

Reflections of a Stoic Emperor

The Stoic line on what constitutes the good for a human being is repeated by no less a figure than the emperor Marcus Aurelius in his *Meditations*, probably written toward the end of his life in 179. He was familiar with the teachings of

Socrates and Epictetus and cites a number of mentors who instilled in him the Stoic doctrines. Among those teachings is the one already familiar to us, that a person in his endeavours achieves all that is good for himself, even if he does not succeed in his goals, as long as he makes the right rational choices. Marcus puts it as follows: "Remember that you made your attempt conditionally, that you did not expect to do the impossible. What then did you expect? To make the attempt as you have done. And you have attained your object, even if the things which you were striving to reach are not accomplished."[55]

There are, however, some aspects of Stoic doctrine that play a large role in Marcus Aurelius's *Meditations* but are not prominent in Epictetus. One concerns the unity of all human beings due to their all sharing a rational nature. This makes them in some way citizens of a single city, one that has a law established by the faculty of reason all humans share. Here is a passage that quite beautifully expresses the idea:

> If the faculty of understanding is common to us all, the reason also, through which we are rational beings, is common. If this is so, common also is that reason which tells us what to do, and what not to do. If this is so, there is a law common to all men also. If this is so, we are fellow citizens and members of some political community, and thus the world is in a way one commonwealth.[56]

Out of Stoicism arose the doctrine of "natural law," a keystone of medieval thinking in the West. We can see in the preceding passage how such a conception fits nicely into the whole Stoic world view, according to which there is a "law common" to all human beings.

Another passage mentions that men do wrong "involuntarily," which will strike the reader as preposterous unless he recalls Socrates's arguments in Plato's *Meno* and elsewhere to the effect that all people seek what is good for them but end up harming themselves by doing what is unjust because of their ignorance of what is genuinely good for them:

> For with what are you discontented? With the wickedness of mankind? Recall to your mind these ideas, that rational animals were

made for one another, that forbearance is a part of justice, that men do wrong involuntarily. Consider how many have already lived in mutual enmity, suspicion, hatred, and conflict, and now lie dead, reduced to ashes; and be quiet at last.[57]

Marcus Aurelius repeats that view frequently as justification for not being angry with wrongdoers. The following nicely sums it up:

> With respect to that which happens in harmony with nature, we ought to blame neither gods, for they do nothing wrong either voluntarily or involuntarily, nor men, for they do nothing wrong, except involuntarily. Consequently we should blame nobody.[58]

There are also cosmological ideas that figure hardly at all in Epictetus but that Marcus Aurelius finds important. One is the relatedness of everything in the universe, a thesis the emperor associates with the view that a single divine reason is present throughout the universe, as the following passage makes clear:

> All parts of the universe are interwoven with one another, and the bond is sacred. Nothing is unconnected with some other thing. For all things have been coordinated and combined to form the same universe. There is one universe made up of everything, and one God who pervades everything, and one substance, one law, one common reason in all intelligent animals, and one truth; perchance indeed there is one perfection for all beings of the same stock, who participate in the same reason.[59]

It is a short step from this notion to the view that whatever happens in the world is for the best once we take into account the whole of the universe; the destruction of parts of that whole may be necessary for the overall good. This thought seems to have been one Marcus took considerable comfort in:

> So accept everything which happens, even though it seems disagreeable, because it leads to the health of the universe and to the

prosperity and felicity of Zeus. For he would not have brought on any man what he has brought, if it were not useful for the whole.[60]

Marcus Aurelius believes that the divine source exercises a providence over all things such that all events, even the immoral behaviour of some people, works to the benefit of the whole, and by implication to the benefit of the parts:

> From providence all things flow. And side by side with it is necessity, and that which works to the advantage of the whole universe, of which you are a part. But that is good for every part of nature which the nature of the whole brings to pass, and which serves to maintain this nature.[61]

The people in this world who complain about what goes on end up contributing to the "advantage of the whole" just as much as anyone else. One does not have to believe in divine providence in order to play inadvertently a positive role in it. This idea that a person in pursuing personal goals may without conscious design on their own part bring about beneficial results for all is one we will see has contributed in important ways to ideological developments in the modern West:

> We are all working together to one end, some with knowledge and design, others without knowing what they do; like men asleep, of whom Heraclitus, I think it is, says that they too are laborers and cooperators in what goes on in the universe. But men cooperate after different fashions; even those who find fault with what happens are cooperating abundantly; for the universe has need even of such men as these.[62]

Another theme Marcus dwells on is that nothing really new ever comes about: a person who has lived a reasonable length of time and observed carefully what is going on will have seen it all. Marcus holds this even though he also emphasizes that everything is in a state of change. Changes evidently keep bringing up the same sorts of things and events that they have in the past and will continue to do in the future. Here are some passages that express these ideas:

> [The rational soul] comprehends that those who come after us will see nothing new, nor have those before us seen anything more, but he who is forty years old, if he has any understanding at all, has seen everything, by virtue of the uniformity of things past and to come.[63]

> Loss is nothing else than change. But the universal nature delights in change, and in obedience to her all things are now done well, and from eternity have been done in like form, and will be such through endless time.[64]

> Nature has this work to do: to shift and to change, to remove from here and to carry there. All things are change, yet we need not fear anything new. All things are familiar and even the distribution of them also remains the same.[65]

The idea that the universe is governed by a powerful rational mind aiming at what is best easily leads to the idea that everything is predetermined and could not really occur otherwise than it does. Marcus adopts this too, encouraging himself to accept without complaint whatever happens to him since it was fated to be. Here are a couple passages that express this thought:

> Willingly give yourself up to Clotho,[66] allowing her to spin your thread into whatever she pleases.[67]

> Whatever may happen to you, it was prepared for you from all eternity; and the implication of causes was from eternity spinning the thread of your being, and of that which is incident to it.[68]

Marcus Aurelius concurred with all the Stoics that detachment from the events of this world did not mean there were no reasons to take action. He himself was likely conducting a frustrating war when he wrote the *Meditations*. Action, even the slaughter of war, can be what reason dictates, and if one's reason dictates it, performing it is in accord with the agent's nature and therefore beneficial to the agent, even if it fails to achieve its goal. Conversely, not to do it would be harmful to the agent as a rational being. This teaching, set in the context of beliefs that the world is already on a predetermined course that inevitably leads to the best, implies that agents should concentrate their ambitions on rightly judging the particular situations in which they find themselves. Thoughts about improving things into the distant future serve no purpose; these are matters to be left to the gods.

Stoicism was very influential among the Greco-Roman elite of the late ancient period, and its ethical and political teachings were largely absorbed into Christianity once it became the religion of the empire. The more the new religion was compelled to develop coherent doctrine in the areas of law and politics, the more it relied on Stoic ideas, adopting even the notion that there is a natural order in the world that reflects God's plan for His creation. Theologians often read into biblical texts these Stoic ideas, so that the orthodox doctrine of the Western Church became heavily imbued with a decidedly Stoic outlook. The idea that there is a divine providence caring for creation—for Christians in particular—percolated down from the theologians to the general populace and became a part of the popular religion of the medieval period in the West.

Ideological Restraints

It is my contention that the outlooks and ethical ideas of the thinkers mentioned above were important in curtailing among the elite any ambitions toward general economic improvement for the civilization Rome governed. To the extent that the governing elite thought about how to make things better in the long term, they focused on military efficiency and the perfection of the law. The latter was certainly inspired mainly by Stoic philosophy, and law may have been Rome's most lasting and beneficial contribution to the culture of the West.

Clearly the limitation on the economic expansion of the Greco-Roman world was not due to a lack of scientific and technological advances. First of all, Greek thinkers in the Hellenistic period (between Alexander's conquests in the late fourth century BCE and the Roman conquest of Greece in the second century) developed a very sophisticated mathematics, particularly in geometry, which they then applied to astronomy. The great genius of this discipline was Archimedes (287–212 BCE), whose proofs of theorems regarding conic sections and solid figures were unexcelled before modern times. He interested himself as well in mechanics, especially as the subject lent itself to mathematical analysis. This led to original work in statics and hydrostatics. Archimedes is credited with practical inventions based on his work, notably the Archimedean screw (for lifting water) and improved systems of pulleys for lifting heavy objects.

Yet according to Plutarch in *Parallel Lives*, where he discusses Archimedes's technological achievements, this genius placed much more value on the pure science of geometry and regarded "the work of an engineer and every art that ministers to the needs of life as ignoble and vulgar."[69] That is why, Plutarch says, Archimedes left no treatise on such practical matters. Whether Plutarch is correct about Archimedes or is more expressing his own prejudices and those of his later era, what he tells us is indicative of a mindset that reflects values that would have undermined any impetus toward a much more technologically oriented civilization.

The Greco-Roman world did not lack for mechanical devices of many kinds: pumps, water clocks, torsion-powered catapults, screw presses, and water mills, to mention a few. There was a fascination with pneumatic devices, especially automata of various sorts. Hero of Alexandria, writing in the first century CE, describes a miniature theatre that was run automatically by a cleverly designed system of a weight and cords attached to rotating drums. Another device used an altar fire to heat air that, in expanding, pulled on cords that opened doors. These and other devices are described by G.E.R. Lloyd in his book *Greek Science after Aristotle* (101–05), which documents advances in medicine, architecture, and engineering as well. But Lloyd acknowledges that after 200 CE there was a gradual decline in the frequency of original scientific advances and that the application of science to the development of practical inventions was very limited. Wealth, he says, was not invested in the research needed to make progress in improving the technologies that would have enabled economic expansion. In explaining this, Lloyd surveys a number of factors, all of which no doubt played a role. And in summing up he makes the following remark, which I find supports the line I have taken: "Neither curiosity nor ingenuity were lacking; but where no great store was set by material progress in the values of society, the potentiality of applied mechanics to achieve such progress was left largely unexplored."[70]

"Material progress" at the societal level was just not an idea that occupied any significant space in the minds of those who controlled wealth. Nor would a wealthy person have thought that investment in researching how to improve technology was likely to be profitable to him, for the dominant outlook decreed that nothing new was likely to appear in the future and that any novel developments that did appear were likely to have unforeseen consequences owing to their interactions with myriad other things. For the most part, wealth was invested in land, the traditional mark of high status and a prerequisite for political influence. As for what a wealthy person aspired to, it was frequently a life of leisure spent studying philosophy, reciting poetry, and attending to the duties consequent on one's privileged position in society.

Any investment in the research needed for technological improvements was going to come, if it came at all, from the state, and in fact considerable work was done on improving technologies of the sort that imperial rule depended on, namely military weapons and machines. The Romans are famous today for their roads and aqueducts, but these were just gigantic applications of technologies already long in existence. Roads were constructed so that the legions could move quickly around the empire; that they facilitated trade and thus economic expansion was an afterthought. Engineers of various sorts were highly skilled, but they had low status in Roman society. On the whole, it appears that the imperial government, while concerned with maintaining urban life, exerted more effort on building temples and public buildings than on any efforts to increase trade, except for military actions such as the elimination of pirates from Mediterranean waters. Certainly, the government showed no significant interest in technological innovations that would have directly increased the efficiency of manufacture or agriculture. This again reflects what Lloyd says, that no great value was placed on material progress, and we have seen how that fits well with the dominant philosophies of the ancient Mediterranean world.[71] Those philosophies consistently disparaged *Kürwille* thinking when it came to material advancement and instead prescribed a focus on the development of moral character.

As noted earlier, the philosophies of Plato and the Stoics were influential only among a literate elite in the Greco-Roman world, especially with those associated with governing. The masses were by and large in the thrall of often fantastic ideas emanating from a wide variety of religious cults. But one of those cults contained a seed of much earlier provenance that engendered an entirely different way of reacting to the trauma of urban civilization, one that had mass appeal. In the next chapter we turn to the origins and development of that alternative ideology.

4

FROM ZARATHUSTRA TO REVOLUTIONARY MILLENNIALISM

> The future is sabotaging the future.
> —Hal Niedzviecki, *Trees on Mars*

Around the middle of the second millennium BCE some Indo-European peoples were making their way from parts of central Asia to the valley of the Indus River; others were migrating from south central Asia into the Middle East, where they became the Hittite nation; still others remained in central Asia, where they lived the pastoral life that had long been their tradition. Among these latter people, usually called Indo-Iranians, arose a prophet whose message would have enormous impact not just in the Middle East but indirectly on the religious imagination of Europe as well. His name was Zarathustra, in Greek "Zoroaster," and hence the religion he inspired is today called "Zoroastrianism." Scholars disagree as to when he lived. Hymns that he supposedly composed, the *Gathās*, are in a language so archaic that it must come from about the time of the first Indo-European migrations into India, but some scholars say that he lived much later, around 600 BCE, and that he used an archaic form of his language for religious effect. The scholar on whom I most depend, the late Norman Cohn, preferred the earlier date, and I shall follow his lead.[1] Cohn thought it likely that Zarathustra lived at a time when his traditional pastoral society was being raided or even invaded by people who had adopted the chariot war machines common in Mesopotamia and who engaged in violent forms of cattle rustling. Certainly the aforementioned hymns show a deep concern with cattle and eulogize the herdsman.

The teachings of Zarathustra and their subsequent development were handed down orally for centuries and probably did not receive written form until the fifth century CE. Because of the gradual destruction of most Zoroastrian communities after Islam conquered the realms they had once dominated, only about one quarter of the original legacy survives. This body of written material is called the *Avesta*, but not all of it is in the original Avestan language; considerable material is preserved only in Pahlavi. The scholarly task of reading and interpreting these materials is enormously complicated, and hence our knowledge of the ancient Zoroastrian rituals and theology is, to say the least, very incomplete and filled with uncertainties.

We do know that this religion became the official faith of the Persian or Achaemenid Empire established by Cyrus the Great in the middle of the sixth century BCE. That entity eventually stretched from the Indus valley in the east to the Aegean in the West. It took in all of the Middle East, including Egypt, and extended north into parts of central Asia north of the Oxus River. The fairly enlightened rule of the Achaemenids brought peace in the region, which, as we saw in chapter 2, had experienced periodic highly destructive conflicts between competing imperial regimes as well as lesser kingdoms. It also facilitated the transit of people, goods, and ideas between the major urban civilizations of the Eurasian world at that time: China, northern India, Mesopotamia, Egypt, and Greece. Until it was conquered by Alexander in the late fourth century BCE, the Persian Empire was without doubt the most advanced and successful imperial regime the world had seen, and the Zoroastrian faith had a privileged position in it. After the Hellenistic kingdoms that resulted from Alexander's conquest and division of his empire had dissolved and regimes such as the Parthians and later the Sasanians had risen, a modified form of the faith persisted as the official religion; but the conquests made by Islam in the seventh century CE put an end to that.

Zoroastrianism was, then, for many centuries one of the world's great religions, and its impact on the peoples who fell under the Persian Empire and on those who had close contact with that empire can hardly be overestimated. Of particular interest to this study is the radical departures from older religions that Zarathustra initiated, for they establish a way of conceiving the universe and humanity's place in it that diverges dramatically from what we have discussed in the previous chapters, and Zarathustra's vision was in the end to have a tremendous impact on Europe and eventually on the Western civilization, whose devastating planetary expansion we are trying to understand.

The Zoroastrian Revision of the Cosmic Combat

The Zoroastrian views in question can, I think, be treated for our purposes as four in number, forming a closely bound package that establishes a world view radically different from anything that went before. I shall briefly describe these four before going on to discuss each in greater detail and to provide texts translated from the *Avesta* that illustrate them. I should warn the reader, however, that Zoroastrianism is not mainly a religion of beliefs; rather, its core is a set of rituals and liturgies only loosely related to dogmas about the nature of the cosmos. What follows, then, must not be viewed as summarizing the "essence" of Zarathustra's teaching or of Zoroastrianism; rather, it isolates certain general beliefs that recur in Zoroastrian liturgy and that would have a profound effect on the West.

First, Zarathustra radically revised how people should think about the various myths of conflict between, on the one side, gods that with human help maintained the cosmic order, and, on the other side, gods that were at work undermining that order. These "combat myths," as Cohn calls them, described in phantastic terms what people deemed a basic feature of the world, one that like the change of seasons was permanent and not to be complained about in any way other than the way people complain about the coming of winter. Zarathustra turned this into a conflict between what was morally right and what was morally wrong, between truth and "the Lie," as he seems to have put it.[2] With this revision of the traditional and nearly universal myth, Zarathustra introduced morality and immorality, righteousness and wickedness, truth and deception, into the basic fabric of the world.

Second, human individuals, now faced with a world in which truth and falsehood were at war, had to make a choice as to which side they were on.[3]

That choice would determine the course of their lives: would they defend righteousness or engage in selfish cruelty to humans and animals? Choice was here operating at a cosmic level where it had never had a place before and determined what sort of person one was going to become.

Third, since individuals determine through their own choices whether they will become moral or not, they are rightfully punished for making the wrong choice and rewarded for making the right one. But such punishments and rewards are often not delivered in this life and so must come in the life the soul has after death.[4] There must, then, be a Hell in which the souls of the unrighteous suffer torments proportionate to their wrongdoing in this life, and a Paradise in which the souls of the righteous receive their due reward. That people have souls that have some sort of existence after bodily death was a common enough idea, and many peoples thought of these souls as having a shadowy existence in some underground place. Zarathustra reworked this idea into a belief in what we now call Heaven and Hell, where those souls get their just deserts.

Fourth, the conflict between Truth and the Lie will eventually come to an end with the total victory of Truth and righteousness. At that moment the world will be utterly transformed into something much better (i.e., more suited to human needs) than what presently exists.[5] The souls of the dead will be given new bodies, and all will achieve immortality. The Lie will totally cease to exist. Zarathustra's followers looked forward to a future in which all their present suffering would be eliminated as long as they chose in their life here and now to align with Truth and righteousness, that is, with the moral side in the cosmic conflict. No previous world view held such a utopian view of the future, and this phantasy had a power over the minds of oppressed and exploited people that none of the more philosophical ideas surveyed in the previous chapter could muster. Whereas the world views previously discussed appealed mainly to the elite, this aspect of Zoroastrianism made it a force among people excluded from the conversations of the rich and powerful, that is, *hoi polloi*, as the Greeks would say. Moreover, in contrast to the *Kürwille* reactions discussed in the three previous chapters, this was an eruption from *Wesenwille*, from natural and unreflective will expressing in extremely phantastic and powerful terms people's deepest longings and resentments.

The above package situates the human individual in a world which is the scene of a gigantic cosmic, moral drama, one in which the individual is called to participate by making a choice between competing values, and one which is moving inevitably toward a final just and happy conclusion. Let us now examine in detail each of these four components.

The Cosmic Combat Becomes a Moral One

Zarathustra believed in a supreme creator deity named "Ahura Mazda," that is, "Lord Wisdom." Among his creations were a number of immortals (*devas*) who assisted him in creating a world in accord with *asha*, that is, with truth and order; but there was also another deity (also created by Ahura Mazda?), named "Angra Mainyu," who with his own assistant *devas* worked to undermine Ahura Mazda's creation and thereby introduce chaos and falsity into the world. This phantastic framework was roughly similar to other mythologies of ancient peoples in the region. But when we look at how this was developed by Zarathustra, we see that he saw the conflict as basically one between morality and immorality. The other mythologies certainly saw the divine agents of order as good, in the sense that they promoted what was conducive to human civilization, and the agents of chaos as bad, in the sense that they promoted what was destructive of human civilization, but they did not see this as a matter of morality and its opposite. Morals arise only in the dealings of humans with one another, although the divine agents of order desire that humans behave morally to one another, this being essential to the human social order.

The flavour of Zarathustra's revision of the ancient mythology is apparent in Yasna[6] 30 of the *Gathās*.

> Truly there are two primal Spirits, twins renowned to be in conflict. In thought and word, in act they are two: the better and the bad. And those who act well have chosen rightly between these two, not so the evildoers. And when these two spirits first came together they created life and not-life, and how at the end Worst Existence shall be for the wicked, but (the House of) Best Purpose for the just man. Of these two Spirits the Wicked One chose achieving the worst things. The Most Holy Spirit, who is clad in

> hardest stone, chose right, and [so do those] who shall satisfy Lord Mazda continually with rightful acts. The Daevas indeed did not choose rightly between these two, for the Deceiver approached them as they conferred. Because they chose worst purpose, they then rushed to Fury, with whom they have afflicted the world and mankind.[7]

The key thing to note here is how the "Wicked One" (i.e., Angra Mainyu) became bad by his own *choice* of promoting what was bad, and the Daevas (= *devas*) deceived by that Wicked One chose what was worst, and from this resulted the violence that afflicted the world. The most basic immoral act, that of deceit and lying, is frequently associated with Angra Mainyu, and truthfulness with Ahura Mazda. By making the introduction of life-destroying elements in the fabric of the world depend on the choice of a divine being, Zarathustra enabled his followers to condemn that being in the same way they would have condemned a human who knowingly chose to lie and deceive; that is, the condemnation was a moral one. And conversely, the divinity that chose what was best was eligible for moral praise. Choice here implied freedom to choose otherwise. The earlier mythologies would not have thought of the gods that defended order and civilization as able to choose not to, or the other gods that tried to corrode same as able to choose to defend order, and hence it would have been inappropriate to think of choice as operating at this cosmic level at all or to adopt moral attitudes toward what the gods were doing. Zarathustra reversed this and inserted morality into the very story of how the gods made the world be the way we find it.

The Crucial Choice

Given the division of the world just described, humans are faced with their own choice as to which side to align with. One can join the forces of Ahura Mazda by imitating his righteousness in one's own conduct, or one can join the forces of the "Wicked One" by imitating his deceitfulness and violence. This is the crucial choice every human must make, and it determines the moral character of their life. Yasna 30 expresses the necessity of this choice as follows:

> Hear with your ears that which is the sovereign good;
> With a clear mind look upon the two sides
> Between which each man must choose for himself,
> Watchful beforehand that the great test may be accomplished in our favour.[8]

An ancient Zoroastrian creed also emphasizes the importance of the believer's choice to follow a righteous life:

> Spenta Armaiti,[9] the good, I choose for myself. Let her be mine! I renounce the theft and raiding of cattle, and harm and destruction for Mazda-worshipping homes...I forswear the company of the wicked Daevas...and the followers of Daevas, of demons and the followers of demons, of those who do harm to any being by thoughts, words, acts or outward signs. Truly I forswear the company of all this as belonging to the Drug,[10] as defiant (of the good)...By the choice of the Waters, the choice of the Plants, the choice of the beneficent Cow, the choice of Ahura Mazda who created the Cow, who created the Just Man, by the choice of Zarathustra, the choice of Kavi Vishtaspa,[11] the choice of Frashaoshtra and Jamaspa,[12] the choice of each of the Saoshyants,[13] bringing about reality, just by that choice and doctrine am I a Mazda-worshipper.[14]

The Zoroastrian emphasis on choice—and here there can be no doubt but that *free* choice is what is meant—was probably the most novel of Zarathustra's religious innovations. It was also to be the most influential in the long run. The doctrine implies that at the most basic level, individual human beings have it in their power to determine the moral character of their own lives. And this means they can be held fully responsible for the moral rightness or wickedness of their lives. Furthermore, that rightness or wickedness aligns with the cosmic conflict that rages between the divinities led on the one side by Ahura Mazda and on the other by Angra Mainyu. Adopting this vision goes a long way to explaining the frequent claims in the *Avesta* that violent attacks on "evildoers" are demanded of the righteous person. Yasna 47 says:

> Whether a man be master of little or of much,
> Let him be good to the righteous, evil to the wicked.[15]

Since morality applies, according to Zarathustra, as much to the gods as to humans, the righteous gods too can be expected to inflict bad consequences on the wicked, both divine and human. This brings us to the third theme where Zoroastrianism diverged from the religions preceding it.

Punishment and Rewards in the Afterlife

Like most peoples of the ancient world, the Indo-Iranians held that each human had their own soul that was the seat of their consciousness and that this soul had some sort of existence after the person's death. One common phantasy was that at death these souls went to some region beneath the earth where they led a disembodied existence. It seems that credit for turning this rather vague idea into what would later be called Heaven and Hell, and making the former into a proper reward for the righteous, the latter into a fitting punishment for the wicked, must be given to Zarathustra, and then the Zoroastrians continued to elaborate in different ways on the story in the centuries after him.

Many passages in the *Gathās* refer to disasters that shall befall the wicked in this life because they have offended Ahura Mazda, but there are some that refer to something that will occur to their souls after their death. There is reference to the "Chinvat Bridge," or "Bridge of the Separator," as we find in this passage from Yasna 51:

> Thus does the evil one's conscience forfeit the assurance of the straight (path);
> His soul [?] stripped naked [?] shall be afraid at the Bridge of the Separator,
> Having strayed from the path of Righteousness
> By its deeds and those of his tongue.[16]

Quite an elaborate and dramatic story seems to have developed in ancient Zorastrianism about what happens at this bridge. A passage from a book titled

The Spirit of Wisdom (*Menog i Khrad*) paints a lively picture of what lies in store for the soul of one who has died:

> It will reach the high and terrible Chinvat Bridge, to which everyone comes, just or wicked. And there many adversaries wait, [such as] Eshm with bloody club, malevolently, and Astvidad, who swallows all creatures and is never sated. And to mediate there are Mihr and Srosh and Rashn. In the weighing Rashn the just, who holds the balance for souls, never makes it dip to one side, neither for the just nor for the wicked, neither for a lord nor for the ruler of a land. He does not swerve by as much as a hair's breadth, and has no regard for persons...When then the soul of the just man crosses that bridge, the bridge becomes as if a mile wide, and the just soul crosses accompanied by the just Srosh. And his own good acts will come to meet him in the form of a girl, more beautiful and fairer than any girl in the world... When a wicked person dies, then for three days and nights his soul scuttles about near the vile head of that wicked one...On the fourth day the demon Vizarsh comes and binds the wicked man's soul in the harshest way, and, in spite of opposition by just Srosh, leads it to the Chinvat Bridge. Then just Rashn will discover that wicked person's soul in its wickedness. Then the demon Vizarsh will seize that wicked person's soul and will beat and torment it scornfully and wrathfully.[17]

The scene is further developed in this passage from the "Religious Judgments" (*Dadestan i denig*):

> The [Chinvat] Bridge is like a sword...one of whose surfaces is broad, one narrow and sharp. With its broad side, it is so ample that it is twenty-seven poles wide; with its sharp side, it is so constructed that it is as narrow as a razor's edge. When the souls of the just and wicked arrive, it turns on that side which is required for them. Through the great glory of the Creator, and at

the command of him who is the true judge and protector of the Bridge, it becomes a broad crossing for the just…; for the wicked it becomes a narrow crossing, just like a razor's edge. The soul of a just person crosses the Bridge, and its way is pleasantness… When that of a wicked person sets foot on the Bridge, because of the…sharpness it falls from the middle of the Bridge and tumbles down.[18]

What the wicked person's soul tumbles down into is vividly portrayed in another work, the *Arda Viraz Nadag*, which relates the account of one Viraz, who has visited both the paradise awaiting the righteous across the Chinvat Bridge and the Hell in store for those who "tumble down." He is accompanied by two just immortals, Srosh and Adar Yazad, who say to Viraz:

Come! That we may show you heaven and hell, and the light and ease and comfort and happiness…of heaven, the reward of the just. And we shall show you the darkness and distress and discomfort and evil…in hell, and the punishments of various kinds which demons and devils and sinners inflict.[19]

When the two Spirits show Viraz Hell, he says:

I saw the blackest hell, dangerous, fearful, terrible, holding much pain, full of evil, foul-smelling. Then I thought it seemed like a pit, to whose bottom a thousand spears would not reach; and if all the firewood which is in the world were placed on the fire in the most evil-smelling, darkest hell, it would never give out fragrance.[20]

A little later he asks his guides:

"What sin had these bodies committed, whose souls suffer such heavy punishment?" Just Srosh and Adar Yazad said: "These are the souls of those wicked people who committed many mortal sins in the flesh, and extinguished Vahram fires, and destroyed bridges over swiftly flowing streams, and spoke falsely and untruthfully, and often gave false witness. And their desire was anarchy; and because of their greediness and miserliness, and lust and anger and envy, innocent and just people were slain. They acted very deceitfully; and now their souls must endure such heavy torment and punishment."[21]

The clear implication is that all this rewarding and punishing is done in a perfectly just manner. The point is made clearly in yet another work, the *Sīh-rōzag*, which tells of the judge, Rašn (= Rashn, mentioned above) who weighs souls in his balance.

> ...[of] the word spoken correctly, increaser of the world the justice of Rašn is this, that for three nights Rašn adjudicates (lit. "reckons") with fairness the souls of humans; and his justice and *hmkw'h* are also this, that if it is possible to distribute, spin and weave fairly, [it is] thanks to him; and he is the holder of the scales at the Passage of lamentation; and at the Future body Rašn will perform the ordeal...[22]

Also in the *Arda Viraz Nadag*, Viraz is told:

> Say to the people of the world: "Do not consider the most trifling good act to be trouble or vexation, for everyone whose good acts outweigh his bad ones goes to heaven, and everyone whose bad acts weigh more, to hell, even if the difference is only three tiny acts of wrongdoing, and those for whom both are equal remain until the future body in this Hammistagan [= The Place of the Motionless Ones]..."[23]

The mention of the "future body" is a reference to Zoroastrian eschatological phantasies that we shall come to in a moment. But before proceeding, let us sum up the basic vision that Zarathustra and later followers gave us of the fate of the disembodied soul. After physical death all the person's good and evil deeds are taken note of, and when the latter predominate the person's soul must suffer according to the decree of a wise and omniscient judge, and the sufferings will be worse the more the person has sinned. On the other hand, a pleasant, comfortable existence awaits the soul of the person whose good deeds are greater than the bad ones. Zarathustra was not above trying to terrify people with this phantasy in order to persuade them to adopt the way of truth and moral rightness. Behaviour, not so much inner motivation, is what is going to count at the reckoning at the Chinvat Bridge. But the phantasy, I think, basically arises from seeing that if the world is created by a being whose chief trait is moral rectitude, then it cannot be that human evildoing, resulting from free choice, can go unpunished in the end.

The "Making Wonderful"

According to Zoroastrian doctrine all the aspects of the world that are destructive of human prosperity, or even obstacles to human comfort, are due not to the righteous creator, Ahura Mazda, but to his evil opponent, Angra Mainyu. Here again there developed an elaborate and dramatic phantasy, this time serving as an explanation for the existence of evil in the world. There exists a work in Pahlavi known as the *Bundahishn*, which consists of interpretive commentary (a "Zand") on lost Avestan texts, and in this we find an extended rendition of the phantasy in question.[24] From the *Bundahishn* we read that in the beginning the two Spirits were entirely separated and that the evil one did not even know of the existence of Ahura Mazda, but Ahura Mazda was aware of the existence and character of Angra Mainyu. For 3,000 years after the creation the Evil Spirit was inactive, but then he awoke and saw the light of Ahura Mazda and attacked it. Seeing that he could not succeed without help he returned to his darkness to create *devs* (= *devas*) who would help him. Ahura Mazda, aware of the danger developing to his own creation, persuaded Angra Mainyu to agree to postpone battle for 9,000 years.

Realizing that eventually Angra Mainyu would assault his creation, Ahura Mazda created time and physical beings as a defence; meanwhile, Angra Mainyu was busy creating his own counter-creation of evil beings. When the

Evil Spirit did attack, he came up from beneath the earth and started his work of destruction, described in the *Bundahishn* as follows:

> Like a fly he rushed upon all creation. And he made the world at midday quite dark, as if it were black night. He made the sky dark below and above the earth...And he brought a bitter taste to the Water. And he loosed noxious creatures upon the Earth. And he brought poison to the Plant, and straightaway it withered. And he loosed pain and sickness upon the Bull and Gayonard [mythical first man]...And so he defiled the whole creation. Hell was in the middle of the earth where the Evil Spirit had bored through the earth and rushed through it. So the things of the material world appeared in duality, turning, opposites, fights, up and down, and mixture.[25]

Thus Ahura Mazda's good creation comes under attack and is deeply compromised by the assaults of Angra Mainyu and his horde of evil *devas*. At this point in the drama we can sympathize with the words of Zarathustra himself in Yasna 44 of the *Gathās*:

> This I ask thee, O Lord, answer me truly:
> If thou hast power, as Righteousness, to avert this from me:
> When the two hostile armies meet, to which of the two
> Wilt thou give victory according to the decrees which thou
>   wilt uphold?
>
> This I ask thee, O Lord, answer me truly:
> Who will be victorious and protect the living by thy doctrine?
> May visible signs be given to me:
> Make known the judge that shall heal existence!
> And may it be given to obey him, through the Good Mind,
> To all those in whom thou seekest it, O Wise One![26]

Of course, the end result is inevitable; the forces of Ahura Mazda will completely win out, and the world will be restored to its original pure state free of the evils introduced by Angra Mainyu. The dead will be resurrected, that is, their souls will be given new bodies, hence the references noted earlier to a "future body." Death will vanish. The process will be facilitated by a kind of saviour figure, called the "Soshyant" (actually, many texts speak of a series of Soshyants arising over time). It also involves another process of judgment on human beings, this time in possession of their new bodies. The *Bundahishn* continues the story as follows:

> Then the assembly of Isdadvastar will take place. In that assembly, everyone will behold his own good or bad deeds, and the just will stand out among the wicked like white sheep among black. Fire and the yazad Airyaman will melt the metal in the hills and mountains, and it will be upon the earth like a river. Then all men will be caused to pass through that molten metal...And for those who are just it will seem as if they are walking through warm milk, and for the wicked it will seem as if they are walking the flesh through molten metal. And thereafter men will come together with the greatest affection, father and son and brother and friend.[27]

As for Angra Mainyu:

> [T]he Evil Spirit, helpless and with his power destroyed, will rush back to shadowy darkness through the way by which he had entered. And the molten metal will flow into hell; and the stench and filth in the earth, where hell was, will be burnt by the metal, and it will become clean. The gap through which the Evil Spirit had entered will be closed by that metal. The hell within the earth will be brought up again to the world's surface, and there will be Frashegird [making wonderful] in the world.[28]

Frashegird, restoring the world to a state of total goodness, follows logically from the premises with which Zarathustra worked: The world is ultimately ruled by a Spirit who desires only what is good, both in the moral sense and in the sense of promoting human prosperity. For this Spirit to rest satisfied with a compromised creation, with sinners suffering torments in hell, and with souls existing without bodies, is unthinkable. In fact, such an alternative is barely distinguishable from the old cosmic conflict myths that Zarathustra set about to radically modify. Zarathustra's phantasy is, of course, a fantasy, but it is a fantasy that has an internal doctrinal coherence that few if any other major religions have ever achieved. Scholars generally think that Zarathustra thought that the Frashegird was imminent, but, as the world failed to fulfil this expectation, Zoroastrians tended to see it as occurring only in the distant future. This delay, of course, made the doctrine more acceptable to political potentates and enabled its acceptance by the Achaemenid rulers of the Persian empire, as well as the later Parthians and Sasanians. As a result, Zoroastrianism for many centuries flourished in a political context that enabled it to spread over most of southwest Asia and influence ideas in areas bordering that region.

Another point to be emphasized is that in contrast to the ideas summarized in the previous chapter, Zoroastrianism appealed not just to an elite but to common folk as well, perhaps even more. The dramatic fantasy we have just reviewed no doubt played an important part in this appeal. It is one that people low on the social totem pole and subject to unjust oppression, if not outright death and destruction, can easily relate to. It expresses in an extremely powerful way the resentment and anger, and consequent desire for just retribution, that such people must feel much of their lives. We can see then that the Zoroastrian fantasy may well have been, and certainly can serve as, another but much different reaction to the transition people were undergoing as *Gemeinschaft*, the traditional custom-ruled community with its relatively egalitarian ways, fell under the domination of an urban-centred *Gesellschaft*, the artificially designed community that always brings with it rule by an elite in a position to exploit the rest of the population. Zoroastrianism is the populist *Wesenwille* reaction; Confucianism, Taoism, Buddhism, Platonism, and Stoicism are all elite *Kürwille* reactions, and the results for society and culture are radically different depending on whether the former or one of the latter is dominant.

The Fury of the Hebrew Prophets
Noman Cohn proposed quite plausibly that Zoroastrianism arose among a people who were being raided and oppressed by outsiders using chariot warfare

in the mid-second millennium BCE.[29] If true, Zarathustra's people were certainly not alone in facing external threats and dominance by foreign powers with invincible military machines. As we saw earlier, what we call the Middle East, including the steppe country north of Iran, was the scene of bloody imperial rivalries and the oppression of smaller and less powerful groups. Imperialism seems to have been the almost inevitable result of the increasing domination of a *Gesellschaft* elite over the general populace still living along *Gemeinschaft* lines, and the imperialist drive reached its most extreme form in this region. Enslavement of whole populations, their removal from their ancestral homelands, and actual extermination were common imperial tactics.

As we also noted, among these less powerful communities was that of the Hebrews, who established their own *Gesellschaft* politics complete with an autocratic king in the early tenth century BCE. But the kingdom broke up into two kingdoms in the latter part of the century, one in the north called Israel, and the other in the south called Judah. The independence of the Hebrews coincides with that period in which the great powers—the Hittites, Assyrians, Babylonians, and Egyptians—went into a temporary eclipse, but by the eighth century these nations were back pursuing their imperial designs, and smaller nations like the Hebrews were under pressure to agree to some sort of vassalage to one or the other of these great powers. In the case of the Hebrews the threats came from Assyria, Babylonia, and Egypt, and this perilous situation called forth many of the poetic creations of the "prophets" of the Hebrew Bible, some of which we sampled in chapter 2.

To understand these prophets in their historical context is a difficult scholarly task that so far has left many questions unanswered. The books ascribed to the prophets were by and large not written by single individuals, nor were they written during a single historical period, and the written texts were assembled after the period of the exile in the late sixth or early fifth centuries BCE. Thus portions of the same book—*Isaiah*, for example—may be responding to situations that existed more than a century apart. Scholars have not reached firm agreement on just how to date the passages in question, and I am certainly not competent to launch into this debate. Much of prophetic writings is in the form of predictions of events that in many cases had already occurred by the time the work was created. This is particularly true of the descriptions of the disasters that were to befall the Hebrew people at the hands of the Assyrians and Babylonians and that the prophets would treat as Yahweh's punishment on his people for having strayed from obedience to his laws. But there are other predictions that speak of a restoration of the Hebrews—and in some passages of all peoples—to a permanent state of peace and prosperity. It is this drama first of great destruction and suffering, followed by a totally transformed, just, and peaceful world, that will be repeated again and again in ever more elaborate forms in the subsequent centuries of Jewish and Christian thought.

Scholars claim that some of *The Book of Amos* contains poetry composed in the mid- or late eighth century BCE and is the oldest of the prophetic compositions. The book opens with Amos reporting the threats made by the Lord against a number of peoples who have strayed into wickedness. These threats conclude with this memorable condemnation of the social inequities of the kingdom of Israel:

Thus says the Lord:

For three transgressions of Israel, and for four, I will not revoke the punishment; because they sell the righteous for silver, and the needy for a pair of shoes—they that trample the head of the poor into the dust of the earth, and turn aside the way of the afflicted; a man and his father go into the same maiden, so that my holy name is profaned; they lay themselves down beside every altar upon garments taken in pledge; and in the house of their God they drink the wine of those who have been fined. (2:4–8)

For such wickedness Yahweh will send the Assyrians or the Egyptians who "shall bring down your defenses from you, and your strongholds shall be plundered" (1:11). Such sentiments echo, of course, the rage felt by the prophets against the *Gesellschaft* domination of the society that we described in chapter 2.

The Book of Micah, parts of which also date from the eighth century BCE, gives vent to similar outrage, this time directed explicitly against the cities of Samaria and Jerusalem.

> What is the transgression of Jacob?
> Is it not Samaria?
> And what is the sin of the house of Judah?
> Is it not Jerusalem?
> Therefore I will make Samaria a heap in the open country,
> a place for planting vineyards;
> and I will pour down her stones into the valley,
> and uncover her foundations. (1:5–6)

As for Jerusalem:

> Therefore because of you
> Zion shall be plowed as a field;
> Jerusalem shall become a heap of ruins,
> and the mountain of the house a wooded height. (3:12)

The Book of Jeremiah, notable for its depictions of the afflictions that befell the Hebrew people, was mostly composed by a single person, the prophet Jeremiah, who includes in the work the story of his own sufferings and persecutions. Jeremiah wrote in the late seventh and early sixth centuries BCE when it was the Babylonians and the Egyptians who were trying to dominate Judah, the Northern Kingdom of Israel having been destroyed by the Assyrians nearly a century earlier. The Babylonians eventually won out against the Egyptians and made Judah a vassal state. Against them there were two revolts, the second in 586 ending in total disaster. The Babylonians had had enough, destroyed Jerusalem and its temple, and removed to Babylon the portion of the population most likely to cause trouble as well as the nation's skilled craftsmen. As Jeremiah says:

> A lion has gone up from its thicket,
> a destroyer of nations has set out; he has gone forth from his place
> to make your land a waste;
> your cities will be ruins without inhabitant.
> For this gird you with sackcloth, lament and wail;

for the fierce anger of the Lord
has not turned back from us. (4:7-8)

Perhaps the most imaginative of the portrayals of why Israel and Judah were to be punished comes in *The Book of Ezekiel*. This prophet was himself exiled as a young man to Babylon after the failed revolt of 597 and apparently spent the rest of his life among the Hebrew exiles in that city. Ezekiel composed an allegory in which two promiscuous women, Oholah and Oholibah, stand for Israel, that is, the Northern Kingdom, and Judah respectively. Oholah "doted on her lovers the Assyrians, warriors clothed in purple, governors and commanders, all of them desirable young men, horsemen riding on horses" (23:5-6). The Lord then says: "Therefore I delivered her into the hands of her lovers, into the hands of the Assyrians, upon whom she doted. These uncovered her nakedness, they seized her sons and her daughters, and her they slew with the sword; and she became a byword among women, when judgment had been executed upon her" (23:8-10).

Oholibah behaves even worse by doting not only on the Assyrians but on the Chaldeans (Babylonians) and Egyptians as well. Once again the Lord turns the wayward woman over to her lovers, who come "with chariots and wagons" (23:24) to wreak judgment on her. They cut off her nose and ears and destroy her children with fire. The Lord addresses her as follows:

> You shall drink your sister's cup; which is deep and large;
> you shall be laughed at and held in derision, for it contains much;
> you will be filled with drunkenness and sorrow.
> A cup of horror and desolation, is the cup of your sister Samaria;
> you shall drink it and drain it out, and pluck out your hair,
> and tear your breasts... (23:32-34)

The harlotry that draws forth such venom from the prophet must stand for the way in which the two Hebrew kingdoms played the great game of international politics, making alliances with the great powers in ways that they hoped would provide them with some security by playing one power off against another. Of course, such alliances often amounted to becoming vassals—or as we now say, "satellites"—of the power with whom they "played the harlot." As we well know, Ezekiel is not the only one of the prophets to look with disgust on this game; inveighing against it is virtually a common theme, one that is especially clear in *Ezekiel*.

Nevertheless, the books of the prophets do not contain just these stark warnings of catastrophe; they also have passages in which the Lord promises a restoration of Israel, a rebuilding of Jerusalem, and a place of honour among the nations for the Hebrew people. These passages may often be creations of the post-exilic period after the Medes and Persians conquered Babylon (539 BCE) and Cyrus, the founder of the Persian Empire, let many of the exiles return home and eventually rebuild the temple at Jerusalem. Isaiah speaks of a "day" of the Lord in which

> He shall judge between the nations, and decide for many peoples;
> and they shall beat their swords into plowshares,
> and their spears into pruning hooks;
> nation shall not lift up sword against nation,
> neither shall they learn war any more. (2:4)

According to this work, on that day Zion will be the place from which God will radiate out his law for all humankind. But the day is also a time when the Lord will take his vengeance on the "proud and lofty":

> And the haughtiness of man shall be humbled,
> and the pride of man shall be brought low;
> and the Lord alone will be exalted in that day. (2:17)

Misrule and wantonness among the people of Israel will lead to a dreadful retribution over the course of which the Lord cleanses the nation; but after this God will erect a protective shield over Jerusalem and its remaining righteous inhabitants so that it is "a shade by day from the heat, and for a refuge and a shelter from the storm and rain" (4:6).

In the final chapters of *Isaiah*, ones that scholars think were probably written after the return from the exile, there are many descriptions of the coming salvation of Israel. Jerusalem will be honoured by all peoples, and the people of Israel will no longer have to fear enemies. This intervention by the Lord in Israel's favour will amount to a whole new creation. The Lord addresses his people as follows:

> For behold, I create new heavens and a new earth;
> and the former things shall not be remembered or come into mind.
> But be glad and rejoice for ever in that which I create;
> for behold, I create Jerusalem a rejoicing, and her people a joy.
> (65:17–18)

After listing the many ways in which He will make his people prosper, the passage ends in these famous words (repeated at 11:6, 9):

> The wolf and the lamb shall feed together,
> the lion shall eat straw like the ox;
> and dust shall be the serpent's food.
> They shall not hurt or destroy in all my holy mountain. (65:25)

We have progressed even within *Isaiah* itself from a coming day of judgment on the wicked in Israel, to a judgment on the nations that have persecuted Israel, to a restoration of Israel's power and prosperity including the holy city of Jerusalem, to finally a utopian new world of peace and harmony that somewhat recalls the Zoroastrian "Making Wonderful." Just how much Zoroastrianism influenced this development is hard to say, but the culmination of history in a defeat of the wicked and the establishment of a new creation better than what has gone on in the past has a distinctly Zoroastrian flavour.

The Book of Ezekiel elaborates on the themes already mentioned by using visions and allegories to an extent not seen in the other prophetic books of the Hebrew Bible. When Ezekiel turns to the Final Judgment of God he resorts to a vision of highly phantastic beings. God rests on winged cherubim; there is a man clothed in white linen carrying a writing case who is assigned to go through Jerusalem slaying the wicked and marking for salvation those who are offended by the wickedness of the inhabitants (9:3–6).

Beside each of the cherubim are four sparkling "whirling wheels" containing eyes and four faces: the face of a cherub, the face of a man, the face of a lion, and the face of an eagle (10:14). Ezekiel notes that the creatures he sees in this vision are the same as those encountered in an earlier one (10:20), and in both cases he uses this image to picture the glory of God by deploying symbolism that we cannot now decipher in any very specific way. It seems that this symbolic mode is something that enters Hebrew prophecy no earlier than the exile in Babylon and that it probably owes much to Zoroastrian influences encountered there.

One feature of Ezekiel's prophetic message that may well stem from direct or indirect contact with the Zoroastrians is the addition of a "Pit" into which the warriors of the foreign oppressors will be thrown when they have been slain by the Lord when he takes his vengeance on them. There is no mention of tortures that these dead warriors will undergo in the "Pit," but it is a place where they will be shamed in comparison to the dignified existence after death that "the mighty men of old" who were buried with their weapons have in Sheol (32:18, 27). Certainly Ezekiel has here introduced the idea of a special place deep in the earth where the dead will receive some sort of punishment for their wickedness, an idea that we saw was important in Zoroastrianism.

Once Ezekiel launches into the Lord's rescue of the people of Israel he uses the traditional metaphor of rounding up a scattered flock of sheep and taking them to good pasture: "I myself will be the shepherd of my sheep, and I will make them lie down, says the Lord God. I will seek the lost, and I will bring back the strayed, and I will bind up the crippled, and I will strengthen the weak, and the fat and the strong I will watch over; I will feed them in justice" (34:15–16).

Contradicting himself a bit, the Lord then says: "And I will set up over them one shepherd, my servant David, and he shall feed them: he shall feed them and be their shepherd. And I, the Lord, will be their God, and my servant David shall be prince among them; I, the Lord, have spoken" (34:22–24). This introduction of a human leader that God will appoint fits in with the much more elaborate version of this theme in *Isaiah*. There we are told that from the offspring of Jesse is to emerge an especially wise, righteous, and just ruler:

> He shall not judge by what his eyes see, or decide by what his
>   ears hear;
> but with righteousness he shall judge the poor,
> and decide with equity for the meek of the earth;
> and he shall smite the earth with the rod of his mouth,
> and with the breath of his lips he shall slay the wicked.
> Righteousness shall be the girdle of his waist,
> and faithfulness the girdle of his loins. (11:3–5)

In chapter 42 a "servant" is described who performs the same function of bringing "forth justice to the nations" and who "will not fail or be discouraged till he has established justice on the earth" (42:1–4). This passage makes evident that the rule of the servant is to extend to all lands, not just to the land of Israel. Indeed, a couple of verses later we find the Lord saying that Israel is "a light to the nations, to open the eyes that are blind" (42:6). There has been a progress in prophesy from the expectation that Israel will be redeemed and made prosperous to the vision of Israel as having a world-redeeming function. This of course goes along with the elevation by the Jewish priesthood of Yahweh to the sole god for the whole world, all the gods of other nations being but idols and fictions. In this too the Jewish prophetic tradition draws closer to the cosmic phantasy of the Zoroastrians. Also, the role of the servant is not unlike that of the Soshyants in the Zoroastrian accounts of how Ahura Mazda will redeem the world, although the stories about them reflect a much earlier mythical tradition than the Jewish prophets would have relied on.

In *Ezekiel* we find as an analogue of the redemption of Israel one of the most memorable of prophetic images, that of the valley of dry bones (37:1–10). In this vision Ezekiel is called upon to prophesy to the bones that the Lord is going to breathe life into them, then cover them with flesh so that the persons whose bones they were live again. And indeed this happens. The Lord says he will open the graves of his people and raise them so that they will live. This image is best read as a metaphor for His bringing the people out of their exile and faithlessness rather than as a literal prediction of the resurrection of the dead, but the use of such a metaphor may well show the influence of Zoroastrianism, which pioneered the whole idea of such a bodily resurrection.

It is helpful to read this passage with one in the preceding chapter that is also about bringing the people of Israel out of their various exiles back to their homeland:

> For I will take you from the nations, and gather you from all the countries, and bring you into your own land. I will sprinkle clean water upon you, and you shall be clean from all your uncleanness, and from all your idols I will cleanse you. A new heart I will give you, and a new spirit I will put within you; and I will take out of your flesh the heart of stone and give you a heart of flesh. And I will put my spirit within you, and cause you to walk in my statutes and be careful to observe my ordinances. (36:24–27)

Here the redemption is that of the people of Israel; it is not as in *Isaiah* a world-encompassing transformation. This reflects Ezekiel's dominant concern to see the exiles returned to Jerusalem and there establish the kind of righteous state they should have had all along. The final chapters of Ezekiel's book are dedicated to a vision of the temple that he hopes to see built once return is accomplished. But he sees that this is going to require a transformation in each of the individuals in the community—their hearts of stone will have to be replaced with hearts of flesh—and this is something only God Himself can accomplish.

But Ezekiel prophesies that before all this happiness can fully emerge the Lord will have to destroy a mighty army led by the rather mysterious Gog of the land of Magog, who will gather a mighty host from lands to the north (38:3–6). Ezekiel's account seems to envision this threat emerging after the people of Israel have returned from their places of exile, and its only purpose seems to be to display before all the nations the justice and power of the Lord of Israel. Gog's force proceeds to plunder the "unwalled villages" and subdue the peaceful people who dwell there, including the people who have returned from exile to resume their traditional life. But God shall oppose this abominable army first with an earthquake, then with pestilence, cloudbursts, and a rain of brimstone. The land of Magog as well as the "coastlands" (frequently cited as enemies of Israel) will be doused in fire, and Gog's host will be destroyed and the bodies disposed of in the "Valley of Hamongog" (39:15). None of the other prophetic books of the Hebrew Bible speak of such an event, but this phantasy along with the characters of Gog and Magog were to figure in apocalyptic literature for many centuries to come.

I have laid out all these texts from the Hebrew prophets to show how vehement was the rage among this relatively small people against the forces unleashed against them by the mighty urban-centred empires of their region and also against their own home-grown urban elite and its *Gesellschaft* ways. But their immensely moving poetry also introduces the vision of a future of peace, justice, and harmony, one in which the world will acknowledge the rightful authority of Israel and its god. This latter side of their message will prove to be extremely important for the theme of this work, and it concurs neatly with the Zoroastrian belief in a coming Frashegird, the Making Wonderful. It is not possible to determine for sure how much the prophets were influenced by the Zoroastrian phantasies, which some of them surely encountered during the exile and afterward; but we *can* be sure that those phantasies were coming from the same place, so to speak, as Zarathustra: life among a weak people living in traditional *Gemeinschaften* but threatened with domination by the might of imperial *Gesellschaft*.

Jewish Apocalyptic Works

Included in the Hebrew Bible, but not as a prophetic book, is *The Book of Daniel*, and indeed it is very different from the prophetic books we have been discussing. Up through chapter 6 we find recounted a legend or legends about a mythical Hebrew seer, Daniel, living among the exiles in Babylon. Because of his extraordinary power to interpret dreams he rises high up in the service of the king, first Nebuchadnezzar and later Belshazzar. The later chapters are composed as though Daniel himself is speaking and are devoted to a series of apocalyptic, that is, revelatory, visions that show him what is to come as the world nears the end of its days. Since the visions give a symbolic account of the wars waged by the Seleucid and Ptolemaic Hellenistic kings, an account that historians agree is accurate up to the reign of the Seleucid Antiochus IV Epiphanes, scholars have concluded that the latter half of the book was composed in the time of Antiochus's persecution of the Jews around 165 BCE. The earlier half is probably a retelling of older legends. The whole book, though, aims at raising the spirits of the Jews, who were at the time rebelling against Antiochus, by assuring them that their god would deliver them from their ordeals.

Daniel always interprets the king's dreams as symbolic of events to come; in this his book resembles parts of *Ezekiel* and illustrates again how likely it is that Ezekiel's mode of prophesy was something the Jews learned during the exile. In the first dream a statue whose body parts are of different materials stands for the succession of imperial powers that would rule over Israel; that same dream concludes with a rock that destroys the whole construction. This rock symbolizes a kingdom set up by God Himself and "which shall never be destroyed" (2:44). In the second dream a wondrous tree that protects and nourishes all the creatures of the earth is ordered to be cut down by a "watcher"[30] from heaven. But the stump is preserved and wrapped with an iron band. Daniel interprets this as a prediction of the mental illness that is to come upon Nebuchadnezzar himself by the will of God, and as giving assurance that his kingdom will be preserved for him to eventually rule over again. The tree stands for the king, and the stump for his realm.

In chapter 7 we have Daniel's own first dream, which is interpreted for him by a heavenly figure in the dream itself. The imagery is extremely phantastic. Out of the sea come four beasts: a lion with eagle's wings, which is made to stand on two legs and receive a human mind; something like a bear with ribs between its teeth; a leopard with four wings and four heads; and a beast with iron teeth that grows horns, one of which has eyes and a mouth "speaking great things" (7:4–8). Next comes an image of a heavenly throng before a throne on which sits "one that was ancient of days" and whose "raiment was white as snow, and the hair of his head like pure wool; his throne was fiery flames, its wheels were burning fire" (7:9). His court consists of thousands and is a court of judgment in which "the books were opened" (7:10). The beasts are destroyed, but then "one like a son of man" comes before the Ancient of Days, who gives to him dominion, one "which shall not pass away" (7:14).

The fourth beast is interpreted as a particularly oppressive imperial power, but the heavenly court brings an end to its rule and establishes the final kingdom of the "saints of the Most High," an everlasting kingdom. Scholars agree that the beast stands for the Seleucid kingdom of Antiochus Epiphanes and that the author is predicting that God himself will bring about its fall and institute a kingdom of the righteous. This will in effect mark an end to history, that is, the history of competing imperial regimes whose conflicts had been so devastating to the the Hebrews' world. Notable is the heavenly throng that surrounds the Ancient of Days; notable as well is that the gathering constitutes a court of judgment. The author is introducing into the drama a whole realm of heavenly beings who involve themselves in judging the earthly events unfolding below them. This too is new in Jewish literature and reminiscent of Zoroastrian beliefs.

Chapter 8 of *Daniel* contains yet another vision that, using a ram and a he-goat as symbols of imperial regimes, recounts the destruction of the Persian Empire (the ram) by Alexander (the he-goat) and the rise of the Hellenistic kingdoms (horns on the head of the goat). It ends with a reference to the chief villain in the world in which the book was composed: Antiochus Epiphanes, whose persecutions of the Jews incited the book's creation. The interpretation of the vision is given by a man of heavenly origin, Gabriel, and begins by his saying, "Understand, O son of man, that the vision is for the time of the end." The vision does not conclude with any redemptive scene, but only with the rampages of the horn that symbolize Antiochus fighting against even the host of heaven and the Prince of that host. Finally, the voice of a holy one predicts that these atrocities will persist for a "thousand and three hundred evenings and mornings," after which the temple will be restored.

At the end of chapter 10 an angelic figure with the appearance of a man tells Daniel what is written in "the Book of Truth" and mentions Michael as a prince come to defend Daniel's people. Chapter 12 continues the angel's revelations with a picture of the End of Days, when Michael shall arise and Daniel's people shall be saved. There is even mention of a resurrection of the dead, a definite sign of the influence of Persian Zoroastrianism. The passage is worth quoting, in part because of the outsize influence it will have later:

> At that time shall arise Michael, the great prince, who has charge of your people. And there shall be a time of trouble, such as never has been since there was a nation till that time; but at that time your people shall be delivered, every one whose name shall be found

written in the book. And many of those who sleep in the dust of the earth shall awake, some to everlasting life and some to shame and everlasting contempt. And those who are wise shall shine like the brightness of the firmament; and those who turn many to righteousness, like the stars for ever and ever. But you Daniel, shut up the words, and seal the book, until the time of the end. Many shall run to and fro, and knowledge shall increase. (12:1–4)

Daniel brings together features of what we might call the apocalyptic style of prophecy. There is an intense effort to recapitulate history in symbolic terms and then make predictions, also in symbolism, about the End of Days, which is deemed to be fairly imminent. Both the heavenly and earthly realms are caught up in the events described, and at the end a judgment is made on the earth's inhabitants by the leader of the "heavenly host." The lively array of symbols used, when combined with the unforgettable stories of the three Jews who survive the fiery furnace and Daniel's own survival in the lion's den, render the book one of the most powerful in ancient literature, and, indeed, it has remained an inspiration for Jewish, Christian, and Islamic believers down to the present day.

Another book in apocalyptic style, a portion of which scholars think was likely composed in the early third century BCE, is *The Book of Enoch*. It divides into several sections: the Book of Watchers (chs. 1–36), the Book of Parables (chs. 37–71), an astronomical book (chs.72–82), the Book of Dreams (chs. 83–90), and the Epistle of Enoch (chs. 91–105). The astronomical book is usually deemed the earliest, dating from the fourth century BCE, but will concern us the least. The Book of Watchers, which probably predates *Daniel*, is of more interest; the dates of the other parts of *Enoch* are even more in doubt, ones having been suggested from the second century BCE to the early second century CE. There is some evidence that the Book of Parables has been emended by Christians; certainly both it and the Book of Watchers were well-known to Christians in the second century. *Enoch* in its entirety exists now only in the ancient Ethiopian language, for the Ethiopian Christians accepted it as part of their canon. Portions of the work exist in Greek, and a few fragments in Aramaic were found in the Dead Sea scrolls. All these fragments are from the Book of Watchers, a finding which indicates that that portion existed before the Christian era.

The whole work pretends to be a revelation given to Enoch, a Hebrew patriarch who *Genesis* says lived before Noah and the Flood and in fact was Noah's great-grandfather. The Book of Watchers is unusual in that it deals mainly with characters from the heavenly realm rather than the earthly, and in this it is hard not to see Zoroastrian influence. The story in *Genesis* 6 about the Sons of God coming down from heaven to impregnate the fair daughters of men is lavishly embellished. Each of the heavenly invaders is named, and each takes just one wife for himself. These unions result in a race of giants who turn against the ordinary humans as well as the other living things. The whole episode is an offence to God, who in the end will mete out punishment to these offending spirits, whom Enoch calls "Watchers," no doubt because they watched the human maidens down below. (It is worth noting that the Watcher mentioned in *Daniel* is not at all a sinful spirit but merely a beneficent messenger. It is possible then that the author of *Daniel* had no knowledge of the Book of Watchers, even though scholars generally think *Daniel* was composed later.)

The Book of Enoch assigns names to around twenty of the Watchers and says they taught humans various arts and sciences such as magic, astrology, cosmetics, the making of weapons, and so on. Evidently none of this leads to prosperity for humans, for when they complain to God about their dire situation, such learning is among the evils they mention. God's reaction is to imprison the Watcher Azazel, who taught the production of arms, in a dark desert where he is covered with jagged stones. Then God orders a proclamation:

> ...and announce the restoration of the earth, for I shall restore the earth, so that not all the sons of men shall be destroyed through the mystery of everything which the Watchers made known and taught to their sons. And the whole earth has been ruined by the teaching of the works of Azazel, and against him write down all sin.[31] (10:7)

Clearly the author has taken the opportunity here to inveigh against the technology of the imperial powers that had devastated the Fertile Crescent and beyond. The Lord's next step is to create war among the sons sired by the Watchers so that they kill one another. The Watchers themselves are imprisoned "under the hills of earth until the day of their judgement and of their consummation, until the judgement which is for all eternity is accomplished."[32] On top of the Flood the author has introduced the now familiar theme of a Final Judgment in which the wicked will be punished and the righteous rewarded. But what is different from the other Jewish works we have studied, yet quite in accord with Zoroastrian doctrine, is that it is the heavenly spirits that are here being judged. The world's troubles originate in the heavenly sphere, and the solution primarily involves the denizens of that realm. Nevertheless, the end result for those on earth will be a world of peace for the rest of eternity:

> And in those days I will open the storehouses of blessing which
> are in heaven that I may send them down upon the earth, upon the
> work and upon the toil of the sons of men. Peace and truth will
> be united for all the days of eternity and for all the generations of
> eternity.[33]

Enoch also describes his visit to the house of the Almighty in especially vivid terms:

> And its floor was fire, and above were lightning and the path of the
> stars, and its roof also was a burning fire. And I looked and I saw
> in it a high throne, and its appearance was like ice and its sur-
> rounds like the shining sun and the sound of Cherubim. And from
> underneath the high throne there flowed out rivers of burning fire
> so that it was impossible to look at it. And He who is great in glory
> sat on it, and his raiment was brighter than the sun, and whiter
> than any snow.[34]

Enoch brings with him a petition for mercy from the Watchers, but the Lord has no patience with them. In what He says to Enoch He describes a starkly dualistic cosmos where the realm of spirit and eternal life stands opposed to the realm of flesh and mortality. Addressing the petitioners the Almighty says:

> And you were spiritual, holy, living an eternal life, but you became
> unclean upon the women, and begat children through the blood
> of flesh, and lusted after the blood of men, and produced flesh and
> blood as they do who die and are destroyed. And for this reason
> I gave them wives, namely that they might sow seed in them
> and that children might be born by them, that thus deeds might
> be done on the earth. But you formerly were spiritual, living an
> eternal, immortal life for all the generations of the world. For this
> reason I did not arrange wives for you because the dwelling of the
> spiritual ones is in heaven.[35]

This dualism is certainly reminiscent of Zoroastrian ideas, but it is not as though the cosmos was divided originally between good and evil. The world's ills arise out of the illicit mixing of the two realms of spirit and flesh by the wantonness of the Watchers.

In another scene Enoch is shown a high mountain and a beautiful fragrant tree. The holy angel Michael explains their significance:

> This high mountain which you saw, whose summit is like the throne
> of the Lord, is the throne where the Holy and Great One, the Lord
> of Glory, the Eternal King, will sit when he comes down to visit the
> earth for good. And this beautiful fragrant tree—and no creature
> of flesh has authority to touch it until the great judgement when he
> will take vengeance on all and will bring everything to a consumma-
> tion for ever—this will be given to the righteous and humble. From
> its fruit life will be given to the chosen; towards the north it will be
> planted, in a holy place, by the house of the Lord, the Eternal King.
> Then they will rejoice with joy and be glad in the holy place; they
> will each draw the fragrance into their bones, and they will live a
> long life on earth, as your fathers lived, and in their days sorrow and
> pain and toil and punishment will not touch them.[36]

The Book of Watchers is not, like *Daniel*, aimed at encouraging the Jewish people in a time of oppression and rebellion, but rather is an effort to give cosmic sense to the whole human condition as the author experienced it, with all its warfare and suffering. There is no mention of a special place for the Hebrews; there is just the divine intervention that will punish the wicked and provide peace and prosperity for the righteous. Certain themes from *Genesis* are included, but the overall scheme draws very little on traditional Hebrew scriptures. Perhaps the work was first composed during the time of the Persian Empire and constitutes an imaginative reworking of Zoroastrian ideas current among the Persians at that time. Certainly it became later a major conduit for apocalyptic phantasy of a non-biblical sort into the Christian world.

The second part of *The Book of Enoch*, the Book of Parables, was, as we said, composed much later than the Book of Watchers, and it may well have been revised by Christians in the first or second century. One element found in this work but not the earlier is the introduction of a special figure, the "Chosen One," the "Son of Man," who is referred to once as the "Messiah," the anointed one, and once as "Son of a Woman" (62:5). To a large extent this figure carries out the role assigned to similar saviours in earlier Jewish literature except that again there is no indication that it is just the Jewish people who are being rescued; rather, the Son of Man comes to establish peace and justice for the whole world by destroying the arrogant kings who presently rule. According to one passage (48:3) his coming was foreordained "before the sun and the constellations were created, before the stars of heaven were made." On him is placed the "whole judgement" (66:27) that distinguishes the sinners from the righteous and condemns the wayward angels to be bound in chains. This subjugation of the "satans" will do away with all corruptibility, the implication being that it was the work of the bad angels that introduced it in the first place (69:29).

The monsters Leviathan and Behemoth are also given an obscure role in the cosmic drama. Leviathan is a sea monster while Behemoth inhabits the land (60:9), and they seem to be instrumental in the Lord's punishment of humans (60:24). "Satans" appear, not as divinely appointed accusers, but, like the Watchers were in the earlier book, as angelic sources of evildoing (65:6). As in the Book of Watchers, wicked angels are enumerated and named (much the same names are used), but those named are just the leaders of a much larger pack of malignant spirits (69:2–3). Sexual intercourse with the daughters of men is mentioned (69:5), as is the teaching of arts and sciences. One art mentioned here but not in the Book of Watchers is that of writing. The angel Penemue:

> ...taught men the art of writing with ink and paper, and through this many have gone astray from eternity to eternity, and to this day. For men were not created for this, that they should confirm their faith like this with pen and ink. For men were created no differently from the angels, that they might remain righteous and pure, and death, which destroys everything, would not have touched them; but through this knowledge of theirs they are being destroyed, and through this power it (death) is consuming me.[37]

The speaker here is Enoch himself, so presumably it is he who is being consumed by the death visited upon humans as a result of learning to write—unless we are to assume someone else wrote down Enoch's words.

The Book of Dreams, the fourth section in *Enoch*, contains one portion (85:1–90:42) that recounts the history of Israel in the terms of a long allegory involving bulls, sheep, wolves, and other animals. Enoch sees all this in a prophetic dream that he relates to his son Methuselah. It is the only section that seems peculiarly directed to the Jewish people; in general, *Enoch* is distinguished by its universality and its preoccupation with the various spiritual inhabitants of heaven, whom it names and describes in endless detail. It provides evidence that among Jews, and probably Christians as well, in the first two centuries CE there were those who were entranced with phantasies about heavenly beings and their relations to humans on earth. The dualism of corporeal existence (flesh) versus spirit is pervasive in the work, as is the robust belief in souls or spirits of humans that survive death and experience what the Lord of Spirits has in store for them after the Great Judgment.

The dualism of *Enoch* is markedly enhanced in another and somewhat later piece of Jewish apocalyptic, *The Apocalypse of Abraham*. Particularly noteworthy is the enlarged role in this work of the angel Azazel as the evil spirit responsible for so much ill in the world. One interpreter says that it seems the author of this work treats Azazel as a "negative counterpart of the deity."[38] Indeed, the entire cosmos seems to be structured so that the evil and good portions mirror each other. It is thought that this work had an important influence on later Jewish mysticism.

Still another late work of Jewish apocalyptic is *The Second Book of Esdras*, and its origins are also very obscure. It has sixteen chapters, but the first two and the last two scholars think were written by Christians, the former in the mid-second century and the latter in the third. The central chapters (3–14), scholars propose, were composed by a Palestinian Jew of the late first century, who used the fiction of a prophet named "Ezra" (the book could be titled "The Second Book of Ezra"), living in Babylon, presumably at the time of the exile. Truths about what is to happen in the future are delivered to Ezra by the angel Uriel, a figure who also appears in *Enoch*, where he has much the same function. But 2 *Esdras* is not concerned much with any host of heavenly beings in the way *Enoch* is. Rather, it foretells how God is going to set things right on earth. It is also deeply concerned with how to justify the ways of God, in particular His allowing the people of Israel to suffer so much at the hands of their enemies.

Here we shall concentrate exclusively on the eschatological passages in 2 *Esdras*, as these are the ones that treat themes relevant to our overall inquiry. In chapter 5, Uriel lets Ezra know that "the days are coming when those who dwell on earth shall be seized with great confusion, and the way of truth shall be hidden, and the land shall be barren of faith" (5:1).[39] There follows a list of evils involving the land, animals, human fertility, and general chaos in human and national relations. This is all recounted again in chapter 6, but there it is followed by a promise that all who remain after the days of destruction will see a radical change:

> And they shall see the men who were taken up, who from their birth have not tasted death; and the heart of the earth's inhabitants shall be changed and converted to a different spirit. For evil shall be blotted out, and deceit shall be quenched; faithfulness shall flourish, and corruption shall be overcome, and the truth, which has been so long without fruit, shall be revealed. (6:26–28)[40]

A Messiah will emerge among the saved remnant of humanity, but after four hundred years he will die and all the saved people with him. After a period of seven days in which "primeval silence" (7:30) will reign, "the world, which is not yet awake, shall be roused, and that which is corruptible will perish. And the earth shall give up those who are asleep in it, and the dust those who dwell silently in it; and the chambers shall give up the souls which have been committed to them" (7:31-32). In other words, everyone who has ever lived will be resurrected, an event that leads directly to the Final Judgment:

> And the Most High shall be revealed upon the seat of judgment, and compassion shall pass away, and patience shall be withdrawn; but only judgment shall remain, truth shall stand, and faithfulness shall grow strong. (7:33-34)[41]

There will then be a "pit of torment" for the many wicked and a "paradise of delight" for the few righteous (7.36).[42]

Death is envisioned as a separating of the spirit of a person from the body, and this spirit is conscious of the spirits of other persons; spirits of persons who led wicked lives will be tormented by knowledge of the rewards in store for the spirits of the righteous, and spirits of persons who lived righteously shall not only enjoy their reward but also find satisfaction in the punishments that await the spirits of the wicked. Ezra is somewhat perplexed by this gruesome fate that awaits evildoers, but he is assured by the angel that he should worry no more about it:

> Therefore do not ask any more questions about the multitude of those who perish. For they also received freedom, but they despised the Most High, and were contemptuous of his law and forsook his ways. (8:55-56)[43]

That they "received freedom" implies that they could have directed their lives otherwise, and consequently they are responsible for their lawlessness and thus deserving of the punishment the Most High imposes on them. This strong notion of personal responsibility was first, as noted earlier, articulated in Zoroastrianism, and it is present in *Ezekiel*. By the time *2 Esdras* was written it had become a foundation stone for the whole doctrine of a Final Judgment by God Himself upon mankind.

In a dream Ezra has a vision of a strange eagle that begins with multiple wings and three heads, but as the dream progresses the beast morphs so that it has only six little wings and two heads, and then one head devours the other. The weird monster obviously symbolizes some series of imperial powers ending with what, given the context in which the work was written, can only be the Roman Empire. The eagle is confronted by a lion, who informs the beast of its coming demise under the vengeance of the "Most High." In the words of the lion:

> Therefore you will surely disappear, you eagle, and your terrifying wings and your most evil little wings, and your malicious heads, and your evil talons, and your whole worthless body, so that the whole earth, freed from your violence, may be refreshed and relieved, and may hope for the judgment and mercy of him who made it. (11:45–46)[44]

The whole dream is much too elaborate to recount here. Suffice it to say that it allegorizes the past history of imperial rule and, as well, what the author hoped would be the eventual outcome. The lion is explicitly said to represent the coming Messiah, who will judge the people, destroy the wicked, and deliver a remnant from the coming destruction of the world. His judgment at this point is not the final one, but something preliminary to the Last Judgment. It is not entirely clear whether the saved remnant will consist just of a minority drawn from the people of Israel or whether the author intends a wider constituency. The former interpretation seems more likely, and in that case the central section of *2 Esdras* must be seen as primarily directed to the Jewish people suffering under the Romans, encouraging them to keep to their traditional faith in trust that God will send a saviour who will destroy their oppressors and provide for those who have been faithful a much improved world where they will prosper.

Reviewing briefly the course of the Jewish literature we have just discussed, we can see that the ancient Hebrew prophetic tradition found in *Amos*, *Micah*, and the older parts of *Isaiah* with its tirades against the sinfulness of the Hebrew wealthy and elite, and its predictions of the nation's coming punishment at the hands of foreign powers acting as instruments of Yahweh's vengeance, gets transformed into a symbolic rendition of human history. An eschatology ensues that envisions some sort of great destruction, followed by a final Divine Judgment that will consign the evildoers to tortures in some sort of pit while providing the righteous with prosperity in a newly created world, a garden of paradise. This intervention by God brings history to an end—it is the End of Days and transforms the world into something incorruptible. In *Daniel* and *Enoch* we find that the heavenly sphere with its host of purely spiritual beings plays a crucial role in the events leading to the end; but only in *Enoch* are they also the originators of the evil that has overtaken mankind. All this operates within the growing use of the dualism of spirit versus flesh and the acceptance that the spirits, or souls, of humans are capable of a full conscious existence apart from embodiment.

I see these elaborate phantasies as very likely the result of the encounters the Hebrews, when in exile in Babylon and after the partial restoration of their state, would have had with eschatological doctrines emanating from Zoroastrianism, the then dominant religion of the Persian Empire. What in the pre-exilic period was an attempt to make sense of the horrific experience of the Hebrew people in the face of brutal oppressors is broadened into a sort of cosmic history that is intended to make sense of such suffering in the world at large by foreseeing the eventual victory of a divine justice, one that will mete out to all the people and nations exactly what they deserve by the standards of morality, that is, God's laws. This victory will be followed by the Hebrew equivalent of the Zoroastrian "Making Wonderful" (the Frashegird), the creation of an incorruptible utopia in which humans will find permanent prosperity and all evildoing will be banished. The Jews, I believe, had found in the Zoroastrian phantasies materials to express their own deep resentments of their oppression by imperial powers and a way to turn their deepest hopes for ultimate restoration into a story of revenge, justice, and total victory for the entire world. It is a *Wesenwille* response, not a *Kürwille* one, in that it erupts from the depths of the soul reacting to the world, not from a self-conscious distancing from the world around one and from one's own self as well. This response was pervasively at work in the milieu in which Christianity was born.

Early Christianity I: Saint Paul

The letters actually written by Paul and found in the New Testament are the earliest Christian writings extant, having been produced around 50 CE. Paul's teachings and writings were immensely influential among the Christians of the first through third centuries, and since being included in the biblical canon, they have formed an authoritative source for Christian theology and piety down through the centuries. What follows is not an attempt to encapsulate the essence of his message and work but merely an extraction of certain themes that emerge in his letters and form the background for the sort of millennialism among Christians that was to come.

Paul had an insight that finds expression in some of the work of sages in many cultures: the worthwhileness of a human life is not to be judged by whether the person adheres to laws or codes of morality but by whether the person is motivated by a spirit of love for righteousness and respect for fellow human beings. It is not outward behaviour but the inner spirit that matters. In this, Paul's insight accords with the words of Plato in *Republic* IV (443d): "The reality is that justice is not a matter of external behavior but the way a man privately and truly governs his inner self." Indeed, it is a thought with which all the major philosophic systems that were sketched in chapter 3, including the ones that were mentioned as arising in India and China, would have concurred. In Paul's case it led to his dismissing as a path leading to sin and death the belief that conscientious and scrupulous obedience to the traditional laws of the Jews would result in justification before God. Rather, one has to be invested with the Spirit of Jesus Christ:

> But you are not in the flesh, you are in the Spirit, if the Spirit of God really dwells in you. Any one who does not have the Spirit of Christ does not belong to him. But if Christ is in you, although your bodies are dead because of sin, your spirits are alive because of righteousness. (*Romans* 8:9–10)

The "fruit of the spirit" consists of character traits—predominantly what might be called *Gemeinschaft* virtues, since they are ones that a traditional, non-urban community (such as those discussed in chapter 2) would have valued:

> But the fruit of the Spirit is love, joy, peace, patience, kindness, goodness, faithfulness, gentleness, self-control; against such there is no law. (*Galatians* 5:22–23)

Such are the characteristics any *Gemeinschaft* must cultivate if it is to stay together very long. These contrast with what Paul calls the "works of the flesh":

> Now the works of the flesh are plain: immorality, impurity, licentiousness, idolatry, sorcery, enmity, strife, jealousy, anger, selfishness, dissension, party spirit, envy, drunkenness, carousing, and the like. (*Galatians* 5:19–21)

Obviously many of these are the very opposites of what a *Gemeinschaft* would need. Paul is thus thinking of the Spirit as something that motivates the traditional values of settled human life. But what about the "flesh"? We have already encountered this term in *The Book of Enoch*, but there it just means a corporeal kind of existence. As such the notion was already found in Zoroastrianism, but neither there nor in Enoch is flesh treated as a source of sinfulness, as it is in Paul's writings.

If we go back to the original Zoroastrian creation myth, we find that Ahura Mazda created the material world as a bulwark against the anticipated attack of Angra Mainyu and his wicked *devas*. These material beings were perfectly good until Angra Mainyu's evil horde wreaked havoc on them. In *Enoch* there is an analogous invasion of the "Watchers," who are spirits, coming down to have their licentious way with the daughters of men. The realm of flesh is in this work considered inferior to that of spirit but not a source of evil. What is wrong is the Watchers, who are pure spirits, involving themselves with beings of flesh. Zoroastrianism envisions that when the world is eventually restored to its pristine state, the material world will resume the beneficent condition it had at its creation. Materiality does not on this conception even imply destructibility, for after the restoration material beings will be indestructible. In the case of Paul, "flesh" seems to have a much more pejorative sense. For a person to be "enfleshed" is for them to be drawn into the ways of the ordinary world, ways that Jesus has warned against. In one place Paul sees flesh as just providing an opportunity for Satan to tempt people into evil ways. Here again we have an evil spirit somehow taking advantage of our materiality and in fact, according to Paul, bringing death upon the person.

> To set the mind on the flesh is death, but to set the mind on the Spirit is life and peace. (*Romans* 8:6)

No doubt Paul speaks metaphorically here of "death" and "life," but there can also be no doubt that he believed that adopting worldly values resulted in the thwarting of one's own life, for the human being is basically a spirit, a being whose life cannot be lived with such values. Here Paul has, in effect, placed humans in the position of the Watchers in *Enoch*—that is, they are spirits who should not involve themselves with flesh. When Paul speaks of the resurrection of the dead, he says they will be given a spiritual body, that is, not one that ties them back to the everyday world and its mores. Paul's disparagement of human physicality does not well accord with the ancient texts of the Hebrews and has been a stumbling block for Christian thinkers ever since.

Paul's doctrine of "flesh," I think, reflects his deep disgust with the morality of the mass of people, as well as their rulers, in his time. It is his way of adopting the attitude of the prophets Amos and Isaiah when they lambaste the decadence of their own people. But he has introduced a dualism that comes close to Plato's visible world of change and inconstancy versus the invisible world of changeless and permanent beings. Just as Plato saw the true home of the human mind in the latter realm, and the former realm as frequently a misleading distraction, so Paul sees humans, himself included, as distracted by the things of the world, which their human flesh desires, away from what their true spiritual self longs for. To this he adds the moral dimension that both Zoroastrianism and the Hebrew prophets insisted on: the deeds one perpetrates while going along with the flesh make one deserving of divine punishment.

This leads us to Paul's eschatology, for he envisions a day of judgment in line with what we have seen in Zoroastrianism and in post-exile Jewish texts.

> But by your hard and impenitent heart you are storing up wrath for yourself on the day of wrath when God's righteous judgment will be revealed. For he will render to every man according to his

works: to those who by patience in well-doing seek for glory and honor and immortality, he will give eternal life; but for those who are factious and do not obey the truth, but obey wickedness, there will be wrath and fury. (*Romans* 2:5–8)

The Judgment is preceded by the arrival of Christ and his angels taking vengeance on all who have not come to have faith in Jesus:

> This [the persecution suffered by the Thessalonians] is evidence of the righteous judgment of God, that you may be made worthy of the kingdom of God, for which you are suffering—since indeed God deems it just to repay with affliction those who afflict you, and to grant rest with us to you who are afflicted, when the Lord Jesus is revealed from heaven with his mighty angels in flaming fire, inflicting vengeance upon those who do not obey the gospel of our Lord Jesus. They shall suffer the punishment of eternal destruction and exclusion from the presence of the Lord and from the glory of his might, when he comes in that day to be glorified in his saints, and to be marveled at in all who have believed, because our testimony to you was believed. (*Thessalonians* 2 1:5–10)

The basic theme is by now familiar to the reader, although, unlike the Hebrew prophets, Paul has the divine revenge fall not on the enemies of Israel but on those who have persecuted the Christian communities; nevertheless, the implication is that what happens in this end of history is of universal significance. In fact, it affects the whole of creation.

> Then comes the end, when he delivers the kingdom to God the Father after destroying every rule and every authority and power. For he must reign until he has put all his enemies under his feet. The last enemy to be destroyed is death. (*Corinthians* 1 15:23–26)

> For the creation waits with eager longing for the revealing of the sons of God; for the creation was subjected to futility, not of its

own will but by the will of him who subjected it in hope; because the creation itself will be set free from its bondage to decay and obtain the glorious liberty of the children of God. (*Romans* 8:19–21)

Paul adopts the idea familiar from the prophets that this restoration must be preceded by an evil time:

> The coming of the lawless one by the activity of Satan will be with all power and with pretended signs and wonders, and with all wicked deception for those who are to perish, because they refused to love the truth and so be saved. Therefore, God sends upon them a strong delusion, to make them believe what is false, so that all may be condemned who did not believe the truth but had pleasure in unrighteousness. (*Thessalonians* 2 2:9–12)

The resurrection of the dead is an important stage in the drama of God's intervention at the End of Days:

> For this we declare to you by the word of the Lord, that we who are alive, who are left until the coming of the Lord, shall not precede those who have fallen asleep. For the Lord himself will descend from heaven with a cry of command, with the archangel's call, and with the sound of the trumpet of God. And the dead in Christ will rise first; then we who are alive, who are left, shall be caught up together with them in the clouds to meet the Lord in the air; and so we shall always be with the Lord. (*Thessalonians* 1 4:15–17)

As for the timing of this great event, Paul thinks it cannot be far off, but it may well surprise everyone when it does come:

> For you yourselves know well that the day of the Lord will come like a thief in the night. When people say, "There is peace and security," then sudden destruction will come upon them as travail comes upon a woman with child, and then there will be no escape.

> But you are not in darkness, brethren, for that day to surprise you like a thief. For you are all sons of light and sons of the day; we are not of the night or of darkness. (*Thessalonians* 1 5:2–5)

Paul does not seem to think that his audience in the various Christian congregations he writes to needs to be convinced of this eschatological phantasy; rather it seems to be what all his brethren in Christ already believe. Their faith in Christ consists in this: They trust that Christ will intervene for them in the Final Judgment and secure their pardon for the sins they have committed simply because they have preserved that faith and loved the life of the spirit. One of the most distinctive Pauline doctrines is that salvation is not secured by good works but by faith, for in fact every person is drawn to varying extent into the works of the flesh just by being enfleshed.

In this Paul differs from all the preceding figures in this chapter. In the Final Judgment God does not weigh up good deeds against wicked deeds in a person's life. If He did that, no one would be saved. What He does is see if the person put their trust in His Son, Christ Jesus, rather than trusting in their own moral goodness. Nor can a person even take credit for their faith, for this, if they have it, is something freely granted to them by God. He compares this gift to the way death came to humans through Adam's original trespass:

> But the free gift is not like the trespass. For if many died through one man's trespass [i.e., Adam's], much more have the grace of God and the free gift in the grace of that one man Jesus Christ abounded for many. And the free gift is not like the effect of that one man's sin. For the judgment following one trespass brought condemnation, but the free gift following many trespasses brings justification. If because of one man's trespass, death reigned through that one man, much more will those who receive the abundance of grace and the free gift of righteousness reign in life through the one man Jesus Christ. (*Romans* 5:15–17)

Add to this the idea expressed in the text quoted above from *Thessalonians* 2:2, namely that God Himself creates delusion in the minds of some, and we see that the central importance of human free choice in determining the worthiness of a person, a doctrine that was the hallmark of Zoroastrianism and implicitly accepted in most later Jewish thought, has been here obliterated. It is a very short step from Paul's conception to the doctrine of predestination as developed centuries later by Saint Augustine. One old prophet, however, laid the groundwork for this shift, Ezekiel. He saw that the people of Israel had to be given a new inner spirit if they were to be restored, and this spirit could only be delivered to them by God Himself. As in Paul, the main agent in the drama of salvation is the deity, not humans, who, in fact, play a mostly passive role in the proceedings. To say the least, it is not clear once this path is taken how God's judgment is still a just one.

Early Christianity II: Jesus's followers
Early Christian literature as found in the New Testament—that is, the canonical gospels and letters attributed to various apostles—reveals that, as with Paul, the underlying assumption that an End of Days scenario involving first a cosmic catastrophe, then the coming of Christ, the defeat of his enemies, the establishment of the Kingdom of God, and finally a judgment by God or Christ that would assign to all people, including those resurrected from the dead, their just deserts—Hell and torture for evildoers who have not repented, and some sort of paradise for those who have accepted the salvation offered by Christ—was the unquestioned background against which people joined the community of followers of the now departed Jesus.

Jesus himself is portrayed in the gospels as holding this belief; indeed, he is pictured as expecting the establishment of the Kingdom within the lifetime of some of those living:

> "For whoever is ashamed of me and my words in this adulterous and sinful generation, of him will the Son of Man also be ashamed, when he comes in the glory of his Father with the holy angels." And he said to them, "Truly, I say to you, there are some standing here who will not taste death before they see the kingdom of God come with power." (*Mark* 8:38–9:1)

> When they persecute you in one town, flee to the next; for truly, I say to you, you will not have gone through all the towns of Israel, before the Son of man comes. (*Matthew* 10:23)

I use texts like these from the gospels not to prove what the historical Jesus actually said and believed but to reveal how the early Christians remembered him; my aim here is simply to show how pervasive among those Christians was this eschatological story. The canonical gospels were written, according to scholars, in the second half of the first century and the early second century, although, of course, what has come down to us may have depended on still earlier texts and oral traditions. In what follows, then, when I speak of Jesus and what he says, I mean only what his early followers took him to be saying; by "Jesus" I refer to the Jesus they held in their minds, without my supposing either that this Jesus accurately represents the historical Jesus or that it does not. That is a question I would not be competent to judge even if it was relevant to this study, which it is not.

The early Christians lived their lives with the assumption that the end might come at any time and that they should be prepared for it. Here is a brief passage citing Jesus's own words, which sound a warning that his followers took very seriously:

> But of that day or that hour no one knows, not even the angels in heaven, nor the Son, but only the Father. Take heed, watch; for you do not know when the time will come. It is like a man going on a journey, when he leaves home and puts his servants in charge, each with his work, and commands the doorkeeper to be on the watch. Watch therefore—for you do not know when the master of the house will come, in the evening, or at midnight, or at the cockcrow, or in the morning—lest he come suddenly and find you asleep. And what I say to you I say to all: "Watch." (*Mark* 13:32-37)

Before Christ returns, however, his followers will suffer from persecution and the whole world will be in a state of chaos and general suffering. Jesus fortells the destruction of Jerusalem (a good indication that some of the gospel texts date from after that event in 70 CE) and many other disasters:

> "Alas for those who are with child and for those who give suck in those days! For great distress shall be upon the earth and wrath upon this people; they will fall by the edge of the sword, and be led captive among all nations; and Jerusalem will be trodden down by the Gentiles, until the times of the Gentiles are fulfilled." (*Luke* 21:23–24)

These bad times will be brought to an end by the arrival of the "Son of man," whom the early Christians assumed would be Jesus himself as Christ/Messiah, "coming in a cloud with power and great glory" (*Luke* 21:27):

> "Immediately after the tribulation of those days the sun will be darkened, and the moon will not give its light, and the stars will fall from heaven, and the powers of the heavens will be shaken; there will appear the sign of the Son of man in heaven, and then all the tribes of the earth will mourn, and they will see the Son of man coming on the clouds of heaven with power and great glory; and he will send out his angels with a loud trumpet call, and they will gather his elect from the four winds, from one end of heaven to the other." (*Matthew* 24:28–31)

This heavenly intervention involves the resurrection of the dead to a new and endless life so that all who have ever lived will be called for judgment:

> The sons of this age marry and are given in marriage; but those who are accounted worthy to attain to that age and to the resurrection from the dead neither marry nor are given in marriage, for they cannot die any more, because they are equal to angels and are sons of God, being sons of the resurrection. (*Luke* 20:34–36)

> Truly, truly, I say to you, the hour is coming, and now is, when the dead will hear the voice of the Son of god, and those who hear will

live. For as the Father has life in himself, so he has granted the son also to have life in himself, and has given him authority to execute judgment, because he is the Son of man. Do not marvel at this, for the hour is coming when all who are in the tombs will hear his voice and come forth, those who have done good to the resurrection of life, and those who have done evil, to the resurrection of judgment. *(John 5:25–29)*

The nature of the judgment is laid out by Jesus in some detail. Here are some excerpts from one of the most famous of the speeches attributed to Jesus:

When the Son of man comes in his glory, and all the angels with him, then he will sit on his glorious throne. Before him will be gathered all the nations, and he will separate them one from another as a shepherd separates the sheep from the goats, and he will place the sheep at his right hand, but the goats at the left. Then the King will say to those at his right hand, "Come, O blessed of my Father, inherit the kingdom prepared for you from the foundation of the world." *(Matthew 25:31–34)*

What follows is Jesus's praising acts of kindness and mercy toward those in trouble as though they had been done to himself. The refusal to perform such acts when the opportunity presents itself is thus a refusal to help him in his hour of need. The sheep are those who did such acts, the goats are those who refused. For the latter, Jesus has these words:

Then he will say to those at his left hand, "Depart from me, you cursed, into the eternal fire prepared for the devil and his angels." *(Matthew 25:41)*

From texts such as these as well as Paul's letters we can see that the early Christians believed that Christ would be there at the Last Judgment to save and reward those who had led a life motivated by values Jesus advocated during his first coming—that is, values that went to an extreme of self-effacement and non-resistance to wrongdoers. It was not that his followers were simply to refrain from doing any harm to others who had harmed them (such as Socrates had demanded of his companions); rather, they were positively to help them—to one who has struck you "turn the other cheek," to the thief who has taken your coat "give your cloak as well," to "love your enemies and pray for those who persecute you."[45] This was not an ethic for effective living in the actual world the Christians found themselves in. But if the expectation was that the whole world would soon end and be replaced by an order in which those, both living and dead, who genuinely honoured such values would be given a home in paradise and those who did not might well be tossed into an "eternal fire"—if that was the expectation—then of course that ethic made total sense. This is not to deny that it has an appeal beyond that expectation, for the ideal espoused comes from the dream of a perfect *Gemeinschaft* where peace, love, and harmony reign supreme. Early Christians turned away from effective action in the surrounding world to try as best they could to fulfil that dream in their various congregations.

Early Christianity III: Apocalypses

We have seen that within the Jewish community out of which the Jesus cult arose and then spread to become the Christian churches, which eventually included more gentiles than Jews, there was a tradition of apocalyptic literature in which all of human history and the future of the cosmos were recounted in highly poetic and symbolic fashion. These works elaborate a kind of basic scenario that almost always includes the following, often in this order:

1. A figure of some sort, usually a very early Hebrew patriarch, to whom things are "unveiled" (= *apocalyphon*) in one way or another.
2. A summary of human history from the creation.
3. Intervention in the world by evil heavenly beings of some sort who corrupt the world and the morals of humans.
4. Persecution of the righteous.
5. A time of dreadful troubles involving the dominance of some peculiarly evil person or being.

6. Cosmic catastrophe.
7. The coming of a saviour figure who defeats the forces of evil.
8. The resurrection of the dead.
9. A judgment by God on all persons both living and those resurrected that separates out the evildoers from the righteous and sends the former to places of great torment and the latter to some sort of happy, everlasting life.
10. A transformation of the whole cosmos into something indestructible and benign.

Christians of the second and third centuries made important contributions to this genre. Here I shall discuss two very briefly—*The Apocalypse of Peter* and *The Sibylline Oracles*—and one at greater length, *The Revelation* (i.e., *Apocalypse*) *to John*, which is part of the canonical New Testament. Unless brought up in a deeply fundamentalist Christian culture, the modern reader is likely to read these works as bizarre, but nevertheless at times very moving, pieces of symbolic phantasy. They have inspired writers and artists in the West down through the centuries with their elaborate images and complex symbolism. In the early centuries CE, however, many ordinary Christians as well as many fathers of the Church took them seriously as history and prediction and fully expected the kind of End of Days that such works forecast to be coming, perhaps in their own lifetimes. It is my thesis that as Christianity became dominant in the West, the belief that these works were describing a perhaps imminent future persisted and permanently moulded how Westerners of all classes viewed the future. From being something that was expected to be largely like the past with no real likelihood of radical improvement, the future became something in which one expected some catastrophic reign of evil, to be followed by a world totally transformed for the better, at least so far as a select group of human beings were concerned. Such were the origins of what today we call "millennialism."

The Apocalypse of Peter existed in the form we now have in the first half of the second century and most likely was first written in Greek. The full version, like *Enoch*, is known only in Ethiopic. It purports to recount what Jesus said to his disciples when they asked him about the Second Coming. Many Christians of the second and third centuries accepted its authority and cited it quite often; in fact, it almost made it into the New Testament canon. Jesus promises that he will come in a cloud of glory:

> Thus I will come in a cloud of heaven with great power in my glory while my cross goes before my face. I will come in my glory while giving out light seven times brighter than the sun. I will come in my glory with all the holy angels when my Father will set a crown upon my head that I might judge the living and the dead. And I will pay back everyone according to his deed.[46]

God will bring forth the dead and reconstitute their bodies, even those that were eaten by birds.[47] This will be followed by a great conflagration, which Jesus vividly describes:

> Cataracts of fire will be opened up and there will be fog and darkness and the whole world will veil and clothe itself. And the waters will be turned and will be given into coals of fire and everything which is in it will burn up and even the ocean will become fire... The children of men who are in the east will flee to the west; they (in the west) will flee into the east. And those in the south will flee north, and those (in the north) to the south. Everywhere the awesome wrath of fire will find them [and] while it pursues them, the flame which does not go out will bring them to the judgment of wrath in the river of fire which does not go out, a fire which flames as it burns.[48]

Most of the remainder of the work is given over to an elaborate portrayal of the tortures awaiting the evildoers. It seems to assume that the audience will take an almost sadistic interest in how various sinners are given appropriately gruesome punishments. Blasphemers are hung by their tongues;[49] sluttish women, by their neck and hair,[50] murderers are put into a fire full of venomous snakes while their victims watch with satisfaction; women who aborted their fetuses are buried up to their necks in what is discharged from the other areas of Hell and viewed by their unborn children who call out to God for vengeance; those who persecuted the righteous are whipped and a worm continuously eats their bowels. And so on.

Those who are saved from these frightful tortures may plead with God for the release of some of those condemned from their just fate, and God will relent, and baptize them in the Acherousian Lake before placing them in the Elysian Fields (a reference to pagan myths about the destination of the dead).[51] As for the happy life provided for the original elect, the *Apocalypse* says little other than that they enter God's eternal kingdom and that there is a fragrant garden with plentiful fruit in which they may reside.[52]

The Sibylline Oracles[53] is one of the most influential of a class of works that were familiar in the early years of the Christian community. These were distinguished by presenting a universal history of the world under the guise of a prophecy by some exceedingly ancient figure, in this case, the Sibyl, well known in Greek literature. Like *The Book of Enoch*, this work begins with the Sibyl poetically predicting the events of early history, starting with the creation, and somewhat revising the narrative in the Hebrew scriptures, but it soon goes beyond that into elements drawn from pagan lore. Also like *Enoch*, it mentions the "Watchers," although the Sibyl does not treat them as heavenly beings but rather as humans who are smart enough to invent the technologies common in the ancient world.

The work developed over time, beginning among Jews living in a Hellenistic kingdom back in the fourth century BCE and undergoing modifications as time went on. The version we have at present probably dates from the second century CE and has obviously been amended by Christians, who, attracted by the basic End of Days story, which the first followers of Jesus had been familiar with from their childhood, wanted to bring that story up to date by giving Christ a role in it. In places it follows closely the scenario of *The Apocalypse of Peter*. It is fair then to treat it as a work reflecting the basic faith of many members of the early Church.

What I want to look at in some detail is the eschatology that is rehearsed at the end of book 2. Like most of these eschatological apocalypses, *The Sibylline Oracles* begins its story of the end with talk of signs of the coming catastrophe:

> ...Piteous fools
> The wicked wretches of the final race,
> Who know not that, when women cease to bear,
> The harvest then falls due for human kind. (2:161–64)[54]

A false prophet appears, Belial, who persecutes the saints as well as the Hebrews. This is followed by a cosmic disaster ending in the melting of everything into one fiery mass:

> And then a vast river of flaming fire
> Shall pour from heaven and ravage every place,
> The earth, the ocean, and the grey-blue sea,
> Lakes, rivers, springs, and Hades hard of heart,
> And heaven's vault, while heaven's fiery stars
> Shall melt into one desolated form. (2:196–205)[55]

The next step in this phantastic scenario is the rescue of human souls, even those of people and mythical figures long consigned to Hades, so that they can all come before the Almighty for judgment on their lives:

> And to the dead, souls, breath, articulate voice
> The heavenly one shall give, and bones fastened
> In all their joints, compact by hand divine.
> Flesh knit to every fleshy part, and nerve
> To nerve, and veins, and skin, their former hair
> Shall grow again; moving and animate,
> Men's bodies on a single day shall rise.
> Then Hades' mighty gates and brazen bars
> Of pitiless, unyielding adamant
> Archangel Uriel shall burst and break
> And bring to judgment every wretched form,
> And foremost there the ancient Titans' shades
> And Giants, and the victims of the flood,
> And those on whom beasts, creeping things, and birds

> Feasted—all these he'll summon to the throne,
> And bodies burned in flesh consuming fire,
> Those too he'll gather to the throne of God. (2:221–37)[56]

The Sibyl has here taken great care to assure the reader that no matter how a person's body was destroyed at death, that person's soul will receive a new body in which the person is to face the Divine Judgment. At this point Christ arrives with a "spotless host" to sit at "God's right hand" and administer the judgment:

> He will condemn and slay. A meet reward
> To pay them back for what they did in life.
> Then all shall pass across a blazing stream
> Of flame unquenchable; wherein the just
> Shall all be saved, the godless be destroyed
> For ever, for the evils that they did. (2:250–55)[57]

The fiery stream has been a recurrent theme from as far back as the Zoroastrians. There follows an uncompromising vision of Hell in which fathers and mothers with their infants and children will all suffer from raging fire. But those who loved justice and lived uprightly will be saved from the fiery stream and placed in a paradise where all their cares are ended. The Sibyl describes this in some surprising ways. Besides unending supplies of wine, honey, and milk, we find the following:

> The earth is one for all, not parceled up
> By walls or fences, and yields up more fruits
> Spontaneous, common produce, boundless wealth,
> No beggar there, no rich man, despot none,
> Nor slave; no longer great nor small exists,
> Nor kings, nor leaders; all are equal there. (2:318–29)[58]

Here is one of the earliest articulations in apocalyptic writings of the ideal of an egalitarian, anarchic community in which private property has no place.

There are hints of this in the old Hebrew prophets, but nothing this explicit has entered eschatological revelations hitherto. With the *Sibylline Oracles* the rage against the privileged and powerful that emerges in all examples of apocalyptic eschatology has moved on to a utopian vision that rejects the whole of the institutions that define settled life. No doubt this reflects the influence of Greco-Roman culture, where the myth of a long-ago golden age in which people lived much simpler lives was very familiar. *The Sibylline Oracles* has transferred elements of that myth about the distant past into a vision of the not so distant future, a change that has had immense implications for Western civilization.

The Sibylline Oracles presents us, then, with a skillful poetic rendering of the sort of End of Days tale we have been surveying, but it has been updated for the second or third centuries, when its readership would have included many brought up in paganism and not entirely comfortable with the exclusively Jewish lore that much of the earlier apocalyptic literature familiar to the first Christians contained. More exclusively Jewish in its outlook is a work that managed to make its way into the New Testament canon and that has had a tremendous impact on Western Christendom through the centuries. I speak, of course, of *The Revelation to John*, henceforth referred to simply as the *Apocalypse*. This work is clearly part of the Jewish apocalyptic genre we have been sampling and was probably first written for a Jewish audience in the late first century after the destruction of Jerusalem by the Romans. It has, however, been modified for the Christian community and was known to them by the middle of the second century.

The author of the *Apocalypse* has created gripping images and complex symbolism that rival those found in *Ezekiel* and *Daniel*. Although what exactly it meant to its first-century audience is largely uncertain, it can easily be seen to convey a bitter attack on the Romans who had recently destroyed the holy city, and then go on to predict the coming fall of that evil empire. But over the centuries it often came to be seen as prophesying events well into the future; in the Middle Ages and modern times, people perceived in it reference to their own historical situations.

The first three chapters of the *Apocalypse* are clearly aimed at Christians, whether Jews or gentiles, for in them John says he is conveying messages from Jesus himself to seven churches. These are said to include "what is and what is to take place hereafter" (1:19), but the revelation of the future really only begins much later. Chapters 4 and 5 describe the vision John is given of the heavenly throne room of God Himself and abounds in the sort of visual imagery we have encountered in other apocalyptic texts. A novel and mysterious element are the four "living creatures" placed around the throne (4:6–8). Each has six wings and a multiplicity of eyes, but one is like a lion, another like an ox, another with the face of a man, and the fourth like an eagle. John sees a scroll sealed with seven seals, which no one is able to open and read (5:1–3); the implication is that on the scroll is recorded what is to come in the future. Then a lamb appears "as though it had been slain" (5:6), and the occupants of the throne room all acknowledge that the lamb is worthy to unlock the scroll, saying "for thou wast slain and by thy blood didst ransom men for God" (5:9). The lamb is, of course, a symbol for Christ, echoing the comparison of the Messiah to a lamb in *Isaiah* (53:7).

In chapters 6–8 the lamb opens up one seal after another. Out of the first four come the famous horsemen, whose significance has been the subject of speculation since ancient times. The last of these, however, is certainly a profoundly menacing figure: Death, followed by Hades (6:8), who the book says will rampage over one quarter of the earth killing with war, famine, and pestilence, as well as wild beasts. Opening the fifth seal reveals under an altar souls of martyrs who plead for vengeance, and when the sixth seal is opened John sees a great earthquake and people hiding from the wrath of God and the Lamb. But there also appear the 144,000 who are to be saved from that wrath, who come from the tribes of Israel, as well as a numberless multitude from every nation, people who have had their sins washed away by "the blood of the Lamb" (7:14).

The opening of the seventh seal reveals the coming cosmic catastrophe, heralded by seven angels blowing seven trumpets successively. One particularly nasty ordeal visited upon those who had not been saved is introduced when a star falling from heaven is given the key to a bottomless pit, which it proceeds to open. Out of it emerges a horde of locust-like creatures whose appearance resembles that of a weird, terrifying cavalry force, except that they have the tails of scorpions, with which they inflict most of their damage (9:1–11).

The twelfth chapter reveals a war in heaven in which Michael and his allied angels defeat a dragon with seven heads, ten horns, and seven diadems and throw him and his allied angels down to the earth, where he is called "Devil" or "Satan." The dragon proceeds to pursue a woman, who gives birth to a male child, "one who is to rule all the nations with a rod of iron" (12:5), but with divine assistance the woman and child elude the dragon's murderous intents, and he then goes off and persecutes righteous Christians (12:17).

The *Apocalypse* moves on to give roles to the traditional monsters of Jewish apocalyptic texts, Leviathan and Behemoth, although the book does not give their names but just says one is from the sea and the other from the land; the latter, however, does have a number, 666, which has also been a huge subject for speculation down through the centuries. Both do the dragon's nefarious work.

In chapter 14, "one like a son of man" (14:14) reaps the earth with a sickle; he is followed by an angel who gathers ripe grapes and throws them in a wine press from which flows blood as the grapes are trodden (14:19–20). (These are the "grapes of wrath" mentioned in much modern Western literature and the title of John Steinbeck's famous novel.) The images continue, always with a connection to the number seven. There are seven bowls of wrath poured out by seven angels. The sixth of these brings on the kings, who are led by demonic spirits who gather for battle at Armageddon (16:14–16). Once the seventh bowl is poured, God's wrath makes itself felt through earthquakes, lightning, thunder, and massive hail storms.

Chapter 17 summons up the image of a harlot luxuriously clothed with whom the kings of the earth have had sex (17:2). She sits on a scarlet beast with seven heads and ten horns. An angel proceeds to interpret the vision: the beast will come from the "bottomless pit," the seven heads are the seven hills on which the woman is seated as well as seven kings; the ten horns are also kings who have not yet ruled. In the end these kings and the beast will destroy the harlot with fire. The angel interprets the harlot as "the great city which has dominion over the kings of the earth" (17:18), no doubt a reference to Rome, whose downfall is predicted. Chapter 18 continues with more detail about the destruction of the "whore of Babylon": kings who have had sex with her will lament her fall and stand in fear; merchants who profited from the trade in luxuries will weep; sea captains and sailors will mourn to see the source of their income liquidated. The *Apocalypse*, in effect, predicts economic collapse in addition to political chaos as Rome's hegemony comes to an end. But this is pictured as welcome to the righteous saints who have suffered so much by the persecution the Romans visited on them.

In chapter 19 there appears a rider on a white horse from whose mouth emerges a sword and whose name is "The Word of God." This figure leads a heavenly army that subdues the nations and defeats the beast and the kings who destroyed the harlot, as well as those misled by a false prophet into following the beast. These two, the beast and the prophet, get thrown into a lake of fire while their followers are simply slain by the sword. In chapter 20 the dragon itself, aka the Devil or Satan, is bound for 1,000 years and thrown into the bottomless pit. There is then a resurrection of the martyrs and others who did not follow the beast, and they reign with Christ for 1,000 years. From all appearances it seems this millennial reign is an earthly one and precedes a second resurrection and the Final Judgment. This whole idea of an earthly millennium where justice rules is unique to the *Apocalypse* within the apocalyptic genre and, as we shall see, was to have revolutionary implications.

The Apocalypse proceeds to events after the 1,000 years are completed. Satan now becomes unbound and deceives nations around the world, who are called Gog and Magog, into attacking the saints, but heaven intervenes and sends fire down to destroy these forces. The dragon himself is thrown into the lake of fire, where he joins the beast and the false prophet. Then it is time for the second and general resurrection followed by the Final Judgment, which consigns those not recorded in the Book of Life to that same lake. Once this is accomplished, the old heaven and earth pass away and are replaced with new ones. God Himself comes down from heaven to live with humans; death is done away with, suffering eliminated. Also from heaven comes a new and resplendent Jerusalem with high walls and three gates on each of its north, south, east, and west sides. Each gate has carved on it the name of one of the twelve tribes of Israel. There are also twelve foundations on which are placed the names of the twelve apostles. The city provides its own light and is never dark; it receives honour from all the nations of the world.

Rarely has a literary work so compellingly given voice to the rage of an oppressed people, to their desire for vengeance and their longing for the triumph of justice and morality, as has the *Apocalypse*. In it comes forth a deep disgust with the whole present order of human affairs as well as the cosmos generally, and a dream that something much better than this has to be possible. In this respect the *Apocalypse* taps into the root of the whole *Gemeinschaft* response to domination by *Gesellschaft* elites, which is basically what we have been exploring in this chapter. In this it is a phantasy entirely different from, and to a degree opposed to, the *Kürwille* reactions of some of the literate elite of the Greco-Roman world that we described in the previous chapter. It has an appeal to the masses of people who remained in *Gemeinschaften*, ran their lives on a *Wesenwille* basis, and often found themselves exploited and derided by the *Kürwille*-minded elites who ran the *Gesellschaften* and who frequently adopted the ideas of the elite *Kürwille* reactions to urban-dominated civilizations we explored earlier.

The appeal is heightened immensely by the visions of a much improved world to come. Once the forces of oppression and injustice are overcome, we move into the "Frashegird," the "making wonderful," the millennium, the Parousia, and establishment of the Kingdom of Heaven. Here is the idea that fundamentally will set the West apart, and, as it finds more and more acceptance in the modern period, fuel the enthusiasm for the kind of expansion that leads to eco-catastrophe. As long as this vision was submerged in the West under the orthodoxy of the Christianized Stoicism that dominated the medieval period, it could exist relatively harmlessly without inciting any radical change. But as that orthodoxy disintegrated, it emerged with devastating results. That is the story we shall explore in the next chapter.

But before we turn to the rather tragic history of how the eschatological and apocalyptic phantasies of the Jews and early Christians were taken up in the West in later centuries, it is good to pause and note how this tradition—the *Apocalypse* in particular—was adopted by extremely oppressed people even in recent times to inspire both their resistance and their sense of their own self-worth. I think here of the Africans brought as slaves to America from the seventeenth to the nineteenth centuries and their descendants. It is hard to imagine a more dehumanizing ordeal than that visited upon these persons, although no doubt there were equivalents in the ancient world. To a lesser degree this oppression exists even now, even after the election of a man with partial African ancestry to the presidency of the United States, as is apparent in the huge numbers of Black Americans in prison and the endemic police violence against Black people in that country.

The late theologian of Black liberation, James H. Cone, was surely right to say that the Black Christian churches of America understood better than the White churches the underlying motivating message of early Christianity, that is, the recognition of oppression as deep injustice, the necessity to resist it, and the faith that in the end justice will triumph. As Cone said:

> White thought on the Christian view of salvation was largely "spiritual" and sometimes "rational," but usually separated from the concrete struggle for freedom in this world. Black thought was largely eschatological and never abstract, but usually related to blacks' struggle against earthly oppression.[59]

Cone railed against scholars who had failed to take literally Jesus's empathy for the poor:

> Because most biblical scholars are the descendants of the advantaged class, it is to be expected that they would minimize Jesus' gospel of liberation for the poor by interpreting poverty as a spiritual condition unrelated to social and political phenomena.[60]

Instead Cone, rightly in my estimation, took the poor to be the powerless in society:

> The poor are the oppressed and the afflicted, those who cannot defend themselves against the powerful. They are the least and the last, the hungry and the thirsty, the unclothed and the strangers, the sick and the captives.[61]

This reading of the gospels brings it into complete alignment with the original motivating force that was at work in the writings of the Hebrew prophets and earlier in Zarathustra. Cone noted too how the eschatological hope for the Second Coming figured large in Black Christian thinking. The following words of a gospel hymn, which I have lifted from the pages of his book, illustrate this:

> I'm going back with Jesus when he comes,
> I'm going back with Jesus when he comes,
> O He may not come today,
> But he's coming anyway
> I'm going back with Jesus when he comes.
>
> And we won't die anymore when He comes,
> And we won't die anymore when He comes.
> O He may not come today,
> But He's coming anyway
> And we won't die anymore when He comes.[62]

Cone goes on to explain how the figure of Jesus, past, present, and future, has figured in Black peoples' fight to preserve their humanity in the face of the dehumanizing ordeal America has put them through:

> When Jesus is understood as the Coming One who will establish divine justice among people, then we will be able to understand why black slaves' religion emphasized the *other* world. They truly believed the story of Jesus' past existence with the poor as told in the Bible. Indeed, their own power struggle to be human was due to the presence of Jesus with them. From his past history with the weak and his present existence with them, black people received a vision of his coming presence to fully heal the misery of human suffering.
>
> Usually when the reality of the political situation dawns upon the oppressed, those who have no vision from another world tend to give up in despair. But those who have heard about the coming of the Lord Jesus and have a vision of crossing to the other side of Jordan, are not terribly disturbed about what happens in Washington, D.C., at least not to the extent that their true humanity is dependent on the political perspective of government officials.[63]

I think we can get some idea of what motivated the belief in the eschatological phantasies of Zoroastrians, Hebrews, and early Christians by understanding this phenomenon of Black resistance and liberation in our own day, as Cone so eloquently describes it. Let me conclude with a portion of a famous gospel hymn that draws directly on the twentieth chapter of the *Apocalypse* and that catches the hope of a better world that has sustained many oppressed people for centuries.

> Oh, what a beautiful city
> Oh, what a beautiful city
> Oh, what a beautiful city
> Twelve gates to the city, hallelujah
> And it's oh, what a beautiful city
> Oh
> Oh Lord, what a beautiful city
> Twelve gates to the city, hallelujah
> There's three gates in the East
> There's three gates in the West
> There's three gates in the North
> There's three gates in the South
> That makes twelve gates to the city, hallelujah.

5

APOCALYPTIC THOUGHT IN THE MEDIEVAL WEST

> But the longer we live in illusion, the worse reality
> will be when it finally shatters our fantasies.
> —Christopher Hedges, *The World As It Is*

Once Constantine made Christianity a favoured religion in the empire, the threat of persecution was lifted from the minds of those adhering to the churches of Christ; and furthermore, when the Church hierarchy achieved real power in the imperial regime, the original anti-imperial, anti-Roman motivations for apocalyptic writing were no longer deemed appropriate by the Church Fathers. It seemed that Christ and his followers had achieved a significant, indeed world-changing, victory over the forces of the Devil that made cooperation with the imperial regime morally possible if not obligatory. In the Latin-speaking West in this period the most important Church apologist was Augustine of Hippo, and since he was through the middle ages in the West the most influential of the Church Fathers, it is worth our examining what he had to say about the *Apocalypse* late in his life (c. 427) as he finished his *The City of God*, while we keep in mind that his views on the subject had many competitors and critics during the 1,000 years that followed.

Augustine's Emasculation of the Millennium

As noted earlier, one of the most original prophecies of the *Apocalypse* was that the Devil would be thrown into an abyss and bound there for 1,000 years. During that millennium the saints who had been martyred would be brought back to life and would reign with Christ. But at the end of this millennium the Devil would be released and would gather an army of people (Gog and Magog) to attack the Christians. One would naturally expect, I think, that this millennium would usher in a period of peace and justice, since the Devil would be confined to his "bottomless pit" and Christ and the saints would be in charge. But this is not the way Augustine saw it. First of all, he takes the passage from the *Apocalypse* in question (20:1–10) not as a prediction of some state still to come but as symbolically describing a situation already existing both in John's day and his own. The millennium began when Christ assumed flesh and came to earth, an event that resulted in the formation of the Christian Church:

> But while the devil is bound, the saints reign with Christ during the same thousand years, understood in the same way, that is, of the time of His first coming.[1]

On Augustine's view, the realm over which Christ and his saints are ruling is the Church, not the whole world, and the Devil's imprisonment in the pit means only that he is restrained to some extent in ways that he was not before:

> But the binding of the devil is his being prevented from the exercise of his whole power to seduce men, either by violently forcing or fraudulently deceiving them into taking part with him.[2]

Still even within this kingdom of God, that is, the Church, the Devil, despite his bound state, is at work to some extent, and as a result we find members of that kingdom who are not living in accord with the true spirit of Christ:

> We must understand in one sense the kingdom of heaven in which exist together both he who breaks what he teaches and he who does it, the one being least, the other great, and in another

sense the kingdom of heaven into which only he who does what he teaches shall enter. Consequently, where both classes exist, it is the Church as it now is, but where only the one shall exist, it is the Church as it is destined to be when no wicked person shall be in her. Therefore, the Church even now is the kingdom of Christ, and the kingdom of heaven. Accordingly, even now His saints reign with Him, though otherwise than as they shall reign hereafter; and yet, though the tares grow in the Church along with the wheat, they do not reign with Him.[3]

The Church as it now is, then, is only imperfectly the Kingdom of God, and only imperfectly ruled by Christ and his saints. The perfect Kingdom will come only after the Last Judgment and will consist only of those who kept the faith. Presently the tares are mingled with the wheat, but one day the tares will have been removed and thrown into the fire.

Augustine interprets the abyss or Bottomless Pit into which the Devil has been thrown as the souls of those who oppose the Church, whose enmity is now increased:

By the abyss is meant the countless multitude of the wicked whose hearts are unfathomably deep in malignity against the Church of God; not that the devil was not there before, but he is said to be cast thither, because, when prevented from harming believers, he takes more complete possession of the ungodly.[4]

We see, then, that Augustine's picture of the millennium is compatible with both persecutions from outside the Church and heresy and hypocrisy within it. In other words, it pretty much describes what the early Church had gone through and its condition in Augustine's own day. What Augustine does not do is equate the imperfect Kingdom of God with the Christianized Roman Empire; it is only the Church that is that Kingdom and that is ruled by Christ and his saints, albeit imperfectly. This refusal to align completely Church and Empire was to have immense consequences in the later Middle Ages. Yet Augustine does not equate the Roman Empire with the Beast or the Whore of Babylon or any of the other nefarious denizens that enliven the *Apocalypse*. His attitude toward the empire is nuanced (but not something we need to investigate here).

But if the Devil while imprisoned in the abyss is able to cause so much evil, what more can he do once he is released at the end of the millennium, and why would he be released at all? Augustine's answer is that he is in his freed state able to war much more powerfully against the Church and raise up the Antichrist[5] to lead the wicked nations against the saints. This is all to demonstrate the power of the Redeemer as he preserves the faithful and in the end destroys the Devil and all his allies:

> And if he were never loosed, his malicious power would be less patent, and less proof would be given of the steadfast fortitude of the holy city: it would, in short, be less manifest what good use the Almighty makes of his great evil…and he will in the end loose him, that the city of God may see how mighty an adversary it has conquered, to the great glory of its Redeemer, Helper, Deliverer.[6]

This victory amounts to the Second Coming of Christ and occasions a second resurrection, the first having occurred after Christ's initial appearance and involving only the souls of living and deceased persons of faith. In this second resurrection the bodies of all who have perished come back to life. Those whose bodies are resurrected at this point but whose souls were not brought to life in the first resurrection are the ones destined to be condemned to eternal punishment. All the others will join Christ in the new world, which will be created after a massive conflagration followed by the Final Judgment. This new world is indestructible and deathless. The saints will receive immortal bodies:

> And by this universal conflagration the qualities of the corruptible elements which suited our corruptible bodies shall utterly perish, and our substance shall receive such qualities as shall, by a wonderful transmutation, harmonize with our immortal bodies, so that, as the world itself is renewed to some better thing, it is fitly accommodated to men, themselves renewed to some better thing.[7]

At this point in his life Augustine was convinced that God had determined from before creation which humans would be among those who would receive the first resurrection and subsequently get to enjoy the new world, and conversely which would be the recipients of the final condemnation. He had argued this against the Pelagians, and indeed the doctrine is strongly foreshadowed, as we saw, in the teaching of Saint Paul.

Augustine's treatment of the Apocalypse, like the work itself, pictures human history as moving inevitably toward an end that is both catastrophic and glorious, but it gives little role for humans in the working out of that fate. Unlike the *Apocalypse* itself, it does not expect a coming reign of Christ before the final days, a reign that will be a marked improvement over what currently exists. There is no allowance for a coming utopia in *this* world; only in the new realm to come will people find a kind of perfect existence. That there were other Christians in Augustine's day who saw differently is evidenced by Augustine's attack on those who envision a future of material plenty, such as was mentioned in *The Sibylline Oracles*. On Augustine's interpretation we must reconcile ourselves to living in this very imperfect world in which injustice and war abound. We are merely "foreign travelers" (*peregrini*) in this world, as we head eventually for the "homeland" (*patria*) in the next life. There is a quite beautiful expression of this idea in Augustine's *On Christian Doctrine,* bk. 1, that is worth quoting:

> It's as if we were foreign travelers unable to live blessedly except in our homeland, indeed made miserable by our foreign travels and desiring that our misery would end, we would want to return to our homeland, and then our job would be to use both land-bound and seafaring conveyances to be able to get back to our homeland, which is what we are to enjoy.
>
> And just as if the amenities of the journey and simply travelling on the conveyances were to delight us, having turned to enjoying what we ought to be simply using, we would not wish to reach the end of our journey too quickly and, entangled in their perverse sweetness, would be alienated from our homeland, the sweetness of which would make us blessed, so, in the same way, as foreign

travelers away from the Lord in the life of this mortality, if we want to return to the homeland, where we could be blessed, this world ought to be used, not enjoyed, so that the invisible things of God, understood through those things which have been made, can be viewed with admiration—that is, so that we might grasp eternal and spiritual things by means of embodied and temporal things.[8]

Among later medieval theologians *viator* (wayfarer) would replace *peregrinus* (foreign traveller) and be the term for referring to all persons still making their way through this mortal life. But the imperative would remain the same: function as needed in the world while keeping your heart and mind set on the return "home." The attractions of this world should remind us of the beauties of the world to come and not seduce us into a life of worldly pleasures. Such a conception allows a person to engage in the needed amount of self-protective and self-interested behaviour in the world, as would a traveller in a foreign country, and so is not fully compatible with the extremely self-renouncing ethic promoted by the Jesus of the gospels, but that gospel ethic, as we saw, makes sense only on the assumption that the arrival of the Kingdom of God in its full glory is imminent. The result in Augustine and in most of the West's later medieval thinkers was that a good portion of Stoic ethics plus some Neoplatonism filled the ethical gap for the "foreign traveller," so far as the intellectual elite was concerned. In this way any revolutionary movements with utopian ideals were either suppressed or sublimated into monasticism or into other communities that separated themselves from the world of ordinary human affairs in order to live a life more in accord with the highly renunciative ethics of the gospels.

Basically, some form of this compromise worked in Western Europe until the late Middle Ages, and it is worth appreciating the sort of mindset it encouraged. Persons who see themselves as *viatores* in this world adopt a certain moderate detachment from the world, its pleasures, its concerns, its everyday travails. One operates within the world, maintains a life in it, and practises care for one's neighbours in accordance with Christ's command to the extent that is practical. But one also keeps reminding oneself of the true home (*patria*) by attending mass, listening to preachers, and gazing at the works of religious art present in chapels and cathedrals. Secular institutions are maintained but not worshipped; kings and emperors are not divine beings but must be tolerated; gross injustices should be remedied, but no radical restructuring of society is to be sought. That is left to Christ when he returns at the end of history. This was the outlook that dominated the lives of most Christians in Western Europe until it all began to unravel from the twelfth century on.

Medieval Counter-Narratives

In the period of transition from ancient to medieval culture, ideas were afloat that would circulate in literate circles from the ninth century on, serving as sources of non-Augustinian ideas about the way the world would end. For example, Saint Jerome, a contemporary of Augustine's, had criticized millennialism just as had Augustine, but he also introduced the notion that between the defeat of the Antichrist and the Last Judgment there would be a brief period of silence and peace. The Venerable Bede in the ninth century produced a commentary on the *Apocalypse* in which he picked up on this interpretation and termed the period Jerome mentioned as the "Sabbath." In this way the idea that before the last days there might be a divinely instituted improvement in life on earth found its way back into the minds of the literate in the Middle Ages despite the dominance of the Augustinian reading of John's *Apocalypse*. Disagreement over the exact length of the Sabbath was common among those who took it seriously as a prediction: some believed it would be as short as a few weeks, some extended it to several years, and, at the other extreme, some equated it with the millennium itself.[9]

Another work well known from the eleventh century on was a prophetic treatise attributed to the "Tiburtine Sibyl."[10] (Works attributed to various Sibyls, in addition to the Sibylline Oracles already discussed, were popular in ancient times and were often translated from Greek to Latin.) This Sibyl introduces the idea of a "Last Emperor" who will reign before the coming of the Antichrist and preside over a period of prosperity. The Sibyl's prediction runs as follows:

> And then there will arise a king of the Greeks whose name is Constans, and he will be king of the Romans and Greeks...And his

reign will end in one hundred and twelve years. In those days there will be much wealth and the earth will yield fruit in abundance so that a measure of wheat will be sold for one denarius, a measure of wine for one denarius and measure of oil for one denarius.[11]

This emperor will rule over all the Christian lands and convert the Jews. But toward the end of his reign, peoples originally imprisoned in the far north by Alexander the Great will break forth to savage the Christian world. (These are the Gog and Magog mentioned in the much earlier Jewish apocalyptic writings already surveyed.) The emperor will defeat these and then proceed to Jerusalem, where he will give up his crown, thus ending the Christian Roman Empire. As the Sibyl says:

> There he will take the diadem from his head and (will divest himself) of all his royal attire. He will surrender the rule over Christians to God the Father and Jesus Christ his son. And when the Roman Empire will cease to exist, then Antichrist will be revealed manifestly.[12]

It is significant that the Antichrist only appears *after* the Roman Empire ceases. It is as though that empire had been holding back the forces of chaos rather than itself being a source of disorder and persecution. It is the empire, according to this Sibyl, that defeats Gog and Magog, those apocalyptic symbols of foreign despoilers of civilization. Many in the later Middle Ages preserved the hope of rescue by such a powerful and benign emperor.

Another early work that calls on a hero-emperor is a prophetic tract falsely attributed by its real author to the early Christian bishop Methodius and hence now referred to as "Pseudo-Methodius."[13] It appears that the actual author lived in Syria soon after the Arab conquest of the region in the seventh century, for it is this event that he has Methodius predict will be reversed by a great Last Emperor. There is no mention of an imperial period of prosperity as in the Tiburtine Sibyl, but, as in that Sibyl's prophecy, Pseudo-Methodius has the emperor giving up his crown in Jerusalem to make way for the Divine Judgment and Second Coming.

What is notably different about these phantasies of a Last Emperor is that they predict that before Christ's Second Coming there will be some sort of restoration of Christian civilization effected by the agency of a single human being rather than by direct divine intervention. We have here early steps toward envisioning a human being bringing a measure of salvation to suffering Christendom, just as earlier Jewish apocalypses predicted a Messiah restoring the Jewish nation. Those in the West who took these works seriously entertained genuine hopes that one, or perhaps more than one, of the Western emperors or kings would fulfil this role. That idea energized some of the popular support for the crusades launched against Islam beginning in the late eleventh century.[14]

Joachim of Fiore

So the hope for some marked betterment in the human condition prior to the ultimate end was alive in the early medieval period even in literate circles. But beginning in the twelfth century ideas come to the fore that were to radically change such apocalyptic views. The transformation largely had its origin in the work of one man, Joachim of Fiore (1135–1202), although his followers in the thirteenth and fourteenth centuries carried the master's conceptions to conclusions he himself would have abjured.

Joachim, a Cistercian monk who became an abbot in Calabria, was a dedicated and imaginative interpreter of the scriptures. For many of us today it is difficult to take seriously that the interpretation of scripture in the light of theological dogmas could be taken as revealing a definite pattern in the whole course of human history as well as reliable predictions about the future. But in the later Middle Ages this was not only possible but generally accepted, for the canonical scriptures were thought to be divinely inspired, and it was to be expected that God would reveal many truths in those works by using symbols that required careful reflection on and comparisons of different texts if they were to be read correctly. Joachim was remarkably creative in this art and was assisted by occasional visions that opened his mind to secret connections. He was particularly adept at comparing stories from the two testaments and finding significant parallels. He also took seriously the kind of mystical respect for certain numbers that we find in John's *Apocalypse*. The result was an outline of the entire course of human evolution from creation up to the final end in the Last Judgment and of the total reform not just of human life but of the entire world.

Joachim divides this evolution into two sets of historical stages (*status*), one of three and the other of seven stages, each encompassing the whole of human development. The three stages correspond to the three persons of the Trinity, the first being that of the Father, the second that of the Son, and the third that of the Holy Spirit. The seven stages correspond to the seven seals and seven angels of the *Apocalypse*. In the three stages there is a progressive spiritualization of human mores, each of the latter two marking a clear advance over the one preceding it. In the third and final stage, "spiritual men" (*viri spirituales*) will lead mankind to a way of life that supersedes without invalidating the way advocated by the Church during the second stage. Joachim envisioned these men to be monks, a group already formed during the second stage but destined to take leadership in the third. That last stage would end with the appearance of the Antichrist followed by Christ's Second Coming, the defeat of the Antichrist, the Last Judgment, and the establishment of the Kingdom of God and the end of history. There is no mention of a Last Emperor. Joachim believed that mankind now stood near the end of the second stage, and he predicted in the near future a renovation of Christendom that would see the spiritual men lead the way to a more perfect life for both individuals and society.

The idea that mankind was living in a divinely ordained course of history, one that was marked by the Fall and the subsequent establishment of the Hebrew Law, the release from the Law that comes with the incarnation of the divine Word in the Christ and with his saving grace, and finally the End of Days commencing with the coming of the Antichrist and ending with the Last Judgment and establishment of the Kingdom of God, was as old as Christianity itself, but Joachim makes some important original contributions to this drama. First of all, he envisions a more or less continual advancement in the moral life of humans who fall within the Judeo-Christian culture; he even subscribes to the idea that the present order will be superseded by something better before Christ's Second Coming. Speaking of the outlook of the groups that were inspired by Joachim's work, the historian Marjorie Reeves said: "To the orthodox the most unpalatable part of this Joachimist doctrine was the belief that the future would transcend the past—a claim that so easily passed into arrogance...it was in the nature of the 'myth' that the future must transcend the past."[15] The myth in question was genuinely Joachim's and not just his later adherents'. Although the orthodox certainly recognized that Christ had somehow transcended the doctrine of salvation through adherence to the Law that, in their view, had marked the Hebrew community from the time of Abraham, they did not expect that there would be any further moral transcending prior to the Second Coming.

This leads to the second important innovation: moral improvement in society as a whole could and would occur in large part through the actions of inspired humans, in Joachim's case, the monks. The myth of the "Last Emperor" had given an active role to a single person, a sort of Messiah figure, but in Joachim's thought a whole class of human beings are given an active role in the progress of mankind; they are not expected to just watch passively as a divinely ordained progress unfolds. In his *Expositio in Apocalypsim* he drew on John's *Apocalypse* when he wrote:

> Wherefore, just as in him who was like the Son of Man there is to be understood a future order of perfect men preserving the life of Christ and the apostles, so in the angel who went forth from the Temple in heaven is to be seen an order of hermits imitating the life of the angels...I think that in that time the life of the monks will be like rain watering the face of the earth in all perfection and in the justice of brotherly love.[16]

Of course, few would have denied that individuals could have some input into their own redemption (although even here the orthodox believed with Augustine that divine grace was necessary and mainly responsible), but the reform and improvement of society as a whole was generally thought to be determined by God's intervention in history, for example, by sending Antichrist to persecute the faithful and then demonstrating the fullness of divine power by destroying him. Joachim, in fact, has melded together two barely compatible strands of thought: on the one hand, the course of history is predetermined by something beyond human control to go in a certain direction and terminate in a certain end, while, on the other hand, humans are free to play their own role in forwarding this progress. The melding of these two ideas is at the core of most millenarian ideologies that were to come later, including ones entirely secular in outlook. For some reason, many humans, it seems, find their motivation to make the effort to work for reform of the world immensely increased by the conviction that the change is inevitable and thus will come whether they personally work for it or not.

A third innovation for which Joachim is responsible is the idea that it is possible to design the form of the improved society in both its social relationships and its physical form. In fact, the physical form, that is, the layout of residences, towns, and cities, should reflect the superior social relationships of this society. In other words, we have here an example of fully utopian thinking, the first in the West since ancient times and the first in a Christian context.[17] Joachim produced drawings of how the residences of his utopia could be arranged, and these reflected the division of the society into contemplatives (monks), lay priests, and the laity. Obviously this goes far beyond the predictions found in some Sibylline works of a future prosperous and egalitarian society. In fact, material prosperity is not something Joachim is particularly interested in. The citizens of the new society, especially the monks, will be too much involved in their spiritual pursuits to concern themselves with producing a cornucopia of material goods. Joachim's utopianism, of course, goes hand in hand with his optimism about human intervention in the social order. His designs for the physical layout of the new community are manifestly human artifacts constructed by a human being using his sense of what would be appropriate for a society of the sort that is to be created.

Joachim's tracts came at a time in Western Europe of great enthusiasm for reform both of the Church administration, including its leaders, and of the way of life of the clergy as well as the laity. The investiture conflict between papacy and emperor, which began in the eleventh century and continued in one form or another for the rest of the Middle Ages, was an effort to free the Church from the domination of secular rulers, and in this it largely succeeded, but at the cost of making the papacy itself a political power and thus compromising its role as a moral exemplar. Moreover, the picture in the gospels of the way Jesus and his apostles had lived became widely accepted as an ideal paradigm for all Christians, although few were expected to come very close to fulfilling it in their own lives. The apostolic way of life was envisioned as placing little or no value on material possessions and no concern for obtaining them, even the necessities of life. Sexual abstinence was always included, as was care for the poor and needy and frequent prayer. In general, egoism was reviled and the tendency toward it regarded as the result of original sin. Rigorous discipline and self-abnegation were required to subdue this manifestation of the Devil within. Monks led the way in enforcing on themselves this way of life, and Joachim himself eventually left the Cistercian order because he considered it not rigorous enough in its renunciations.

Francis and the Radical Franciscans

Of course, this conception of the apostolic life contrasted sharply with the growth of the unequally distributed affluence of Western Europe in the twelfth century. One who became deeply aware of and troubled by this contrast between the few rich and the many poor was Giovanni di Pietro di Bernardone, the young scion of a wealthy Italian family of Assisi, who after a short but disastrous career as a knight underwent a process of adopting what he saw as the way of life lived by Christ himself; by his own example he set out to challenge the self-indulgent ways of the rich and powerful. This man went on to be known as Francis, and, after canonization in 1228, as Saint Francis (1181–1226). His example attracted many followers, and with the blessing of Pope Gregory IX he established the Order of Friars Minor, that is, the Franciscans.

It is important for our purposes to understand something of the ideas motivating Francis's attachment to asceticism and the extremes to which he adopted it. We are fortunate, then, to have guidance in the form of an excellent essay by Gordon Leff,[18] according to whom (and my own readings confirm this) Francis thought human beings were all very deeply deranged by original sin, with the consequence that the human personality was dominated by an egoism that demanded satisfaction of a person's desires for material affluence, sexual pleasure, social prestige and power. As Leff reports,[19] Francis was motivated by such scriptural passages as this one from the gospel of Mark:

> For out of the heart of man come evil thoughts, fornication, theft, murder, adultery, coveting, wickedness, deceit, licentiousness,

envy, slander, pride, foolishness. All these things come from within, and they defile a man. (7:21–23)

Fundamentally, these faults, Francis concluded, all arise from the desire to benefit and protect oneself, and hence the way to a holy life required the extirpation of this desire by humbling oneself. This was best facilitated by accepting without complaint or rebuff the persecutions and tribulations that others and the world in general visited upon one. It also meant associating with and helping the most disadvantaged in life, like lepers. Nor should one simply bear such hardships in Stoic silence; rather one should rejoice that they have entered your life, for they provide the necessary lessons in humility that will reduce, or at least constrain, one's own self-love. Leff puts it well:

> To be poor in spirit thus consists in more than submission to prayer and religious devotion or bodily mortification; it means self-hate, and love of those who do one injury; it can only be attained when the self is no longer held dear and so can no longer be affronted.[20]

The result is a twofold impetus: On the one hand, the sincere convert must detach from or entirely renounce the world, but, on the other, he does what he can to assist and console the destitute and sick. The detachment consists in no longer seeing the world as the theatre for fulfilling one's self-esteem; one does not concern oneself with the world in that way. The friar is not to "take thought for the morrow"[21] by preparing the next day's meal (and thus he lives in accord with the "lilies of the field" spoken of in Matthew 6:28); if tomorrow comes and no food is available, he can beg as do the destitute, if his physical need is that great. But the most important renunciation is to have as little in the way of possessions as is consonant with survival. It was Francis's conviction, and that of all the persons who joined his order, that Christ and the apostles had led a life without possessing anything other than their clothes and necessary utensils. In this way they joined the ranks of the lowest in society. This is what it meant to be "poor in spirit," those who Jesus said would belong to the Kingdom of Heaven (*Matthew* 5:3).

On the other hand, just as Christ had spent much of his ministry healing the sick and disabled, so a friar should be concerned to help the needy in his own society, perhaps by begging for alms on their behalf. But for this to manifest the true spirit of Christ it had to be done out of a spontaneous love for human beings, one's fellow travellers (*viatores*) making their way through the world to the "homeland" (*patria*), that is, the next life with Christ and the Saints. Needless to say, to engage in such charity entirely without thought for the ultimate benefits for oneself in terms of spiritual development, or even for the esteem of one's confreres, let alone the general public's, is difficult and probably impossible in a completely pure form.

Francis has taken the most radical of Christ's ethical injunctions in the gospels and made them councils of perfection in living a Christian life. That these precepts were originally given in the context of expecting in the near future the establishment of the Kingdom of Heaven, and can only be taken seriously as an ethic for everyone given belief in that future, is not something that Francis and his more radical followers understood, but neither should we think that they condemned those who found themselves unable to accept such an abstemious and altruistic existence. Francis himself recognized his own sinful tendencies and knew he relied on divine forgiveness. He was not likely, then, to deny that others who also fell short of perfection could be forgiven as well.

Nevertheless, such rigorous standards, particularly regarding the command of poverty, were not realistically compatible with a large movement, and even in Francis's lifetime he had to combat those who wanted them relaxed, particularly the rules condemning any acquiring of possessions beyond rude necessities. After his death and toward the middle of the thirteenth century the Order was torn by sharp disagreement between the "Conventuals" and the "Spirituals," the latter trying to preserve the original intent of the founder and the former accepting a certain compromise, one that consisted in distinguishing *ownership* of things from *use* of things. True, it was said, a friar should not *own* anything but the merest of necessities, but he could *use* many other things as long as he did not *own* them. To enable this compromise to work the Church took ownership of things that were not personal necessities and allowed the friars to use them. In this way the friar himself was impoverished, he owned almost nothing, but he could make use of lots of things that he did not own, such as shelters, books, supplies of food and drink, although even the Conventuals thought such use had to be very limited.

The Spirituals saw through this piece of scholastic sophistry and demanded poverty in use (*usus pauper*), not just poverty in ownership. Only with the former could a person genuinely be living the sort of life Christ and Francis had led and advocated, and I think there can be little doubt that on this point they were correct. But the sophistry was necessary if the Order were to continue as a major force in European society, including in the universities, where Franciscans became by the late thirteenth century some of the most astute thinkers in theology and philosophy the Middle Ages were to produce. (Francis himself entirely disdained scholastic book learning.)[22]

It is into this intensifying dispute that the works of Joachim of Fiore, as well as ones falsely attributed to him, found their way. Franciscans, particularly the Spirituals, were much attracted to the idea that they were the "spiritual men" who Joachim said would lead the way into the reformed world of the third stage. The brilliant philosopher/theologian Peter John Olivi (c. 1248–1298), the leading polemicist on behalf of the Spirituals, deployed Joachim's sevenfold series of stages to place his own time near the transition from the fifth to the sixth. Bernard McGinn nicely describes Olivi's thought here as follows:

> The fifth period, that of laxity, and the sixth, the time of evangelical renewal and the persecution of the Antichrist, overlap; the seventh period will see the age of interior peace and spiritual understanding before the coming of Gog and the Last Judgment. The concurrence of the fifth and sixth periods in his own time is visible in the conflict between the carnal Church, the body of evildoers in Christendom, and the spiritual Church, the true followers of poverty.[23]

The Spirituals were much given to describing the Church outside their own coterie as the "carnal Church," the Church of those who had failed to detach themselves from the world and its temptations. Of course, they could find much of this "carnality" to point to, given the increasing wealth and indulgent lifestyle of highly placed ecclesiastics, including the Pope himself. (The Latin word here is *carnalis*, which derives from the word for flesh and thus resonates with the term translated as "flesh" in the English versions of the New Testament, especially by Saint Paul, and in earlier works, some of which were discussed in the preceding chapter.) Olivi also developed the idea of two quite different Antichrists, a mystical one who would be a false pope and would attack the true Spirituals, and another, the Great or Open Antichrist, who would be the one defeated at the End of Days.[24] In Olivi's own day popes were less than enthused about the radicalism of the Spirituals, and eventually the latter suffered papal condemnation. Olivi's own work was consigned to the fire in 1326. The Italian Ubertino of Casale (c. 1259–c. 1330) went on to identify the Mystical Antichrist with Popes Boniface VIII and Benedict XI because of their hostility to the Spirituals.

In this heated polemical atmosphere, the Joachimist framework proved very attractive to the Spirituals, for it gave them a key place in a cosmic, progressive evolution that would inevitably lead to a better, more spiritual humanity. Saint Francis was regarded as the forerunner of this transition and treated almost as a second Christ. The more the Spirituals became convinced that they were the vanguard of this reform, the more they saw the ecclesiastical authorities who resisted them as controlled by Satan or as servants of Antichrist. In 1323 Pope John XXII declared that the doctrine of apostolic poverty was mistaken, thereby offending not just the Spirituals but the Conventuals as well. This led to a large-scale rebellion in the Franciscan Order against the papacy, in the course of which a number of Franciscans, including Michael of Cesena, Minister General of the Order, and the philosopher/theologian William of Ockham, both Conventuals, sought the protection of the emperor while they campaigned against the Pope.

By then there were groups so incensed by papal denunciations of the Spirituals and their conception of apostolic poverty that they longed for a violent overthrow of the "carnal" Church. In the first decade of the fourteenth century a coterie known as the Apostolic Brethren came to be led by the fantasizing prophet Fra Dolcino, who convinced his followers that the Last Emperor was about to return, demolish the carnal Church, and inaugurate a purified era in which the Apostolic Brethren would take the lead. An inquisitor named Bernard Gui, involved in the inquiry that led to Dolcino's suffering an execution especially cruel even by medieval standards, described his views as follows:

> Further, he [Fra Dolcino] holds that the secular clergy along with many of the populace and the rulers and tyrants are his enemies and the ministers of the devil. The same is true of all the religious, especially the Preachers and the Friars and others who persecuted him, and the followers who held to the sect he calls a spiritual and apostolic congregation...He says that all its persecutors along with the prelates of the Church will soon be slaughtered and destroyed. Those who are left will be converted to his sect and united to him. Then he and his sect will prevail over all.[25]

Among the Franciscans themselves there were in the later fourteenth century radical extremists looking forward to the violent overthrow of the current ecclesiastical regime. The most notable of these was John of Rupescissa (c. 1310–c. 1365), who combined the fantasy of a Last Emperor with that of a reforming or "Angelic Pope" in his prophecy of a coming violent destruction of the current structure of society. He wrote a popular book called *Companion in Tribulation*, from which Bernard McGinn has extracted the following:

> Within these five years will arise a popular justice. It will devour the treacherous and tyrannical nobles with a two-edged sword, and many princes, nobles, and powerful men will fall from their positions and from the glory of their wealth. The affliction among the nobility will be beyond belief. The potentates, who by their betrayal despoiled an afflicted people, will be plundered.[26]

Here we see a return to one of the ancient motivations for apocalyptic thought: righteous anger at the oppression by the rich and powerful of the poor and weak, coupled with the belief that cosmic forces will not allow this injustice to continue forever and will in some way exact just vengeance on the oppressors.

In Italy there arose groups of Franciscans known as the Fratticelli who carried on the ideals of the Spirituals and bitterly attacked Pope John XXII, as this extract from their "Letter to the Citizens of Narnio" shows:

> The Abomination of Desolation is the principal source from which have come all the temporal and spiritual evils that have reigned, remained and grown wonderfully strong in the world for a long time now…What is this Abomination of Desolation which stands in the holy place, the Church? We respond with a sorrowful soul that this Abomination of Desolation is the condemnation of the life of Christ, of his poverty and that of his apostles made by Pope John XXII thirty years ago and confirmed through his many supporters in a variety of ways.[27]

The work goes on to treat John as a forerunner of the soon to be expected Antichrist:

> Therefore Christ says in Matthew 24;15: "Let him who reads understand," that is, let him read in such a way that he understands lest he be led into error and eternal damnation by the Abomination. Do we not see what Christ said there about false Christs, that is, false pontiffs and prelates, arising, and also about false prophets, that is, false teachers and doctors, fulfilled almost to the letter? It will not be completely fulfilled until the Great Antichrist comes. Without doubt we await him very soon, because John and all his supporters without number are his messengers and chief disciples, just as the true prophets, Isaiah, Jeremiah, and the others were the messengers and precursors of our Lord Jesus Christ, the crucified man of poverty.[28]

Clearly, by the latter half of the fourteenth century the ideological atmosphere of Western Europe was roiling with very extreme resentment and bitter sense of betrayal, and this found expression in the apocalyptic phantasies of old with their uncompromising division between the righteous, on the one side, and the followers of Satan, on the other, their predictions of the coming catastrophic warfare between these two, and their grand finale in the eventual total victory for the good and terrible retribution upon the wicked. That all this was usually directed against the Church establishment from the local priest to the Pope himself meant that it was potentially revolutionary in its implications.

Hussite and Other Rebellions

In the late fourteenth century the papacy fell into the crisis of the Great Schism in which two men each claimed to be the legitimate Pope. In the early fifteenth there were actually three pretenders. A Church Council was convened at Constance in 1415 to resolve the dispute, and it did depose two of the contenders and persuaded the third to retire, thus clearing the way for its own nominee to become Pope Martin V. The council also took on the job of stamping out heresies propagated by radical proponents of reform, and among its victims were the Czechs John Hus (burned at the stake in 1415) and his close associate Jerome of Prague (similarly disposed of the following year). Neither Hus nor Jerome was any more motivated by apocalyptic thought than most Christians of the time; but they were radical proponents of Church reform in Bohemia, deploying a close reading of the New Testament and Christ's recorded teachings to condemn the current ecclesiastical practices. Their executions, however, sparked developments in Bohemia in which those sympathetic to Hus and Jerome went far beyond what the original pair of heretics had envisioned. These followers tapped into the tradition of apocalyptic prophecies to motivate many ordinary clerics and lay people to take up arms in a fight for revolutionary change.

The ideas of the English reformer John Wycliffe (c.1330–1384) became influential at the Charles University in Prague late in the fourteenth century, and both Hus and Jerome promoted his beliefs. With Wycliffe they condemned the decadence of the clergy and the Church hierarchy, convinced that only the overthrow of Roman domination could bring the Church back to the true faith.[29] After Hus's and Jerome's executions the Bohemian Church began to go its own way, and when King Wenceslaus IV tried to rein in his clergy, there was open revolt in Prague. This insurrection manifested the deep popular support for the Hussite reform movement, but it also brought to light a split within its ranks between moderates and radicals. Both supported Utraquism, the taking of both the bread and the wine in the Eucharist, but the radicals proposed a social revolution that went far beyond the ecclesiastical reforms advocated by the moderates.

Wycliffe had held to the view that classification of things in the world reflected archetypes existing in the divine mind on the basis of which the world had been created. This "metaphysical realism" lent to the severe moral standards on which Hus and Jerome, and their followers, condemned the laxity of the current Church hierarchy, as well as that of professedly Christian secular potentates, the status of regulations eternally established and admitting of no compromise.[30] Jerome was particularly keen to attack the *via moderna*, that is, the nominalist school of thought, which took classification to be the result of human cognitive acts resulting in signs each of which grouped many individual things into a class. This school eschewed the idea of eternal archetypes as a form of the Platonism that Aristotle, the chief ancient authority in philosophy, had rejected. In fact, both Hus and Jerome were much more attracted to Plato than to Aristotle, and Jerome, who travelled widely among the universities of Europe giving disputations, offended the established scholastic teachers, usually partisans of the *via moderna*, wherever he went. The reputation he earned in this way contributed in no small measure to his condemnation at Constance.

Given the gross inequities of medieval society, it is not too surprising that an uncompromising, gospel-based moralism of the sort Hus preached would be seen by some among the oppressed populace as having implications in the secular as well as the ecclesiastical realm. It is at this point that apocalyptic thinking had a very significant role to play. The radical Hussite program evidently had great appeal among elements of the Bohemian peasantry, and the development of the movement, particularly in the years 1419–20, abundantly illustrates how the full range of medieval apocalyptic thought could motivate a persecuted group. Howard Kaminsky in his very judicious history of the Hussite revolution[31] has sorted out the influences on the movement and the stages in its evolution. What follows depends heavily on his work.

The Hussites in southern Bohemia who were attracted to the radical program gathered on a hilltop to partake of the Eucharist in both forms and to listen to the preaching of the radical clerics. This hill they named Mount Tabor after the mount on which the gospels said Christ underwent the transformation. The radicals thus became known as Taborites, and it is necessary to keep them and their doctrines quite separate from those of Hus as well as those of the Hussites, who after Hus's execution were active in Prague. The fifteenth-century chronicler Laurence of Březová, a harsh critic of the Taborites, notes the following when recounting the events of early 1420:

> During this time certain Taborite priests were preaching to other people a new coming of Christ, in which all evil men and enemies of the Truth would perish and be exterminated, while the good would be preserved in five cities. For this reason certain cities in which communion in both kinds could freely be given refused to enter into any agreement with the enemy, and especially the city of Plzeň.
>
> ...They urged that all those desiring to be saved from the wrath of Almighty God, which in their view was about to be visited on the whole globe, should leave their cities, castles, villages, and towns, as Lot left Sodom, and should go to the five cities of refuge.[32]

One of the Taborite prophets has left a letter in which we find the following appeal:

> The time of greatest suffering prophesied by Christ in his scriptures, the apostles in their letters, the prophets, and St. John in the Apocalypse, is now at hand; it has begun; it stands at the gates! And in this time the Lord God commands His elect to flee from the midst of the evil ones, through Isaiah 51: "Go out from their midst, my people," so that each may save his soul from the wrath of God and be spared His blows. And so that your heart may not perhaps soften, and that you may not stand in fear of the dreadful sound that will be heard on earth. And through St. John, Rev. 18 [4], the Lord says: "Go out of it my people, so that you may not share in their sins; for their sins have reached the heavens."[33]

Here appear apocalyptic themes the reader will recognize from previous discussions: the condemnation of the surrounding society as morally evil, the imminent catastrophe in which all these sinners will be destroyed, the necessity for the righteous to separate themselves from the condemned. All this will occur, of course, as a prelude to the Second Coming of Christ and the Final Judgment. Kaminsky believes that at this stage of their development the Taborites called on the ideas of the Waldensians, a heretical movement of the thirteenth century that had lingered in Bohemia long after its extermination in Western Europe. But in the face of royal armies marching to eradicate them the Taborites did not persist in Waldensian pacifism. Tabor was turned into a fortified town, and the Taborites constructed a formidable fighting force of their own and brought several towns in southern Bohemia under their control.

At this point the Taborites in imitation of the apostolic churches introduced communism, another familiar apocalyptic dream, into the community they had constructed at Tabor. John Příbram, an enemy of the Taborites, wrote in 1429 about the events of 1420 as follows:

> They [the Taborite priests] preached and ordained in the city of Písek, to those people who had fled to them on the mountains, that all the brethren should pool absolutely everything, and for this purpose the priests set up one or two chests, which the community almost filled up for them.[34]

This development is closely associated with the introduction of millenarianism (or chiliasm), that is, the belief that the catastrophes mentioned will not be followed directly by the end of the world, but by a period, perhaps a thousand years, in which Christ and his elect will rule a reformed and renovated world, much improved morally and socially compared to the one prior to the catastrophes. Again, John Příbram gives a description of how the Taborite priests presented this idea derived from John's *Apocalypse* to the populace:

> At this point the false seducers thought up a new lie somehow to console the people, and they said that the whole Christian church was to be reformed in such a way that all the sinners and evil

people were to perish completely, and that only God's elect were to remain on the earth—those who had fled to the mountains. And they said that the elect of God would rule in the world for a thousand years with Christ, visibly and tangibly. And they preached that the elect of God who fled to the mountains would themselves possess all the goods of the destroyed evil ones and rule freely over all their estates and villages. And they said, "You will have such an abundance of everything that silver, gold and money will only be a nuisance to you." They also said and preached to the people, "Now you will not pay rents to your lords any more, nor be subject of them, but will freely and undisturbedly possess their villages, fishponds, meadows, forests, and all their domains."[35]

The theme of abundance in the millennium is one we have seen in some of the oracles attributed to the Sibyl and was no doubt a powerful fantasy especially among the common people, who often faced extreme hardship.

This millenarian fantasy and other doctrines were biblically supported by the Joachite technique of interpreting the New Testament by reference to the Old and vice versa. And this is not the only evidence of Joachite influence on the Taborites. Some of the radicals also adopted Joachim's three-stage understanding of human history and placed themselves at the beginning of the third stage in which both testaments would be superseded by a new spiritualism. Příbram found all this most offensive:

> If it were true, that there would be no sin in the renovated kingdom, then there would be no penance, because no sin; no merit, because no resistance [to sin]; no sacraments, because no wounds [of the soul]; indeed the Lord's Prayer would cease, for they would not have to pray, "Forgive us our debts as we forgive our debtors theirs, and lead us not into temptation, but free us from evil." Nor is this all: the greater part of the Old and New Law, if not all, would cease on the basis of the most perfidious opinion, along with almost all the scriptures teaching us to pray, to repent, to give alms, to fast, and to do the works of mercy.[36]

These most extreme ideas among the Taborites Kaminsky thinks very likely came from the influence of Beghards who were attached to the Brethren of the Free Spirit, a movement that had been present in Europe since the thirteenth century.[37] It was not particularly apocalyptic in its outlook, but rather stressed the possibility of individual humans achieving such a state of spiritual perfection in this life that they no longer need be guided by laws or any external authority. To achieve this state a person must first imitate Christ's life of poverty, charity, and suffering in order to cleanse their soul, but after that nothing the person willed to do would be sinful and the traditional rites of the Church were no longer appropriate for them.[38]

We can see from this brief account that the Taborite movement brought together just about all the powerful phantasies of the apocalyptic tradition as it had developed in medieval Europe. I think it is fair to say that without the motivating force of these phantasies the Taborite revolution would never have occurred, or at least it would not have been able to long survive the military onslaught which King Sigismund, who was also Holy Roman Emperor, supported by the power of the Roman Church, brought against it. True, the mass of followers had many valid grievances against Church, the nobles, and the king, and had suffered much under the current social dispensation. They had reason to be bitter and vengeful. But to maintain the movement the way the Taborites did required their viewing themselves as playing an active part in a drama with cosmic dimensions leading inevitably to the fulfilment of a dream of moral goodness and material plenty. Apocalyptic phantasies, particularly that of the millennium, provided this, for instead of predicting merely a strange existence in some heavenly, non-earthly kingdom, the millennium promised an earthly, easily imagined utopia akin to the Garden of Paradise. Once this whole phantasy is fully adopted, it justifies violence on the surrounding society and the people in it, for they can be seen as opposing the divine will and persecuting the truly righteous, God's elect. This wholesale rejection of society as it exists, to the point of working for its total destruction, is the bitter core of apocalyptic thought and had been there since its beginnings in the teachings of Zarathustra and in some of the harangues of the Hebrew prophets.

The Taborite movement had a number of remarkable military successes under the inspired leadership of John Žižka, who was killed in 1424, but in

1434 the moderate Hussites defeated it in battle, and it soon thereafter ceased to exist as an organized society. Many of its doctrines, however, became well known in Central Europe and persisted there well into the next century. Among those who came under Taborite influence was Thomas Müntzer (c. 1489–1525), a well-educated cleric who attached himself to Luther in the early days of the Reformation but went on to develop his own theology and disagree sharply with some of Luther's teachings. He shared, of course, Luther's condemnation of the corruption in the Catholic Church, but he put much less reliance on the authority of the scriptures than did Luther and much more on the believer's inner spirit. He held strong apocalyptic beliefs, which show the influence of the Taborite program. Norman Cohn described these as follows:

> What most appealed to Müntzer in this programme was the war of extermination which the righteous were to wage against the unrighteous. Abandoning Luther, he now thought and talked only of the Book of Revelation and of such incidents in the Old Testament as Elijah's slaughter of the priests of Baal, Jehu's slaying of the sons of Ahab and Jael's assassination of the sleeping Sisera.[39]

Obviously, Müntzer had been drawn into the idea that the End of Days scenario required violent action by the righteous against the wicked. As with the Taborites, this view was combined with a belief that the poor people were much more likely to be the true people of God than were the rich and powerful. The sense of the injustice of the contemporary order, in which the rich nobility exploited and oppressed the impoverished serfs, was keenly felt by this man of prophetic temperament. He could not abide Luther's outlook, according to which the Christian gospel was not to be taken as a call to action against the injustices of the world but only as a guide to spiritual improvement.[40] At the end of his life, Müntzer allied himself with the German Peasant Rebellion of 1524–25, helping to lead its military campaigns. That rebellion was suppressed in very bloody fashion, and he was caught and executed.

This sort of violent radicalism continued during the sixteenth century among some Protestant groups, particularly the Anabaptists, some of whom had participated in the peasant revolt. Anabaptists came to power in the west

German town of Münster in 1534, and their leaders had thoroughly imbibed apocalyptic and millenarian ideas.[41] One of them, Jan Matthys, declared the town to be the "New Jerusalem," and a kind of communism was adopted by the community. Lutherans and Catholics were expelled, adult baptism prescribed, and the wealth of the rich redistributed. When the local bishop attempting to suppress the radicals gathered an army and laid siege to the town, Matthys was killed leading a few men out against the besiegers in the belief that God would give victory to them as He had to Gideon, as recorded in the Hebrew Bible. Leadership now fell to Jan Bockelson (also known as John of Leyden), who made himself king and established compulsory polygamy. As the military situation worsened and the population starved, Bockelson resorted to a reign of terror to maintain order. The town was captured by the besiegers in 1535, and Bockelson and other Anabaptist leaders were tortured and executed.

In these events occurring at the end of the Middle Ages and the beginning of the modern period, apocalyptic and millenarian ideas were not the only ideological forces at work, but they were certainly important and provided a cosmic historical framework into which other ideas could be fitted and thought to have a predestined role. Norman Cohn's work, already cited, amply elaborates on this. Apocalyptic thought combines outrage over current social injustice with the conviction that divine power will not allow this to go on much longer and that the result will be a horrendous cleansing of the world followed by its replacement with something much better, including just punishment of the wicked. The medieval reformers combined outrage at the corruption of the Church with the expectation of divine vengeance (involving the Antichrist) and the inevitable establishment of a more righteous community. Increasingly they saw a role for humans, or a special class of humans, in this cosmic process. How easy it was for the reform effort to slip over into demonizing its opponents and justifying violence against them. How powerful a motivating force was the myth that all this was part of an inevitable unfolding of history. And so it is with any utopian millenarianism that advocates radical moral and social reform. But in the modern period millenarian thinking was to take forms different from those just described, including totally secular ones.

6

REFORMATION AND UTOPIA

> The truth that survives is simply the lie
> that is pleasantest to believe.
> —H.L. Mencken, *A Little Book in C Major*

As we said earlier, the basic commonly accepted wisdom of Europe's medieval period is caught by the image of humans as *viatores*, wayfarers, on their way to the *patria*, the homeland, that is, heaven and eventually, after the Second Coming, a physical paradise. Thinking of themselves in this way meant that enthusiasm for engaging in mammoth projects of renovation and improvement in their society and lives was limited to radical thinkers, such as those described in the previous chapter, and minorities among the clergy and laity who followed those radicals. Most people viewed the world they were in as not their real home; eventually something better would be provided, but not chiefly by human effort. We saw in the previous chapter that radical challenges to this outlook erupted as Europe began its transition to modernity. The millenarian vision of John's *Apocalypse* coupled with the conception of history as spiritual progress put forth by the Joachimites led some to believe that human action in the world could usher in a vast transformation of Christian society, if not of the whole world. The results, as we saw, were attempts at violent revolution followed by brutal suppression. The Protestant Reformation in the sixteenth century adopted the view that humans were not just wayfarers and that they could enact fundamental change in the world, but, at least in its mainstream, it did not countenance social revolution. In this chapter we are going to look at the development in the sixteenth and seventeenth centuries of Protestant attitudes as well as full-fledged utopian visions that emerged in Protestant milieux and were utterly inconsonant with the outlook of a *viator*. Some of those visions were to provide both the impetus and outline for the ideological justification of Western expansion.

The Protestant Reformation

We saw in the previous chapter that the late medieval struggles for reform operated on several levels at once. There was the insistence that the way of life practised by Christ and the apostles was the one to which all Christians were called and that this way entailed a rigorous personal asceticism. This was joined to a vision of a reformed Christian society awaiting the Second Coming. And, finally, the practices of the Church had to be brought in line with its original spiritual calling. In the two mainline Protestant churches established by the reformation of the sixteenth century, the Lutheran and the Calvinist, these elements were retained, but the radical social aims of those highly motivated by the apocalyptic phantasies we described in the previous chapter were cast aside. Luther, for example, condemned the German Peasant Revolt of 1525 and had no scruples about directing his appeals for support of reform to the German nobility. Nevertheless, Luther and Calvin shifted the aims of these reforms in important ways and in doing so envisioned a direction for European society quite different from that of the late medieval reformers.

Some of the earlier reform movements adopted profoundly anticlerical and antimonastic stances, and in extreme cases this led to slaughters of the despised groups. Luther and Calvin adopted the position that all believers were priests and that the idea that an especially ascetic outward life, one that could be practised only by a small minority of particularly holy people, was the paradigmatic Christian way, was in fact not biblical at all and a deviation from what God wanted of his faithful. This shift had two results. The first was that the ascetic impulse was turned inward rather than outward so that what mattered was the spirit in which one lived one's life, not so much the outward expression of that life. The believer was enjoined to base life in a love of Christ, a love that led to service to one's fellow humans and a sharp restriction on love of self. In particular, Lutheran and Calvinist preachers strongly rebuked love of riches and lust for carnal pleasures.

The second result was that the doctrines of Luther and Calvin encouraged the believer to enter into the surrounding world and express in that world this spirit just described, not withdraw from it in the way monks had. This led to what Max Weber called "innerworldly asceticism."[1] The Protestant is ascetic in not being motivated by any love of carnal pleasure, but he still tries to operate successfully in the surrounding world in a way that is governed by his love of God and Christ. The Protestant can marry, indeed is encouraged to do so, but not from a love of sexual pleasure. The Protestant can work at a trade or as a businessman, indeed is encouraged to do so, but not out of a love of accumulating wealth. He or she is ascetic in their inner motivation but not in their outward behaviour.

This whole direction is strengthened by the doctrine that a Christian should have a "vocation," that is, something he feels called by God to work at and succeed in. Worldly occupations thus receive a divine sanction as long as the believer sees how those occupations can be a vehicle for expressing and fulfilling in action their love of God, Christ, and their human neighbours. In this vocation the believer is to exercise to the full their mental capacities to accomplish as successfully as possible whatever it is their occupation aims at. Thus, even merchants must exercise their rational thinking so as best to succeed in buying and selling. If this means they become wealthy, then well and good as long as they don't attach any value to the accumulation of that wealth in itself, but view it as a means for carrying out works of charity and beneficence to their fellow humans. Thus, often in the sixteenth and seventeenth centuries there were wealthy Protestants who made sure that in their dress and lifestyle they gave no appearance of indulging in or enjoying a lifestyle of overt affluence. Restricting asceticism to the "innerworld" left the Christian free, then, to pursue and succeed in the accepted occupations of the secular world, and by and large Protestants did not feel they had to challenge the basic economic and social structure of that world.

Among Calvinists the doctrine of predestination figured importantly in motivating a conscientious effort to achieve success in one's vocation. According to this teaching, only a relatively few people would be saved at the Last Judgment, and although God had decided before all creation who those few were to be, we humans in this life could not be sure who they were. All humans were deeply corrupted by sin and deserved damnation, but God graciously decided to forgive that sin in some for reasons known to Him alone. The individual believers, however, could rest assured of their salvation if the proper spirit came to dominate their life and they felt the call to some occupation. Moreover, God was keen to see those whom he had decided to save succeed in their vocations, so success too was a sign of being among the favoured. Protestant believers took very seriously—perhaps more seriously than medieval Catholics—the prophecy of the Final Judgment and relegation of a few saints to paradise and the rest to eternal suffering in Hell. Given this, it is easy to imagine how anxious these believers were to find in themselves and in their lives signs of being among the former retinue, as well as to avoid signs that they were among the reprobate. Although Protestant theologians insisted that salvation depended on receiving the proper spirit as a gift of God's grace, not as a product of one's own efforts, many were driven to try to engender that spirit, as well as to succeed in a vocation, by their own efforts of rational will. And in those people there arose a marked tendency toward self-discipline, a subject well discussed recently by Charles Taylor.[2]

Calvinist divines were keen to see society in general be governed by persons who had received the proper spirit and were thus moved to act in accordance with God's will. This led to the society they did in fact rule, the one in Geneva, being governed by laws that enforced on the general citizenry prohibitions on activities that manifested sin, particularly unruly pleasures of the flesh. In contrast to medieval Catholic society, which had allowed space for outbursts of lasciviousness and drunkenness,[3] Calvinists saw these as breakdowns in the order demanded by God and thus deserving of civic prohibition. There was, then, among many Protestants an effort to reform and improve morally society as a whole, even though most people were crippled by sin and destined for Hell. As a consequence, there arose calls for a stricter form of social discipline than earlier medieval society had demanded. In this way the old millenarian hopes for society as a whole re-emerged, and this time the conscious role for righteous humans in bringing about the required reforms was clearly acknowledged and encouraged. In other words, Protestants no longer saw themselves as mere *viatores* in this world, but rather as fully engaged actors on the world's stage in front of an audience of one, their highly judgmental creator.

Thomas More and the Humanist Utopia

During the century preceding the Reformation scholars had been at work in universities and elite circles introducing changes in the focus of advanced education, changes that included a more comprehensive appreciation of ancient Greek and Roman literature and culture. Whereas in the earlier medieval period a knowledge of Greek among scholars was rare and familiarity with ancient Greek literature very limited, from the fifteenth century on more and more scholars learned Greek, as well as Latin, of course, and often translated Greek works, such as the satires of Lucian, into Latin. As a result, the scholastic fixation on the works of Aristotle and his Islamic commentators was loosened and even deplored, Platonism was reborn (recall how John Hus and Jerome of Prague favoured Plato), and much literature from ancient times outside of philosophy was given an important role in education.

This was all part of what we now call the rise of "humanism," but rather than address this entire movement, it will serve our purposes to focus just on certain aspects of the work of two famous proponents: Thomas More (1478–1535) and Justus Lipsius (1547–1606). We begin with the former.

More was a friend of the famous humanist Erasmus, and like him had learned Greek and translated some of Lucian's works. He served as chancellor under the tyrannous Henry VIII, who in the end had More beheaded for not acceding to his marriage to Catherine of Aragon. Our interest here is entirely on More's most famous work: *On the Best State of a Commonwealth and on the New Island of Utopia*, or simply *Utopia*, composed in Latin and first published in 1516.[4] More's book takes the form of a letter to his friend Peter Giles pretending to recapitulate a conversation he and Peter, as well as others, had had with the fictional character Raphael Hythloday, who is supposed to have travelled to a newly discovered island named Utopia. Raphael proceeds to relate to the others the sort of society he found there. The plan of the book enables More to attribute to Raphael his own misgivings about contemporary European society while at the same time distancing himself from the radical solutions that he has Raphael say he found in Utopia and would have liked to see instituted in Europe, although Raphael sees no real prospect of this happening. Nevertheless, that More takes the Utopian arrangements as at least a candidate for "the best state of a commonwealth"[5] shows how aware he was both of the deep failings of his own society and of the in-principle possibility of humans' instituting a much better alternative. In accord with ancient millenarian hopes, More envisions this alternative as something brought about independently of any divine intervention such as the Parousia (i.e., the Second Coming).

A deep bitterness emerges in what More has Raphael say when he describes current European practices. More's fictional traveller has no time for the nobility and the rich, whom he deems to be exploiting and oppressing the common people who do society's necessary work:

> First there is a great number of gentlemen who cannot be content to live idle themselves, like drones, on that which others have labored for: their tenants, I mean, whom they shave and cut to the quick by raising their rents (for this one kind of frugality do they practice, men who else through their lavish and prodigal spending may bring themselves to very beggary).[6]

He is also scathing when it comes to the "idling" classes generally. When comparing Europe to what he has found in Utopia, where none but the disabled are idle, he argues that all that is necessary for a comfortable life for everyone can be produced, as in Utopia, without imposing on anyone very onerous labour, as long as idleness, like that found in Europe, is not tolerated:

> And this you also shall perceive, if you weigh and consider with yourselves how great a part of the people in other countries live idle. First, almost all women, who are half of the whole number; or else if the women be anywhere occupied, there most commonly in their stead the men are idle. Besides this how great and how idle

a company is there of priests and religious men, as they call them. Add thereto all rich men, especially all landed men, who are commonly called gentlemen and noblemen. Take into this number also their servants: I mean all that flock of stout bragging swashbucklers. Join to them also the sturdy and lusty beggars, cloaking their idle life under the color of some disease or sickness.[7]

Raphael is no less bitter in his condemnation of how the law and its punishments enforce a basically unjust social order:

For great and horrible punishments are appointed for thieves, whereas much rather, provision should have been made to provide some means whereby they might get their living, so that no man should be driven to this extreme necessity, first to steal, and then to die.[8]

And yet, in addition to this, the rich not only by private fraud, but also by public laws, every day pluck and snatch away from the poor some part of their daily living. So whereas it seemed previously unjust to recompense with unkindness the toils that have been beneficial to the public weal, the rich have now to this their wrong and unjust dealing—which is much worse act—given the name of justice, yea, and that by force of law.[9]

There had been a peasants' revolt in fourteenth-century England that nurtured such radical views, including those expressed by the preacher John Ball, author of the famous rhetorical question: "When Adam delved and Eve span who was then the gentleman?" Among those joining the Taborites in the Hussite rebellion, resentments similar to Raphael's surfaced in violent fashion for a time. The sentiments Raphael expresses, then, were definitely familiar in late medieval Europe, but More's literary expression of them is remarkable for its forthrightness and vehement indignation. Nothing earlier compares with it in this respect unless we go back to the Hebrew prophets.

Ordinary Europeans do not entirely escape Raphael's wrath unscathed, as the following passage speaking of the attitudes of Utopia's inhabitants shows:

> But much more do they marvel at and detest the madness of those who give honor to those rich men, in whose debt and power they are not, but because they are rich; although they know them to be such niggardly skinflints that they are sure that as long as they live not one farthing's worth of that heap of gold shall come to them.[10]

Unlike Europeans of More's day the Utopians have little regard for affluence and its trappings. How have they come to possess an attitude that seems so bizarre to many of More's contemporaries? Here is what Raphael says he found:

> These and such like opinions have they conceived, partly through education, being brought up in that commonwealth, whose laws and customs are far different from these kinds of folly, and partly through good literature and learning. For though there are not many in every city who are exempt and discharged from all other labors, and appointed only to learning; that is to say, in whom even from their very childhood they have perceived a singular forwardness, a fine wit, and a mind apt to good learning; yet all, in their childhood, are instructed in learning. And the better part of the people, both men and women, throughout all their whole life do bestow on learning those spare hours, which we said they have free from bodily labors.[11]

Being raised in a community that has such values is part of the explanation, and More is keen to point out the importance of customs in directing a community's values. But there is also education in the literature of the culture, an education that is not at all limited to the elite, nor just to males. Among the works of literature studied are philosophical texts, and Raphael says that the Utopians carry on a vigorous discussion of philosophical issues with different views being put forth in the area of ethics. Not surprisingly, given More's own education, the philosophical views explored have a strong resemblance to those expressed by the ancient Greeks:

> In that division of philosophy which treats of manners and virtue, their reasons and opinions agree with ours. They discuss the good qualities of the soul, of the body, and of fortune, and whether the name goodness may be applied to all these, or only to the endowments and gifts of the soul. They reason of virtue and pleasure. But their chief and principal question is in what thing, be it one or more, does the felicity of man consist. On this point they seem almost too much given and inclined to the opinion of those who defend pleasure, in which they say either all or the chief part of man's felicity rests.[12]

However, the Utopians do not approve of just *any* sort of pleasure. The above Epicurean thrust is qualified by a decidedly Stoic amendment:

> But now, sir, they do not think felicity is in all pleasure, but only in that pleasure that is good and honest, and that to it, as to perfect blessedness, our nature is allured and drawn even by virtue, to which alone they that are of the contrary opinion attribute felicity. For they define virtue as a life ordered according to nature, and say that we are hereunto ordained by God; and that a man follows the course of nature, when in desiring and refusing things he is ruled by reason.[13]

But they do not think their morality is based solely on reason; religion undergirds it as well:

> And (which is more to be marveled at) the defense of this so dainty and soft an opinion they derive even from their grave, austere, sober and rigorous religion. For they never discuss felicity or blessedness without joining to the reasons of philosophy certain principles taken from religion; without which for the investigation

of true felicity they think reason alone weak and imperfect. Those principles are these and such like: that the soul is immortal, and by the bountiful goodness of God ordained to felicity; that for our virtues and good deeds rewards are appointed after this life, and for our evil deeds, punishments. Though these ideas belong to religion, yet they think it right they should be believed and confirmed by proofs of reason. But if these principles should be condemned and annulled, then without any delay they would pronounce no man so foolish as not to put forth all his diligence and endeavor to obtain pleasure by right or wrong, avoiding only this error, that the less pleasure should be a hindrance to a bigger, or that he should labor for a pleasure which would bring after it displeasure, grief and sorrow.[14]

Nevertheless, the Utopians, following the lead of the founder of their Commonwealth, Utopus, are tolerant of diverse religious views, as long as they are not held in a fanatical way:

[Utopus] made a decree that it should be lawful for every man to favor and follow whatever religion he would, and that he might do the best he could to lead others to his opinion, so long as he did it peaceably, gently, quietly, and soberly, without haste and contentious rebuking and denouncing others. If he could not by fair and gentle speech induce them to accept his opinion, still he should use no kind of violence and should refrain from unpleasant, seditious words. For him who would vehemently and fervently strive and contend for this cause was decreed banishment or bondage.[15]

Utopian attitudes, then, as to what is valuable in life are grounded in the early inculcation of the customs of the community and reinforced by an education that includes philosophical and religious buttressing of those attitudes. More's picture here is a complex one in which different elements, rational, quasi-rational, and non-rational, all work together to preserve a reasonable stability of attitudes while allowing for a goodly measure of discussion and debate.

The result is a morality in which altruism and egoism support each other in a rather elegant way:

> And that secondly, it [reason] moves and encourages us to lead our life free of care in joy and mirth, and to help all others in the fellowship of nature to obtain the same. For there was never a man so earnest and painstaking a follower of virtue and hater of pleasure, who would so enjoin you to labors, watchings, and fastings, but he would also exhort you to ease, and lighten, to your power, the poverty and misery of others, praising the same as a deed of humanity and pity.
>
> Then if it be a point of humanity for man to bring health and comfort to man, and especially (which is a virtue most peculiarly belonging to man) to mitigate and assuage the grief of others, and by taking from them the sorrow and heaviness of life, to restore them to joy, that is to say, to pleasure, why may it not then be said that nature incites every man to do the same for himself?[16]

The praise here given to the virtue of "humanity" shows the kinship of the ethic here ascribed to the Utopians with the one that Chinese Confucians promoted. Among the latter, "humanity" (*jen*), in the sense More gives it, was the greatest of the virtues.[17] I think there can be little doubt that More, at least when he wrote *Utopia*, deeply sympathized with this outlook,[18] although, of course, he had no knowledge of Confucian teachings.

As for development of the natural sciences, this is carried on in order to create greater appreciation of the works of Nature and of the Creator. The Utopians take little notice of the practical ends of scientific knowledge:

> For while by the help of philosophy they search out the secret mysteries of nature, they think that they not only receive thereby wonderful great pleasure, but also obtain great thanks and favor from the author and maker thereof. For he, they think, according to the fashion of other artificers, has set forth the marvelous and gorgeous frame of the world for man to behold, who alone has the

wit and capacity to consider and understand the excellence of so great a work. And therefore, they say, he bears more good will and love to the careful and diligent beholder and viewer of his work and marveller at the same, than he does to him, who like a very beast without wit and reason, or as one without sense or motion, pays no regard to so great and wonderful a spectacle.[19]

The Utopians proceed to organize their society in a way that most fulfils these values, and that, according to them, means doing away with private property and money. All the citizens are provided with what they need for a comfortable, but not luxurious, life, from what the community holds in common. The advantages of this system Raphael is keen to point out:

> For in other places they speak still of the commonwealth, but every man procures his own private wealth. Here, where nothing is private, the common interests are earnestly looked to. And truly on both accounts they have good cause to do as they do. For in other countries, who knows that he will not starve for hunger, unless he make some private provision for himself, even though the commonwealth flourish never so much in riches? And, therefore, he is compelled even of very necessity to pay regard to himself rather than to the people, that is to say, to others. Contrariwise, where all things are common to every man, it is not doubted that no man shall lack anything necessary for his private use, so long as the common storehouses and barns are sufficiently stored. For there nothing is distributed in a niggardly fashion, nor is there any poor man or beggar. And though no man owns anything, yet every man is rich. For what can be more rich than to live joyfully and merrily, without grief and worry, not concerned for his own living, nor vexed and troubled with his wife's importunate complaints, nor dreading poverty for his son, nor sorrowing for his daughter's dowry?[20]

Freed from cares about their own survival and prosperity, Utopians have the leisure to concern themselves with the affairs of the commonwealth and with securing a good living for all citizens, not just themselves and their own family. We have seen that the roots of this communist ideal go back deep into ancient Christian and pagan thought. Early Christians practised communal living, the myth of the golden age pictured humans living without private ownership of anything, and *The Sibylline Oracles* sometimes looked forward to such a development. We also noted that the Taborites for a while experimented with such an arrangement in their community. More would then have been quite familiar with the proposal. At the very end of *Utopia*, however, he distances himself from it:

> When Raphael had thus made an end of his tale, many things came to my mind, which in the manners and laws of that people seemed to be instituted and founded on no good reason...and chiefly, that which is the principal foundation of all their ordinances, that is to say, the community of their life and living, without any use of money, by which practice alone all the nobility, magnificence, worship, honor and majesty, the true ornaments and honors, as the common opinion is, of a commonwealth, are utterly overthrown and destroyed.[21]

I tend to think that More is being ironic here in picturing himself as going along with popular opinion and finding the communist proposal as "founded on no good reason." He may also, of course, be protecting himself against the wrath of his royal employer. Be that as it may, he has constructed a generally attractive account of Utopia and acknowledged that communism is the "linchpin" in the way of life of that community. It is another question, however, whether More would have countenanced promoting such radical views among Europe's ruling elite. Toward the end of Book 1 of *Utopia*, More has himself express this view about Raphael's radical communism:

> And to speak as I think, truly I cannot approve the offer of such information, or the giving of such counsel, as you are sure will never be regarded or received. For how can such strange information be profitable, or how can it be beaten into their heads, whose minds are

already prejudiced with wholly contrary persuasions. This school philosophy is not unpleasant among friends in familiar conversation, but in the councils of kings, where great matters are debated and reasoned with great authority, these things have no place.[22]

The More of *Utopia* goes on to defend working in the "councils of kings" to make better policies without challenging those views which the king or other advisers would never abandon, however grossly mistaken one knows them to be. It is a beautiful statement of why you should work "within the system," as we say, even if you think the system is perverse. More says the following:

> If you cannot, even as you would, remedy vices which habit and custom have confirmed, yet this is no cause for leaving and forsaking the commonwealth. You must not forsake the ship in a tempest, because you cannot rule and keep down the winds. No, nor must you labor to drive into their heads new and strange information, which you know well will be all disregarded by those that are of wholly contrary minds. But you must with a crafty wile and subtle art endeavor, as much as in you lies, to handle the matter wisely and handsomely for the purpose, and that which you cannot turn to good, so order that it be not very bad.[23]

Raphael's response to this is sharp:

> "By this means," quoth he, "nothing else will be brought to pass, but that while I go about to remedy the madness of others, I shall be even as mad as they. For if I would speak things that are true, I must needs speak such things. But as for speaking false things, whether that is a philosopher's part or no, I cannot tell; truly it is not my part."[24]

This is followed by appeals to Plato and Christ as urging us to have nothing to do with such compromises as More proposes. In all this the real More, I think, is revealing his own ambivalence about his actual career as an adviser to the king and a civil servant. His mind is divided: part of it thinks as does the More of *Utopia*, and part as does Raphael. But I think we can say that, despite continuing to operate much as the More of *Utopia* recommends and persecuting cruelly those who propagated in England the Protestant rebellion against the Catholic Church, he did not, as Raphael predicted, end up as corrupt as his associates or as villainous as his master. Instead of losing his mind, he lost his head.

Utopia is an urban-centred society, and rational planning has been crucial in its development. The *Kürwille* mentality, manifested in rational planning and design and behind the formation of all urban societies, is evident. But it is not dominant in Utopia. Rather, it operates in the context of what is basically an agrarian *Gemeinschaft*, the sort of community that is valued for its own sake and governed by custom, and, consequently, Utopia comes across as a way of avoiding domination by a *Gesellschaft*, an association viewed primarily as a means to something else and governed by rational planning, while preserving the advantages of urbanism, to describe it in the terms from Tönnies we have adopted in this study. But Utopian life is a way built on established customs and thus does not offer itself as the goal for any program for quick reform of More's own society, whose customs he admits are quite opposed to those of the Utopians. Unless one believes in the feasibility of "cultural revolution" (as had been tried in Bohemia) to dramatically change customs within a few years—and More was certainly not in that camp—comparison with Utopia can only serve to highlight some of the worst features of European society, ones that might be mitigated somewhat through legislative action. Nevertheless, with this work More launched among the literate elite of Europe an attractive vision of a radically different sort of society, established by human rather than divine powers.

Justus Lipsius and the Revival of Stoicism

Another, quite different view of human communities arose in conjunction with humanism through the revival of ancient Stoicism. Its chief propagator in early modern Europe was Justus Lipsius (1547–1606), a very learned scholar of ancient Greek and Roman literature, who taught at several universities, ending at Louvain. His times were turbulent to say the least, and his adoption of a Christianized form of ancient Stoicism was in part his way of coping with the war and destruction he saw about him, especially in his native Flanders.[25] His written works received wide circulation, especially *De Constantia* (*On Constancy*), in which he presents arguments and observations, mostly arising out of ancient Stoicism, particularly the works of Seneca, to convince himself that his deeply felt lamentations over the fate of his native land, not to mention his own consequent troubles, are not befitting a truly virtuous human being.

On Constancy is a dialogue in which a young Lipsius fleeing war-torn Flanders is tutored in Stoic philosophy by the fictitious older and wiser Langius, but there is no doubt that Langius's words present the considered views of the work's author, that is, the older Lipsius. It is interesting to see, then, the kind of argument that Langius presents for rejecting the legitimacy of grief over the destruction of the political state in which one grew up as well as over the sufferings of its citizens. In the dialogue the young Lipsius claims that such grief is natural, and flows from the natural love of one's native country (in Tönnies's terms, from *Wesenwille*, the motivating force behind all *Gemeinschaften*). But Langius insists it arises from custom. It turns out, on his view, that the state or "commonwealth" is an artifact required to preserve those common institutions that are necessary for the welfare of all, and consequently each citizen sees that his own safety and well-being are tied to the success of the commonwealth:

> When men saw the chief stay of each person's safety to consist in this, laws were enacted for the succour and defence of it, or at the least such customs were received by tradition from the predecessors to their posterity that grew to be of like force as laws. From this it comes to pass that we rejoice at the good of the commonwealth, and be sorry for her harm—because our own private goods are secure by her safety, and are lost by her overthrow.[26]

Once we see that the commonwealth is established for a valuable purpose and that the affection for it arises from customs adopted to protect it, then, according to Langius, the attitude that Reason would have us adopt toward it excludes emotional patriotism but prescribes loyalty:

> No, no, our country is not as you take it, but it is some one state, or as it were one common ship, under the regiment of one prince, or one law, which I confess we ought to love, to defend, and to die for. Yet must it not drive us to lament, wail and despair. Well said the poet,
>
> > A happy quarrel is it and a good,
> > For country's cause to spend our dearest blood.
> > (Horace, *Carmina*, 3.2.13)
>
> He said not that we should weep and lament, but die for our country. For we must so far forth be good commonwealth men, that we also retain the person of good and honest men, which we lose if we take to childish and womanlike lamentations.[27]

This is all sound Stoic doctrine. What is good for a person is the preservation of their virtue, and this means that we obey the dictates of accurately informed Reason, which in this case commands that we be willing to sacrifice our lives for the safety of the state, since the state preserves what is in accord with nature, viz., the communal life of human beings, which is in turn necessary for each individual's welfare. But should the state succumb to internal or external enemies, as long as we have done what is rationally demanded in its defence, no good for us is lost, and thus no lamentation is in order.

In his *Guide to Stoic Philosophy* Lipsius quotes Seneca to nail down the Stoic view that virtue is the only good:

> The supreme good is that which is honourable; and, what you may find more remarkable, that which is the only good." (Seneca, *Epistolae* LXXI.4) Here you have both principles: the first which I have proposed and affirmed, and the second, which follows automatically from it.[28]

The thesis that virtue arises from following Reason Lipsius defends by drawing a stark contrast between the soul and the body of a human being. The rule of

Reason is the perfection of the soul because it blocks the power of "Opinion," which Lipsius thinks arises from the impulses of the body, and in his mind the body is filthy and inferior in the way earth is to heaven. But since Reason is a faculty common to all humanity, we should, he thinks, see our true community as that of all human beings, not just those in some limited terrain:

> The whole world is our country, wherever the race of mankind is sprung of that celestial seed. Socrates, being asked of what country he was, answered, "of the world." For a high and lofty mind will not suffer itself to be penned by Opinion within such narrow bounds, but conceives and knows the whole world to be its own.[29]

This is to be what we now call a "citizen of the world," but that is to distance oneself from any actual, real-world *Gemeinschaft*, for all those are local, in favour of a *Gemeinschaft* that exists only in some other world, one that only our Reason, not our bodies, can access.

When the youthful Lipsius in an impassioned speech defends feeling pity for his countrymen, the elder Lipsius has Langius offer an orthodox Stoic reply:

> "What then? Are we so unkind and void of humanity that we would have no man to be moved at another's misery?" "Yes, I allow that we be moved to help them, not to bewail or wail with them. I permit mercy, but not pitying. I call mercy an inclination of the mind to succour the necessity or misery of another. This is that virtue, Lipsius, which you see through a cloud, and instead of which pity intrudes herself into you.[30]

Reason sees that it is right and in accord with nature to help one's fallen comrade, and abiding by that judgment is virtuous and good, but it is only Opinion that leads one to grieve at your comrade's suffering and pity him, an Opinion that arises from the impulses of the vile body.

On the Stoic view, Reason is that capacity nearly all humans have in varying degrees to stand back from perceptions and feelings that arise in us automatically as responses to the situations we encounter. We can then take advantage of that psychological distance to pass judgments on those feelings and perceptions using criteria such as natural appropriateness, moral correctness, utility, aesthetic appeal, and so on. It is, as the Stoics say, our "hegemonic" faculty, that is, one which can rule the deliverances of the other faculties. In total accord with ancient Stoic thought, Lipsius believes that allowing any of our automatic reactions to block the operation of Reason in this function is despicable, a capitulation to the lower part of our nature. Lipsius adds a very Platonic note to this Stoic thesis when he treats the lower part, that is, the body, as something vile, not part of our true nature at all. A person is truly controlling their own life only when they are acting on the basis of what their Reason judges to be in order.

To sustain this view, Stoicism must claim that Reason takes its criteria for judgment from itself and not from any of the automatic impulses it is supposed to pass judgment on. But once we allow that the internalization of customs arising from early upbringing in a particular culture can result in automatic reactions to what we observe and contemplate doing, it can be maintained that some, if not all, of the criteria Reason deploys actually arise from those automatic reactions that have been inculcated in us by custom and thus amount to what Lipsius calls Opinion. Reason, then, serves the very things it is supposed to rule over. But again, in accord, this time, with Plato more than the Stoics, Lipsius views a person's true home as Heaven, not earth, and thus Reason by its very own constitution brings with it the criteria by which it judges. As he has Langius say:

> Last of all, Lipsius, I would have you learn this one hidden and deep mystery, that if we respect the whole nature of man, all these earthly countries are vain and falsely so termed, except only in respect of the body, and not of the mind or soul, which descending down from that highest habitation, deems all the whole earth as a jail or prison, but heaven is our true and rightful country.[31]

Just as Lipsius's contrast of the real knowledge produced by Reason as against misleading Opinion echoes Plato's contrast of the kind of knowledge we find in mathematics as against mere "belief," so in treating Heaven as our true native land he is adopting Plato's view that our true self is Reason and that Reason finds its real rest and satisfaction in the realm of the eternal Forms, those archetypes that things in the visible world only dimly resemble. The visible world of things that come to be and pass away is not, according to Plato, something Reason enjoys studying or getting involved with, and since the unchanging, precise Forms are just on account of those features perfect ideals, the visible world is inferior; indeed, it does not even fully exist. Here is the Platonic source of Lipsius's disparagement of the earth as opposed to Heaven.

But the Christian side of Lipsius's outlook leads to the conclusion that the human, earthly communities we become attached to through custom are not our true home. Here the medieval *viator* makes a reappearance. Armed, however, with Stoicism's overwhelming confidence in Reason, the wayfarer is now emboldened to see any earthly state as an artificial device for maintaining the material welfare of its citizens. It becomes, to use Tönnies's term, a *Gesellschaft*, an association that exists to forward some further end. Reason demands that we endeavour to preserve it because it is a means to that natural end, but it is a short step from that to seeing the state as something that can be redesigned so that it more effectively serves that end. Lipsius himself does not take that step; he is no utopian, but he has opened that door.

To so alienate a person's real self from the world that physically surrounds them and from the worldly culture in which they were brought up is a fateful step that we encounter in some of the Indian Vedic traditions, in Platonism, and to some extent in ancient Stoicism; but it is Lipsius who fully propels this view onto the modern European stage. To some degree it was present in medieval Christian dogma, largely on account of Platonic influences, but in Lipsius we find Reason rendered independent of the rest of the human psyche, promoted as the true self, with the remainder of what we ordinarily take to be human relegated to the vile body. Such a view of what humans are cannot but have radical results in the life of anyone who tries to live up to it. Followers of Lipsius will be in their waking hours constantly engaged in taking psychological distance from the impulses and impressions that keep erupting from their despicable bodies, and also in assessing their legitimacy—a task that for nearly all of us requires considerable effort and discipline. Of itself Lipsius's is a view that certainly tends to counteract any longings for worldly improvement such as we have found in millenarianism. But at the same time it places the human mind, and in particular the mind of the Christian *viator*, in a position of complete superiority to the world it finds itself in, and this stance is needed by anyone attempting to design a radically better world that overthrows the established and traditional mores and structures of the existent society: in Tönnies's terms, substituting a *Kürwille*-planned *Gesellschaft* for *Gemeinschaften* in which *Wesenwille* dominates. Here now is a way for devout Christians, without adopting the excesses of millenarian fantasies, to think that envisioning utopias is not a useless effort. And utopian thinking among Protestant Christians of the seventeenth century will be a crucial element in the ideology we are uncovering.

Protestant Utopias

More's Utopia was based on the ideas of the ancient pagan world. Could there be a similar phantasy but based solidly in reformed Christianity? Johann Valentin Andreae (1586–1654) produced such a utopian vision and published it in 1619 in Latin under the title *Republicae Christianopolitanae Descriptio* (henceforth: *Christianopolis*). That work bears many similarities to More's: in each, the account of a utopia is given by a sailor shipwrecked on a hitherto unknown island, communism is practised, money is not used except in trade with external neighbours, much is made of abjuring luxury and promoting a simple life, and education in morals is emphasized. But Andreae's Christianopolitans are first and foremost Christians relying heavily on the gospels and traditional Christian theology to direct their lives. A sort of poverty in imitation of Christ and his disciples becomes a virtue. The following passage describing the ways of the inhabitants is representative of numerous others:

> It is not sufficient for Christians to be good according to the teachings of ethics and government, but they choose as their model Christ Himself, a far higher Master. As He is the most perfect embodiment of the highest virtues, He deserves to have imitators. Moreover, these virtues go beyond human excellencies and are included under the symbols of the cross: and those, who have devoted themselves closer to man, have called these Christian

poverty, by which we renounce even the things that are permitted the world, that we may possess only Christ.32

Just how much importance the Christianopolitans place on moral character and breadth of learning is illustrated by the questions an examiner asks their visitor almost as soon as he has arrived:

> He asked me, in most pleasant terms it is true, to what extent I had learned to control myself and to be of service to my brother; to fight off the world, to be in harmony with death, to follow the Spirit; what progress I had made in the observation of the heavens and the earth, in the close examination of nature, in instruments of the arts, in the history and origin of languages, the harmony of all the world; what relation I bore toward the society of the church, toward a compendium of the Scriptures, the kingdom of heaven, the school of the Spirit, the brotherhood of Christ, the household of God.33

Concerns like these with the spiritual life of the inhabitants are forwarded by an elaborate educational system, which is the most novel part of Andreae's utopia, although in this regard Andreae was probably influenced by Campanella's *Città del Sole*.34 A common and very central feature of the utopian thought of the Protestant reformers is the emphasis on education as the vehicle that can carry humanity to the promised land. The aims of the education of the young are described by Andreae as follows:

> Their first and highest exertion is to worship God with a pure and faithful soul; the second, to strive toward the best and most chaste morals; the third, to cultivate the mental powers—an order, reversed by the world, if any thought of God still remains among the inhabitants of the latter.35

This process of education is divided into several schools, the first of which is devoted to the study of language and languages. Hebrew, Greek, and Latin are all taught, as well as oratory and modern languages. In a second school we find teachers of logic, useful for the evaluation of arguments and the detection of fallacies but not to be considered sufficient for all learning. The same school teaches metaphysics, where "they look at the true, the good, the beautiful, unity, order, and the like,"[36] as well as an even higher discipline, theosophy, which, it seems, deals with revelations about God not available to philosophical inquiry.

Still a third school is shown to our visiting sailor, one that deals with all things mathematical. Here the influence of Plato's *Republic* makes itself felt, for the subjects include arithmetic and geometry, to which Andreae adds algebra, a relatively recent import to Europe, showing that his Christianopolis is abreast of the latest intellectual advances. On top of these disciplines we find the study of "mystic numbers" which God has used in constructing the world. The idea that God is a kind of architect figures importantly here, and it is worth quoting a passage that constitutes an early deployment of this metaphor, one that would become extremely popular in the modern West.

> God has His numbers and measures, and it is fitting that man should regard them. Surely that supreme Architect did not make this mighty mechanism haphazard, but He completed it most wisely by measures, numbers, and proportions, and He added to it the element of time, distinguished by a wonderful harmony. His mysteries has He placed especially in His workshops and typical buildings, that with the key of David we may reveal the length, breadth, and depth of divinity, find and note down the Messiah present in all things, who unites all in a wonderful harmony and conducts all wisely and powerfully, and that we may take our delight in adoring the name of Jesus.[37]

A fourth school teaches music, but here one must first have mastered arithmetic and geometry, since music "depends to a considerable extent upon measure and number,"[38] Andreae says, echoing Plato's Pythagorean thoughts. But, again like Plato, Andreae warns against forms of music that lead to corruption of morals, assuring us that such practices are banned from Christianopolis:

> Yet the world has not been able to keep from abusing the legitimate joy of heaven with the evil of Satan, and subjecting it to deceit. So it comes that we have the madness of dancing, the frivolity of vulgar songs, the wickedness of roisterers. All of these things have been long ago driven out of this republic and are now unheard.[39]

In a fifth school our sailor finds astronomy being studied. Without any sort of degradation of the earth, such as we found in Lipsius, Andreae finds the study of the heavens ennobling to humans. A sixth school is devoted to natural science, or natural philosophy, as it was then called. Andreae has his sailor rhapsodize eloquently about the objects of this study:

> All these, forsooth, are very beautiful things, and it is below his dignity for man not to know them, after the faithful investigations of so many men. For we have not been sent into this world, even the most splendid theater of God, that as beasts we should merely devour the pastures of the earth, but that we might walk about observing His wonders, distributing His gifts, and valuing His works. For who would believe that the great variety of things, their elegance, advantage, and maturity, and in short, the utility of the earth, had been granted to man for any other reason than for his highest benefit.[40]

Note the belief, Stoic in origin and common enough in Western thought, that the natural world has been created for the benefit of the human race.[41] The study of its wonders reflects on the beneficence of its creator while at the same time revealing the creation's usefulness to us and thus inspiring our gratitude to God. History, particularly Church history, has its place as well in this sixth school. As with all the other subjects, Christianopolitans see a moral benefit from its study:

> For as the study of human history makes man gentle, humble, and careful, so the ignorance of it keeps him crude toward himself and others, proud, and hasty toward his own and the state's undoing.[42]

Other rooms are given over to more practical and empirical endeavours. There is a laboratory whose instruments and methods obviously owe much to the alchemists and in which what we would call experimental science is carried out. There are also "ingenious ovens" and contrivances "for uniting and dissolving substances":

> Here the properties of metals, minerals, and vegetables, and even the life of animals are examined, purified, increased, and united, for the use of the human race and in the interests of health. Here the sky and the earth are married together; divine mysteries impressed upon the land are discovered; here men learn to regulate fire, make use of the air, value the water, and test earth. Here the ape of nature has wherewith it may play, while it emulates her principles and so by the traces of the large mechanism forms another, minute and most exquisite.[43]

Careful observation is practised in order to ensure that old theories about what in fact occurs in nature are properly tested:

> Whatever has been dug out and extracted from the bowels of nature by the industry of the ancients, is here subjected to close examination, that we may know whether nature has been truly and faithfully opened to us.[44]

High in the esteem of this society are the artisans who combine with their productive activity a deep interest in how nature works and engage in the careful empirical work necessary to understand it. Andreae has combined into one the occupations of artisan and scientist in a way that, as we shall see, would surely have pleased Francis Bacon.[45] He has already foreseen that marriage of technology and science that Bacon would laud, but in *Christianopolis*, unlike in Bacon's utopia, which we will come to, the marriage is consummated within individuals and realizes in them their inner spark of divinity, as well as providing material benefits to the citizens.

There is also a pharmacy, but its employment is of much broader scope than the term seems to imply:

> Whatsoever the elements offer, whatever art improves, whatever all creatures furnish, it is all brought to this place, not only for the cause of health, but also with a view toward the advancement of education in general.[46]

The practical aim of this education, however, is emphasized, and Andreae does not miss the opportunity to make an invidious comparison with the scholastic learning he would have known full well from his studies in the universities of the day:

> For what a narrow thing is human knowledge if it walks about as a stranger in the most wholesome creations and does not know what advantage this or that thing bears to man, yet meanwhile wanders about in the unpleasant crackle of abstractions and rules, none the less boasting of this as a science of the highest order.[47]

The educational program that Andreae puts forward here as the practice of Christianopolis is an amalgam of three different cultural materials: There is first a rigorous pietism that places the worship and reverence of God and imitation of Christ as both the foundation and goal of the whole program. Second, there is the incorporation of humanist learning based on the ancient classics read in the original languages. And third, we have a full acceptance of the new observational and experimental science that has only recently found approval among Europe's educated elite. Although it has to be said that these three components do not sit all that happily with one another, the mix is a very potent one, for it satisfies the desire for religious reform of society by the improvement of morals, while also raising the hope that the physical well-being of humans can be bettered by advances in the understanding of how nature really works, nurtured by the new observational methods of investigation. It is ironic that such a work would appear at the very moment that Europe was heading into one of the worst periods in its history, the wars of religion. But just as Plato's utopia was in part a reaction to the debacle of Athens's war with Sparta, perhaps utopian thinking generally gets a strong impetus from tumultuous times.

Another Protestant utopian vision emerges in a little noticed work of the mid-seventeenth century, *Nova Solyma*, composed in Latin by Samuel Gott, who was a student at Cambridge between 1630 and 1633, later a Member of Parliament between 1645 and 1648, and then again in 1660 and 1663 (the "Convention Parliament," which prepared the way for the restoration of Charles II). He was a Puritan but opposed to the more radical elements in the Puritan revolution that led to Cromwell. *Nova Solyma* was published in 1648 and responds to Puritan desires for a society reformed along the lines of Protestant Christian values. Its literary form is unusual in that it is partly a novel incorporating a romantic love story and partly an adventure involving bandits and narrow escapes. There is also a considerable amount of straight philosophy and theology, along with frequent poetic interludes. The title is the name of a fictitious city founded on the site of ancient Jerusalem by Jews who have converted to Christianity, and it is this city that is Gott's ideal republic. The novelistic form, which the author admits is a departure from past practice, fits Gott's philosophy of education, which holds that poetry and imaginative stories are effective ways of instilling Christian values.

The city of Nova Solyma does not have the communism and heavy emphasis on equality we found in both More's and Andreae's utopias. In fact, radical reform of the social structure of human communities is explicitly rejected by the Head Teacher in Nova Solyma, whose words in the following passage can I believe be taken as describing Gott's purposes for writing the very work we are reading:

> The author...has not the impudent audacity of those rash reformers[48] who are for tearing up the old foundations, for putting civil and political life on a new basis, and for carrying out specious schemes which are as costly as they are dangerous, in order to overturn what has stood the test of many generations.[49]

Accordingly, we find that Nova Solyma does not differ in its class structure all that much from Gott's England: there are differences in wealth and in status, and the educational system is designed to produce an elite who will guide the commonwealth. The Head Teacher, Alphaeus, describes the two-tier system of education as follows:

> And it has always been no slight recommendation to any candidate for public service or the magisterial office if he has taken his degree with us...There are technical schools as well, and public workshops where the children of the poorer classes are taught the meaner occupations, or, if they show ability, are instructed in the mechanical arts and crafts...The education of all these goes no farther than reading, writing, arithmetic with geometry, and other such studies as are a help to the mechanical arts, for the higher culture is considered out of place in their station of life, and even prejudicial, from its tendency to make the working classes dissatisfied with their humble duties, if once they have tasted the dignified "sweetness and light" of the intellectual life. But as regards morality, military drill, and religious exercises, these are inculcated on all without exception.[50]

It is fair then to view Gott as interested in practical reform in his home country, mainly in the area of education, but not at all in social structure, and that *Nova Solyma* was an effort to attract people to that cause. Indeed, we know that Gott at Cambridge would have moved in a circle of men like Richard Hartlib, John Dury, Commenius, and Milton, who were aware of Andreae's work and devoted to educational reform.

The upbringing of youths in Nova Solyma is oriented toward curbing unruly passions and seduction by worldly pleasures, a goal quite in line with Andreae's Christianopolis's ideal, but the method of going about this is different, and Gott is keen to make it clear that he is innovating. He has the main character in his story, Joseph, explain this to a couple students from Cambridge, after they have heard the mentor to Joseph's two much younger brothers tell the boys a dream she has concocted to point out the dangers of unrestrained pleasure-seeking:

> I think this aged teacher has desired to point out to her pupils
> how (as the tale goes of Hercules) they may distinguish right from

> wrong by the critical faculty alone without perilous experiment, and why she relates their fall is for their protection in like event; and to make a deeper impression she veils the lesson under the pleasing guise of a mythic tale...As a matter of fact...not only in teaching proper behaviour, but in instilling the first principles of religion, we also make use of this device. It is not our practice to compel children to learn by rote what they hardly understand, nor do we administer their religious pabulum minced up into short questions and answers; we rather season it to their taste and age, and, like birds, prepare and digest it ourselves first...[51]

Here we find the emphasis on cloaking the lesson to be inculcated in something entertaining. Rote learning is avoided as well as the use of catechisms.

Adolescents are taken to a boarding school where they are largely isolated from the outside world for periods of time. The goal of the education there is to prepare them for leadership in the community, and this gives priority to instilling the principle that the good of the whole republic comes before any personal benefit. The Head Teacher, Alphaeus, puts it as follows:

> The founders of our republic, in their zealous enquiry how best to establish it on a sound basis, put the education of the rising generation in the very forefront of all means to that end...They thought it would not be an easy, natural thing for citizens to act for the common weal unless from their youth up they were accustomed to restrain their natural evil desires, and to learn that habit of mind by which they would willingly, in their own interests, keep inviolate the laws of God and their country, and put the advantage of the republic before any private or personal benefits whatever.[52]

Alphaeus makes much of working with the differing natural inclinations that the students bring with them to the school. The remarkable aspect here is that the education is tailored to each individual; differences are not erased in a futile attempt to produce a uniform product. Alphaeus explains:

> My method is this: I first search out the boy's natural disposition and character, his vices, generally due to the weakness and compliance of youth, his virtues, and his accomplishments. With proper attention his levity may be changed into quickness of comprehension, his choler into valour, his credulity into faith and obedience. Having thus modified his bad qualities, we can also bring out and improve the natural virtues of modesty, simplicity, and the like... And besides this, I seek to discover each one's peculiar disposition and genius. Some are so evenly and happily gifted by nature that all good things come alike to them. They are like very fertile soil, which deserves the best seed, and requires checking rather than forcing...In fact, we find that the majority of those who are pressed to undertake uncongenial studies get lazy and careless until they return to what they naturally prefer.[53]

This recognition of the desirability of individual differences fits nicely with the attitude taken toward the texts of classical antiquity. Instead of reading them as ideal moral guides, the teacher encourages his pupils to take a critical attitude:

> We also encourage them to give their own opinions and to judge for themselves. And in my lectures on general history I lay before them the methods and meaning of the old authors, where their remarks are just, and where their judgment is at fault, and why it is that so much which is in accordance with the traditions of other times is at variance with our present views. I am careful to do this, lest their boyish ardour should be attracted by the examples of antiquity, and, without true discernment, be induced to follow them.[54]

In rhetoric, too, the student is encouraged to advance in his own way. No set of rules for the art can dictate the way to proceed; the individual's own spirit must emerge:

> Rhetoric cannot be tied down to ordinary rules, though what I have said forms the foundation of the art. It will be found that a

noble mind will best follow its own course, and pour forth new
figures of speech, new surprises, and new intellectual feats, as
the occasion for them arises, for the right expression at the right
moment can hardly ever be made a certainty by any rule or by any
speaker.[55]

What is remarkable here is the belief in the basic goodness and creativity of human beings as we find them, coupled with a recognition of individual talents and proclivities. The youths must be encouraged to think for themselves and develop their own styles of speech and writing. In this Gott was a century ahead of his time.

The education system is basically a literary one, with much emphasis upon classical authors and especially poetry. The study of nature is not mentioned as a subject in school except for what might come from the reading of classical philosophers. But the worthwhileness of this study and the beauty and wonder of nature itself is something the work emphasizes. In book 2 there is a discussion between Joseph and his two student friends from Cambridge on the comparative value of art versus nature, and Joseph defends in the most uncertain terms the superiority of the latter:

> And this leads me to my main contention, which is, that we should
> esteem everything according to its proper value and order, taking
> care lest, by dwelling too intently on the beauties of art, we rob
> that Divine energy which we call Nature of her highest honours,
> and deprive ourselves too of that great and constant pleasure
> which she is so able to afford; lest also, when privileged spectators
> of that wondrous and varied scene wherein the whole universe is
> put before us as on a stage, we should only care to bestow a casual
> or superficial glance upon it, only caring to use our outward eyes,
> not deeming the spectacle worthy [of] the deeper considerations of
> the inward eye of the soul.[56]

One of the students, Politian, tries to defend the superiority of works of art and in frustration asks Joseph the following sarcastic question, which elicits a reply:

> "Do you therefore...wish us all to become philosophers and adepts in the chemistry of Nature, and in these studies to wear away our lives?"
>
> "Yes, indeed I do," said Joseph, "if you are such adepts as to be able to extract the meaning of the Divine goodness, and such philosophers as to look at common things with no common views. The average sensual man measures every pleasure by his desire and lust, and so grows dull to the sense of God's goodness, which should be the supreme whet to all our joys."[57]

We see that in the end nature is valued for the evidence it provides of God's beneficence, and this produces a joy of its own on top of the mere sensual delight in nature's beauty. As there had been in Andreae's *Christianopolis*, we find here a deep religious motivation for studying nature, but what is missing from *Nova Solyma* is any interest in developing this study in the direction of improvement in the mechanical arts. In fact, in another passage Joseph is quite disdainful of those arts. He associates them with the gluttonous desire for worldly wealth as opposed to the development of the mind and soul:

> All this excessive wealth is a product of the labour of the poor, and depends upon it. It is not the mind that requires these things, for the mind neither hungers nor thirsts, nor has it to pay the doctor's bill: it is the body that is such an expensive glutton, and such a bad and hard master as well; it is the body that commands us to come and go with all speed on its behests, to suffer toil and danger and work ourselves almost to death, all for its sake. Hence the great attention given to the mechanical arts, to the neglect of pure science and culture. The great mass of mankind weighed down with this great burden, have to spend the whole of their life in procuring the necessities of living, nor is their life much above that of mere animals.[58]

The reference here to the body is Platonic and akin to the sentiments we found expressed by Lipsius. Indeed there is more than a modicum of Stoicism in

Joseph's pronouncements, but it is placed in an almost mystical context of Christianized Platonism, as the following passage makes evident:

> For it is our nature, so to speak, to cast forth rays of love towards that which is beautiful outside us, and to attract it to ourselves; and while we thus crave after ideal beauty and perfection, we never reach it till we find it in God Himself, and drink our fill, as far as we may now, from that fathomless well of the Water of Life which He offers to our thirsty souls. All worldly substitutes are vain: the more we use them the more our burning thirst consumes us; they add but fuel to our flames. This union with God alone satisfies our craving, this alone stills our restless wants, or rather, I would say, it gives them most abundant liberty to wander at will through the vast expanse of God's infinite love.[59]

This belief in the basic human craving for "beauty and perfection" underlies the educational system just discussed, but it has to be balanced by the Christian recognition of the effects of original sin, a balance that has bedeviled Christian theologians from the early Church on. The problem is addressed in a lecture by a moral philosopher that Joseph and his friends attend. The lecturer tries to blend a typically Stoic theme with the Christian doctrine of the Fall.

> But the heart of a wise man is under his own control, and he can mould and alter it even as a workman can fashion with his strong right hand the material beneath it...So said the old philosophers, and they made the discipline of the soul almost a religion, and so far the Word of God bears them out; but from Revelation we know what the philosophers least of all imagined, that man is by nature corrupt, fallen, and unable to raise himself to God, though he has still left to man somewhat of his original justice, strength, and nobleness of mind...Nor is this dignity of character inconsistent with or opposed to Christian humility, for this last Christian virtue is really a sense of shame at the great fall from our first estate, and this begets a desire in us to recover the native dignity

we have lost, and so the two apparent extremes of character are found to be harmoniously consistent.[60]

The lecturer goes on with a discourse that is pure Epictetus:

> Therefore continually practise this self-government, even in the most trivial matters, for the least loosening of the reins of control may make a firm command no easy matter to regain...Therefore I say, obey the rules you lay down for yourself more implicitly even than if they were laws with the King's sanction, and, like an athlete, keep always in training and practice. Do not forget that we can modify our natural disposition. Socrates was ugly—that could not be mended; his disposition was not naturally good, but by self-control he made it so.[61]

The direction of these thoughts clashes, I think, with Joseph's sentiments, which are much more at ease with the idea that our nature is basically good and leads us in the right direction. In commenting on the lecture, Joseph remarks:

> "It is a true saying," said he, "that a philosophic composure of mind is, in all our troubles, the one earthly thing that brings back happiness and proves to be a physician for every woe..."[62]

In other words, Joseph trivializes the lecturer's Stoic message as recommending something like a therapy for dealing with life's woes. Which represents Gott's own view, or was he unaware of the conflict? I do not think it is possible to say, and perhaps Gott wished his readers to appreciate the tension between basic human nobility and deeply ingrained corruption, and then live with it in a way that still promotes moral improvement both in individuals and in society.

The author of *Nova Solyma*, unlike Johann Andreae, expresses no interest in the new science that was already well established by his time. There is no mention in the work of the need for experiment or the usefulness of mechanical equipment for scientific exploration. In this respect *Nova Solyma* is old-fashioned even for its own day. Its innovations are mainly in the realm of education; this faith in the ability of proper education to improve life it shares with *Christianopolis,* and like that work too it sees the benefit as being mainly in improved character and good government. All three of the utopias explored above have this in common: genuine improvement in human affairs is achievable only through improvement in human character. In this respect they are a throwback to the ideals of the elite in the Greco-Roman culture of antiquity. They point in a direction that had it been followed would definitely have curtailed the future growth of Europe's economy, in just the way that Platonic–Stoic ideals had constrained the growth of the ancient economy in the Mediterranean world, and Confucianism in China.

But there is another theme to be noted that is common to the Protestant utopias (though not More's) as well as to Lipsius, and that is the power of human reason to concoct solutions to pressing problems and the need for inner discipline to ensure that reason remains in control of behaviour. *Nova Solyma* moderates this theme by its emphasis on poetry, feelings, and the imagination; but reason, our ability to judge after psychologically stepping back and examining matters in their full context, remains hegemonic. We are entering the European Enlightenment, and not for nothing has it been called the "Age of Reason."

Charles Taylor has noted how, particularly in Calvinism, the drive for discipline was carried over from the realm of one's personal life to that of the ordering of society.[63] What we have seen in the two Protestant utopias surveyed above is a desire, indeed, to improve society, but the way they recommended to achieve this was to first improve individual human souls. In both, educational reform is the key to this effort. Taylor notes that Calvinist divines inclined to another route: legislation of good behaviour, and rigorous enforcement. The spirit is quite different. As was noted earlier in a passage from *Nova Solyma,* the work is "the history of a life that is free" but well brought-up. The author's utopia relies on the internalizing of principles of conduct by individuals, not on the external enforcement of rules.

Bacon and Puritan Reform in Britain

Since the fifteenth century Europe had seen remarkable change in both scientific thought and technological practice. In science the geocentric conception of the universe had been challenged by Copernicus and then Galileo. The latter had revolutionized the physics of matter in motion. Descartes had laid the foundations of analytic geometry. William Harvey had discovered the circulation of blood and the true function of the heart. In technology somehow the idea of printing with movable type had made it to Europe from China; there had been improvements in mining; gunpowder had radically changed warfare. The compass, another Chinese invention, had revolutionized navigation, and with its help voyages had made known to Europe the existence of the Americas and the millions of people inhabiting them, who were already suffering the cruel effects of that encounter. Alchemists had experimented with chemicals and furnaces. One only need look at the drawings of Leonardo depicting machines and even submarines to realize that the spirit of technological innovation was vigorously alive even before 1500.

The utopia of *Christianopolis* recognized the importance of this flood of innovation, but like those of More and of *Nova Solyma* its hope for improvement of society relied mainly on inculcating a higher level of moral character in its citizens. Education was important in all three of the utopias just discussed, but its aim in all three was not so much to increase knowledge of nature and the practical arts as to instil better character in those to whom it was offered. In this respect these utopias bore a resemblance to the Confucian philosophy of China and reflected a self-conscious return to some of the philosophy of the ancient Greeks and Romans. Stoicism was also revived by Lipsius, albeit in a quite non-utopian form, yet laying the philosophical basis for rational modification of political arrangements. More and Andreae also recognized the deleterious impact of the way people accepted wealth inequality and evaluated things in terms of money. Such radical social ideas are absent from Gott's *Nova Solyma*, however. None of this phantasizing about a better world would have led in the direction of the rampant economic development that the West was to pursue in later centuries. On the contrary, it was profoundly antithetical to such a vision, just as Confucianism had been and still was in China, and Platonism and Stoicism had been in the ancient Mediterranean world.

It was not, then, this sort of utopia that was in the end to enthrall and dominate the intellectuals of the modern European world. Rather it was a utopia that put the new science and technological innovation at the very centre of efforts to improve society and the prosperity of humankind while neatly side-stepping calls for moral improvement. This was the kind of utopia imagined by Francis Bacon (1561–1626) in his *New Atlantis*, written in 1624 and left unfinished at his death. The work came at the end of a series of efforts by Bacon to convince his king, James I, for whom he served as Lord Keeper of the Great Seal and later Lord Chancellor before being impeached in 1621, that he and his domain would be greatly served by royal support for a new kind of education and method of investigating nature. At the time Britain was decidedly behind the continent in both scientific theory and technological practice, but, on the other hand, Britain in the early seventeenth century was peaceful compared with the devastation being wreaked on the continent by the wars of religion. However, even though Bacon had chosen a timely moment to launch his appeals, they did not succeed in gaining the desired support. Their fruit would come later, at the end of the century.

Bacon believed that advances in learning could only be made if the scholasticism that dominated the universities and the humanism taught in the schools were largely abandoned in favour of more empirical work with a practical end in view, that end being the "relief of man's estate," that is, the mitigation of poverty and ignorance among the people generally. His attack on scholasticism is instructive: he incessantly lambasted the practice of arguing and disputing, which was at the core of scholastic methodology, as well as its unrelenting reliance on the works of ancient authorities, primarily Aristotle. In place of that he would emphasize, so far as the study of nature was concerned, observation and experiments with tools and instruments such as were being used by the alchemists. He wrote as follows in *The Advancement of Learning* (1605):

> In general, there will hardly be any main proficience in the disclosing of nature, except there be some allowance for expenses about experiments; whether they be experiments appertaining to Vulcanus or Daedalus, furnace or engine, or any other kind; and therefore as secretaries and spials [spies] of princes bring in bills for intelligence, so you must allow the spials and intelligencers of nature to bring in their bills, or else you shall be ill advertised [informed].[64]

Experiments, and costly ones at that, would replace the methods of the scholastics. It is important to understand how deep this overthrow of the scholastic tradition runs so far as our conception of knowledge is concerned. The scholastics had developed out of the dialectical method of Plato a highly sophisticated approach to securing knowledge, one that involved consulting the revered opinions of people like Aristotle and the Islamic thinkers Avicenna (Ibn Sina) and Averroes (Ibn Rushd) and then arguing among themselves how these works were to be interpreted and how corrected. There was no slavish following of Aristotle among the thirteenth- and fourteenth-century scholastics in the medieval universities. Rather there was continuous debate about the merits of his views in natural philosophy, ethics, and politics. Plato had tried to establish the process of thesis and refutation followed by a more refined thesis, a method called dialectic, as the way to eventually arrive at what rational minds would agree had to be the truth. Only what survived rigorous debate could be entirely trusted—only that, in his terminology, could be viewed as genuine knowledge and not just opinion. Plato himself had a skeptical view about what appeared to us through the senses; Aristotle and the scholastics who followed him, however, held that observations of obvious facts about the world we experience around us were useful, but such facts only established what were the "phenomena" that had to be explained by theory. To get to the correct theory, if this were possible, one had to construct some explanatory scheme, whose merits would then have to be compared with those of other schemes and argued about until one scheme survived as the only tenable one, if indeed such a happy result could be reached at all. (In the realm of philosophy of nature Plato himself seems to have settled for "likely stories.")

If the process of debate reached the desired conclusion, then each of the participants was in a position to know the victorious theory to be true and to understand why it had to be accepted as true, since each of them had followed the course of the arguments that had led to the disposal of all the other theories people could propose. In this it was a bit like proofs in mathematics, in that the person who understands the proof not only knows its conclusion to be true but also knows why it must be true, for he has followed the line of argument in the proof. The inquirer has in both cases become wiser; his own mind has been furnished with what is needed to reason convincingly about the matters investigated. Hence both Aristotle and Plato can think that the life of the person who has gained such knowledge, when it is about truly noble things like the heavenly bodies, is an extraordinarily worthwhile endeavour, perhaps the most worthwhile of all the kinds of achievement available to individual humans. In this respect the Platonic conception of knowledge is not unlike the one held by Indian sages, although they thought that such a condition was achievable through rigorous mental and physical exercises and were not impressed with the efficacy of argument.

The scholastic conception had to reduce the role of observation down to just those facts that were so obvious that nearly everyone knew them. If instead inquiry required reliance on observations that could be made only by those few who had special equipment, then those who could not make such observations had to rely on the testimony of those who could, and such reliance was incompatible with genuine knowledge since it was not self-reliant. Bacon's approach overturned this conception entirely. He believed in trusting the reports of observations made by people using equipment that only a few could possess, although, no doubt, he advocated other inquirers' reproducing the experiments involved so that charlatans could not mislead the whole community of inquirers. He also held to very naive ideas about how proper methodology and training of the mind could lead to inferring from gathered observations a correct theory about what was causing nature to behave in the way it was observed to behave. But now the locus of knowledge really shifts from the individual inquirer to the community of inquirers, for each individual must trust the others to be reporting and testing observations in such a way that erroneous reports are weeded out. It is this cooperation among numerous inquirers that underpins any claim to know the truth of some explanatory theory; thus knowledge is really a virtuous state of the community rather than of any particular member. Any claim that the inquirer's own activity is leading to some intrinsically noble state of their own mind is undercut. The classical idea of the "sage" disappears so far as being wise about the external observable world is concerned.

If self-improvement ceases to be a motive for scientific investigation, what is? Bacon's answer is that it is the desire to benefit mankind in its struggle to attain prosperity in the face of a recalcitrant nature. The practice of the Christian virtue of charity now figures as what scientific endeavours are supposed to result in. Hence the concurrence of Christian ethics with scientific and technological enterprise. Here is one of many passages from Bacon's works that stresses this theme:

> But the greatest error of all the rest is the mistaking or misplacing of the last or furthest end of knowledge. For men have entered into a desire of learning and knowledge, sometimes upon a natural curiosity and inquisitive appetite; sometimes to entertain their minds with variety and delight; sometimes for ornament and reputation; and sometimes to enable them to victory of wit and contradiction; and most times for lucre and profession; and seldom sincerely to give a true account of their gift of reason to the benefit and use of men.[65]

Note in the above passage how all but the last of the motivations are petty or even despicable. Missing entirely is either the awakening and enlightenment of the mind so as to produce a "sage," or the increased awe for the Architect of a nature now discovered to be so marvellous in its design. Bacon has shifted the status of scientific knowledge from being one of the great end goals of the development of a human individual to that of a very estimable means to human prosperity.

And there is this passage, taken from Bacon's *Masculine Birth of Time* (*Tempus Partus Masculus*, ca. 1602) in which he addresses a pupil and stirs hopes of an elite of scientists practising a method of direct observation of the world who will find ways to cure the main sources of human suffering:

> My dear, dear boy, what I purpose is to unite you with *things themselves* in a chaste, holy, and legal wedlock; and from this association you will secure an increase beyond all the hopes and prayers of ordinary marriages, to wit, a blessed race of Heroes or Supermen who will overcome the immeasurable helplessness and poverty of the human race, which cause it more destruction than all giants,

monsters, or tyrants, and will make you peaceful, happy, prosperous, and secure.[66]

It was this charitable aim, joined to the idea of "a race of Heroes or Supermen" leading humanity on the way out of poverty, that was to enthrall the minds of those who read his works, for it tied the investigation of nature to the enthusiasm for reformed Christianity that was being felt among many intellectuals in seventeenth-century England and elsewhere. In addition it positioned the envisioned inquirers at the forefront of a world-transforming movement, analogous to Joachim of Fiore's *viri spirituales*, although the transformation promoted was entirely different. From an ideological point of view, this conception was Bacon's *tour de force*, and it was to resonate down through the ensuing centuries to the present day.

Bacon's unfinished utopian fiction, *New Atlantis* (published in 1626), makes clear what his ultimate aim was. Like More's and Andreae's utopias, the story is told by someone who has by chance been stranded in a land presently unknown to Europeans, in Bacon's case somewhere in the Pacific Ocean west of Peru. The name of the country located there is "Bensalem," and since the Bensalemites had had contact with ancient civilizations in the long distant past, they were familiar with some of the languages of that world. In addition, they had more recently sent small clandestine expeditions to Europe, and so were able to communicate with their visitors in their native Spanish.

Bensalem is Christian despite having been isolated from Europe and Asia since long before the birth of Jesus. One of the governors of the country explains to the visiting sailors how many centuries ago a pillar of light appeared in the harbour of their capital; when that pillar finally dissolved it left an ark on the water containing a book that held the Holy Scriptures, including the full New Testament, even though at that time some of those books were not yet written. The leader of the country accepts this bizarre event as a miracle and acknowledges the book's divine providence. The episode reflects Bacon's oft expressed view that the edicts of the divine will are known only through revelation and that this sort of knowledge has an entirely different basis than that of natural science.

But before this, the king who founded Bensalem had established the basic ruling institution of the country, Salomon's House. The informant introduces it as follows:

> Ye shall understand (my dear friends) that amongst the excellent acts of that king, one above all hath the preeminence. It was the erection and institution of an Order or Society which we call "Salomon's House"; the noblest foundation (as we think) that ever was upon the earth; and the lanthorn of this kingdom. It is dedicated to the study of the Works and Creatures of God.[67]

He also describes its purpose:

> The End of our Foundation is the knowledge of Causes, and secret motions of things; and the enlarging of the bounds of Human Empire, to the effecting of all things possible.[68]

In other words, through the acquisition of knowledge of how nature works, human control over the world will be extended to the limits of what is humanly possible.

The full members of Salomon's House constitute a highly educated elite, no doubt the Heroes and Supermen prophesied earlier in *Masculine Birth of Time*, who are exalted above the rest of the populace. Bacon gives us a detailed description of the way in which one of the principals in this elite makes his appearance in the capital city:

> He was carried in a rich chariot, without wheels, litter-wise; with two horses at either end, richly trapped in blue velvet embroidered; and two footmen on each side in the like attire. The chariot was all of cedar, gilt, and adorned with crystal; save that the fore-end had panels of sapphires, set in borders of gold, and the hinder-end the like of emeralds of the Peru colour. There was also a sun of gold, radiant, upon the top, in the midst; and on the top before, a small

cherub of gold, with wings displayed. The chariot was covered with
cloth of gold tissued upon blue.[69]

Clearly Bacon has nothing to do with the disgust exhibited by More and Andreae toward ostentatious luxury, nor is he in the least sympathetic to their egalitarian ideals. Reform of society is to come not by some sort of communism but by the aristocratic rule of the scientifically educated.

Later the exalted figure from Salomon's House lays out the work that this institute engages in. Its scope is extremely broad; a few examples will have to suffice to give the reader some estimate of this. There are observation towers:

> We use these towers, according to their several heights and situations, for insolation, refrigeration, conservation; and for the view of divers meteors; as winds, rain, snow, hail; and some of the fiery meteors.

There are pools for desalination and the reverse:

> We have also pools, of which some do strain fresh water out of salt; and others by art do turn fresh water into salt.[70]

There are orchards and vineyards maintained not so much for their beauty as for the useful products that can be obtained from them. Also, experiments with modifying the nature of various plants are carried out in the belief that art can improve on nature:

> And we make (by art) in the same orchards and gardens, trees and flowers to come earlier or later than their seasons; and to come up and bear more speedily than by their natural course they do. We make them also by art greater much than their nature; and their fruit greater and sweeter and of differing taste, smell, colour, and figure, from their nature. And many of them we so order, as they become of medicinal use.[71]

Powerful engines are constructed as well as ordinance for war.

> We have also engine-houses, where are prepared engines and instruments for all sorts of motions. There we imitate and practise to make swifter motions than any you have, either out of your muskets or any engine that you have; and to make them and multiply them more easily, and with small force, by wheels and other means: and to make them stronger, and more violent than yours are; exceeding your greatest cannons and basilisks. We represent also ordnance and instruments of war, and engines of all kinds: and likewise new mixtures and compositions of gun-powder, wildfires burning in water, and unquenchable.[72]

Salomon's House periodically sends out small expeditions to the rest of the world to gather information about the progress made there, without, however, letting their origin be known:

> For the several employments and offices of our fellows; we have twelve that sail into foreign countries, under the names of other nations (for our own we conceal); who bring us the books, and abstracts, and patterns of experiments of all other parts. These we call Merchants of Light.[73]

Research is carried on in a succession of levels. At one level there is the gathering of records of experiments others have carried out. Then there are those who try new experiments, followed by those who draw all of these results together:

> We have three that draw the experiments of the former four into titles and tables, to give the better light for the drawing of observations and axioms out of them. These we call Compilers.[74]

The division of labour becomes still more evident when we encounter a level of researchers who go through all this information so carefully organized to see what of use can be drawn from it, both what has practical value and what provides clues to the underlying causes of phenomena:

> We have three that bend themselves, looking into the experiments of their fellows, and cast about how to draw out of them things of use and practice for man's life, and knowledge as well for works as for plain demonstration of causes, means of natural divinations, and the easy and clear discovery of the virtues and parts of bodies. These we call Dowry-men or Benefactors.[75]

Still another level, taking advantage of what has so far been learned, designs new experiments. Then comes a level whose members conduct these experiments and report the results. Finally, we have those who interpret all the resultant material so as to arrive at general principles governing nature. The whole operation employs others to carry out the more menial tasks involved.

Bacon here has done nothing less than conceive the idea of scientific research as an industry exhibiting a minute division of labour whereby different aspects of the work of acquiring knowledge are assigned to different people, all of whom depend on one another for their own success. Salomon's House is in effect a clearing house for the scientific researches of many people, even those in foreign lands. (It was to serve as the model for the Royal Society when it was formed toward the end of the century.) Bacon has also placed experiment, often with sophisticated techniques and equipment, at the heart of the enterprise. He fully realizes that Europe has seen much progress in the development of the mechanical arts and in horticulture, that this sort of practical knowledge can be of benefit to our basic understanding of nature, and that that understanding can in turn call forth new advances in technology. We have here the prescient idea of a marriage of science and technology, a union that a couple of centuries later would totally remake the world. There can be no doubt that Bacon's general idea for reform of how knowledge was obtained and used was far more powerful than the scholastic method it sought to replace, both in terms of generating insight into how the natural world works and in coming up with ways to improve the human condition.

What Salomon's House is not, however, is an educational institution, a school for disseminating knowledge among the general populace. In this it is totally unlike Andreae's *Christianopolis,* and this is because Bacon does not see scientific knowledge as improving human moral character or Christian piety, in the way Andreae did. Salomon's House is a "research and development" hub, not a university, and its goals are intensely practical, "the relief of man's estate."

In a much earlier work Bacon was keen to justify his advocacy for the advancement of knowledge against the objections of some Christian divines. He focused then on how to interpret the Genesis account of the Fall. It was not knowledge of nature that the serpent tempted Adam and Eve with, but the knowledge of good and evil:

> For behold it was not that pure light of natural knowledge, whereby man in paradise was able to give unto every creature a name according to his propriety, which gave occasion to the fall; but it was an aspiring desire to attain to that part of moral knowledge which defineth of good and evil, whereby to dispute God's commandments and not to depend on the revelation of his will which was the original temptation.[76]

The implications of Bacon's reading of the biblical story are quite enormous. Ethics rests not on reasoning about what we observe in this world but on the Holy Scriptures, which reveal what sort of life God wants us to live, namely the life of charity. Seeking to find some other source for this knowledge is what brought about the Fall. But the knowledge of the natural world is something we are free to undertake, and it can be pushed to the limits of human possibilities. Bacon is clear in this treatise that mixing the inquiries into nature with those into the divine nature and will is a recipe for disaster:

> To conclude, the prejudice hath been infinite that both divine and human knowledge hath received by the intermingling and tempering of the one with the other; as that which hath filled the one with heresies, and the other with speculative fictions and vanities.[77]

Bacon goes so far as to deny that from natural philosophy any inferences about the nature of God can be inferred:

> It is true that the contemplation of the creatures of God hath for end (as to the natures of the creatures themselves) knowledge, but as to the nature of God, no knowledge, but wonder; which is nothing else but contemplation broken off, or losing itself... And this appeareth sufficiently in that there is no proceeding in invention of knowledge but by similitude; and God is only self-like, having nothing in common with any creature, otherwise than as in shadow and trope.[78]

Knowledge of nature, in contrast to knowledge of God, is something man's mind has been fitted for in its original creation:

> So as whatever is not God but parcel of the world, he hath fitted it to the comprehension of man's mind, if man will but open and dilate the powers of his understanding as he may.[79]

In fact, the advancement of knowledge of nature is the recovery of what man had as his natural endowment before the Fall. In this Bacon aligns himself with an idea as old as the ninth century in the thought of John Scotus Eriugena.[80] Bacon writes as follows:

> And therefore it is not the pleasure of curiosity, nor the quiet of resolution, nor the raising of the spirit, nor victory of wit, nor faculty of speech, nor lucre of profession, nor ambition of honour or fame, nor enablement of business, that are the true ends of knowledge; some of these being more worthy than others, though all inferior and degenerate: but it is a restitution and reinvesting (in great part) of man to the sovereignty and power (for whensoever he shall be able to call the creatures by their true names he shall again command them) which he had in his first state of creation. And to speak plainly and clearly, it is a discovery of all operations

and possibilities of operations from immortality (if it were possible) to the meanest mechanical practice.[81]

Note that in this passage Bacon is very clear that knowledge means power over the other creatures (a restoration of the dominion that God had given mankind) and the discovery of "operations," that is, of the means of improving human life, even possibly of finding a way to immortality. We see then that Bacon viewed his energetic appeal for support for the sciences as playing an important role in the great Judeo-Christian cosmic drama whereby mankind is working its way out of its disastrous Fall.

Viewing Bacon's efforts in the light of his interpretation of the Genesis account of the Fall, we can see that his warnings in his treatise *Novum Organum* about the various "idols" of the mind are an attempt to clear away the obstacles to human understanding that were visited on humanity as a result of Adam's original sin in the Garden of Eden. Note how in the following passage Bacon speaks of a "restoration" of man's faculties:

> The idols and false notions that have hitherto occupied the human understanding, and lie deep-seated there, have not only so beset men's minds that their approach to truth becomes difficult; but even when access to it is given and conceded, they will present themselves and interfere in that very restoration of the science, unless men are forewarned and protect themselves against them as far as possible.[82]

Indeed, "restoration" is probably the most accurate English translation of *instauratio* as it appears in the title of Bacon's great unfinished work *Instauratio Magna*. It was not just a desire to increase the prosperity of King James's realm and its subjects that motivated Bacon, but a vision of his work as playing a pivotal role in the ancient cosmic drama of the Fall and Redemption of humanity as he viewed it.

Bacon believed that the scriptures prophesied that in the last days there would be such a revival of learning. In this, he relied on a passage we noted earlier from the Book of Daniel, which was referred to frequently in seventeenth-century England:

> For to my understanding, it is not violent to the letter, and safe now after the event, so to interpret that place in the prophecy of Daniel where speaking of the latter times it is said, *Many shall pass to and fro, and science shall be increased*; as if the opening of the world by navigation and commerce and the further discovery of knowledge should meet in one time or age.[83]

Bacon, then, embraced many of the millenarian aspirations that, as we have seen, were revived in the late medieval period. But whereas then it was largely the oppressed masses who found in these phantasies a ground for hope and even for resistance against oppressive elites, now it was a paradigmatic member of the elite who was attracted to this cosmic picture.

And yet Bacon was aware that knowledge could be abused.

> Wherefore seeing that knowledge is of the number of those things which are to be accepted of with caution and distinction…I thought it good and necessary in the first place to make a strong head or bank to rule and guide the course of the waters; by setting down this position or firmament, namely, *that all knowledge is to be limited by religion, and to be referred to use and action*.[84]

Religion, then, is to be relied on to supply the ethical constraints that science might threaten to breach, and it does this by decreeing that knowledge must be used for the benefit of mankind, just as we noted earlier in a passage from *The Advancement of Learning*. Natural science cannot overthrow the ethical demands of the Christian religion, since those demands depend on revelation, not observation and reason. As long as the scientist respects those demands, he is free to explore all "the operations and possibilities of operations" that arise from his investigations. Since, as we saw, the natural scientist can have no grounds on which to challenge those ethical demands, the realm of ethics remains autonomous and secure against any inroads by the natural philosophers. Herein lies the true significance of the way the Bensalemites in *New Atlantis* have received the Christian religion. It is handed down from on high in a visible miracle that is acknowledged as authoritative by the head of

Salomon's House. The story symbolizes the acceptance by science of the ethical constraints established by God himself on the practice of scientific investigation. Thus Bacon has outlined one possible solution to the supposed conflict between science and religion: science may proceed full throttle with its investigations and amassing of knowledge as long as it directs that endeavour and its results solely to the "relief of man's estate," that is man's increased prosperity and dominance over nature, which are the divinely revealed goals for mankind. But it has to acknowledge its own inability to ground any alternative ethical framework, let alone knowledge of God's will.

Shortly after the publication of *New Atlantis*, two scholarly interpretations of biblical prophecies about the Last Days appeared and excited interest in the sort of millenarian ideas that, as we have seen, were already present in Bacon's world view. These were Joseph Mede's *Clavis Apocalyptica* and Johann Heinrich Alsted's *Mille Annis Apocalypticis Diatribe*. Mede was a professor at Cambridge and taught both John Milton and Henry More. Milton could be extremely florid when it came to the possibilities that were open to the progress of mankind:

> He [i.e., Man] will indeed seem to be one whose rule and dominion the stars obey, to whose command earth and sea hearken, and whom winds and tempests serve; to whom, lastly, Mother Nature herself has surrendered, as if indeed some god had abdicated the throne of the world and entrusted its rights, laws, and administration to him as governor.[85]

Here it is not just the earth and its living creatures that fall under man's possible dominion but the starry heavens as well.

Milton was for a time part of a circle that gathered around Samuel Hartlib (1600–1662) and John Dury (1596–1680), who together tirelessly promoted educational reform and the unification of the various Protestant sects before, during, and after the Puritan revolution in Britain.[86] Hartlib and Dury firmly believed in education as the chief means to both spiritual and material reform, and like Bacon they opposed medieval scholasticism, whose remnants still dominated the universities. In its place they advocated a much more empirical approach to natural science and an appreciation of the mechanical arts. In the grammar schools they proposed new methods for the teaching of languages, inclusive of Latin, Greek, and Hebrew, and produced textbooks for this purpose. They had a strong interest in the improvement of the conditions of poor people and in general shared Bacon's thesis that learning in the natural sciences should aim at the improvement of man's material prosperity.

In these efforts they were joined in 1641 by another ardent enthusiast of Bacon's ideas, the Moravian Jan Amos Komensky (1592–1670), better known as Comenius, who had quite grandiose ideas for a "pansophia," that is, an encyclopaedic knowledge based in Neoplatonism and infused with deeply millenarian beliefs. Pansophia went far beyond anything Bacon had proposed in its idea of the harmony of all nature and in its attempt to unify knowledge from three great sources: sense, reason, and revelation. Bacon's ideas for the "advancement of learning" were decidedly secular; Comenius's ideas brought together spiritual and religious aims with the goals of material progress. Hartlib and Dury had grown dissatisfied with Bacon's secularism and became enthusiastic supporters of Comenius's ideas for reform.

Also strongly influencing this group of reformers were the utopian works of Johann Andreae, whose *Christianopolis* we have already discussed. Andreae had the idea of a society of learned Christians who could be advisers to a utopian state that would institute the sort of educational system described in *Christianopolis*. According to the great scholar of intellectual movements in seventeenth-century Britain, Charles Webster, this constituted a good part of the inspiration for a utopian fiction, *Macaria*, which was written in 1641 by Gabriele Plattes, a close associate of the Hartlib circle, as part of an effort to sell the British Parliament on its program of educational reform.[87]

Macaria takes the form of a dialogue between a scholar and a traveller who comes bearing a tale of a land he has just visited that is unknown to Europe, called "Macaria." The traveller puts heavy emphasis on the advances Macaria has made in husbandry so that a much enlarged population may be supported on the available land. He suggests that England could do the same:

> I will propound a book of Husbandry to the high Court of Parliament, whereby the Kingdome may maintaine double the

number of people, which it doth now, and in more plenty and prosperity, than now they enjoy…

…Why should not all the inhabitants of England joyne with one consent, to make this country to bee like to *Macaria*, that is numerous in people, rich in treasure and munition, that so they may bee invincible?[88]

Unity of religious belief is also highly valued in Macaria, where stringent measures are taken to suppress any ideological novelties, although once a year anyone who wishes to introduce new ideas is given a chance to present them before a "Grand Councell," which proceeds to pass judgment on them.

Comenius eagerly joined in the effort to get support for Hartlib and Dury's proposals by writing *Via Lucis* (*Way of Light*), in which he promoted the idea of a "Universal College" made up of good Christians who would direct religious and educational reform. He advocated providing education not just for the well-off but for the poor as well, not just for men but for women too, and of course that education would be guided by the principles of his pansophia.[89] His vision is otherwise not unlike Bacon's Salomon's House. He writes as follows:

For this task fit men will be chosen from the whole world, men of quick and industrious temper, of piety, warmly devoted to the welfare of the people, taken indifferently from laymen engaged in public affairs and of ecclesiastics; these must be set, as it were, in a watch-tower, to look out for the well-being of mankind, and to see every possible way, means, or occasion of seeking whatever will be beneficial to all men.[90]

In addition, Comenius recommended the formation in England of a clearing house for communications from all over Europe and America relating the course and results of investigations and progress undertaken to serve the advancement of learning. All these efforts by the Hartlib circle were interrupted by the outbreak of civil war in 1642; but once the supremacy of Parliament was secured, the proposal was revived in the form of advocating for an "Office of Address," something Hartlib and Dury conceived in

1646 and made public in 1647.[91] The office was to be divided into one for "Accommodations" and one for "Communications," the former concerned with a kind of learned labour exchange and the latter being a clearing house for reports of investigations. Hartlib and Dury, joined at this time by Robert Boyle and other natural scientists, became almost entirely concerned with this Office of Communications. The information to be collected would concern "matters of Religion, of Learning, and of all Ingenuities, which are objects of Contemplation and delight unto the Mind, for their strangenesse and usefulnesse unto the life of Man."[92] By "Ingenuities" was meant "the most profitable Inventions"—profitable, that is, to the state.

Efforts were made in 1649 to persuade Parliament to fund this agency and assign it care not only of correspondence but of all schools and schoolmasters. At first the proposal seemed to be having some success, but the Irish War distracted Parliament, and it was only after its conclusion that a new version received serious attention. This time the agency's concerns were almost entirely secular. Part of its mandate was "for the making some further progresse & Advancement in a useful improvement of Experiments, to the more cleare elucidation as well of things Naturall as Artificiall."[93] These efforts too had no immediate success, but after the restoration of the monarchy the idea for a Royal Society was approved by Charles II and given a charter in 1660. Its aims were entirely along the lines of developing the natural sciences and mathematics. Although the original inspiration for such a society had come from the Hartlib circle, Hartlib and Dury were not among the founders, and the founding members of the society were loath to acknowledge that connection since they wanted to avoid contentious issues of religion and politics. Bacon's secular vision of Salomon's House had won out.[94] Although on the continent Leibniz indefatigably promoted a utopian vision that combined reverence for science with a universal Christianity that would unite all the peoples of the world, his was, as the Manuels say, "the last great utopian vision that derived its meaning from the love of God and the exploration of His world."[95] Other Christian utopias of the late seventeenth and early eighteenth centuries, like those of Fénelon and Fleury, were adamantly opposed to the modern and argued for a return to some mythical Arcadian existence. They would not significantly influence the trajectory of Western culture.

The implications of the victory of the secular but millenarian approach to natural science, whose ultimate results for human civilization would not emerge for another two centuries, can be gauged if we draw a comparison between the Baconian utopian vision, the road taken, and the utopia first discussed in this chapter, that is, Thomas More's, the road rejected.

First, More's Utopia rests on a social regime radically different from that of early modern Western Europe. Utopia is socially egalitarian to the point of being communistic. The Bensalem of Bacon's *New Atlantis*, in contrast, is based on rule by an elite, and except for the fact that that elite is made up of learned men, especially natural scientists, rather than monarchs and feudal lords, it is not all that different from what Europe exhibited in Bacon's own day.

Second, material prosperity is maintained in More's Utopia by having every able-bodied person work at the tasks necessary for provisioning the community amply, but not luxuriously. In this system the hours any one person works are few enough to make possible a great deal of leisure time to pursue educational activities. In Bacon's Bensalem prosperity is achieved through the development of the practical arts by the application of the results of scientific research. In other words, improved technology relieves people of most heavy work and makes possible a very luxurious life style, at least for some. The citizens of Utopia have a positive distaste for luxury and disdain those who are enamoured of it. Bensalemites, in contrast, are deeply impressed by the luxury of their rulers. The attitude among Utopians is that time is wasted on the production of luxuries, and this mild asceticism enables them to have more leisure hours.

Third, the virtues of good moral character are emphasized in Utopia, while in Bensalem priority is given to maintaining material prosperity for all citizens. There is an obvious difference here in the conceptions of what a good human life consists in: Utopians have returned to the doctrines of the ancient philosophers, while the only virtue espoused in Bensalem is Christian charity.

Fourth, knowledge of nature in More's Utopia is valued chiefly because it inspires wonder and appreciation of God's creation, not for any practical benefits. In Bensalem, in contrast, the chief aim of investigations into natural science is practical benefit for the citizens.

Fifth, and finally, knowledge in Utopia is supposed to reside in and improve the individual possessor. In Bensalem the work of scientific investigation is so divided among many people that only the corporate body of inquirers is improved, not the individuals.

Neither *New Atlantis* nor *Utopia* put forward reforms that could be carried out quickly in the European society of the times in which they were written, although both in effect suggested some steps toward reform that could have been adopted fairly soon. Raphael, the sailor who relates the account of Utopia, rages against the extreme punishments meted out in the Europe of his day to the poor caught stealing, a cruelty that could have been corrected by legislation. Bacon's proposal for gathering the results of scientific and technological experiments from many quarters was actually put into effect with the founding of the Royal Society four decades after his death. What is really important to see in these writings is that very different routes for change and improvement in society are clearly envisioned by the authors. One of these routes, More's, would surely in the end have led to economic stasis and a technological development that would probably have come to rest in pretty much the condition of the practical arts and sciences that Europe was to attain in the middle of the eighteenth century, that is, something that would have been about as advanced as what China already had when More wrote. Although, no doubt, this would have occasioned considerable ecological damage in Western Europe itself, it would no more have led to planetary eco-catastrophe than had China's development.

But More's vision was not the one that would eventually be followed. Rather, as we shall see, by the mid-nineteenth century it was clear that Bacon's vision, now totally secularized and bereft of the religious constraints that Bacon himself advocated, was the one the West was following, and that this program was vastly more economically and technologically powerful not only than anything the Utopian way could have produced but even than what Bacon himself and his followers could have dreamed of. Bensalem did indeed possess the potential for planetary ecological disaster. But it is quite possible that moderate measures along the lines Bacon suggested could have been carried out in a carefully circumscribed way without such dire environmental results. And indeed for some time they were adopted, albeit in a limited fashion, and Western Europe and its American colonies were, on the whole, none the worse for it. The rest of our story is largely one of how the Baconian program was released from the ideological (i.e., philosophical and religious) bonds that helped keep it in check.

At the same time, there are two facts about the program that from the start tended to impel it to ever grander goals. The first was its embedding in the millenarian cosmic drama that we have already described in some detail. People working in all the practical arts as well as natural philosophers could envision themselves as part of a magnificent divinely sanctioned enterprise aimed at restoring human beings to the dominant place for which they were originally intended. Once they thought of themselves in that way, the participants in the program were not likely to think that barriers to its progress were in any way legitimate. They were much more likely to see such barriers as manifestations of the very ignorance and prejudices they were trying to overcome.

The second fact was that the program was one devised by the elite and to be carried out by the elite in the service of humanity in general. As such it had great appeal to the *Kürwille* mentality that characterizes the *Gesellschaft* elites of any urban-dominated civilization. Theoretical science is itself paradigmatically a sophisticated refinement of rational thinking about the world, and its marriage partner, the practical arts, are, of course, examples of *Kürwille* at work designing means to reach practical ends. More than that, the ideal of Bensalem suggests that theoretical science coupled with practical technology should be put to work designing a new sort of society. Of course, designing society through technical expertise had been the force behind the earliest development of cities and the urban-centred civilizations of Mesopotamia, and a hallmark of all such civilizations ever since. It is much easier to see Bacon's project as one readily adapted to *Kürwille* thinking and planning than the other utopias we have discussed, all of which put much emphasis on education and improvement of character. Such an endeavour lends itself to some extent to rational planning, but the ends in view are so much harder to define in any precise way than the ends of mechanical arts are, that it is not clear how to design the means to achieve them. In the case of More's Utopia there is the added problem that the improvements envisioned rest on already existent customs that the people long ago adopted. Changing people's customs is not something one can accomplish through a premeditated, well thought-out plan, as the failures of so many efforts of that sort in history demonstrate. And this is, I suggest, the most fundamental difference between More's vision and Bacon's: the former is not millenarian, More is not proposing any practical proposal for radical change, but Bacon is, and he views his proposals as forwarding a divine, providential plan for humanity.

In conclusion, we can see that the Baconian vision for the future fit much better than More's, or Andreae's, or Ott's with the *Gesellschaft* dominance that characterizes any urban-centred civilization. (Indeed, pursuing the other visions might well have undermined that dominance.) Couple this with the wide acceptance of its role in a phantastic cosmic story relating that it was God's plan that through implementation of Bacon's vision humanity would be uplifted to its rightful place as Lord of the physical universe, and you have an idea with an appeal to the affective imagination unequalled since John's *Apocalypse*; and this time the appeal is mainly to the elite, who can actually effect some of what they project, and not so much to the oppressed masses, whose efforts are either ineffectual or lead to grotesque social disasters like the one on Mount Tabor in the 1420s or the one in Münster in 1535.

7

SECULARIZING THE MILLENNIUM

> The great aim of modern life has been to improve the future—or even just to reach the future, assuming that the future will inevitably be "better."
> —Wendell Berry, *The Unsettling of America*

Although at the end of the seventeenth century Bacon's vision of material improvement of human life through science and technology was gaining adherents, the Puritan appeal for education leading to moral improvement and greater adherence to pietistic standards of conduct was still central to most conceptions of what improvement was to consist of. As long as that held sway, the utopian vision people held contained a serious counterweight to any emphasis on technological advancement and economic expansion. The belief in the original Fall of humans in the Garden of Eden was usually taken to mean that within all people thereafter there was an inherent tendency toward immorality and wrongdoing, not to mention cowardice and folly. Human nature may have been created noble and upright, but it now suffered from serious corruption. Where Bacon had thought that the result of the Fall had been the loss of knowledge of the natural world and of the practical arts, most Christians, and especially Protestants, thought it had been an inability to refrain from sin. Corrupted human nature needed moral reform if any substantial improvement in life was to occur, and the way to this was proper education.

As Western Europe moved into the eighteenth century and into what we in the West like to call "the Enlightenment," many thinkers left behind the mythical background for speculation about real human nature and its fallen condition and attempted to form entirely secular theories. Those theories were to have a profound impact on how utopian thought and practice were to evolve. In the end they facilitated the liberation of the originally religious impulse toward material progress from the emphasis on moral improvement through education that the religious context had placed on it, and gave that impulse permission to seek an entirely secular version of the millennium.

Mandeville's Fable

In 1705 Bernard Mandeville, a Dutch physician who had immigrated to England, published a poem called "The Grumbling Hive: or, Knaves Turn'd Honest," which later became the core of his *The Fable of the Bees*, published in 1714. This extraordinary work promotes the idea that the sophisticated prosperity of advanced societies is dependent on and in part promoted by moral vices and would be lost if virtue were to entirely extirpate its opposite. The poem recounts a fable in which, in the manner of La Fontaine, bees substitute for humans and their hive for a human society.

At the beginning of the poem the hive is described as very prosperous by the standards current in Western Europe of the time:

> A Spacious Hive well stock'd with Bees,
> That lived in Luxury and Ease;
> And yet as fam'd for Laws and Arms,
> As yielding large and early Swarms;
> Was counted the great Nursery
> Of Sciences and Industry.[1]

The engine of the hive's prosperity is linked to the "lust and vanity" of its members and to the fact that prosperity is not shared equally.

> Millions endeavouring to supply
> Each other's Lust and Vanity;
> Whilst other Millions were employ'd,
> To see their Handy-works destroy'd;
> They furnish'd half the Universe;
> Yet had more Work than Labourers.
> Some with vast Stocks, and little Pains
> Jump'd into Business of great Gains;[2]

Furthermore, there is plenty of exploitive cheating going on:

> As sharpers, parasites, pimps, players,
> Pickpockets, coiners, quacks, soothsayers,
> And all those, that in enmity,
> With downright working, cunningly
> Convert to their own use the labour
> Of their good-natur'd heedless neighbour.
> These were call'd Knaves, but bar the name,
> The grave industrious were the same:
> All trades and places knew some cheat,
> No calling was without deceit.[3]

The priesthood is no exception:

> Among the many priests of love,
> Hir'd to draw blessings from above,
> Some few were learn'd and eloquent,
> But thousands hot and ignorant:
> Yet all pass'd muster that could hide
> Their sloth, lust, avarice and pride;[4]

But all these human vices and morally despicable behaviours play an indispensable role in creating the affluence and power of the hive:

> Thus every Part was full of Vice,
> Yet the whole Mass a Paradice;
> Flatter'd in Peace, and fear'd in Wars
> They were th'Esteem of Foreigners,
> And lavish of their Wealth and Lives,
> The Ballance of all other Hives.
> Such were the Blessings of that State;
> Their Crimes conspired to make 'em Great;
> And Vertue, who from Politicks
> Had learn'd a Thousand cunning Tricks,
> Was, by their happy Influence,
> Made Friends with Vice: And ever since
> The worst of all the Multitude
> Did something for the common Good.[5]

The much derided vices of avarice, lust, and pride are engines of industry and trade:

> The Root of evil Avarice,
> That damn'd ill-natur'd baneful Vice,
> Was Slave to Prodigality,
> That Noble Sin; whilst Luxury
> Employ'd a Million of the Poor,
> And odious Pride a Million more.
> Envy itself, and Vanity
> Were Ministers of Industry;
> Their darling Folly, Fickleness
> In Diet, Furniture, and Dress,
> That strange, ridic'lous Vice, was made
> The very Wheel, that turn'd the Trade.[6]

To sum up, what we today call "progress" is due not to the increasing virtuousness of humanity but in large measure to those evils moralists have tried to expunge as much as possible from their fellow human beings:

> Thus Vice nursed Ingenuity,
> Which joind with Time; and Industry
> Had carry'd Life's Conveniencies,
> It's real Pleasures, Comforts, Ease,
> To such a Height, the very Poor
> Lived better than the Rich before;
> And nothing could be added more.[7]

As in any fable, Mandeville supplies a moral that reveals the real opponents the story is meant to skewer:

> T' enjoy the world's conveniences,
> Be fam'd in war, yet live in ease,
> Without great vices, is a vain
> Eutopia seated in the brain.
>
> So vice is beneficial found,
> When it's by justice lopp'd and bound;
> Nay, where the people would be great,
> As necessary to the state,
> As hunger is to make 'em eat.
> Bare virtue can't make nations live
> In splendor; they, that would revive
> A golden age, must be as free,
> For acorns as for honesty.[8]

It is those advocating a morally pure utopia that still contains all the affluence, cultural advances, worldly power, and full employment of the poorer classes, who Mandeville thinks totally misunderstand human nature and what creates a great society. Mandeville makes the point crystal clear in the Preface to the *Fable*:

> For the main design of the Fable...is to show the impossibility of enjoying all the most elegant comforts of life that are to be met

> with in an industrious, wealthy and powerful nation, and at the same time be blessed with all the virtue and innocence that can be wished for in a golden age, from thence to expose the unreasonableness and folly of those that desirous of being an opulent and flourishing people and wonderfully greedy after all the benefits they can receive as such, are yet always murmuring at and exclaiming against those vices and inconveniences that from the beginning of the world to this present day have been inseparable from all kingdoms and states that ever were famed for strength, riches, and politeness, at the same time.⁹

The target of Mandeville's story was, of course, the Puritan divines who were trying to combine in their utopias the absence of vice with the presence of affluence. But when we view it in relation to the ideas discussed in chapter 3 of this work, might we not see it as equally an assault on the Platonic ideal of a state where education has brought into existence a morally selfless ruling class and a populace willing to follow it, or on the Stoic idea of happiness lying entirely in the internalization of rational canons of behaviour, or on the Confucian ideal of the sage disciplined in the virtue of humanity? To be blunt, is it not an attack on those very modes of thought about human well-being that unwittingly restrained Chinese and Mediterranean civilizations from pursuing material advances to the point of endangering the whole planet's ecosystem?

Probably not. Certainly Plato, and the Stoics, would not have been troubled to find that moral purity was incompatible with the kind of affluence Mandeville's hive enjoys. That was not for them the ideal sort of society. And perhaps it was not for Mandeville either. In the Preface to the *Fable* he makes this confession:

> In the same manner, if laying aside all worldly greatness and vainglory, I should be asked where I thought it was most probable that men might enjoy true happiness, I would prefer a small peaceable society, in which men, neither envied nor esteemed by neighbours, should be contented to live upon the natural product of the spot they inhabit, to a vast multitude abounding in wealth and power

that should always be conquering others by their arms abroad and debauching themselves by foreign luxury at home.[10]

The passage is preceded by a short description of the filth and congestion that confronts the person who travels the streets of early eighteenth-century London and by Mandeville's observation that all this ugliness cannot be lessened without making London less flourishing. His point here is that the same can be said of moral impropriety and that just as noting the inevitability of garbage-strewn streets in a flourishing city does not entail being in favour of filth and congestion and ceasing to do what one can to reduce them, so noting that moral impropriety cannot be lessened without decreasing a society's "flourishing" does not entail being for immorality and ceasing to advocate against it. In this way Mandeville can defend himself against the charge of being an unabashed advocate for vice. But the passage just quoted seems to imply that in Mandeville's own judgment all this flourishing leads away from the "true happiness" of human beings, and that is a sentiment Plato and the Stoics would have fully approved. Is that his real view, or is it a ruse to avoid the official censure of the authorities?

It is certainly the case that Mandeville thinks a good measure of justice and morally respectable behaviour is a necessary condition for the gathering of humans together into a society. In the moral of the poem itself he says that for vice to be beneficial it must be "by justice lopp'd and bound." By Mandeville's own argument, society can only survive if humans learn to restrain many of their self-regarding passions and appetites. It emerges from later works that Mandeville believed that to render humans sociable to one another they must hide these appetites from others. From infancy they are taught to be hypocrites and to deny that they experience such desires. This is reinforced by the inculcation of the concepts of virtue and vice, ideas originally sponsored by wise politicians who saw that people were easily susceptible to flattery and thus could be brought around to the view that they were superior to the beasts on account of their distinctive rational faculty, and that to succumb to the base appetites humans have in common with animals generally was to betray this superiority. The passion of pride was thus drawn upon to restrain such appetites, and people became ashamed of capitulating to them and even feeling them to any marked degree. Since reason grasped the utility of society for human existence, any acts that were purely self-regarding, rather than taken to forward the general good, came to be viewed as contrary to humanity's superior nature. The impulse to forward the common good even when contrary to one's own appetites was termed "virtue," while the impulse to promote one's own benefit was named "vice." But reason would have little effect on our conduct were it not bolstered by pride in this mythical superiority, and pride is itself a self-regarding passion. Thus, one passion is used to curb others and make a human being fit for a well-run, reasonably orderly society.

In his *Inquiry into the Origin of Moral Virtue* (which forms part of a later edition of the *Fable*), Mandeville speculates that this whole process was contrived by avaricious "politicians," who saw the benefit that would come to them from manipulating people into the frame of mind where it seemed to them shameful to go about satisfying one's own appetites at the cost to society in general. He makes this quite clear in the following passage:

> It being the interest then of the very worst of them, more than any, to preach up public-spiritedness...they agreed with the rest to call everything, which, without regard to the public, man should commit to gratify any of his appetites, VICE; if in that action there could be observed the least prospect that it might either be injurious to any of the society or even render himself less serviceable to others; and to give the name of VIRTUE to every performance, by which man, contrary to the impulses of nature, should endeavour the benefit of others or the conquest of his own passions out of a rational ambition of being good.[11]

He concludes with a famous summation:

> And the nearer we search into human nature, the more we shall be convinced that the moral virtues are the political offspring which flattery begot upon pride.[12]

It is then the weakness humans generally have to think well of themselves, that is, to be proud, that seduces them into thinking there is something shameful about giving way to appetites shared with beasts, that is, passions of a self-regarding sort. They are so enchanted with the view of themselves as elevated far above the other animals that they take pride in curtailing what they share with them and, in general, restraining anything purely self-regarding. But pride is itself self-regarding, so in the end respect for morality itself results from a self-regarding passion. The supposedly virtuous persons then are really a species of hypocrite in that they proclaim the shamefulness of self-regarding behaviour while themselves engaging in it.

All this might be thought a mere cynical appraisal of the human condition, but Mandeville puts this twist upon it: A society with a decent amount of order is impossible without this hypocrisy, and society is well advised to promote it. So in the end it is something reasonable to espouse as long as you are interested in such a society, and who is not? On the other hand, it is unwise for a society interested in grandeur to carry it so far as to extinguish all vice, for a fair measure of envy, avarice, laziness, gluttony, fickleness, and even a certain amount of cheating also promote and are necessary for the affluence that Mandeville saw around him in Western Europe.

It is interesting from our own standpoint to note how much Mandeville defends vices on account of their contribution to what we call economic prosperity, that is, increased trade and full employment. A couple of examples drawn from his remarks on his own poem will suffice to show how he argues this point. Here he defends envy:

> We all look above ourselves and, as fast as we can, strive to imitate those that some way or other are superior to us...
> To this emulation and continual striving to outdo one another it is owing that after so many various shiftings and changes of modes, in trumping up new ones and renewing of old ones, there is still a *plus ultra* left for the ingenious; it is this, or at least the consequence of it, that sets the poor to work, adds spurs to industry, and encourages the skilful artificer to search after further improvements.[13]

This is surely a familiar theme: most of us are driven not simply by the pleasure of using comforts and conveniences but by the desire to be at least equal to all others in acquiring them. Furthermore, styles continually change just to satisfy the desire to excel others in some way, and this makes what has been produced now obsolete, thereby creating a demand for what is new and different. Without such an impetus, invention, industry, and employment would hardly be as extensive as they are. Another example is the fickleness of women:

> The variety of work that is performed and the number of hands employed to gratify the fickleness and luxury of women is prodigious, and if only the married ones should hearken to reason and just remonstrances, think themselves sufficiently answered with the first refusal, and never ask a second time what had been once denied them...the consumption of a thousand things they now make use of would be lessened by at least a fourth part...I do not speak now of profuse and extravagant women, but such as are counted prudent and moderate in their desires.[14]

Mandeville has fully grasped some important truths: the economy of a modern commercial nation is highly dependent on a high level of consumption among the well-off; such a level can only be maintained if such people in large measure disregard the strictures of moralists about self-indulgence; and, finally, a high level of consumption is needed to maintain full employment among the working class. Thus people who engage in these vices (and Mandeville genuinely believes they are vices) in promoting their own pleasures actually also promote general affluence without intending it. This old idea of the unintended but beneficial results of things we think of as bad would come to have a tremendous influence on Western thought later in the century.

Mandeville's analysis of the human condition places moral virtue in a very ambiguous position. On the one hand the general respect for moral virtue, or at least the usual partial acquiescence to its demands, is essential to any human society and a comfortable life. But on the other hand, the motivation to respect it is founded in a belief in human reason's huge superiority to the capacities of other animals, a belief that Mandeville thinks is groundless and has been foisted on us by self-interested political leaders. His view is that human beings are governed by passions and appetites just as are other animals and that reason by itself is powerless unless some passion or other is brought to its aid. Here we have the direct opposite of the Stoicism we saw promulgated by Justus Lipsius. Such an estimate of human nature has remained a viable philosophic option down to the present day, and the conflict with variants of Stoicism has never been resolved.

The most important consequence of Mandeville's analysis, however, is to cast doubt on any utopian dream that tries to combine moral purity with material affluence. That was certainly the dream of some of the Puritan reformers of the preceding century. His analysis also dispensed with the myth of the Fall. Human nature is of itself inevitably prone to self-regarding desires and habits, and the only way to tame it into something fit for social living is to turn one of these habits against the others. How much you want to promote this kind of self-effacement depends on how much you also want material affluence and grandeur, for the latter will not be much satisfied if the former is given total sway.

Rousseau on the Evils of Civilization

If Mandeville is somewhat ambivalent regarding the benefits of an advanced civilization, the French thinker Jean Jacques Rousseau (1712–1778), who wrote in the mid-eighteenth century, is not. His conclusion is that it has been an unmitigated disaster and that humans were much more admirable and better off when they lived in some very simple and unsophisticated society in which they were allowed to express their innate impulses.

In his 1750 essay *Discourse on the Sciences and the Arts*, Rousseau, while declaring that the study of man needs further work, maintains that the development of the sophisticated sciences and arts has led to a decline in people's moral character by helping to enslave them. Here we find a neat twist on the myth of the Fall. What Christianity had attributed to a just punishment for choosing to seek godlike knowledge Rousseau sees as a result of the knowledge that humans themselves have created:

> While the government and the laws see to the safety and well-being of assembled men, the sciences, letters and the arts, less despotic and perhaps more powerful, spread garlands of flowers over the iron

> chains with which they are burdened, stifle in them *the sense of that original liberty for which they seem to have been born*, make them love slavery, and turn them into civilized peoples. [my emphasis]¹⁵

According to Rousseau in this essay, the development of the arts had led to people's real characters being less transparent:

> Before art had fashioned our manners and taught our passions to speak an affected language, our mores were rustic but natural, and differences in behavior heralded, at first glance, differences of character.¹⁶

In other words, the sophistication of our way of life has led to more dissimulation, pretence, and hypocrisy than when we were in a more natural state. Furthermore, science has thrust us into luxury, dissolution, and slavery. We should never have involved ourselves in the tiresome effort to uncover nature's secrets:

> Peoples, know then once and for all that nature wanted to protect you from science just as a mother wrests a dangerous weapon from the hands of her child; that all the secrets she hides from you are so many evils from which she is protecting you, and that the difficulty you find in teaching yourselves is not the least of her kindnesses.¹⁷

Here is an astonishing declaration that science, and sophisticated arts in general, do not come naturally to humans, but are something that is actually *against* basic human nature. Note the radical departure from the idea that the arts were innately possessed before the Fall. And then, further, Rousseau claims that nature was beneficent to us in making it so hard to acquire them. Nothing more opposed to the Baconian dream explored in the previous chapter can be imagined.

Rousseau is especially contemptuous of luxury, which he says "seldom thrives without the sciences and the arts, and they never without it":

> Precisely what, then, is at issue in this question of luxury? To know whether it is more important for empires to be brilliant and fleeting, or virtuous and long-lasting. I say brilliant, but by what luster? The taste for ostentation is hardly ever combined in the same souls with the taste for honesty. No, it is not possible for minds degraded by a multitude of futile needs ever to rise to anything great; and even if they had the strength, they would lack the courage.[18]

The claim seems to be that the simple virtues are what give strength to the state and that sophistication leads to decline. Rousseau is particularly concerned about the decline of the "military virtues":

> The Romans admitted that military virtue died out among them in proportion as they had begun to become connoisseurs of paintings, engravings, goldsmiths' vessels, and to cultivate the fine arts.[19]

Citizenship is neglected, even despised:

> We have physicists, geometers, chemists, astronomers, poets, musicians, painters; we no longer have citizens.[20]

Rousseau expressed a nostalgia for simpler times, a revulsion against the changes and supposed improvements in the culture of his day. He asks: Isn't what is necessary to know for a genuinely good life something fairly simple that is innate in us?:

> O virtue! Sublime science of simple souls, are there so many difficulties and so much preparation necessary in order to know you? Are your principles not engraved in all hearts, and is it not enough, in order to learn your laws, to commune with oneself and, in the silence of the passions, to listen to the voice of one's conscience?[21]

What is innate in human nature, then, is not the arts and sciences, or even a proclivity for them, but a basic sense of moral right and wrong. That sense is obscured by all the sophistication of civilization.

Rousseau's belief that basic human nature is good and is only corrupted by civilization comes out even more clearly in his *Discourse on the Origin of Inequality* (1755). He begins by pleading for the study of man:

> Of all the branches of human knowledge, the most useful and the least advanced seems to me to be that of man; and I dare say that the inscription on the temple at Delphi alone contained a precept more important and more difficult than all the huge tomes of the moralists.[22]

But to understand humans you have to get back to the way nature first formed them before all the changes introduced by society:

> And how will man be successful in seeing himself as nature formed him, through all the changes that the succession of time and things must have produced in his original constitution, and in separating what he derives from his own wherewithal from what circumstances and his progress have added to or changed in his primitive state?[23]

Rousseau thinks he sees two principles that were originally implanted in human beings and that suffice for providing a good but simple life. These are each person's interest in their own well-being and self-preservation, and "a natural repugnance to seeing any sentient being, especially our fellow man, perish or suffer."

Putting humans into society is like domesticating a wild animal:

> It might be said that all our efforts at feeding them and treating them well only end in their degeneration. It is the same for man himself. In becoming habituated to the ways of society and a slave, he becomes weak, fearful, and servile; his soft and

> effeminate lifestyle completes the enervation of both his strength and his courage.[24]

> In instinct alone, man had everything he needed in order to live in the state of nature; in a cultivated reason, he has only what he needs to live in society.[25]

Rousseau speculates that the formation of society goes hand-in-hand with the institution of property. In order to secure a more reliable means of subsistence, people began to develop tools and hunting equipment, and individuals appropriated to themselves such things. They learned then that matters could be improved in many situations by cooperation, and this led to family life. Rousseau also thinks that language was an invention of this stage. Invidious distinctions between people began to be made as some were esteemed and others not. Nevertheless, Rousseau holds that probably this initial state of society was the best period for human beings.

Once metallurgy and agriculture appear, however, property becomes much more significant and rules for what belongs to whom become necessary. This is the origin of justice. The natural differences among men lead to inequalities in property, and a gap between the rich and the poor opens up. From this come conflict and violence. In order to restore peace the rich say to the poor:

> Let us institute rules of justice and peace to which all will be obliged to conform, which will make special exceptions for no one, and which will in some way compensate for the caprices of fortune by subjecting the strong and the weak to mutual obligations. In short, instead of turning our forces against ourselves, let us gather them into one supreme power that governs us according to wise laws, that protects and defends all the members of the association, repulses common enemies, and maintains us in an eternal concord.[26]

We have here Rousseau's answer to our question of what made people first establish urban-centred civilizations. Despite all his errors, Rousseau at least saw that civilization was something needing explanation. But Rousseau is far from thinking that the resulting society is desirable. He makes it sound very much like the society of the ancient urban-dominated civilizations we discussed in an earlier chapter:

> Such was, or should have been, the origin of society and laws, which gave new fetters to the weak and new forces to the rich, irretrievably destroyed natural liberty, established forever the law of property and of inequality, changed adroit usurpation into an irrevocable right, and for the profit of a few ambitious men henceforth subjected the entire human race to labor, servitude and misery.[27]

A pithier description of the initial trauma of urban civilization could hardly be devised. Rousseau carried his bitterness over this transition into his critique of his own Western European urban civilization. Like the ones before it, it has fettered, debilitated, and morally corrupted human beings, and this degeneration of humankind itself is not made up for by all the sophisticated arts, sciences, comforts, and conveniences this civilization provides; it is only deepened by them.

While Mandeville certainly had considerable appreciation of all these "benefits" of advanced civilization and would not have joined Rousseau in his Romantic diatribes against them, the real difference between the two lies in their views of human life before socialization, when humans were in the "state of nature." Mandeville realized that humans would have a very precarious existence at best without socialization. The remedy required first the summoning of pride to repress natural desires, and then this artificially induced pride provided the impulse to the moral behaviour socialization demands. He would have deemed totally naive Rousseau's belief that a basic sense of right and wrong was natural to humans. Rousseau's contribution to the story we are telling is his broaching the idea that in human life what is natural is good and what is artificial is bad. Mandeville realized that the artificial has brought with it most of the vices we deplore in humans, but he had no sympathy for the view that humans would be better off without the artificial. Rousseau was one with those philosophers of ancient times who thought human well-being lay in internalizing basic virtues, not in material comforts and sophisticated arts and knowledge. On that view, of course, the introduction of all the vices of civilization is an unmitigated disaster. But the question arises whether we can somehow combine the millennium of material progress with the idea that what is natural will better achieve that millennium than what is artificial. We shall see how an affirmative answer to this query comes to have increasing respect.

Adam Smith: The Natural Way is Best

Eighteenth-century Western Europe coupled with its colonies in the Americas had a civilization that many among the educated thought had achieved a hitherto unknown high level of prosperity and sophistication—this despite the prevalence of slavery, war, genocide, and marked inequality of affluence and power between the ruling class and the masses. In other words, all the major dysfunctions of all previous urban-centred civilizations were still present and unabated, but the educated saw themselves as liberated from the strictures of medieval religion and scholasticism, while indeed encountering greater affluence for a larger percentage of the population than Europeans had known at least since the days of ancient Rome. It could be expected, then, that thinkers would arise who objected to the ways that Mandeville and Rousseau, differently of course, had cast aspersions on that achievement. Adam Smith (1723–1790) was such a theorist.

His key work, at least for the purposes of this chapter, is his *Theory of Moral Sentiments*, first published in 1759 but successively revised by him right up to near his death in 1790. The chief aim of this work is to show that Stoic virtue is the perfection of something very natural to humans and that it arises out of a faculty for "sympathy" with the feelings of others, a faculty that human society could not exist without. What Smith means by "sympathy" is what we now call "empathy," that is, to so imagine what it is like to be "in someone else's shoes" that we in a way experience the feelings the other person might well be feeling in his or her situation. If we find that what we feel through imagining ourselves in that person's situation is very much the same as what that person is feeling in reality, we approve of that person's feelings and the behavioural reaction that accords with it. On the other hand, if we find that our reaction is a lot different from the other person's, we feel disapproval of their emotional state and behaviour. For example, if I witness someone accidentally spilling a glass of wine on another person's lap, and the latter flies into a violent fit of anger, while I, on the other hand, find that, when imagining myself in the victim's place, my reaction is much more given to regret and patience, consequently I, mentally at least, will be appalled at the person's reaction. In contrast, if the person who spilled the wine shows tremendous regret, apologizes profusely, and promises to pay for cleaning, my empathy with them engenders a similar reaction in me and I approve of the person's feelings and behaviour. This sort of approval and disapproval is for Smith the foundation of what we take to be right and wrong. Smith says the following:

> What is agreeable to our moral faculties, is fit, and right, and proper to be done; the contrary, wrong, unfit, and improper. The sentiments which they approve of are graceful and becoming; the contrary, ungraceful and unbecoming. The very words, right, wrong, fit improper, graceful, unbecoming, mean only what pleases or displeases those faculties.[28]

Following his friend David Hume, Smith does not think moral judgments have any claim to truth or falsity apart from human "sentimental" reactions to the situations they experience. This is not to say there is no real place for disagreement and argument between people making moral judgments, but resolving such disputes must always end up appealing to people's ability to empathize and emotionally react to the positions other people find themselves in.

But that is only the beginning of Smith's theory. He also finds it natural in almost all humans to feel discomfort when other people do not through empathy share much the same reaction to a situation as they do. They know then that the others are to one degree or another disapproving of their reaction, a knowledge that is naturally disturbing to the knower to one degree or another. This sort of feeling can lead people to restrain their displays of emotion so as to bring about the approval of others. Such dissimulation is the very thing Rousseau found so lamentable among people who had been "socialized" and is hardly very admirable even if it does conduce to polite interactions. Smith's theory agrees and moves beyond it by claiming that we have an even more powerful desire to bring our reactions in line, not so much with what our acquaintances will approve, but to bring them in line with what we, if we were to be an unbiased spectator to our own reactions, would approve of. To take up this position of psychological distance from ourselves and imagine that we are someone not directly involved in the situation we are in fact involved in, and then to ask ourselves what empathetic reaction we would have, is for Smith to consult one's conscience. He describes this capacity at length:

> We either approve or disapprove of our own conduct, according as we feel that, when we place ourselves in the situation of another man, and view it, as it were, with his eyes and from his station, we either can or cannot entirely enter into and sympathize with the sentiments and motives which influenced it. We can never survey our own sentiments and motives, we can never form any judgment concerning them, unless we remove ourselves, as it were, from our own natural station, and endeavour to view them as at a certain distance from us...
>
> We suppose ourselves the spectators of our own behaviour, and endeavour to imagine what effect it would, in this light, produce upon us. This is the only looking glass by which we can, in some measure, with the eyes of other people, scrutinize the propriety of our own conduct.[29]

> Man...desires not only praise, but praise worthiness; or to be that thing which, though it should be praised by nobody, is however, the natural and proper object of praise. He dreads, not only blame, but blame-worthiness; or to be that thing which, though it should be blamed by nobody, is, however, the natural and proper object of blame...
>
> Emulation, the anxious desire that we ourselves should excel, is originally founded in our admiration of the excellence of others. Neither can we be satisfied with being merely admired for what other people are admired. We must at least believe ourselves to be

admirable for what they are admirable. But, in order to attain this satisfaction, we must become the impartial spectators of our own character and conduct.[30]

The desire to bring one's own reactions into accord with this "impartial spectator"—"the man within the breast, the great judge and arbiter of their conduct," as he elsewhere calls it—is what we term the love of virtue. We now love what is right because it is right and not merely because it is approved of; we love what deserves to be approved of, not just what in fact is approved of. In this way Smith brings the Stoic virtues back into ethics within a distinctly un-Stoic meta-ethical framework based on a sort of empirical psychology of sentiments. In doing so he makes those virtues natural in a way that the nature-obsessed thinkers of the Enlightenment could understand, not in the way Christian scholasticism had proclaimed the naturalness of virtues. Stoic virtues arise out of practising reflection on and regulation of our feelings and resultant behaviour, as we noted in discussing Justus Lipsius. But with Smith the motivation for this often difficult regulation arises not from intellectual appreciation of a realm beyond this earthly one, as Lipsius held, but from an appreciation of what unbiased but very human spectators of our reactions would approve and disapprove.

That said, we have to acknowledge, nevertheless, that the "Author of Nature" figures importantly in Smith's theory and dilutes somewhat its secular approach to ethics. Smith claims that the existence of the sentiments that promote moral behaviour has a purpose that has been set by divine providence, namely the persistence of the social life that is necessary for the happiness of human beings. These sentiments are the most effective way of achieving this end:

> By acting according to the dictates of our moral faculties, we necessarily pursue the most effectual means for promoting the happiness of mankind, and may therefore be said, in some sense, to co-operate with the Deity, and to advance, as far as in our power, the plan of providence.[31]

It is particularly important that the sentiment that finds certain behaviour deserving of punishment, that is, that promotes retribution for acts that inexcusably harm others, be followed as part of justice. Punishment of such acts is necessary for the preservation of society and consequently human happiness, but the Author of Nature has not left it up to our reasoning capacity to see this connection in order for punishment to be carried out. Smith puts it this way:

> The very existence of society requires that unmerited and unprovoked malice should be restrained by proper punishments; and consequently, that to inflict those punishments should be regarded as a proper and laudable action. Though man, therefore, be naturally endowed with a desire of the welfare and preservation of society, yet the Author of nature has not entrusted it to his reason to find out that a certain application of punishments is the proper means of attaining this end; but has endowed him with an immediate and instinctive approbation of that very application which is most proper to attain it.[32]

And so it is in general. Morality facilitates social interaction and, through that, human happiness, which is the goal of the deity. But even if we accept that the deity operates as a beneficent utilitarian and that morality exists in order to serve that purpose, we ourselves should not become utilitarians and think that meting out punishment on wrongdoers is right simply because it serves that utilitarian end, or that expressions of gratitude for favours others give us is laudable simply because it makes social life a lot easier. The sentiment favouring the happiness of all humans exists in most people, but it is a weak impetus, often overridden by self-love. Instead we should rely on the stronger motivation arising out of our desire to be approved of by an impartial spectator, that is, by our own conscience. Smith puts it well in the following:

> When we are always so much more deeply affected by whatever concerns ourselves than by whatever concerns other men; what is it which prompts the generous upon all occasions, and the mean upon many, to sacrifice their own interests to the greater interests

of others? It is not the soft power of humanity, it is not that feeble spark of benevolence which Nature has lighted up in the human heart, that is thus capable of counteracting the strongest impulses of self-love. It is a stronger power, a more forcible motive, which exerts itself upon such occasions. It is reason, principle, conscience, the inhabitant of the breast, the man within, the great judge and arbiter of our conduct…It is a stronger love, a more powerful affection, which generally takes place upon such occasions; the love of what is honourable and noble, of the grandeur, and dignity, and superiority of our own characters.[33]

In this way Smith avoids the utilitarianism of Hume while preserving the idea that Nature, or the Author of Nature, has created in us the sentiments and faculties that make possible and provide incentive for moral behaviour for the very same end that the utilitarian believes should be the sole basis for our moral judgments, that is, the goal of promoting human happiness. We are not to believe that by taking on the position of the deity and guiding our behaviour as He does His, we will end up better off than if we simply relied on the judgments that arise from the natural faculties and feelings, which that all-wise deity has bestowed upon us for our own welfare.

It is an interesting question whether Smith's theory can survive jettisoning the Author of Nature and His divine providence. If we do eliminate that theological premise, we are left simply saying that we, or at least most of us, naturally have feelings that cause us to value having the sentiments we feel are shared by others around us, and ultimately feel ashamed when we discover that upon taking up the position of the impartial spectator we cannot empathize with our own feelings and reactions. But it is a commonplace that we often critically reject our natural reactions in the light of finding that they lead to behaviour destructive not only to ourselves but to others as well. Why not apply that kind of rational criticism to the feelings and reactions Smith says we should uncritically follow? If we can somehow conclude that generally speaking these natural sentiments help us form social units, and then suppose that that effect is the sole or main justification for indulging them, it would then seem quite irrational to continue obeying morality on those occasions when it is quite obviously destructive of social relations to do so. In other words, unless we are convinced that the sentiments leading to morality are placed in us by a divine providence that with infinite wisdom sees that in the long run unquestioned obedience to the dictates of the impartial spectator always leads to greater human happiness, it would seem that those sentiments and the deliverances of the spectator, that is, our conscience, ought to be open to rational critique as much as any other feelings. In fact, maybe it will seem rational to adopt the position of utilitarianism, the very one Smith rejects.

The phrase "invisible hand" occurs several times in *The Theory of Moral Sentiments* (= TMS) to indicate the way in which some natural reaction directed solely toward ends such as retribution for unjustified harms to others in fact leads to unintended but good consequences such as peace and order in society. Here Smith is making a point analogous to the one Mandeville made when he tried to show that vices that aim at nothing more than the pleasure of the agent can lead to full employment and economic growth. It is popularly thought that the "invisible hand" is called upon in Smith's later and longer work *The Wealth of Nations* (= WN), but in fact Smith makes no use of the phrase there. What he does say is that competition in markets among a relatively large number of self-interested entrepreneurs with fairly equal resources, governed by rules of fair behaviour, where conspiring with each other to hold down wages or raise prices is not allowed, will result in a "natural" level of prices, wages, and investment in resources, and that this in turn will result, without anyone aiming at it, in greater economic prosperity than would any top-down, "artificial" effort to organize and control economic activity. The "natural" level here is natural only in the sense that it results when "artificial" ways of influencing market activity are excluded.[34] These counterproductive ways would include collusion among businessmen to reduce the risks inherent in investing in enterprises that have to operate within a highly competitive market, as well as, of course, governments' establishing monopolies like the East India Company. As is well known, Smith, like many of the Enlightenment thinkers, favoured free trade, and his doctrine was meant in part to defend the adoption of that policy.

Smith holds that competition of the "natural" sort, if not curtailed by limits on free trade, inevitably tends to increase the size of the market in which goods and services are exchanged, and that a larger market means that greater division of labour leading to greater labour productivity becomes possible. It is this increased productivity as jobs become more and more specialized that makes possible economic growth.[35] Smith was aware in his own day of the debilitating effects on the human spirit of high levels of specialization in work, but, writing before the Industrial Revolution had fully begun, he does not foresee the effects of mechanization and of labour-saving technology generally on the situation of workers. Nevertheless, Smith's point that increases in the size of markets make possible higher labour productivity would certainly apply as well to increases in productivity through the introduction of expensive machinery, and, indeed, he says as much chapter 1 of book 1 of *WN*.

At this point the doctrines of *TMS* and *WN* come together, for what more, it can be asked, conduces to general human happiness than economic prosperity? And now we see that economic prosperity is best pursued by maximizing the freedom for self-interested market behaviour of capitalist entrepreneurs. Moreover, it could be maintained that when moralists appear on the scene to condemn such behaviour and to demand its curtailment, morality itself only exists to promote human happiness and so ought not be allowed to get in the way of what in a world built around commerce most promotes that happiness, that is, the freedom of entrepreneurs to pursue their own interests. Of course, there were few who publicly argued in this way; ordinary people, not entirely imbued with the sophisticated thinking of the Enlightenment, would have been appalled at such notions, especially given the continued prominence of a moralizing Protestant Christianity in the populace of the countries at the forefront of economic development. But this line of thought is there and, no doubt, in some form or other at the back of the minds of those pursuing wealth and grandeur through investments in the market economy, as well as in the thoughts of the often self-interested defenders of the wealthy capitalist class found among political and intellectual elites.

Sophie de Grouchy and the Hedonist Revision of Smith

Smith's *TMS* was well known in France prior to the revolution, and Sophie de Grouchy (1764–1822), one of a number of women at the centre of philosophical salons in France at that time, appreciated the work and published a translation of it in 1798. But de Grouchy was not satisfied with the approach Smith had taken and wrote a response to it that takes a quite different line on the whole question of the origins of morality and the prospects for improvement of mankind. This response took the form of eight letters addressed to "my dear C***" that accompanied her translation of *TMS*. It is not clear from the letters themselves who "my dear C***" is, but it may well have been her brother-in-law, P.-J.-G. Cabanis, a physician prominent in the French Ideologue movement of the time.[36]

Whereas Smith's work is an attempt to found a Stoic ethic in easily observed features of human psychology, de Grouchy attempts to base ethics in a sort of Epicurean psychology in which pleasures and pains are the fundamental motivating forces. De Grouchy was not happy with Smith's citing features of psychology without seeking out their deeper roots, roots that are embedded in basic human nature and consist in automatic pleasurable or painful reactions to what we experience. She makes use of Smith's concept of "sympathy" in order to explain how we move from our own physical and "moral" (i.e., mental) pleasures and pains to taking pleasure in or being pained by the joys or distresses of others. It is our "sentient" capacity, or "sensibility," that enables us to have this sympathy:

> You see, my dear C***, that the first causes of sympathy derive from the nature of the sensations that pleasure and pain cause us to experience, and it is first and foremost as sentient beings that we are capable of sympathy for physical ailments, the most common afflictions among men.[37]

Sensibility, however, requires "reflection" in order to produce in the human heart what is needed for genuine moral motivation:

> And just as reflection prolongs ideas which the senses bring to us, so it extends and preserves in us the effects of the sight of pain, and one can say that it alone makes us truly human. Indeed, reflection fixes in our soul the presence of an injury which our eyes have only seen for a brief moment, and reflection leads us to try to relieve misfortune in order to efface the painful and unwelcome idea of

> it...And finally, reflection conditions our sensibility by prolonging its activity and so installs humanity in our souls as an active and permanent sentiment that, eager to apply itself, spontaneously seeks the happiness of men through works of science and meditations on nature, experience, and philosophy...The feeling of humanity is thus in some way a seed lodged in the interior of man's heart by nature and which the faculty of reflection will nurture and develop.[38]

Our natural distress on being made aware of pain in another person motivates us to help relieve that person's pain. But we are also capable of being moved by an abstract notion of pain and thus come to have a desire to alleviate pain in general by removing its causes. Similarly, but with less intensity, we are positively motivated to promote happiness in another. The realization of having been the cause of thus helping others is itself a source of pleasure to ourselves:

> If the pleasure of contributing to the happiness of others is always more intense than being a passive witness, then the one we experience in comforting the ills of others is always more intense because it is enjoyed with even more reflection and is always accompanied by the pleasant sensation one feels when one is freed from the idea of pain...
>
> We thus take personal pleasure in the recollection of someone else's happiness. But for this recollection to recur often in our memory, it must be linked to our existence and to our own trains of thought, and this is what happens when we are the cause.[39]

The motivation to enhance the happiness of others extends itself when through the abstract notions of pain and pleasure we arrive at the general notions of good and evil. This all requires cultivation from early childhood on, and, if all goes well, this development, which only perfects what nature provides, leads to the truly moral person exhibiting the full virtue of humanity:

> Not only are the sight or memory of the moral or physical pains or pleasures of others accompanied by pain and pleasure in us, but

also, as we already explained, this sensitivity, once awakened and excited in our souls renews itself solely at the abstract idea of good or evil. As a result, we have an internal and personal incentive to do good and to avoid doing evil. This incentive is an extension of our natures as both *sensory and rational beings*. In delicate souls it is capable of both monitoring our conscience and driving us towards virtue.[40] (de Grouchy's emphasis)

De Grouchy sees the notions of *just* and *unjust* arising out of such sentiments when reason leads us to accept certain rules about the pernicious or beneficent results of certain types of behaviour. This is connected to seeing persons acquiring rights which it is unjust to violate. She gives the following example, which is largely taken from John Locke:

You have seen, my dear C***, that when accompanied by reflection, the sentiments awakened in us when we do good or harm to others impart the abstract idea of moral good and evil. From this idea is born that of the *just* and the *unjust*. And, the latter differs from the former only in that reason's assent to a just action must be grounded on the idea of *right*, that is to say, a preference commanded by reason itself in favor of a particular individual... Thus, for example, a man who, in the state of nature, has taken the trouble to cultivate a field and to oversee its harvest has a *right* to this harvest...This preference is based on *reason* and on the necessity of a general law that serves to regulate actions, that is common to all men, and that precludes considering the details of each particular case. This preference is likewise founded on sentiment since, the effect of injustice being more harmful to the party involved than the effects of a simple wrong, it must inspire a greater repugnance in us.[41]

We can see that de Grouchy's main concern is to firmly establish morality in human nature, seeing it as a natural result of the cultivation of human sensibility and reason. In this she believes she has improved on Smith's theory, which she evidently views as merely describing the phenomenon rather than seeking the underlying causes. But if moral sentiments and behaviour are so natural, why is it that so many people become vicious? Here de Grouchy echoes the critique Rousseau had launched against civilized society, that is, the claim that it degraded the human spirit. She sees many of the institutions of current European society as corrupting the human heart, especially those institutions that perpetuate wide inequalities between humans: the wealthy over the poor, the powerful over the enslaved, men over women. Out of this emerges her utopian dream of a society in which the natural sentiments and reason are not fettered and perverted by social institutions but allowed to develop toward their natural perfection:

> But let all faulty institutions be abolished from one end of the earth to the other, let only necessary and reasonable laws remain, and let arbitrary power that sinks its victims into misery and servitude and reduces them to ignorance and credulity disappear forever, and human reason will reemerge healthy and vigorous from beneath its chains. It will predominate in all classes and will itself shape public opinion...The present social order amongst all peoples whose government is not based on the natural rights of man is thus the single cause of the obstacles that ambition and vanity oppose to the stirrings of conscience.[42]

In this way de Grouchy aligns herself with some of the ideals of the French Revolution, even though a few years earlier it had led to the death of her husband, the celebrated mathematician and political activist the Marquis de Condorcet, and to her own impoverishment. It is not her view, however, that mere institutional change is sufficient. Some of the most eloquent passages in her *Letters* are devoted to emphasizing the cultivation in the young of their natural sensibility. Witness the following passage:

> Fathers, mothers, teachers, you have virtually in your hands alone the destiny of the next generation! Ah! How guilty you are if you allow to wither away in your children these precious seeds of

sensibility that need nothing more to develop than the sight of suffering, the example of compassion, tears of recognition, and an enlightened hand that warms and coddles them! How guilty you are, if you are more concerned with the outward success of your children than with their virtues, or if you are more impatient to see them please a social circle than to see their hearts roil with indignation in the face of injustice, their foreheads pale before sorrow, and their hearts treat all men as brothers![43]

Without, I think, her entirely realizing it, de Grouchy's effort to ground morality in a hedonist psychology has led to an entirely different ethic than that advocated by Smith. In fact, it really ends up in the utilitarianism that Smith strove to avoid, for the whole of morality, so far as de Grouchy is concerned, lies in the spirit of rational benevolence or humanity, that is, in being motivated to promote the good of one's fellow humans as well as oneself and curtail the evils. Because of de Grouchy's hedonist psychology it is tempting to conclude that this means promoting general pleasure or happiness and curtailing pain, that is, making an increase in pleasure and a decrease in pain the goals to be obtained by ethical behaviour. What is clear is that de Grouchy thinks that our own pleasures and pains are what motivates our actions and that the sight of pleasure in others naturally incites our approval, while the sight of pain inspires our urge to relieve it. Is this not tantamount to accepting pleasure as the supreme good to be obtained both for ourselves and for others? I think not. It is possible to maintain that all that this shows is that our pleasure in certain things is a *prima facie* sign that those things are good, and, conversely, our displeasure or pain with certain things is a *prima facie* sign that they are bad. They are such signs simply by virtue of the motivating force intrinsic to them. But it is the things we react to in this way that are being judged good or bad, not just the pleasure or pain themselves, although there can of course be a certain reflective pleasure taken in pleasure and pain in pain. In other words, pleasure and pain are at most items among a large list of goods and evils, and not the most prominent either.

Nevertheless, this is a fairly subtle position that is not easily kept from slipping over into plain hedonistic utilitarianism, and, as we shall see in a later chapter, it did indeed in many "enlightened" minds do just that, with notable consequences for Western society. De Grouchy, however, does not, I think, slip into that sort of utilitarianism, although, seemingly unaware of that danger, she does not clearly disavow it either. What she has done is construct a hedonist psychology that seems to make utilitarianism, but not necessarily *hedonist* utilitarianism,[44] the ethical theory that most accords with our natural impulses and thus has a foundation in human nature itself, without any recourse, as in Smith, to some sort of divine author of that nature.

Turgot: Inevitable Progress through "Violent Fermentation"

Many of the thinkers in Western Europe that we have reviewed imagined how their societies might progress in the ordinary sense of the word, that is, what changes might be made in their societies that would make life better in one way or another for people generally. Joachim of Fiore had even seen such progress as part of a divine plan that had been unfolding throughout history and that would inevitably reach its climax in a state of perfection. Of course, the improvements he envisioned were mainly spiritual, whereas the progress Bacon and his admirers envisioned was in large measure a matter of making life easier, the "relief of man's estate," as Bacon put it. In what follows we will see the idea that Joachim had promoted of an inevitable progress of the whole of humanity now applied through entirely secular means to completely secular goals.

This idea of progress in human history underwent a remarkable transformation in France during the latter half of the eighteenth century, and this development arose largely out of the imaginative work of a nobleman educated to be a cleric, Anne Robert-Jacques Turgot (1727–1781). In 1750 he gave two lectures at the Sorbonne, then the citadel of Catholic intellectualism; the second of these, titled *Tableau philosophique des progrés successifs de l'esprit humain* (*A Philosophical Review of the Successive Advances of the Human Mind*), became the guiding beacon for progressivist thought for the rest of the century. Composed at about the same time but not published until well after his death was Turgot's unfinished sketch of a history of human progress (*Plan de deux discours sur l'histoire universelle*), that in English goes by the title *On Universal History*. These two pieces articulate a vision of human history as a story of gradual *but inevitable* improvement in all aspects of human life despite frequent interruptions and regressions.

Turgot was well aware that the record of events in history is full of horrors and obscene behaviour, often perpetrated by the powerful of the day; but this, in his view, did not permanently obstruct the overall upward trend. In the *Philosophical Review* he wrote:

> Self-interest, ambition, and vainglory continually change the world scene and inundate the earth with blood; yet in the midst of their ravages manners are softened, the human mind becomes more enlightened, and separate nations are brought closer to one another. Finally commercial and political ties unite all parts of the globe, and the whole human race, through alternate periods of rest and unrest, of weal and woe, goes on advancing, although at a slow pace, towards greater perfection.[45]

From Turgot's *Universal History* we learn that he actually thought that these ugly elements in history were in the long run conducive to the progress he believed was inevitable:

> And the ambitious themselves, in forming great nations, have contributed to the designs of Providence, to the progress of enlightenment, and thus to the increase in the happiness of the human race, with which they were not concerned at all. Their passions, even their fits of rage, have led them on their way without their being aware of where they were going.[46]

Here we see a theme already familiar to us from Mandeville and Smith: Often there can be good consequences of actions undertaken without any intention of bringing about such consequences. But how in this case is it possible that enlightenment and prosperity are forwarded by wars and brutal pursuit of power by ambitious men? Turgot's most frequent answer to this query is that any disruption to the established order in a society provides an opportunity for innovation, for new ideas to be considered and put into action. Such occasions enable geniuses, those persons of extraordinary talents, who are rare but present with roughly the same frequency in all nations, to bring forth the innovations that mark genuine progress in some field, be it technology, science, art, politics, or manners.

> Amidst this complex of different events, sometimes favourable, sometimes adverse, which because they act in opposite ways must in the long run nullify one another, genius ceaselessly asserts its influence. Nature, while distributing genius to only a few individuals, has nevertheless spread it out almost equally over the whole mass, and with time its effects become appreciable.[47]

Progress in the political realm is particularly one in which advances have to be preceded by calamities, as he says in the following passage from *On Universal History*:

> It was only after centuries, and by means of bloody revolutions, that despotism at last learned to moderate itself, and liberty to regulate itself; that the situation of states at last became less fluctuating and more stable. In this way, then, through alternate periods of rest and unrest, of weal and woe, the human race as a whole has advanced ceaselessly toward perfection.[48]

Given this line of thought, it is not surprising that Turgot inveighs frequently against all conditions that tend to stabilize the situations and ideas that people are allowed to encounter. This is particularly the case in the development of science. In this same work he accuses the Chinese of promoting a particularly conservative view of the scientific ideas they had once arrived at and thus stultifying further development of their theories:

> The Chinese were stabilised too soon. They became like those trees whose trunk has been lopped and whose branches grow close to the ground; they never escape from mediocrity. There was so much respect among them for their barely sketched-out sciences, and they retained so much for the ancestors who had caused these first steps to be taken, that it was believed that

nothing remained to be added, and that it was no longer a question of anything but preventing this wonderful knowledge from being lost. But to limit oneself to preserving the sciences in their existing state is equivalent to deciding to perpetuate all the errors they contain.[49]

As one might expect from a classically educated Westerner of the eighteenth century, Turgot contrasts the Chinese unfavourably with ancient Greece in its innovative period and with Italy of the Renaissance:

> Fortunately the situation in which Greece found itself, divided as it was into an infinity of small republics, allowed genius all the freedom and all the competition of which it had need in its endeavours. The perspectives of men are always very narrow in comparison with those of nature. It is much better to be guided by the latter than by imperfect laws. If the sciences have made such great progress in Italy, and consequently in the rest of Europe, they undoubtedly owe this to the situation in which Italy found itself in the fourteenth century, which was rather similar to that of ancient Greece.[50]

Note in the above the recommendation to follow nature rather than "imperfect laws." It is no surprise, then, that despotic government is a frequent target for Turgot's contempt on the grounds that it tends to narrow the range of activity and experience of its subjects. It "enslaves men's minds," as Turgot says in this excerpt from *On Universal History*:

> The peoples who were preserved from despotism were those who remained shepherds or hunters; those who formed small societies; and the republics. It was among such people that revolutions were useful; that nations participated in them and thus drew gain from them; that tyranny was unable to consolidate itself sufficiently to enslave men's minds; that the profusion of particular bodies of law and of revolutions which pointed out the errors of the founders of

the state, and the fall of an old and rise of a new sovereign authority which brought about a re-examination of the laws, in the long run perfected the laws and government. It was among such peoples that equality was maintained, that intellect and courage showed great activity, and that the human mind made rapid progress. It was among them that manners and laws in the course of time learned how to direct themselves towards the greatest happiness of the people.[51]

As an example of peculiarly virulent despotism Turgot picks on the dreaded Turks and their "barbaric" religion. Speaking of Islam he says in the same work:

This religion [Islam], which does not allow any laws other than those of the religion itself, opposes the wall of superstition to the natural march of improvement. It has consolidated barbarism by *consecrating* that which existed when it appeared, and which it adopted through national prejudice. [Turgot's emphasis][52]

"Consecrating" what already exists, this is the great sin against progress. According to the Manuels in their very illuminating discussion of Turgot's utopian ideas, he carried this spirit into action when later in life he was serving as part of Louis XVI's civil service, a career that culminated in his holding the high office of Contrôleur Général des Finances from 1774 to 1776. Here is a short excerpt from the Manuels' chapter on Turgot:

He had a pervasive psychological horror of the static, his friends have reported, and in public office he was always impatient of any curbs on his zeal to reform and rearrange whatever ancient practices came within his jurisdiction...The past had to be overcome, brushed aside, lest it gain a stranglehold on the unborn. Living meant an eternal breaking out of old forms, an emancipation, a liberation...Whatever was fixed, set, hardened, a religious dogma or an economic restriction, literally anything that might block new combinations of ideas, was a source of evil, deadly.[53]

In philosophy Turgot shared the assessments of most of his contemporaries in his high admiration for the genius of Descartes as a breaker of the stranglehold of tradition and as an innovator in how we are to think about the world. Bacon he treated as the initiator of the rebellion against Aristotle and his abstract essences; Kepler and Galileo figured as laying foundations for the new through their observations; and then:

> But it was DESCARTES who, bolder than they, meditated and made a revolution. The system of occasional causes, the idea of reducing everything to matter and movement, constituted the essence of this lively philosopher, and presuppose an analysis of ideas of which the Ancients had provided no example at all.[54]

Nevertheless, not even a genius like Descartes escapes from Turgot's critical gaze. Immediately after the above he qualifies his praise:

> In shaking off the yoke of their authority, he still did not challenge sufficiently the knowledge which he had first received from them... One might say that he was frightened by the solitude in which he had put himself, and that he was unable to endure it. All at once he throws himself back into the very ideas which he had been able to divest himself.[55]

In the sciences the inability to "shake off the yoke" of past ideas is a recipe for stagnation and ultimately for being surpassed by peoples who began without any sophisticated scientific tradition at all:

> Woe betide those nations, then, in which the sciences, as the result of a blind zeal for them, are confined within the limits of existing knowledge in an attempt to stabilise them. It is for this reason that the regions which were the first to become enlightened are not those where the sciences have made the greatest progress.[56]

Stability, then, is, from a philosopher's point of view, to be avoided, for the philosopher approaches human history in order to see what are the determinants of its overall course. As he says at the beginning of *On Universal History*:

> To unveil the influence of general and necessary causes, that of particular causes and the free actions of great men, and the relation of all this to the very constitution of man; to reveal the springs and mechanisms of moral causes through their effects—that is what History is in the eyes of a philosopher.[57]

And what this inquiry reveals is that humanity has progressed hardly at all through rational planning and design but rather through the often destabilizing vicissitudes of history coupled with humans' natural, passionate reactions to them. Turgot is quite vehement on this point, so far as the propelling force for progress is concerned, as the following passage from *On Universal History* makes clear:

> Thus the passions have led to the multiplication of ideas, the extension of knowledge, and the perfection of the mind, in the absence of that reason whose day had not yet come and which would have been less powerful if its reign had arrived earlier... Reason and justice, if they had been more attended to, would have immobilised everything, as has virtually happened in China. But what is never perfect ought never to be entirely immobilised. The passions, tumultuous and dangerous as they are, became a mainspring of action and consequently of progress; everything which draws men away from their present condition, and everything which puts varied scenes before their eyes, extends the scope of their ideas, enlightens them, stimulates them, and in the long run leads them to the good and the true, towards which they are drawn by their natural bent...In the same way, violent fermentation is indispensable in the making of good wine.[58]

It is not merely that "reason and justice" were in such a primitive state that they could have little propelling force; rather, if they had been motivating people they would have "immobilised everything," as he says. China is brought forth again as the example of this sort of paralysis. The "violent fermentation" that history has often visited on societies and that has elicited the fears, hopes, and outrage of their peoples—that is, the passions that propel them forward to betterment—would only have been stifled if reason and justice had had their way. He explains this point further as follows:

> Reason, which is justice itself, would not have taken away from anyone what belonged to him, would have banished wars and usurpations for ever, and would have left men divided up into a host of nations separated from one another and speaking different languages. As a result the human race, limited in its ideas, incapable of that progress in all kinds of understanding, and in the sciences, arts, and government, which takes its rise from the collective genius of different regions, would have remained for ever in a state of mediocrity.[59]

In other words, if humans had been directed by their reasoning they would have avoided all the brutal conquests and cruel injustices that fill history books and thereby, albeit inadvertently, kept themselves from the kinds of interactions among various nations that make for progress. We arrive then at a kind of theodicy, for Turgot is no atheist. "The whole universe proclaims to us a supreme Being. Everywhere we see the print of the hand of a GOD," he says near the start of *On Universal History*.[60] And God in his wisdom has so constructed the natural world, as well as human nature itself, that this creation will inevitably proceed toward the *perfection* of humankind, admittedly in an irregular fashion. Viewed philosophically, that is, from a viewpoint that encompasses the whole course of history, that story attests to the supreme wisdom that created the human participants in the historical drama as well as the world stage on which it is performed:

> If we look at the world from a broad point of view, then, and see it in the context of the whole concatenation of events which has characterised its progress, it becomes the most glorious witness to the wisdom which presides over it.[61]

All the "fermentation," all the tribulations, which humans have suffered throughout history are thus seen to be justified from the philosophical point of view. Although the "Author of Nature" has so set things up that they will take this in the end benevolent course, Turgot does not at all deploy that Author and his wisdom *within* history. Rather, the human story unfolds of its own accord, driven ultimately by the passionate reactions of humans to the catastrophes that rationally motivated people would have evaded, but which allow for the eruptions of the genius that a few humans naturally possess and that are required for humans to reach the perfection of which they are capable. In this aspect of Turgot's vision we see something very similar to the way the Author of Nature figured in Smith's *Theory of Moral Sentiments*, where the Author has endowed us humans with certain imaginative capacities and feelings that naturally lead us purposefully to moral behaviour, but also by that behaviour *unintentionally* to the happiness of the human race, which was the divine Author's original goal, although not our own. For both Turgot and Smith, God has made it utterly unnecessary for humans to seek consciously the goal of either the happiness or the perfection of the human race; indeed, both think that efforts to figure out in a logical fashion what humans need to do to reach that goal and then act on that reasoning are counterproductive. Better is the design of the all-wise Author.

Or at least that is the line Turgot most often puts forward in the works discussed here. On occasion, however, he hints at a late stage of human progress in which reason comes to be the dominant factor determining the course of history. This development occurs when in the course of progress the softer emotions come to dominate over the more violent ones:

> Men who are taught by experience become more and more humane; and it would appear that in recent times generosity, the virtues, and the tender affections, which are continually spreading, at any rate in Europe, are diminishing the dominion of vengeance and national hatreds.[62]

No passage exactly says this, but it would seem that in Turgot's mind, once the softer sentiments dominate, reason and justice become relatively stronger in relation to the passions and thus can come to direct human behaviour. Otherwise how do we account for Turgot's exclamation in the *Philosophical Review*?

> Time, spread your swift wings! Century of Louis, century of great men, century of reason, hasten![63]

This remark is followed by a catalogue of the advances in learning and science that have been made in recent times in Europe. Although Turgot acknowledges that human society is still quite far from perfection, he perhaps sees grounds for hope that soon people will be able to make progress by following the dictates of reason and so draw more quickly near to that divinely ordained goal.

Turgot's concept of human perfection certainly includes the softening of manners, the respect for justice, the advancement of the sciences, as well as innovations in technology and the mechanical arts that lead to an easier life, and he sees all this going along with the spread and deepening of civilization. There is in Turgot's mind no conflict between sophisticated civilization and this perfection of human life, that is, the sort of conflict that Rousseau saw as inevitable. He is a confirmed optimist about the future of his own civilization; its achievements have laid the foundation for still further improvement in human well-being in all its aspects. And all of this has arisen through an entirely natural process in which humans of genius have taken advantage of the calamities into which humanity naturally falls.

Condorcet: Endless Progress toward Absolute Perfection

One of Turgot's staunchest admirers, both while Turgot was alive and after his death, was Antoine Nicolas de Condorcet (1743–1794), a nobleman who became famous in his own day for his mathematical discoveries, particularly in the theory of probability, and also for his advocacy of an end to slavery and for the equality of women. He and his wife, the aforementioned Sophie de Grouchy, were at first supporters of the revolution that began in 1789. Condorcet participated in the Legislative Assembly that took over the reins of government after the overthrow of the monarchy, and he crafted its educational reforms. But in the end he had to flee from the Jacobin "terror," a victim of the very revolution to whose ideology he had contributed so much. He died in prison in 1794, possibly by suicide.

Condorcet took Turgot's notion of progress and transformed it into the doctrine that in many ways was to become the dominant ideology of the Western world and remains so to this day.[64] Like Turgot, he saw human history as a story in which there are both periods of advance and periods of regress, but in which the arc, in the long run, bends upward toward human perfection. But his view of what propels this overall advance is quite different from Turgot's. While on the run from the Jacobin authorities he composed *L'Esquisse d'un tableau historique des progrès de l'esprit humaine* (*Sketch for a Historical Picture of the Progress of the Human Mind*), an outline for a longer work that he hoped eventually to publish and that would have presented in detail the history of human development from prehistoric times to his own day and then predicted the future course of that development. Condorcet firmly believed that humanity's history was subject to natural laws analogous to the way the physical world had been shown to be so ordered by the Newtonian revolution in physics; furthermore, these laws made it possible to predict humanity's future in general outline on the basis of its past course. On this lawfulness he remarks as follows:

> The sole foundation for belief in the natural sciences is this idea, that the general laws directing the phenomena of the universe, known or unknown, are necessary and constant. Why should this principle be any less true for the development of the intellectual and moral faculties of man than for the other operations of nature?[65]

This is probably the basic difference between his view of how progress is maintained and Turgot's, for the latter was definitely opposed to the idea that the mode of explanation in the natural sciences was appropriate to understanding human affairs. At the very beginning of the *Philosophical Review* Turgot wrote:

> The phenomena of nature, governed as they are by constant laws, are confined within a circle of revolutions which are always the

same. All things perish, and all things spring up again, and in these successive acts of generation through which plants and animals reproduce themselves time does no more than restore continually the counterpart of what it has caused to disappear.

The succession of mankind, on the other hand, affords from age to age an ever-changing spectacle.[66]

Turgot goes on then to elaborate on his theory of progress, showing that progress would be impossible if humanity was governed by natural laws in the way Newton had shown matter in motion to be. Condorcet, on the other hand, viewed the sciences of man to be as much dependent on the discovery of natural laws as were the natural sciences; indeed, the science of man, he declared, *is* a natural science.

It is not that Turgot was unaware of how the economy can operate as a kind of machine tending to produce an equilibrium between the various factors of investment, employment, production, and consumption.[67] There is a certain lawfulness in such a system, and left on its own free from artificial meddling by governments, for example, it would tend to stabilize itself. But stability, as we saw, was in Turgot's mind evil so far as progress was concerned, and he would as a philosopher have been pleased to see outside forces upset the economic applecart. The "laws" governing the economy, then, are, in contrast to the laws governing nature, ones that operate only so long as some human contrivance is allowed by humans to continue to exist unobstructed. There is no suggestion in Turgot's thinking that the economy or any other social contrivance is the propelling force behind progress. What is required, rather, is random chaos.

Neither is it part of Condorcet's theory that progress occurs in some mechanical fashion. His view is that the minds of individual human beings are impelled by their very nature toward a certain sort of growth, although this development can be blocked by external influences. Here is his account from the *Sketch* of how the human being interacts so as to promote social progress:

> Finally, as a consequence of his capacity and of his ability to form and combine ideas, there arise between him and his

> fellow-creatures ties of interest and duty, to which nature herself has wished to attach the most precious portion of our happiness and the most painful of our ills...This progress is subject to the same general laws that can be observed in the development of the faculties of the individual, and it is indeed no more than the sum of that development realized in a large number of individuals joined together in society.[68]

It is this natural impulse in individuals toward growth of their faculties that in the end propels the curve of human development upward toward perfection, not the chaotic "violent fermentation" so admired by Turgot. Nor does Condorcet think that his emphasis on natural laws implies some cyclical view of history. Having explained his aim as showing through an examination of the actual course of human history that laws governing human nature compel advancement, he remarks as follows in the *Sketch*:

> Such is the aim of the work that I have undertaken, and its result will be to show by appeal to reason and fact that nature has set no term to the perfection of human faculties; that the perfectibility of man is truly indefinite; and that the progress of this perfectibility, from now onwards independent of any power that might wish to halt it, has no other limit than the duration of the globe upon which nature has cast us.[69]

Note that Condorcet places no inherent limit on the degree to which perfection might be achieved. On his view, we go on perfecting ourselves as long as the earth remains in existence. How broad a conception of improvement Condorcet has in mind is revealed in this later passage from the same work:

> The real advantages that should result from this progress of which we can entertain a hope that is almost a certainty, can have no other term than that of the absolute perfection of the human race; since, as the various kinds of equality come to work in its favour by producing ampler sources of supply, more extensive education,

more complete liberty, an equality will be more real and will embrace everything which is really of importance for the happiness of human beings.[70]

In the above passage Condorcet notes two features of the progress of humankind, both of which increase with time and are crucial in maintaining the general advance: equality and liberty. The *Sketch* frequently returns to these values as both constitutive of and productive of the advancement he deems inevitable. In the political realm he is very clear about this:

> After long periods of error, after being led astray by vague or incomplete theories, publicists have at last discovered the true rights of man and how they can all be deduced from the single truth, that *man is a sentient being, capable of reasoning and of acquiring moral ideas.* [Condorcet's emphasis]
>
> They have seen that the maintenance of these rights was the sole object of men's coming together in political societies, and that the social art is the art of guaranteeing the preservation of these rights and their distribution in the most equal fashion over the largest area. It was felt that in every society the means of assuring the rights of the individual should be submitted to certain common rules, but that the authority to choose these means and to determine these rules could belong only to the majority of the members of the society itself; for in making this choice the individual cannot follow his own reason without subjecting others to it, and the will of the majority is the only mark of truth that can be accepted by all without loss of equality.[71]

It is mental capacities common to all that ground human rights, and the purpose of society is to guarantee these rights to all in an equal fashion. He then moves on to the system of governance that, while subjecting people to "common rules," will preserve people's freedom as much as possible, and the suggestion is that majoritarian democracy is such a system. Immediately after the above passage he comments as follows:

> Doubtless there are issues on which the decision of the majority is likely to be in favour of error and against the interests of all: but it is still this majority that must decide which issues are not to be subjected to its own direct decision; it is the majority that must appoint those persons whose judgment it considers to be more reliable than its own; it is the majority that must lay down the procedure that it considers most likely to conduct them to the truth; and it may not abdicate its authority to decide whether the decisions they take on its behalf do or do not infringe the rights that are common to all.[72]

The majority may delegate their decision-making, but they always retain the right to overrule decisions made by their delegates if they judge them to "infringe the rights common to all." It is not entirely clear what rights Condorcet thought were common to all, but they must be quite extensive, as a subsequent paragraph makes clear:

> Men, therefore, should be able to use their faculties, dispose of their wealth and provide for their needs in complete freedom. The common interest of any society, far from demanding that they should restrain such activity, on the contrary, forbids any interference with it; and as far as this aspect of public order is concerned, the guaranteeing to each man his natural rights is at once the whole of social utility, the sole duty of the social power, the only right that the general will can legitimately exercise over the individual.[73]

The above passage immediately follows the question below and assumes that that question is rhetorical and is not so much a query as an expression of wonder at an established fact.

> How...is it that, by a universal moral law, the efforts made by each individual on his own behalf minister to the welfare of all, and that the interests of society demand that everyone should understand

where his own interests lie, and should be able to follow them without hindrance?[74]

He believes, then, that some law guarantees that persons each working in their own true interests will result in conditions beneficial to all. In this way Condorcet combined a radical libertarianism with majoritarian democracy, a mix that was to continue to inspire thousands among not just some of the elite but among the masses as well. Of course, he is not saying that the beneficent effects of individual liberty happen automatically. If people work simply for what they *believe* to be their own best interests, they can be mistaken about those interests, and so for the results to be to the welfare of all, people must be brought to a state of enlightenment about their own interests. From this it follows that knowledge of what is genuinely useful must become widespread before the equality and freedom he advocates can be forces promoting human happiness.

Accordingly, Condorcet ascribes great importance to the spread of knowledge not just among an educated elite but among the masses too. Indeed, it is the spread of knowledge and the erasing of ignorance that most promotes the advancement of human life, as the following passage indicates:

> We have indeed arrived at that point of civilization where the mass of the people profit from knowledge not only through what they owe to the more enlightened members of their community but through the uses to which they themselves put it, in defending themselves against error, in anticipating or satisfying their needs, in preserving themselves from the troubles of life or in mitigating them by new pleasures.[75]

Conversely, it is the forces of established institutions, particularly religion, that by promoting ignorance most obstruct the natural advancement of humanity:

> If we were to confine ourselves to showing the benefits that we have derived from the sciences in their immediate uses or in their applications to the arts, either for the well-being of individuals or

for the prosperity of nations, we should display only a very small portion of their blessings.

The most important of these, perhaps, is to have destroyed prejudices and to have redirected the human intelligence, which had been obliged to follow the false directions imposed on it by the absurd beliefs that were implanted in each generation in infancy with the terrors of superstition and the fear of tyranny.

All errors in politics and morals are based on philosophical errors and these in turn are connected with scientific errors. There is not a religious system nor a supernatural extravagance that is not founded on ignorance of the laws of nature.[76]

Condorcet's contempt for the Christian religion of his time is virtually boundless and arises from his viewing it as doctrinally opposed to the natural science of his day and as promoting a fantastic theology and cosmology, as well as an equally erroneous view of human nature, all of which are refuted by rational thinking based on observation of the facts. The Manuels sum up this aspect of Condorcet's vision vividly as follows:

> History has been a worldly battleground between those forces advancing real utility and those suppressing it in the name of religion, a philosophic system, or a tyrannical lust for domination...More explicitly than in Turgot, religious bodies in all ages harbored evil antiprogressive elements and their opponents were the legions of the good...The historic, almost Zoroastrian combat between enlightenment and obscurantism had been marked by a series of great technological and scientific discoveries, which became the natural benchmarks of Condorcet's world tableau...For Condorcet the world was still witnessing a death struggle between Christianity and progress, the great irreconcilable polar opposites both in scientific and in moral values.[77]

Given this outlook, Condorcet, of course, felt no need for a theodicy, as had Turgot, but the theme of a conflict between the forces of darkness and those of enlightenment, a theme we have seen arise out of Zorastrianism and pass over through Judaism into Christianity and thence in various forms into the subterranean culture of medieval Europe, emerges here in a totally anti-religious garb.

Despite his vehement assault on the institutions of the *ancien régime*, and on all systems of institutionalized inequality, Condorcet is not of Rousseau's opinion that civilization itself corrupts human morals and promotes dissimulation and hypocrisy. The vices of civilized life arise from the ignorance and superstition that corrupt institutions have engendered, and these can be overcome by increases in knowledge leading to a civilization in which human beings are perfected, not corrupted:

> We shall see that the rough and stormy passage from a crude state of society to that degree of civilization enjoyed by enlightened and free nations is in no way a degeneration of the human race but is rather a necessary crisis in its gradual progress towards absolute perfection. And finally we shall see that it is not the growth of knowledge but its decadence that has engendered the vices of civilized peoples, and that knowledge, so far from corrupting man, has always improved him when it could not totally correct or reform him.[78]

But what does the "absolute perfection" of the human race consist in? It includes, Condorcet thinks, improvement not just in material prosperity and affluence but more basically perfection of human beings' moral and intellectual faculties. Here he is in accord with his wife's ideas on the importance of cultivating "sensibility" and reason, and he is also on board with the same hedonic or Epicurean psychology she relied on in her *Letters*. In fact, Condorcet makes evident the Epicurean origins of the theory in the next passage, which also shows how he saw morality as independent of dogmatic religion:

> This resemblance between the moral precepts of all religions and all philosophical sects suffices to prove that their truth is something independent of the dogmas of these various religions and the principles of these different sects; that it is to the moral

constitution of man that we must look for the foundations of his duties and the origins of his ideas of justice and virtue; a truth to which the Epicureans were closer than any other sect, and it is perhaps for this reason more than any other that they drew down on themselves the hatred of hypocrites of all classes for whom morality is but an object of trade whose monopoly they contest.[79]

Moral improvement is of a piece with the break from obscurantist religion and other institutions of repression that constrain mental development. Knowledge, then, is not just valuable for its advancement of technology and the "relief of man's estate," although this is certainly another way in which Condorcet thought it advances human life. No doubt Condorcet had in mind the way in which Epicurus, and later Lucretius, had based their ethic on their atomistic materialism, which consigned the gods to a place where they had no effect on or concern with human life. He may well have thought of himself as proposing for eighteenth-century Europe a reform of the Epicurean sort where physical science leads the way in removing the superstitions of the past and thus opens the path to a more satisfactory morality.

We also see here how totally different Condorcet's conception of how science can lead to progress is from Bacon's. The author of *The New Atlantis* had taken great care to secure for morality a place impervious to the investigative methods of science by lodging it completely under the purview of divine revelation. Condorcet, following the skepticism of the French *philosophes* toward religion generally and Christianity in particular, rejects revelation as superstition and seeks to apply the scientific methods of the physical sciences to humanity itself. Out of this effort he thinks has already come a new foundation for morality and human society. The methods of the new Western science, already shown to be so successful in mechanics and currently being applied in investigations of all areas of the physical world, could now expand to encompass what was then called "moral philosophy" as well. In other words, no area was now excluded from its domain. In our next chapter we shall see how this claim worked its way into the ideology of the nineteenth century.

It should not be thought, however, that Condorcet believed he was promoting ideals applicable in his day only to Europe or the more advanced nations of Europe and their offshoots in North America. He had a truly planet-wide vision and was ready to chastise the Europeans for violating human rights in their colonial empires. Scientific advances could improve humanity as a whole only when those abuses were ended:

> But these discoveries will have repaid humanity what they have cost it only when Europe renounces her oppressive and avaricious system of monopoly; only when she remembers that men of all races are equally brothers by the wish of nature and have not been created to feed the vanity and greed of a few privileged nations; only when she calls upon all people to share her independence, freedom and knowledge, which she will do once she is alive to her own true interests.[80]

It is clear, too, that he wants to see an active role for Europeans in positively proselytizing for the ideals he promotes as well as for the scientific insights that Europeans have achieved. The following passage makes this clear but also reveals a threatening side to Condorcet's enthusiasm:

> Zeal for the truth is also one of the passions, and it will turn its efforts to distant lands, once there are no longer at home any crass prejudices to combat, any shameful errors to dissipate.
>
> These vast lands are inhabited partly by large tribes who need only assistance from us to become civilized, who wait only to find brothers amongst the European nations to become their friends and pupils; partly by races oppressed by sacred despots or dull-witted conquerors, and who for so many centuries have cried out to be liberated; partly by tribes living in a condition of almost total savagery in a climate whose harshness repels the sweet blessings of civilization and deters those who would teach them its benefits; and finally, by conquering hordes who know no other law but force, no other profession but piracy. The progress of these two last classes of people will be slower and stormier; and perhaps it will even be that, reduced in number as they are driven

back by civilized nations, they will finally disappear imperceptibly before them or merge into them.[81]

Once Europe has rid itself of the religion-induced prejudices and fully adopted the science-given enlightenment that was increasing in his day, it must spread the truth among the peoples not yet arrived at this advanced state of civilization but still wallowing for various reasons in ignorance and hardship. Hopefully most of these races will convert easily and quickly to the truth, but there may be some that are so resistant that their fate can only be to "disappear" from the earth.

Condorcet's vision is the secularized version of not just the millennium but also the Kingdom of God that Christians had longed for over the centuries. Even the old idea that human nature is good and, if not for the original sin, would have total knowledge of the creation finds its analogue in the belief that tyrannical institutions have corrupted human morals and kept people in ignorance and that this has temporarily deprived them of the destiny their own nature longs for and that it will achieve once it is freed from its institutional fetters. Just as the ancient and medieval beliefs in the millennium inspired calls for radical reform of society, so the ideas Condorcet espouses in his *Sketch* inspired the imaginations and passions of those who supported the French Revolution and its efforts to overturn the whole structure and culture of eighteenth-century France, and in some measure the whole of Europe. Indeed, it provided a rationale for spreading the blessings of enlightened Europe to the rest of the entire world.

But like some of the social millenarian movements of late medieval Europe, the utopian ideas of the French Revolution could have a dark side. Utopians always come upon those who do not share their ideals, who have not yet been introduced to the truth, who wander in darkness and error, who must be educated and in some cases subdued by force. In so promulgating the virtues of their own enlightenment the utopians view themselves as promoting a cause that is backed by divine or impersonal forces that make inevitable their eventual success. They are part of a drama that has been destined to play itself out since the origins of the human race. This arrogance can in its treatment of the "unbelievers" lead to disregard of the very moral sentiments the utopian is so keen to promote. Such an attitude was to be present in much of the European treatment of Indigenous Peoples in the Americas and other lands where the Europeans in their expansion around the globe came to conquer or colonize. Condorcet was himself appalled at the way Europeans were dealing with "unenlightened" peoples around the globe; he was a vigorous opponent of slavery. But this is the paradox of utopian movements: the utopians' conviction that they are right and on the right side of history can lead them to treat those unconvinced in a most dystopian manner.

It is ironic that as he was writing his *Sketch* Condorcet was himself suffering from just such a ghastly turn in the French Revolution. Of course he thought that the ideals he embraced could be and would be eventually restored in practice. But in fact what ensued was the rise to autocratic power of a conniving, narcissistic, power-hungry man who under the guise of promoting the ideals of the Revolution would preen himself as emperor of all Europe and bring the horrors of war to the entire continent from Madrid to Moscow. In the course of that madness he was able to persuade many among the educated elite, at least for a time, that he was the vanguard of a great and needed renovation of European politics and society. Recall that Beethoven wrote the *Eroica* symphony in celebration of this man's victories. We see then how utopian ideals can so inflame even an educated person's passions that they become unable to see what is actually happening in the name of those ideals. How could something so bad actually be occurring in the name of something so good?!

Both Turgot and Condorcet embraced the idea that humanity, by the very nature of what it is to be human, was set on a path of inevitable progress, but they saw the driving force of this differently. Turgot envisioned persons of genius reacting creatively to the disasters civilization brings on itself when left free of premature rational regulation. Condorcet placed his faith in the growth of the human mind toward ever greater knowledge of the world and of human life itself. Both men had totally jettisoned the need for any divine assistance. To their disciples these views meant that humanity, once made aware of its true innate potential, could proceed to greater and greater achievements with total self-confidence. This vision would increasingly motivate Westerners in the coming century.

8

THE CULT OF SCIENCE

> The notion that one can discover large patterns
> or regularities in the procession of historical events
> is naturally attractive to those who are impressed
> by the success of the natural sciences in classifying,
> correlating and, above all, predicting.
> —Isaiah Berlin, *Historical Inevitability*

Although thinkers like Turgot and Condorcet applauded the advancement of science that had been occurring in Western Europe since the sixteenth century, they praised it mainly for its intellectual achievements and moral consequences, not so much for its contribution to "the relief of man's estate," to return again to Bacon's memorable phrase. They had not engaged with the Bacon who argued for the marriage of science with the practical arts, although they certainly had no sympathy for Rousseau's total antipathy toward science and the arts. But the development of that side of Bacon's vision was to be crucial to the kind of economic expansion that would bring on planetary eco-catastrophe. Without science and the technologies that benefited from science, the economy of the West would never have had the power to be so enormously destructive to the home that nature had placed humanity in at the beginning of the Holocene. How then did the West come to have so much enthusiastic faith and hope in science that it thought the enormous expense and effort involved in advancing it were justified? This chapter attempts to fill in the ideological side of that story.

Henri de Saint-Simon: Science in the Service of Industry

There can be no doubt, and it is universally acknowledged, that the French Revolution, culminating in the disaster of Napoleon, had enormous consequences for the culture of the modern West, including its offshoots in the Americas and Australasia. One thinker on whom that impact is very obvious and whose ideas exemplify in several ways an ideology that was to gain prominence during the nineteenth century, and even more so in the twentieth, was Henri de Saint-Simon (1760–1825). His thinking carries forward in a particularly enticing direction ideas that had already in the eighteenth century become common currency among the *philosophes* like Turgot and Condorcet. My reason for introducing Saint-Simon here is that I believe the particular direction he took was significant in clearing an ideological path toward the expectation that *applied* science could lead the way to the secular millennium. That step was crucial to the acceptance of the advances in industry that led to the catastrophic destruction of what I have called the "home" that nature bequeathed to our race.

During the period leading up to the French Revolution, Saint-Simon had a career as a soldier that took him at one point to the battle at Yorktown, Virginia, where he was part of the French force that combined with an American army to defeat the British under Cornwallis and in effect secure the independence of Britain's American colonies. But a military career was not one he was satisfied with; his contact with the Americans, he says, inspired him with more elevated ambitions:

> My calling was not at all to being a soldier. I was meant for a very different sort of activity, a contrary one I might say. To study the progress of the human mind, to work then for the perfecting of civilization, this was the goal I set for myself. From then on I would devote myself to it completely, I would consecrate my whole life to it, and from then on this new work would begin to take up all my efforts.[1]

This exalted calling, however, did not emerge immediately thereafter in his life. For a while he promoted canal-building schemes, and then during the revolution he became involved in very profitable real estate transactions enabling him for a time to enjoy a lavish lifestyle in Paris. During the Terror he fell afoul of the Jacobins and narrowly escaped the guillotine. It was only after the rise of Bonaparte that his messianic inspiration manifested itself, and it remained dominant for the rest of his life as he tried in one way or another to interest powerful people in his schemes to reform the political and social life of Europe. It is certainly fair to view Saint-Simon as a secular millennialist, for he became convinced that inevitably, and in the not too distant future, a much improved ordering of human society would emerge. In 1814 he and his enthusiastic assistant Augustin Thierry wrote as follows in their essay on how to reorganize European society after the collapse of Napoleon's empire:

> The golden age of the human race is not at all behind us; it lies ahead; it lies in the perfection of the social order. Our ancestors did not at all get to see it; our offspring will get there one day; it's up to us to clear for them the path to it.[2]

In 1802 and 1803 Saint-Simon wrote two letters, eventually published, that lay out themes that were to recur in his writings from then on. The first letter proclaims his belief that an elect of persons of genius—in particular, *scientific* genius—must be given respect and independence so that they can lead the way to intellectual and cultural reform. He outlines a plan to give a monetary reward to three mathematicians, three physicists, three chemists, three physiologists, three authors, three painters, and three musicians, who will then take advantage of their financial independence to provide the cultural leadership for a new society. When in the first letter he addresses men of property to enlist their support, the crucial motivation for the proposal emerges:

> Gentlemen, by adopting the project which I am proposing you will reduce the crises which these peoples have been destined to suffer (without it no power in the world would be able to prevent them) to some simple changes in their government and in their finances, and you will save them from that general fermentation with which

> the people of France have been stricken—a sort of fermentation in which all the relations that exist among the individuals of the same nation become precarious, anarchy, the worst of all scourges, freely wreaks havoc to the point that the state of misery in which it thrusts the whole of the nation on which it weighs engenders in the soul of the most ignorant of its members the desire for the reestablishment of order.[3]

At this point, in his mind, the French Revolution had been a disaster, but it had been, nonetheless, a response to a situation in Europe that demanded change. His proposal would enable such reform through "simple governmental and financial changes" that avoided the chaos of full-scale revolution. For the rest of his life Saint-Simon will continue to elaborate on these "simple" changes and advocate for their enactment.

In these letters Saint-Simon grants scientists an especially exalted status:

> A scientist, my friends, is a man who foresees. It is because science provides the means for predicting that it is useful, and that scientists are superior to all other men.[4]

Science, as he asserts, enables its possessor to predict, and that is what makes it useful. In the second of these letters he makes clear that potentially science can predict everything and that this capacity is not limited to the physical sciences but applies to the "moral" ones, that is, the sciences of human life and society, as well:

> Suppose that you have obtained knowledge of the way in which matter is situated at some time or other and that you have made a map of the universe which indicates by certain numbers the quantity of matter which each of the portions of the universe contains. You will then clearly see that once you apply the law of universal gravitation to this map you will be able to predict (just as precisely as the state of your mathematical knowledge permits) all the succeeding changes which would occur in the universe.

> This supposition puts your intelligence in a place where all the phenomena come before it with the same appearance; for when you examine on the map of the universe the portion of space occupied by your own individual self, you will not find any difference between the phenomena which you called moral and those which you called physical.[5]

Saint-Simon had been greatly impressed with Condorcet's *Sketch* and believed that it laid the foundations for a science of human mental advancement that would show progress in knowledge, and hence morality, to be inevitable. This is why in the second letter he equates his proposal to a new religion, the "Religion of Newton," one in which "the obligation is imposed on everyone to constantly use their personal powers for the benefit of humanity." "For Newton will certainly not allow any workers to remain useless on this planet."[6]

Science, in contrast to theology and metaphysics, is "positive," that is, it obeys the injunction that "*men should believe only those things avowed by reason and confirmed by experience*," a principle he believes Descartes first established in Western thought.[7] (Saint-Simon continues the sanctification of both Bacon and Descartes, which had been common among the *philosophes*.) This method contrasts with that of scholastic metaphysics, which the clergy still clung to and which persists in obstructing the inevitable progress of the human mind. But the *philosophes* and scientists had certainly breached the walls of this retrograde citadel in the previous century, as he remarks in this colourful passage:

> I imagine the principles of the theological system as solidified into ramparts with the clergy taking refuge within this fort. I see the natural scientists forming an army busy battering a breach in those ramparts. Finally, I envisage Diderot and d'Alembert as the generals who have ordered the natural scientists to make a full-scale assault against the place defended by the theologians.[8]

Science's exalted mission in the progress of the mind will be fully realized only when science achieves such a level of understanding that it will acknowledge a single overarching principle from which all less general principles can be derived. Saint-Simon declared that science had two moments in its investigations: one was analytic and delved deeper into the particular facts of the world, and the other was synthetic and sought to encompass these facts under principles of greater and greater generality. The ultimate would be a single principle encompassing everything. In an encomium to Socrates, Saint-Simon expressed both these ideas:

> Socrates is the greatest man who has ever existed. None of the men who will exist will be able to equal Socrates, because this supreme genius produced the most powerful concept the human mind can possibly give birth to...When I analysed the concept Socrates produced, I found that it consists of two general and elementary ideas: One, that a system should be a totality organized in such a way that the secondary principles are to be deduced from a single general principle, and tertiary principles from the secondary ones... The other idea involved in his concept was that men, if they are to organize their system scientifically...have to proceed alternatively *a priori* and *a posteriori* in the coordination of their ideas.[9]

Saint-Simon sums up the implications of this line of thought as follows:

> The overall system encompassing our areas of knowledge will be reorganized; its organization will be based on the belief that the universe is ruled by just one immutable law. All the applied systems, such as the systems of religion, politics, morals, civil legislation, will be made to accord with the systemization of our areas of knowledge.[10]

No wonder, then, that at one point in his career Saint-Simon sees the scientists as replacing the clergy, or at least the clergy as being trained in science rather than the theology currently taught in his day.

Around 1813 Saint-Simon was convinced that the Law of Gravitation was the "single immutable law" that science should acknowledge as the basis of our understanding of all reality. In his *Travail sur la gravitation universelle* he imagines Francis Bacon upbraiding the French Academy as follows:

> You have presidents and secretaries. Yet you do not form a scientific body; you are merely a gathering of scientists. And your studies have no unity; they are merely series of ideas which are joined together, because they are not related to any general conception, and because your association is not organised systematically... Select an idea to which you can relate all others and from which you can deduce all principles as consequences. Then you will have a philosophy. This philosophy will certainly be based on the idea of Universal Gravitation.[11]

But not long thereafter Saint-Simon's focus shifted from science to production, from scientists to *industriels*, and the organization of the economy became his foremost concern.[12] In his *Lettres à un Américain*, which appeared in *L'Industrie*, vol. 2, 1817, Saint-Simon is perfectly clear about what his chief priority is:

> Yes, sir, in my opinion the sole goal at which all thoughts and efforts ought to aim *is the organization most favourable to industry*, i.e., to industry in the broadest sense of the term, which encompasses all types of useful work: theorizing as much as applications, works of the mind as much as those of the hands. By "organization most favourable to industry" I mean a government where the political power takes no action and deploys no force except what is necessary to prevent useful work from being disturbed...a government which is such that society, which alone can know what agrees with it, what it wants and what it prefers, is to be the sole judge of the worth and usefulness of works; and, consequently, the producer would expect payment for his work and recompense for his service solely from the consumer. [emphasis in original][13]

At this point Saint-Simon is arguing for the liberal cause, and he is quite adamant in his support of freedom for the *industriels*—that is, all who engage in genuinely productive work—from interference by governments. The above passage makes society itself, not some political elite, the judge of what production is genuinely useful, and he intimates that the consumers will by what they decide to purchase decide what goods on the market merit further production.

Idleness is for Saint-Simon a social and moral disease, and the idle classes, the nobility and the clergy in the main, are a drag on industrial efforts and thus on progress. In *Declaration de principes*, which also appeared in *L'Industrie*, vol. 2, 1817, he becomes quite vitriolic on this point.

> But there surrounds society, there circulates in its heart, a crowd of parasitic people, who, while having the same needs and the same desires as other people, have not been able like them to get over the laziness natural to everybody, and who, while producing nothing, consume or want to consume as if they were producing. It is by force that these people live off the labour of others, either on what is given them or on what they take. In short, we have idlers, which is to say thieves.[14]

The role of government then becomes the elimination of this sort of idleness, which if allowed to flourish will only lead to class warfare. And this is all that government should be concerned with:

> Idleness, that is the subject matter for government. As soon as its actions are applied beyond that, it becomes arbitrary, domineering, and, consequently, tyrannical and hostile to industry... Every time an action superior and foreign to industry involves itself in industry and what pertains to governing it, it hinders and discourages it...
>
> What industry needs is to be governed as little as possible, and there is only one way to attain that: to be governed in the cheapest way possible.[15]

The reader might well infer from such a passage that Saint-Simon is in favour of a totally unregulated economy based on competition in a free market, in other words, *laissez-faire*; but in fact, this is not the case, and it is just on this issue that Saint-Simon makes perhaps his most prescient recommendation. He believes in some sort of ruling body whose main task is drawing up a budget. This he considers an "administrative" task and one which is best carried out by the leading *industriels* themselves in collaboration with their bankers. He writes in *Considérations sur les mesures à prendre pour terminer la revolution* (1820):

> In the present state of civilization the premier political capacity is the capacity for administration; the most important minister is the minister of finance; and the government which would acquire the greatest reputation would be the one which would produce the best budgetary program, which is to say the program of a sort which most accords with the interests of the farmers, the businessmen and the manufacturers.
>
> Now, of all the Frenchmen it is the industrials who are the most learned in administration, because their capital is always in action, because their capital, on account of their credit, is triple in value that of what they possess.[16]

Administration as opposed to ruling becomes an ever more important theme in Saint-Simon's works, with the former holding the place of honour. Here is a passage from *L'Artiste, le savant et l'industiel; dialogue, Opin. Litt.*, published in 1825 not long before his death. In this dialogue the artist is speaking:

> God forbid, nevertheless, that I hold those who govern as useless! Responsible for giving society its regulations they perform for it very important and very real services, once they see that the high administration of public affairs is entrusted to positive capacities and they are led to regard their functions as merely secondary and to recognize that there has to be between them and the men of industry, of science, and of the fine arts, the same distance which exists in the schools between the supervisors and the teachers.[17]

Note the reference to "positive" capacities, that is, to knowledge gained through observation and reasoning, the method of the positive, that is, genuine, sciences. Five years earlier in *Deuxième extrait de mon ouvrage sur l'organisation sociale, L'Organisateur,* pt. 2, Saint-Simon had described the new political order and its goal:

> Thus, we believe it possible to propose in principle that in the new political order social organization must have as its sole and permanent goal the best possible application of the fields of knowledge acquired in the sciences, in the fine arts, and in the arts and crafts to the satisfaction of human needs.[18]

And shortly after we learn this:

> All the questions which are troubling in such a political system... and all those which these can give rise to are eminently positive and answerable; decisions can only be the result of scientific proofs that are absolutely independent of all human will and susceptible of being discussed by all those who have the degree of learning sufficient to understand them.[19]

Government in the traditional sense has given way to scientific administration. The goals are given. They would have been well summed up as the "relief of man's estate," to use Bacon's phrase. All that remains is to determine the best means of achieving those goals, and this is where the science of man comes into play, and it is a science just as "positive" as the physical ones:

> Henceforth, the science of societies should be treated in the same way as all other sciences, by employing no other means but reasoning and observation. On the basis of purely human principles man should establish what he ought to do, what he should avoid, what is proper for society, what is harmful to it.[20]

Politics will be turned over to scientists, who will exclude from the discussion those who have no expertise in the science required:

> But when politics has risen to the rank of an observation-based science, something which today is not far off, the state of capacities will become clear and definite, and the political culture will be exclusively assigned to a special class of scientists who will impose silence on all the twaddle.[21]

But what is this a science of? Since in his mind the welfare of society depends almost entirely on the promotion of production and full employment, it is a matter of knowing how best to accomplish those goals. In other words, it is economics that should now assume the dominant place in the administration of society. In the eighth of his *Lettres à un Américain* Saint-Simon at first lauds the economist Jean Baptiste Say (1754–1836),[22] quoting him at length, before criticizing him for distinguishing *political economy* (Say's field) from *politics*:

> It can be seen clearly that M. Say here views politics and political economy as two distinct and separate things. On the other hand, those who have read his work or heard his public lectures will know what importance he attaches to the science which he deals with, and how often he repeats that it alone has given to morals and politics any certainty and positiveness they might have.
>
> This contradiction proves that the author has sensed vaguely, almost in spite of himself, that political economy is the true and sole foundation of politics, but that he has not seen it in a precise enough manner, since he in fact makes it known only in the details of his work and not in his general considerations.[23]

And in a footnote Saint-Simon is even more explicit:

> With still a little more courage, a little more philosophy, and soon political economy will be born to its true place. At the beginning it gets applied to politics, and politics will come to be

based on it, or rather it itself will be the whole of politics. This moment is not far off.[24]

Saint-Simon proceeds to tell us what the science of political economy will one day establish as incontrovertible truths. First:

> The production of useful things is the sole reasonable and positive goal which political societies can set for themselves; and, consequently, the principle of *respect for production and for producers* is infinitely more fruitful than the principle of *respect for property and property owners*. [emphasis in the original][25]

Saint-Simon had no time for *rentiers*, that is, idle people who live off the proceeds from their investments while doing no work themselves; hence his remark about who deserves respect. But the most radical part of this passage comes in the first sentence, which contends that production is the sole goal of political society and thus of politics. This, of course, makes a science of the organization of society's productive resources the science of politics.

A second soon to be revealed truth is that "governments should restrict themselves to protecting industry against every kind of trouble and impediment," in other words, the liberal ideology we noted earlier. But then comes the third truth, which tells us who should be regulating society:

> Since producers of useful things are the only useful people in society, they are the only ones who ought to be involved in its progress. Since they are the only ones who really pay taxes, they are the only ones who should have the right to vote them.[26]

Could this be the origin of Marx's famous quip about government in capitalist society being the executive committee of the capitalist class? Probably not, but even if so, it has an opposite meaning, for by the "producers" Saint-Simon means people who are doing work, and no doubt he has especially in mind the managers of large enterprises including farms, mercantile companies, and manufacturing companies. (See the passages above on pp. 283–85.) Certainly, too, bankers must be included, for Saint-Simon was well aware of the capacity of banks through lending and interest rates to exercise a good deal of control over the economy as a whole. These people do the regulating, not the government (now reduced to maintaining the peaceful social order that industry requires in order to thrive), and they do it by learning the science of political economy.

Saint-Simon holds that like any well-developed science, this one must reduce back to one basic principle, and he knows what that principle is going to be:

> There is an ordering of interests, which everybody senses, the interests which concern the maintenance of life and of well being. This ordering of interests is the only one to which all people listen and would need to be in accord with, the only one on which they would have to deliberate, to take common action. It is the only one, then, on which politics would be able to concern itself and which ought to be used as the sole standard when criticizing all institutions and all things social.
>
> Politics is, then, to be brief, *the science of production*, that is to say, the science whose object is the ordering of things that is most favourable for all the kinds of production.[27] [emphasis in the original]

Society, on this view, has become an enterprise to create a full life and well-being for all its citizens, and we will soon have a science of how to do this, for the goal is achieved simply by the production of goods and services, as we say now, and the science needed, political economy, is well on its way to fully "positive" status. But is that all that human well-being requires, we might ask? What about our relations with others, morals in the sense of the term Saint-Simon uses? Well, our science has an answer for that too. The sixth of the truths Saint-Simon says it will shortly deliver to us runs as follows:

> Morals improve at the same time as industry is perfected. This observation is true whether one looks at the relations of one people to another or at the relations among individuals.

> Consequently, education spreads, ideas strengthen in all minds; rendered everywhere dominant are those which tend to increase in each person productive activity and respect for other people's productive activity.[28]

The improvement in morals is in part a by-product of the decrease in idleness brought on by increase in industry, for we know what Saint-Simon thinks of idleness. But our science is going to prescribe the sort of education that makes youngsters honour productivity and all those who forward and exhibit it. Productivity is coming close here to being not just a means to the good life but also a prominent constituent of the good life, something to be valued for its own sake, for now it is really the essence of human virtue, the sort of life we come to admire and desire.

At the end of his life Saint-Simon attempted to enlist his own version of Christianity as a motivator for honouring productivity. Like a number of Enlightenment figures he would reduce Christianity to what he takes to be the central moral tenet of the gospels. In *Nouveau christianisme; Diologuies entre un conservateur et un novateur; Premier dialogue* (1825), he offers up this proposal put into the mouth of the innovator:

> God has said: *People should treat one another as brothers*. This sublime principle contains all there is that is divine in the Christian religion...
>
> Now, according to this principle which God gave to men as a rule governing their conduct they must organize their society in the way which would be able to be most advantageous to the greatest number; they should set as the goal of all their works, of all their actions, the quickest and most complete amelioration possible of the moral and physical existence of the most numerous class. [emphasis in the original][29]

I do not think we should doubt that Saint-Simon all along was concerned about the welfare of the "most numerous class," that is, the poor, but his sudden discovery that this was what Christianity was really about, and not all that metaphysical-theological phantasy the Enlightenment had debunked, I suspect, is a desperate last-ditch effort to enlist support from those who had not entirely deserted the traditional faith. Saint-Simon's later life was spent in large part trying to attract sympathy from unlikely sources. Later Saint-Simonians were keen to promote this particular tactic, and no doubt it met with a modicum of success. But Saint-Simon's basic vision, the one described so forthrightly in that eighth letter to an American, remains the same: society should maximize production and turn its management over to those who understand the science of political economy. It's just a matter of how to get people to sign on to it.

My contention is that later in the century and even more in the century to follow, powerful people did sign on to it, but that was only after the promised science of political economy actually appeared in full scientific garb, or at least people thought it did. That is a story we will come to in the next chapter.

Auguste Comte: Science a Remedy for Cultural Anarchy
Saint-Simon was assisted in his propagandizing between 1817 and 1824 by a young man who had been educated in science at the prestigious *École Polytechnique* and who found the older man's vision and determination to rescue European civilization from the chaos induced by the French Revolution consonant with his own aspirations. This was Auguste Comte (1798–1857), who was to push the scientific millennialism of Saint-Simon to its full completion. The latter had, of course, promoted "positive science," and Comte turned this basic faith into a whole philosophy, which he called "positivism." Its eventual (and inevitable) adoption would be, he thought, the salvation of a Europe plagued with intellectual anarchy. As he says near the beginning of the first of his two mammoth multi-volume works, the *Cours de Philosophie Positive* (published between 1830 and 1842)[30]:

> The positive philosophy offers the only solid basis for that social reorganization that must succeed the critical condition in which the most civilized nations are now living.[31]

The positive philosophy basically authorizes as the sole way of understanding the world the observation of facts and reasoning upon those facts so as to uncover the laws governing the phenomena of that world. In the "positive state" he says:

> the mind has given over the vain search after absolute notions, the origin and destination of the universe, and the causes of phenomena, and applies itself to the study of their laws—that is, their invariable relations of succession and resemblance. Reasoning and observation, duly combined, are the means of this knowledge.[32]

He contrasts this way of proceeding with two other ways that had been practised in the past and still were by some: the "theological" and the "metaphysical." The former makes use of the agency of supernatural beings and was dominant in ancient society. He describes it as follows:

> In the theological state, the human mind, seeking the essential nature of beings, the first and final causes (the origin and purpose) of all effects—in short, absolute knowledge—supposes all phenomena to be produced by the immediate action of supernatural beings.[33]

The "metaphysical" approach, on the other hand, relies on abstract entities rather than supernatural agents:

> In the metaphysical state, which is only a modification of the first, the mind supposes, instead of supernatural beings, abstract forces, veritable entities (that is, personified abstractions) inherent in all beings, and capable of producing all phenomena.[34]

Prime examples of these "abstract forces" would be the substantial forms of Aristotelian science as practised by the scholastics. But Comte makes of this threefold division not just a basis for classifying modes of scientific thought but the ground for three different types of civilizations. This is based on a fundamental assumption he shared with Saint-Simon:

> It cannot be necessary to prove to anybody who reads this work that ideas govern the world, or throw it into chaos—in other words, that all social mechanism rests upon opinions. The great political and moral crisis that societies are now undergoing is shown by a rigid analysis to arise out of intellectual anarchy.[35]

In other words, it is how people describe the world to themselves that determines the way a civilization carries on. When these ideas are in chaos, life in the whole society is as well. The development of the mental faculties is basic, as he says in his early *Plan of the Scientific Operations Necessary for Reorganizing Society* (THIRD ESSAY, 1822):

> Civilization properly so called consists on one hand in the development of the human mind, on the other in the result of this—namely, the increasing power of man over nature. In other words, the component elements of civilization are science, the fine arts, and industry.[36]

As we shall see, it is our understanding of the world, a civilization's "science," that is primary for Comte, and out of this arises "the increasing power of man over nature", and thus the development of the civilization. In the same work he traces the results right down to the political arrangements:

> For if it is clear that the political order is the exponent of the civil order, it is, at least equally apparent that the civil order itself is merely the exponent of the state of civilization.[37]

Comte's idea is simply that civilizations are products of the dominant way in which the people in them view the world they inhabit as well as their own place in it. The theological way produces one sort of civilization: the militaristic. The metaphysical way produces the society based on laws. But this latter is only a way station leading to what is now in the process of formation, the civilization based on the philosophy of positivism. The earlier philosophies relied on imagination more than reason and observation; now, positivism will eliminate imagination from the method we employ to determine how the world operates:

> The theological and metaphysical states of any science possess one characteristic in common—the predominance of imagination over observation. The only difference that exists between them under this point of view is that in the first the imagination occupies itself with supernatural beings and in the second, with personified abstractions.[38]

In the most original of his dogmas, Comte claims that these modes of understanding follow each other historically in a necessary sequence, which accordingly results in a sequence of three types of civilizations. Europe has been through the first (the ancient world), is emerging from the second (medieval Christian Europe), and is moving toward the third and final positivist civilization. Comte believes the sequence is necessary in all cultures, although Europe is further advanced in it than others. Furthermore, he postulates that we have here a law of nature in the same sense that Newton's laws are laws of nature, and that this law is discovered by observation of human history. The law is fundamental to the now developing positive science of human society, i.e., sociology:

> From the study of the development of human intelligence, in all directions, and through all times, the discovery arises of a great fundamental law, to which it is necessarily subject, and which has a solid foundation of proof, both in the facts of our organization and in our historical experience. The law is this: that each of our leading conceptions—each branch of our knowledge—passes successively through three different theoretical conditions: the theological, or fictitious; the metaphysical, or abstract; and the scientific, or positive.[39]

The law guides the positive study of society so that it sees the institutions of that society as the result of the stage of advancement of the ruling ideas of that society:

> The scientific doctrine of politics...[notes] the constant tendency of man to act upon nature in order to modify it for his own advantage. It then considers the social order as aiming at a collective development of this natural tendency, so as to give the highest possible efficiency to this useful action. This being settled, it endeavors, by direct observations on the collective development of the race, to deduce from the fundamental laws of human organization the evolution it had undergone...this doctrine regards the improvements reserved for each epoch as necessitated, without resorting to any hypothesis, by the stage of development that the human race has reached. Thus in reference to each degree of civilization, it views political combinations as merely intended to facilitate natural tendencies where these have been sufficiently ascertained.[40]

Note well the claim that improvements in society are "necessitated" by the "stage of development." Here is an important source for the talk still current today of "developed" and "underdeveloped" countries, and how "improvement" of the latter depends on their "developing" the way the former already have. As is implied in the preceding passage, the law of the sequence of the three stages is not the only law operative here. There are two economic laws regarding the accumulation of capital that explain the motive force promoting the development of a society:

> Of these two economic laws, one may be called subjective, the other objective; for the former concerns man, the latter concerns the world without. They consist of these two truths: first, each individual can produce more than he consumes; second, products can be preserved for a longer time than is necessary to reproduce them...Having ascertained these two elementary conditions of labor, we shall see that by their joint operation the accumulation of temporal wealth is possible.[41]

Comte's idea here is that production tends to outstrip consumption and that the surplus can be preserved for a longer time than it takes to produce it. The result is the accumulation of wealth, which in turn can be used to facilitate greater production and greater surpluses. Comte believes that the efficient administration of this wealth requires its accumulation in a few hands and that this leads to central government and hence to the creation of genuine civilization. But how people go about generating that wealth is largely determined by the way in which they understand the world, by the sort of "science" they have. There is no tendency in Comte, as there is in Marx, to make the economic laws determine the "spiritual" (i.e., intellectual) development. Ideas develop according to their own law, that of the sequence of the three stages, and ideas, as we noted, are in Comte's view fundamental in determining the course of a civilization's development. The natural human desire for material prosperity provides the driving force, but ideas do the steering.

The development of human society that results in accord with these laws is, Comte holds, progressive in the strict sense of leading to greater and greater improvement in human life. He speaks of "ameliorating" that life, and his conception of just what that "ameliorating" consists in is far broader than that of many "progressives," both in his day and our own. It is definitely not a matter of an increase in "happiness," as he makes clear in this passage from the *Cours*:

> We have nothing to do here with the metaphysical controversy about the absolute happiness of man at different stages of civilization. As the happiness of every man depends on the harmony between the development of his various faculties and the entire system of the circumstances that govern his life, and as, on the other hand, this equilibrium always establishes itself spontaneously to a certain extent, it is impossible to compare in a positive way, by either sentiment or reasoning, the individual welfare that belongs to social situations that can never be brought into direct comparison.[42]

Individuals are happy, he is saying here, to the extent that the use of their faculties harmonizes with the circumstances in which they find themselves, and this harmony can occur in all civilizations regardless of how far advanced they are. There is no sense in trying to determine between civilizations whether people in one were happier in this way than those in another.

Rather, the amelioration of human life is to be seen in objective conditions that include not only the increase in the ease with which humans procure the material means of life, although that is part of it and Comte thinks progress in this area is evident in the historical record of development, but also the perfecting of human natural faculties. He puts it as follows:

> Taking the human race as a whole, and not any one people, it appears that human development brings after it, in two ways, an ever-growing amelioration, first, in the radical condition of man, which no one disputes, and, next, in his corresponding faculties, which is a view much less attended to.[43]

In particular, human moral faculties have improved with the advancement of civilization.

> In regard to morals, particularly, I think it indisputable that the gradual development of humanity favors a growing preponderance of the noblest tendencies of our nature.[44]

In fact, it is this development of our faculties that is the summit of the amelioration Comte envisions. The philosopher will account material progress as of little worth if it does not lead to perfecting morals and our mental life:

> Taking, then, this point of view, we may say that the one great object of life, personal or social, is to become more perfect in every way—in our external condition first, but also and more especially in our own nature...A nation that has made no efforts to improve itself materially will take but little interest in moral or mental improvement. This is the only ground on which enlightened men can feel much pleasure in the material progress of our own times.[45]

When it comes to the improvement of human faculties Comte applies what amounts to an Aristotelian view of amelioration, but he places it in the whole context of animal life:

> If we regard the course of human development from the highest scientific point of view, we shall perceive that it consists in educing, more and more, the characteristic faculties of humanity, in comparison with those of animality; and especially with those that man has in common with the whole organic kingdom. It is in this philosophical sense that the most eminent civilization must be pronounced to be fully accordant with nature, since it is, in fact, only a more marked manifestation of the chief properties or our species—properties that, latent at first, can come into play only in that advanced state of social life for which they are exclusively destined…This comparative estimate affords us the scientific view of human progression, connected, as we see it is, with the whole course of animal advancement, of which it is itself the highest degree.[46]

Our species stands at the summit of a continuum of animal life with "properties" characteristic of humans alone that can be expressed and developed only in a community and by participation in the life of that community. The progress in social institutions is enabled and is facilitated by progress in the development of these human capacities that can be exercised only in social life.

Comte acknowledges that the irrational desires and emotions motivate us much more than our reason does. Initially they set the goals, which reason then pursues. But our advancement consists largely in reason coming more and more to direct the course that humans and human society take, and it is in this that we come to surpass all the other animals:

> If our reason required at the outset the awakening and stimulating influence of the appetites, the passions, and the sentiments, not the less has human progression gone forward under its direction. It is only through the more and more marked influence of reason over the general conduct of man and of society that the gradual march of our race has attained that regularity and persevering continuity that distinguish it so radically from the desultory and barren expansion of even the highest of the animal orders.[47]

This process will be markedly strengthened once the positive philosophy has been generally accepted, for it will show with scientific certitude that respect for moral rules is essential for the operation of an advanced civilization and thus give an "energy and tenacity" to them that they had lacked previously:

> In our present state of anarchy, we see nothing that can give us an idea of the energy and tenacity that moral rules must acquire when they rest on a clear understanding of the influence that the actions and the tendencies of every one of us must exercise on human life...the intellectual unity of that time will not only determine practical moral convictions in individual minds but also generate powerful public prepossession, by disclosing a plenitude of assent, such as has never existed in the same degree, and will supply the insufficiency of private efforts, in cases of very imperfect culture, or entanglement of passion.[48]

But now, what does morality of the sort Comte endorses so enthusiastically teach us? The answer becomes quite clear in Comte's later *opus magnum*, his *Système*. The following passages deserve a close reading.

> The chief problem of human life was thus shown to be the subordination of egoism to altruism...the whole of social science consists therefore in duly working out this problem, the essential principle being the reaction of collective over individual life.[49]

Humans need to arrive at a morality that promotes each individual's concern for the welfare of his fellows as against concern for his own personal needs. No doubt Comte believes that this is the culmination of a progress from minimal to greater and greater interdependence among members of a society for the fulfilment of everyone's needs. The science of society will reveal this interdependence and how it enables not just the satisfaction of material needs but the full development of the human faculties mentioned earlier.

Nevertheless, the satisfaction of the personal material needs of individuals is a prerequisite for the higher developments, and once this is achieved those egoistic impulses can be easily controlled:

> Although the personal instincts greatly predominate in the constitution of the brain, the paramount place they hold is due chiefly to the constant stimulus of physical wants. Were this removed, they would be easily restrained by forces arising from the varied contact of society. The natural course of human relations would dispose us all to cultivate the only instincts that admit of a perfectly universal and almost boundless expansion.[50]

By those latter instincts Comte can only mean the altruistic ones, whose expansion cannot but be conducive to social life. But Comte goes even further by advocating for the curtailment of what we deem material necessities so that the development of those faculties distinctive of humans and that elevate us above the rest of the animal kingdom, among which will be our moral instincts, can be perfected:

> The hypothesis assumed brings us therefore to the general conclusion that the continued suppression of our material necessities would result in a more simple and more perfect type of humanity, and render its development more free and speedy.[51]

Morality, then, basically teaches benevolent love of our fellow humans. In the *Système* this ethic is extolled in hyperbolic fashion, as Comte constructs for humanity a full-scale religion to replace the medieval Catholicism that had once unified Western Europe. And like that morality of the fast-disappearing metaphysical state of civilization, the new morality endorsed by positive science needs an objective base, something in the cosmos that renders it objectively justified. Comte give us this too. Let us follow another passage from his *Système*, one that lays out this thought in some detail.

> The first condition of unity is a subjective principle, and this principle in the positive system is the subordination of the intellect to the

> heart...But this first condition, indispensable as it is, would be quite insufficient for the purpose, without some objective basis, existing independently of ourselves in the external world. That basis consists for us in the laws of order of the phenomena by which humanity is regulated.[52]

Although the feeling of love for humanity must come to be our dominant motivation, we need besides this subjective grounding for morality something objective "in the external world," and this is the laws of nature that relate to humans and their societies and that the positive science of society is discovering, or at least Comte is discovering. But how does this work?

> The subjection of human life to this order in incontestable, and as soon as the intellect has enabled us to comprehend it, it becomes possible for the feeling of love to exercise a controlling influence over our discordant tendencies. This, then, is the mission allotted to the intellect in the positive synthesis; in this sense it is that it should be consecrated to the service of the heart...The social instincts would never gain the mastery were they not sustained and called into constant exercise by the economy of the external world, an influence which at the same time checks the power of the selfish instincts.[53]

Our feeling of love for our fellow humans would be unable to dominate the chaos of our emotions, and altruism would never get the better of egoism, were we not to see intellectually that the immutable laws of nature governing human life demand that in the end the rule of the social feeling is required for the inevitable advancement of human civilization and way of life:

> Now the benevolent affections, which themselves act in harmony with the laws of social development, incline us to submit to all other laws, as soon as the intellect has discovered their existence. The possibility of moral unity depends, therefore, even in the case of the individual, but still more in that of society, upon the necessity of recognizing our subjection to an external power...

> That basis is, that all events whatever, the events our own personal and social life included, are always subject to natural relations of sequence and similitude, which in all essential respects lie beyond the reach of our interference.[54]

Comte envisions that the realization that there is in nature itself something to whose direction of human progress we must submit works symbiotically with the rise of the social motivations and feelings, each supporting and motivating the other:

> On the one hand, it is requisite that our minds should conceive a Power without us so superior to ourselves as to command the complete submission of our entire life. But on the other hand, it is equally indispensable that our moral nature be inspired within by one affection capable of habitually combining all the rest. These two essential conditions naturally tend to work as one, since the sense of submission to a Power without necessarily seconds the discipline of the moral nature within, and this in turn prepares the way for the spirit of submission...[55]

Our submission is to a pre-established order that compels humans to an ever more interdependent social nexus and thus to the need for social feelings, that is, altruistic ones, to preserve the unity of that nexus. Comte can thus view this order as a sort of "providence" exercised by "the true Great Being" whereby our egoistic desires are gradually brought under the rule of the altruistic ones:

> But while we offer blessings to the fatality that becomes the chief source of our real greatness, we must refer all the benefits we receive from it to the active providence, first spontaneous and then systematic, by means of which the true Great Being renders more and more salutary a bondage once found so oppressive. This transformation of life, the chief triumph of our species rests necessarily on the gradual substitution of the social for the personal character

in the whole of our practical existence, the instrument by which it is effected being the steady concentration of capital.[56]

The reference to the "concentration of capital" as the "instrument" by which all this is brought about reaffirms what was noted earlier: the motivating force for the progress of humanity is the constant pressure to make more efficient use of economic surplus by bringing it under the control of a small number of people operating for the good of the whole society. Comte would certainly admit that the progress thus engendered would have to pass through periods of human history in which gross inequalities and injustices existed, including slavery and wars, but in the end the most efficient mode of operation would be one in which a morality that suppresses egoistic motivation in favour of concern for the welfare of all in society rules people's lives. Thus economic pressure will eventually and inevitably lead to that result.

Comte's vision marks the intellectual apex of secular millenarianism in the Western world. Given Comte's affection for medieval Christianity it is not too surprising to find striking parallels between his view of history and that of the twelfth-century monk Joachim of Fiore, whom we discussed in an earlier chapter. Both saw human history as a story of predetermined progress, both saw it as advancing through three stages, both saw their current society as near the end of the second stage, both were much more concerned with moral and "spiritual" progress than with material, and both believed that a certain class of "spiritual" persons would be instrumental in bringing about the final stage— monks in the case of Joachim, scientists in the case of Comte. Furthermore, both visions suffer from a tension between the inevitability of progress as determined by some irresistible "providence," on the one hand, and the crucial role of certain human beings in bringing progress to fruition, on the other.[57]

When we view Comte's proposals and dogmas as part of the long millenarian tradition in the West, we can understand why it could have a genuinely religious hold on his followers and why his motto, "Order and Progress," could become a slogan for progressivist activism, finding its way even onto the flag of Brazil. But Comte's version of the millennium still had a strong moral and intellectual component and actually contained material affluence, mainly because it was a *sine qua non* of moral advancement. His ideology was not, then, entirely what was needed to justify the environmental destruction that the West had by his time already embarked on. It had little sympathy with the wholesale concentration on producing wealth in the sense the word has when Adam Smith speaks of the "wealth of nations." In this respect, it differs markedly from the dogma of his early mentor, Saint-Simon. Another shift in thinking had to occur, and, in fact, was already occurring in Comte's day, as we shall see in what follows here and in the next chapter.

The Engineers as the Vanguard of Progress

In his *Cours* Comte had taken note of the rise of a new class of scientists:

> Meantime, an intermediate class is rising up whose particular destination is to organize the relations of theory and practice, such as the engineers, who do not labor in the advancement of science, but who study it in its existing state, to apply it to practical purposes... Already, Monge,[58] in his view of descriptive geometry, has given us a general theory of the arts of construction...The time will come when out of such results a department of positive philosophy may arise, but it will be in a distant future.[59]

These scientists, that is, the engineers, were interested in applying theoretical science to practical problems, but Comte thought that the theoretical side was not yet sufficiently developed to render these efforts fully scientific. He seems unaware of how within the nascent engineering profession itself a vision of this class was already developing that would radically change the focus of scientific endeavours over the next two centuries.

In the above passage Comte mentions Gaspard Monge, whom he must have known, for Monge was one of the founders during the Revolution in 1794 of the *École Polytechnique*, where Comte himself studied and gained his broad familiarity with the sciences of his day. David F. Noble has noted that Monge was a Freemason, as were the three other men who formed the commission that guided the establishment of the *École*.[60] Freemasonry in the eighteenth and nineteenth centuries promoted the practical arts and applied sciences with a virtually religious zeal often associated with millenarian beliefs. In America, Stephen van Rensselaer (1764–1839), founder in 1824 of the school in Troy, New York, that would become

Rensselaer Polytechnic Institute, the first engineering school in the anglophone world, was a Mason and Grand Master of the Grand Lodge of New York between 1824 and 1829. David F. Noble has cited many other instances of Masons promoting the engineering profession in nineteenth-century America.[61]

By and large Masons of that time in America were fervent Protestants and inheritors of the reforming Protestant views of seventeenth-century Great Britain that we have described earlier. These men were infected to one degree or another with millenarianism in the Baconian mode.[62] Speaking of the Masonic lodges in Britain and other organizations in the period leading up to and including the French Revolution, a recent scholar of Masonry, Margaret Jacob, has said the following:

> By 1790 the lodges have ceased in the minds of their opponents to be centers of religious fanaticism; they are now the Enlightenment fanaticized. They retain the sectarian quality of the enthusiasts, we are told, only now they have adopted a secular political and religious agenda. They are in effect the old revolutionary Puritans of the seventeenth century transformed into new revolutionary philosophes.[63]

The Masons in Britain and on the Continent, however, were not political revolutionaries like the Jacobins of revolutionary Paris. For most Masons the revolution had already occurred in 1688 with the deposition of Charles II and the institution of a constitutional monarchy in Britain. Nor were Masons from the lower classes. After the formation of the Grand Lodge in London and the ascendency of "speculative" Masonry in 1717, aristocrats, intellectuals, government bureaucrats, and other educated men dominated the movement. These individuals were interested in promoting the rule of Parliament, respect for a constitution, the maintenance of general order, and the welfare of society as a whole. Margaret Jacob points out how the Masons tried to practise within their own lodges the political principles they espoused:

> Although entirely private and avoiding any discussion of religion or politics, the typical eighteenth-century British masonic lodge was in effect a microcosm of the ideal civil polity. With an almost utopian

> sense of what is possible...the lodges sought to make a better society through the virtue each brother practiced within a constitutional setting...Within this sociable meritocracy lies the first self-conscious attempt to create societies governed by the abstract principles of British constitutionalism.[64]

The lodges of the period emphasized fraternal harmony within their ranks and were interested in seeing that harmony established in society as a whole. This vision was backed by the high prestige of Newtonian science with its world governed by divine laws. Again Margaret Jacob notes this aspect of Masonry and acknowledges the tensions it involved:

> The early Newtonians laid great emphasis upon order, stability, and the rule of law. The belief in the order proclaimed by science in turn encouraged masonic fantasies about the possibility of creating perfect harmony in human society, if only within the confines of the lodge. Yet the Newtonian model also explicitly proclaimed a rigid spiritual hierarchy within nature, and by implication within society: spiritual forces, "active principles," rules over "brute and stupid" matter. Not surprisingly, masonic aspirations for stability and perfectibility were not always compatible.[65]

To gain a fuller insight into the impulses motivating Masons in the nineteenth century, when they were so influential in promoting engineering and practical science generally, it will be useful first to go further back into the history of the movement, even back to late medieval times. In those days there were guilds of stonemasons who formed quasi-religious organizations that established rules for those who could practise the craft and that governed how they would be trained. Heavily emphasized was the art of geometry as handed down from Euclid, and no doubt knowledge of this area of mathematics was useful in construction projects besides giving the masons a form of expert knowledge not widely disseminated among the people of the time and thus a source of considerable prestige. A poem in Middle English, which has come down to us in a late medieval manuscript, called the "Regius" ms., dates from the late fourteenth century and describes in fabulous terms the origin of masonry, connecting it directly with geometry and Euclid.[66] According to the poem "great lords and ladies" lacking much income sought training for their children from some "clerks" in some art whereby they could maintain their lives. The poem then continues:

> In that time, through good geometry,
> This honest craft of good masonry
> Was ordained and made in this manner,
> Counterfeited of these clerks together;
> At these lords' prayers they counterfeited geometry,
> And gave it the name of masonry,
> For the most honest craft of all.[67]
>
> This great clerk's name was called Euclid,
> His name was spread both far and wide.
> Yet this great clerk ordained still more
> To him that was higher in this degree,
> That he should teach the simplest of wit,
> In that honest craft to be perfect;
> And so each one should teach the other,
> And love together as sister and brother.[68]
>
> In this manner, through good knowledge of geometry,
> Began first the craft of masonry.
> The clerk Euclid in this wise founded
> This craft of geometry in Egyptian land.[69]

The poem shows that two important traits of Masonry that were to persist into modern times, the respect for applied science (in this case, geometry) and the evocation of the spirit of brotherly love, were present long before Masonry took its modern form in the eighteenth century.

Another ms. called the "Matthew Cooke" ms., dating from the early fifteenth century, in a preface to eighteen "charges" (i.e., regulations), provides an even more elaborate story of masonry's origins, this time pushing them back to before the Flood. We need not detain ourselves with that except to note that it too presses the connection with geometry and finds a place for Euclid as the teacher of the craft. What is more interesting is the theological introduction to the work, which I quote in full from the translation by G.W. Speth:

> Thanked be God, our glorious Father, the founder and creator of heaven and earth, and of all that therein are, for that he has vouchsafed, of his glorious Godhead, to make so many things of manifold virtue for the use of mankind. For he made all things to be subject and obedient to man. All things eatable of a wholesome nature he ordained for man's sustenance. And moreover, he hath given to man wit and the knowledge of divine things and handicrafts, by which we may labor in this world, in order to therewith get our livelihood, and fashion many objects pleasant in the sight of God, to our own ease and profit.[70]

From this text we gather that the Masonic theology believed in a Creator who was from the start very friendly toward humans. He had placed in his creation many items useful to them; He had made them the lords of that creation, so that all other things were "subject and obedient" to them. Finally, He had given them knowledge of the practical crafts (chief among which was, of course, masonry) and expected humans to use those crafts to produce things that were not only pleasing to the Creator but also useful to humanity. There is, moreover, a notable omission: the Fall and the affliction of sin. This absence too is a feature of Masonry that persists down through the centuries; there is among Masons a basic optimism about humanity's ability to improve itself, and there is no mention of having lost the knowledge God gave Adam and Eve in the Garden when they committed their act of rebellion. In this the Masons differed from many of the Christian millenarians we treated earlier, and thus they were in a better position to accept the secularization of the millennium that took place in the eighteenth century. The Masonic view of humans is that they have been equipped by the Creator with the intelligence, knowledge, and skills to improve both their world and themselves, and that it would be an act of defiance against that Creator not to proceed on that path.

The transition of Masonry away from "operatives" toward "speculatives"—that is, from guilds of practising masons to lodges containing people who were not masons at all but educated men (and a few women) interested in science, its practical applications, and how it could be used to the benefit of humanity—began in the seventeenth century and was completed early in the eighteenth. It is likely that during this transition the ideas of the Rosicrucians had an impact on Masonry. Certainly both movements had great expectations of science, and both encouraged charitable works. The symbolic rituals of Masonry show what could very well be borrowings from those of the Society of the Rosy Cross, which itself took over a lot of lore from Hermeticism. The scholarship in this area does not, however, admit of drawing any solid conclusions.

Returning to the nineteenth century, we note in Masonic writings a strong emphasis on the unifying of humanity in universal love as the paramount aim of the brotherhood. Here are the words of John Hamilton Graham (1826–1899),[71] who was Grand Master of the Grand Lodge of Quebec, taken from the eulogium he contributed to the History of Masonry published in 1898 and referenced above in note 62:

> Freemasonry proclaims itself to be, and is, a Universal Fellowship. It knows no distinctions among men but those of worth and merit. It is founded upon the equality of man in his inherent and inalienable rights. Its great aim is the amelioration, in all things, of the individual, the family, the neighborhood, the State, the Nation, and the race. All are included in its grand design. Reverencing and utilizing the past, it acts in the living present, and ever strives after a more glorious future. Envious of none, it gladly welcomes the cooperation of all who love their fellow-men.[72]

Note how Graham builds into his conception of Masonry the Enlightenment ideals (promoted as we saw by Condorcet) of equality of all humans and their "inalienable rights." These had been part of European Masonry from the eighteenth century on and have their roots in the medieval guilds as well as in the

British constitutional revolution of 1688. Graham continues in this essay to set Masonry's aims in a cosmic context:

> Freemasonry is a system of symbolic architecture. The grand superstructure to be erected is the cosmic temple of humanity. Therein, labor is nobility and all is dedicate[d] to work and worthship. Man, the rough ashlar,[73] is symbolically taken from the quarry of life,—is hewn, squared, polished, and made well-fit for his place in the great living temple whose chief foundation stones are truth and right; whose main pillars are wisdom, strength, and beauty; whose adornments are the virtues; the key-stone of whose world-o'erspanning arch is brotherhood; and whose Master Builder is The Great Architect of the Universe.[74]

It is humanity itself that Masonry aims to hew into proper moral shape so that humans can take their place in the harmonious order constructed by the Great Architect Himself. And how is this goal to be achieved? Graham answers in the immediately following paragraph:

> Freemasonry is a system of human culture. It inspires a desire for, inculcates a knowledge and teaches the use of, all the liberal arts and sciences. Chief among these is the science of mathematics. Geometry, its most important branch, is the basis of the Craftsman's art, and in ancient times was its synonym. It is taught to be of a divine or moral nature, enriched with the most useful knowledge, so that while it proves the wonderful properties of nature, it demonstrates the more important truths of morality. It teaches a knowledge of the earth, and sun, and moon, and stars, and of the laws which govern them. It is the basis of astronomy, the noblest of the sciences. Above all, it teaches the Craftsman to know and love, to adore and serve, the Grand Geometrician of the Universe.[75]

Graham exhibits here the faith evident as far back as the medieval guilds of masons that there is a connection between geometry and morality whereby knowledge of the former inculcates the latter. This, I think, is the central message of Freemasonry: science and its application in the material world fully support and indeed inspire a morality that seeks the improvement of human life. There is no hint here of doubt, any entertaining of the possibility that science and morality might be entirely disparate and perhaps even at odds. In this regard Masonry is one with the vision of Comte, even though it retains a kind of theological context that Comte would have seen as cast aside by the progress of ideas. Graham explicitly denies that Masonry is a religion, and certainly its theology is not fully Christian. Rather it sets forth a minimum of dogmas that it thinks all theists can accept. Here is Graham again:

> Freemasonry is not a religion or a system of religion. It is the handmaid of all seeking truth, and light, and right. It is a centre of union of good and true men of every race and tongue, who believe in God and practise the sacred duties of morality.[76]

Perhaps this position can be maintained, but only so long as some views that are not officially espoused by Masonry are not also officially denied. I have mentioned the lack of any reference to the doctrine of original sin, a cardinal dogma of orthodox Christianity, both Catholic and Protestant, and one that is profoundly at odds with the humanistic optimism that flows from all accounts of Masonic culture. This optimism emerges in the firm belief that the progress of human scientific knowledge and its practical applications cannot overall but sustain and encourage an improvement in the morals of mankind and thus lead to "peace, prosperity, uprightness, enlightenment, and unlimited good will."[77] It is this belief that energized the Masons who spurred on and directed the rise of the engineering profession and that no doubt inspired many who joined that profession's ranks.

In France the development of such a profession was first formally encouraged in the *École Polytechnique*, although there education in the sciences was oriented very much toward theory rather than practical applications. It also included study of literature and aimed at producing men with a broad education fit for government service, be it civil or military. Technological advances and the changes these introduced in industry led some scientifically educated men to see the need for a more practically oriented education. One result was the founding in 1829 of the *École Centrale des Arts et Manufactures*, which quickly became the leading school for the new profession of engineers, men who went on to ply their expertise in the service as much of private entrepreneurs as of governments. In a book published in 1982[78] John H. Weiss described the establishment of the *École Centrale* and the spirit of its founders, thereby documenting the school's importance for the rise of the profession. What follows is heavily dependent on Weiss's work.

According to Weiss the ideas of Saint-Simon about the importance of the *industriels* and *science industrielle* definitely had an impact on the founders,[79] although the graduates did not generally join in the Saint-Simonian movement. Theodore Olivier (1793–1853),[80] one of the founders of the *École Centrale*, based the importance of applied as opposed to pure theoretical science on the centrality of work in human life, a sentiment that is certainly very Saint-Simonian. Weiss quotes him as follows:

> The pure scientists thus forget, like nobles of all species and countries, that *work* is the condition imposed on man, that that work useful for humanity must be honored and rewarded more than amusements that men devise as mental games or circus tricks. [emphasis in the original]
>
> There is not a single human science that does not owe its birth to the fact that labor is a necessity of the human condition. It is always the need to satisfy an earthly need that has led human intelligence to create in succession all the sciences taught in schools. [81]

Olivier believed that only persons with their roots in technology could teach theoretical science with success. The engineer's mission was to mediate between ideas and the world of material effects, and education at the *École Centrale* aimed at producing men who were broadly trained so that they could carry out this task in all sorts of industries and practical projects.[82] The *science industrielle* combined theory and practice in a way that enabled science to produce the material benefits so necessary for human progress. Weiss assesses this view of the *École* as follows:

> The *École Centrale* stood...as an autonomous and even morally superior institution, the sole repository of the salutary union of theory and practice. One may suggest, then, that the claims made for *la science industrielle* served not so much to sum up the intellectually rigorous rationale of a program of study as they did to assert this faith in a special mission.[83]

Writing on the fiftieth anniversary of the school's founding, Charles de Comberousse (1826–1897),[84] a graduate and later professor at the *École*, drew this picture of the results of a training at the *École Centrale* in which he stresses the graduate's ability to react creatively to a wide variety of demands:

> To pass through the *École Centrale* is to undergo a special kind of tempering. One is now ready for all contingencies. One can leave tomorrow for Asia or America, Japan or Australia, Suez or Panama, sure of being able to face all difficulties, to fulfill all sorts of tasks... In short, he is a generalist first and foremost; he only becomes a specialist by necessity...To adapt the available means in the most rational manner to the assigned goal, with neither unintelligent prodigality nor damaging parsimony; to calculate everything, to prepare everything in advance; to forget nothing; to achieve the most useful, convenient, and least expensive solution with the aid of ingenious combinations; such is the Centrale civil engineer, the brain that sets in motion all efforts destined to create the projected ensemble.[85]

De Combreuse's vision amply shows how his graduates embodied the perfection of what we, using Tönnies's term, have referred to as the *Kürwille* mentality, which emphasizes planning, calculation, ingenuity, and efficiency in obtaining useful ends. Those activities and virtues were the ones that the engineering profession adopted at its birth and that it reveres to the present day.

While the social utility of the work of engineers was emphasized by Olivier, de Comberousse, and others, the moral benefits to be obtained from the profession were not entirely neglected. Weiss notes that supporters of the *École* saw their education as supporting a "moral order":

> In the view of the Centrale spokesmen, science helped in three ways to strengthen the moral order in which emerged their new technological elite: by the personal effectiveness that technical competence gave to the engineer, by the way its enterprises channeled students away from more dangerous careers, and by the general uplift produced by common participation in the acquisition and application of scientific knowledge.[86]

There was also the thought that by increasing productivity, and thus enlarging the "pie" from which the benefits of progress were to be drawn, protest against the inequalities of society would be moderated. This was one of the arguments deployed by the engineer and scientist Walter de Saint-Ange (1793–1851) in praising the education received at the *École*.[87]

The French engineering profession was created, then, in an atmosphere in which many saw the practical applications of science as leading the way to a greatly improved society, both in material terms and in terms of social stability. The engineers, as the translators of progress in scientific theory into practical advances, were the avant-garde of the progressive forces in the world working to fulfil many of the dreams of Saint-Simon and Auguste Comte. Walter de Saint-Ange expressed this messianic view of science vividly as follows:

> It does not suffice that science exists; it must be propagated. It must be summoned to every place that it is currently applicable so that the country may profit from its blessings. It must branch out in all directions to carry everywhere its light and its continual ameliorative powers, to take everywhere its moral, civilizing force.[88]

Comte had to some extent seen it coming, and the engineers became his analogue of Joachim of Fiore's *viri spirituales*, and thus the whole meaning of "progress" was bent in the direction of what the engineers with their *Kürwille* virtues could accomplish for society and humanity.[89] They became the "Heroes and Supermen" whom Bacon had heralded two centuries earlier, and they stood ready to bring the Baconian vision to fulfilment.[90]

9

THE VULGARIZATION OF THE MILLENNIUM

> There will always be a part, and a very large part of every community, that have no care but for themselves, and whose care for themselves reaches little further than impatience of immediate pain, and eagerness for the nearest good.
> —Samuel Johnson, *Taxation No Tyranny*

The recent immense expansion of the Western economy, and of the West's culture generally, has been marked by demand for continual economic growth through mass consumption. Without that impetus we would hardly be facing planetary ecological catastrophe today. Comte's vision of fulfilling material needs only to the degree necessary and then focusing on the spiritual, and even the Masonic ideals of equality, brotherhood, and moral improvement, to some degree constrained any drive for growth and mass consumption. In this chapter we see how an ideology justifying the removal of such constraints came into existence and how that ideology achieved the status of the science Saint-Simon had so desired.

From Smith to Ricardo: Growth Becomes a Necessity

In the first book of his much celebrated *Inquiry into the Nature and Causes of the Wealth of Nations* (= *WN*),[1] Adam Smith entered into a long discussion of what circumstances would increase the relative price of labour, that is, the value of the wages of working people in real terms. Smith was fully aware that most workers in England, and in most European countries, lived only a little above what was required for their subsistence, despite the fact that those countries, and England in particular, were much wealthier than they had been in the not so distant past. This led him to conclude that it is not the level of wealth—what we might call the degree of affluence—in a society that leads to relatively high wages; rather, the fact that that level is *increasing* is what compels wages to rise in real value.[2]

Following his usual mode of inquiry, Smith seeks confirmation for this claim in the actual conditions in various countries. Britain's American colonies, he notes, grant their workers much higher wages than they would get in Britain itself, even though Britain is wealthier (i.e., more affluent). Accordingly, the level of affluence in Britain, if increasing at all, is doing so at a much slower rate than in those prospering colonies. Likewise, China, where the conditions of the labouring class are quite lamentable compared even to those in Britain, even though China's wealth is enormous, remains in a "stationary" state so far as increase in wealth is concerned. In Bengal he finds the masses starving despite great overall wealth, but there the level of wealth is actually declining. (He attributes this to the dominance of "the mercantile company which oppresses and domineers in the East Indies."[3])

Smith was not among those who thought the conditions of the working class were irrelevant to the prosperity of the whole society. In his discussion of the wages of labour he says the following:

> Is this improvement in the circumstances of the lower ranks of the people to be regarded as an advantage or as an inconveniency to the society? The answer seems at first sight abundantly plain. Servants, labourers, and workmen of different kinds, make up the far greater part of every great political society. But what improves the circumstances of the greater part can never be regarded as an inconveniency to the whole. No society can surely be flourishing and happy, of which the far greater part of the members are poor and miserable. It is but equity, besides, that they who food, clothe, and lodge the whole body of the people, should have such a share

of the produce of their own labour as to be themselves tolerably well fed, clothed, and lodged.[4]

We see then that although Smith's great effort in *WN* was to show how a nation can increase its wealth (i.e., affluence), it is not, in his view, so much wealth itself that leads to a happy and prosperous country, as the circumstance of *increasing* wealth. Once wealth stops increasing, the real wages of labour start decreasing toward the minimum needed for subsistence,[5] the number of the poor increases along with their misery, and thus the society as a whole ceases to flourish, although, of course, there will be a minority who are very well off indeed.

It was also Smith's view that the return on the capital that was used to put people to work—that is, the profit received by the owners of capital—did not vary in the same way as did the wages of labour. He thought that in a society advancing in its level of wealth, the rate of return on capital investments would be on average lower than in a stationary society or even in one that was declining. The reason for the low rate in an advancing society Smith explained as follows:

> As capitals increase in any country, the profits which can be made by employing them necessarily diminish. It becomes gradually more and more difficult to find within the country a profitable method of employing any new capital. There arises in consequence a competition between different capitals, the owner of one endeavouring to get possession of that employment which is occupied by another...The demand for productive labour, by the increase of the funds which are destined for maintaining it, grows every day greater and greater. Labourers easily find employment, but the owners of capitals find it difficult to get labourers to employ. Their competition raises the wages of labour and sinks the profits of stock. But when the profits which can be made by the use of a capital are in this manner diminished, as it were, at both ends, the price which can be paid for the use of it, that is, the rate of interest, must necessarily be diminished with them.[6]

In the advancing society, which naturally attracts capital investment in industry, the competition between the different capitalists for workers to employ raises the level of wages and thus diminishes the profits to be made from the end product produced by the labourers. (The general rate of interest, which Smith thinks tends to reflect the returns on capital, thus falls.) Of course, the workers in this situation thrive, and thus the society as a whole flourishes. All of which led Smith to note that of the three great classes in his society—the landlords, the labourers, and the owners of capital—the interests of the first two were generally in line with the interests of the whole society, but this could not be said of the interests of the third class:

> But the rate of profit does not, like rent and wages, rise with the prosperity and fall with the declension of the society. On the contrary, it is naturally low in rich and high in poor countries, and it is always highest in the countries which are going fastest to ruin. The interest of this third order, therefore, has not the same connexion with the general interest of the society as the other two.[7]

Although in this passage Smith has failed to make his own distinction between riches and *increase* in riches, between poverty and *decrease* in riches, the point is clear enough, when he notes that profits are usually very high in countries fast going to ruin (as in Bengal).

Unfortunately, Smith noted, the landlords and the labourers, for different reasons, are ignorant of what is genuinely to their own advantage, for if they genuinely pursued that, they would, even without intending it, forward the increase of general prosperity. On the other hand, no one is more aware of what is to their own advantage than the owners of large capital. He goes on, in a beautiful example of British understatement, to make the point that, though they are smart in that regard, their sagacity in respect of the interest of society as a whole is not to be trusted:

> Merchants and master manufacturers are, in this order, the two classes of people who commonly employ the largest capitals, and who by their wealth draw to themselves the greatest share of the

public consideration. As during their whole lives they are engaged in plans and projects, they have frequently more acuteness of understanding than the greater part of country gentlemen. As their thoughts, however, are commonly exercised rather about the interest of their own particular branch of business, than about that of the society, their judgement, even when given with the greatest candour (which it has not been upon every occasion) is much more to be depended upon with regard to the former of those two objects than with regard to the latter. Their superiority over the country gentleman is not so much in their knowledge of the public interest, as in their having a better knowledge of their own interest than he has of his…To widen the market and to narrow the competition, is always the interest of the dealers. To widen the market may frequently be agreeable enough to the interest of the public; but to narrow the competition must always be against it, and can serve only to enable the dealers, by raising their profits above what they naturally would be, to levy, for their own benefit, an absurd tax upon the rest of their fellow citizens.[8]

In the preceding passage Smith brings to bear two of the themes so widely associated with his economic ideas: the widening of markets and the encouragement of competition. Both play important roles in his ideas about how wealth can be increased. To understand how he thought about wealth creation, one has to go back to the "myth of origin" to which he subscribed. Smith believed that long before there was anything we could call civilization humans lived solitary lives, with each person providing for their own needs. But luckily humans have been endowed by nature with a disposition to "truck and barter," for it is this that leads to increasing division of labour, the chief source for increasing wealth.

> This division of labour, from which so many advantages are derived, is not originally the effect of any human wisdom, which foresees and intends that general opulence to which it gives occasion. It is the necessary, though very slow and gradual

consequence of a certain propensity in human nature which has in view no such extensive utility; the propensity to truck, barter, and exchange one thing for another.[9]

This is, of course, a fine example of Smith's belief that more often than not reliance on propensities built into us by nature (i.e., by the Author of Nature, if we use the language of *The Theory of Moral Sentiments* [= *TMS*]) leads us in directions more conducive to general human well-being than does dependence on the calculations of practical reasoning. This is an example of what *TMS* calls "the invisible hand." Bartering, once it becomes dependable through the institution of a market, makes it possible for individuals to rely on others to produce some of the things they need, and the more parties to the bartering that there are the more each individual can specialize in producing certain specific marketable products, which they can then exchange for the produce of other people's labour:

> Every workman has a great quantity of his own work to dispose of beyond what he himself has occasion for; and every other workman being exactly in the same situation, he is enabled to exchange a great quantity of his own goods for a great quantity, or, what comes to the same thing, for the price of a great quantity of theirs. He supplies them abundantly with what they have occasion for, and they accommodate him as amply with what he has occasion for, and a general plenty diffuses itself through all the different ranks of society.[10]

Division of labour makes work more productive, Smith argues, by improving "dexterity in every particular workman," by saving the time that would otherwise be expended in transferring between different employments, and by encouraging "the invention of a great number of machines which facilitate and abridge labour."[11] Real increase in a society's wealth comes from getting more product from less labour. We today are inclined to think that this is mainly achieved by using more and more sophisticated machines, but, although Smith too views machines as important here, he holds that it is dividing labour down into more and more specific tasks that encourages workmen to invent machines that can do those simple tasks.[12]

From this view of how wealth can be increased it is easy to see how expanding the market for what workers produce leads to what we can call economic progress. The larger the market the more product that can be profitably sold, and thus the more workers who can be employed in its production, and thus the greater the opportunity for dividing the work into separate specific tasks, and thus the more opportunity for deploying labour-saving machinery. Once machinery gets into the picture, capital becomes more and more important, and the larger the market for what is produced the more the capitalist will be willing to spend large amounts of capital buying the expensive machinery needed to set the labourers to work in the most productive ways.

But if competition, particularly among the capitalists, is artificially restricted (as by ill-conceived government regulation or the establishment of monopolies, as well as by agreements among the capitalists themselves), then the rate of return on capital increases and thus also the price of the product on the market, since the capitalist is grabbing for himself more of the difference between the costs of production and the end sale price. The benefit of the product to people generally is then limited to a narrower class. Also, competition forces capitalists to put their capital where it will get the greatest return, that is, answer to the greatest demand and thus do the most good. Without that competition capital will refuse to move to those areas where it would be invested in producing what buyers are asking for, that is, are willing and able to pay for.

As is well known, Smith was a proponent of free trade as against the mercantilist policy of using a mix of tariffs and monopolies to increase the nation's favourable balance of trade by encouraging exports and discouraging imports. His argument here is much the same. The important thing is to expand the market and then let competition among traders determine how capital is invested in trading ventures, thereby ensuring that it tends to go to the ventures that are likely to provide the greatest rate of return on that capital. Carried out this way, international trade will lead to improvements in wealth for all parties. In domestic markets in which every party is free to come forth with whatever products they think will exchange for the most goods they want, and competition is not artificially hindered, everybody tends to profit in the long run and general prosperity is the result; the same applies to international markets. The chief obstacles on this road to universal affluence are governments. Returning to his theme that reliance on natural propensities rather than artificial contrivances is usually best, Smith puts his point in this memorable remark:

> The uniform, constant, and uninterrupted effort of every man to better his condition, the principle from which public and national, as well as private opulence is originally derived, is frequently powerful enough to maintain the natural progress of things toward improvement, in spite of the extravagance of government and of the greatest errors of administration. Like the unknown principle of animal life, it frequently restores health and vigour to the constitution, in spite, not only of the disease, but of the absurd prescriptions of the doctor.[13]

It would be out of place in this work to indulge in a critique of the ideas described above; suffice to say that numerous economists and scholars have found those ideas at many points unconvincing, as do I. Nevertheless, it is a fact that prosperity for society as a whole since Smith's time has only been obtained during periods of what we call economic growth, or what Smith would term "increase in wealth." We see this today when failure of a society's economy to grow always results in unemployment and hardship for many (though certainly not all). Smith may not have entirely understood why this should be, but he observed it and acknowledged it, and it is a rule that has stood the test of time. It may well be that the rule holds only for market-driven economies, but such were the only ones that Smith thought could sustain economic growth and material prosperity in the long run. What I have called his "myth of origin" is just the initial point of departure for a whole view of human history, one that views the progress of civilization as propelled by individual humans each seeking to better their material conditions and indulging in their propensity to "truck and barter." His aim is to see these motivators freed of societal controls on economic activity, including the restraints imposed by cartels and monopolies, excepting only those required for justice, that is, those that keep individuals from directly harming one another and that maintain the sanctity of property and contracts.

Smith's view of human nature certainly did not see economic activity as the entire or even the most honourable part of human life, but he rightly saw it as foundational. Improperly run, such activity could lead to great injustices, among which was the sort of wealth inequality that meant those who worked hardest for the prosperity of society participated least in that prosperity. Smith was revolted by such failures. No doubt religious convictions concerning the ways of divine providence backed up in his mind the validity of the peculiar cure he prescribed for these economic ailments, but we need not speculate further on what exactly they were. What we need to keep in focus is that in Smith's mind his prescriptions were aimed at raising the level of affluence of the working class (i.e., the masses) by enabling them to purchase and consume more of what was being produced. This, he maintained, required a state of continuous growth in the economy as a whole.

Without much in the way of religious convictions at all,[14] David Ricardo (1772–1823), writing during and after the Napoleonic Wars, was also alarmed at the way the economy of Europe, and Britain in particular, left the labouring masses in misery despite greater social affluence than ever since ancient times. As we shall see, he too viewed this as remediable only by economic growth. His concerns are clear in what follows:

> The friends of humanity cannot but wish that in all countries the labouring classes should have a taste for comforts and enjoyments, and that they should be stimulated by all legal means in their exertions to procure them. There cannot be a better security against a superabundant population. In those countries, where the labouring classes have the fewest wants, and are contented with the cheapest food, the people are exposed to the greatest vicissitudes and miseries. They have no place of refuge from calamity; they cannot seek safety in a lower station; they are already so low, that they can fall no lower. On any deficiency of the chief article of their subsistence, there are few substitutes of which they can avail themselves, and dearth is attended with almost all the evils of famine.[15]

How to grow an economy is, then, as central a question for Ricardo as it was for Smith, and his answer relies a great deal on Smith's analysis in WN. Where Smith had claimed that the exchange value of a commodity was the quantity of labour required to produce and bring to market the goods the commodity could be exchanged for,[16] Ricardo simply says that the commodity's exchange value is the quantity of labour required to produce *it* and bring *it* to market. After noting that in a relatively rude economy,

> the exchangeable value of the commodities produced would be in proportion to the labour bestowed on their production; not on their immediate production only, but on all those implements or machines required to give effect to the particular labour to which they were applied.

He goes on to say that basically the same rule holds in a much improved economy:

> If we look to a state of society in which greater improvements have been made, and in which arts and commerce flourish, we shall still find that commodities vary in value conformably with this principle: in estimating the exchangeable value of stockings, for example, we shall find that their value, comparatively with other things, depends on the total quantity of labour necessary to manufacture them and bring them to market.[17]

Indeed, provided that the market in question is large and flexible enough, Smith would have to agree, since, if the labour required to produce the commodity is *greater* than the labour required to produce and market what it can purchase on the market, then producers, all of whom are constantly trying to produce what will purchase goods that require more labour to produce, will switch from producing that commodity to producing something else, and thus the supply of it will fall and its price will rise until it is able to purchase goods whose production involves no less than what is involved in its own production. Likewise, if the labour involved in its production is *less* than that involved in what it can purchase, producers will switch to producing the latter and as its supply increases its price will fall until it can be exchanged only for what is produced with no more labour than what is involved in its own production and marketing. In modern terms, the market left to itself tends constantly to a sort of equilibrium in which there is no reason for rationally self-interested producers and traders to change what they are doing since they are always trying to get the most purchasing power on the market for the least expense of their own labour, and at the point of equilibrium no change would improve their position. Smith's and Ricardo's way of putting this is to speak of the "natural price" or the "ordinary price" of a commodity. On this analysis the natural or ordinary price of a commodity will have to be both the quantity of labour required to produce it and the quantity of labour required to produce what it purchases, since these will be the same.

Treating labour itself as a commodity, Ricardo concludes that its exchange value is determined by the value of the commodities required to sustain the labour force and their families. Labour's "natural price" then is the price of those commodities:

> Labour, like all other things which are purchased and sold, and which may be increased or diminished in quantity, has its natural and its market price. The natural price of labour is that price which is necessary to enable the labourers, one with another, to subsist and to perpetrate their race, without either increase or diminution…The natural price of labour, therefore, depends on the price of the food, necessaries, and conveniences required for the support of the labourer and his family…With the progress of society the natural price of labour has always a tendency to rise, because one of the principal commodities by which its natural price is regulated, has a tendency to become dearer, from the greater difficulty of producing it.[18]

The tendency of the price of these commodities by which labouring people are sustained (primarily the corn, i.e., grain, that is turned into bread) to rise is explained by the increase in population that will naturally occur if the labouring masses are reasonably well fed. This generates the need to bring more land into cultivation, which means that less and less fertile land will have to be used; hence, the average productivity of farm labour will decrease and more and more labour will have to be deployed to produce each bushel of corn.[19] But, if more labour must be deployed, then those crops will have more exchange value, that is, be more expensive; hence sustaining the labour force will be more expensive, that is, the natural price of labour will rise basically because more labour is required to maintain the same number of labourers.

Ricardo was especially keen to prove that it was not the rising rent of arable land that was causing the increase in the price of necessities and thus the price of labour. His idea here was that the labour required to raise crops on the last piece of land brought into cultivation, that is, the least fertile piece in cultivation, controlled what rent could be demanded on the rest of the land, that is, the more fertile pieces. A landlord can only demand rent from a farmer if his land is more fertile than what that farmer could obtain elsewhere for nothing, and he can only demand as much rent as is compatible with that farmer's profiting at a rate comparable with the average rate of profit on capital investments, otherwise the farmer will turn to other employments. Consequently, it is because the cost of producing crops is increasing on account of having to bring land with less fertility into cultivation that the landlord can increase his rents; the higher rents are thus the effect, not the cause, of more expensive foodstuffs. Ricardo says, "The clearly [sic] understanding this principle is, I am persuaded, of the utmost importance to the science of political economy."[20]

Then, since the price of any commodity divides itself into returns to no more than three parties—the landlord collecting rent, the labourer collecting wages, and the capitalist collecting profit—Ricardo concludes that profits will always be less as wages rise, since rents are predetermined in the way just described:

> If the farmer gets no additional value for the corn which remains to him after paying rent, if the manufacturer gets no additional value for the goods which he manufactures, and if both are obliged to pay a greater value in wages, can any point be more clearly established than that profits must fall, with a rise in wages.[21]

Now, in an "advancing society" (i.e., a growing economy), capitalists will always be competing for more and more labourers, and thus the market price of labour will rise, and the general rate of profit will fall. But this prosperity for the working class will increase its numbers and thus, in the way described above, increase the costs of the agricultural products that sustain the workers, and so further increase the price of labour, until no further capital is being invested;[22] and so the demand for labour levels off, and with the number of people seeking work increasing, we fall into a situation in which there is unemployment and falling wages, and consequent misery for the masses. In this way the "advance" naturally tends to kill itself off. This pessimistic conclusion of Ricardo's was in large measure why the study of political economy came to be known as the "dismal science."

In fact, all Ricardo intended to show was that, given no developments *external* to the market to jolt the economy out of its ordinary rut, it would eventually fall into such a miserable state. Maxine Berg has argued, effectively I think, that all of this pessimism about what happens "naturally" is meant as an argument for free trade and the introduction of more and more sophisticated machinery into the productive process, that is, for bringing these external factors to bear on the market. She writes as follows:

> I will argue that Ricardo, in fact, drew a sharp distinction between this "natural world" and the socio-economic world he was attempting to analyse. This model of "natural tendencies" had a negative purpose. It was counterfactual, set up precisely in order to emphasise the significance of the factors from which Ricardo abstracted—free trade and technological improvement.[23]

That Ricardo was an ardent supporter of free trade is, of course, well known. Basically he just restated Adam Smith's argument. And while he certainly subscribed to the view that machinery made the end product less expensive by reducing the labour required,[24] he did add one caveat: importing luxury goods or using machinery to produce these rather than goods for general consumption would not have the desired effect:

> It has been my endeavour to shew throughout this work, that the rate of profits can never be increased but by a fall in wages, and that there can be no permanent fall of wages but in consequence of a fall of the necessaries on which wages are expended. If, therefore, by the extension of foreign trade, or by improvements in machinery, the food and necessaries of the labourer can be brought to market at a reduced price, profits will rise...but if the commodities obtained at a cheaper rate, by the extension of foreign commerce, or by the improvement of machinery, be exclusively the commodities consumed by the rich, no alteration will take place in the rate of profits.[25]

Why the caveat? Because making luxury goods, which the labourers do not depend on, less expensive, will have no effect on the price of labour, whereas cheaper goods aimed at general consumption (like corn) will lower the price of labour (while leaving a labourer's standard of living the same) and thus increase the rate of profit. Capital will then be attracted and the economy will grow, and growth, as we saw, by increasing the demand for labour, increases its market price and thus improves the standard of living of the labourers. We see then why Ricardo was also a vigorous proponent of the repeal of the "Corn Laws," which had placed tariffs on the importing of that staple of the labourer's diet.

Ricardo claimed that if we investigate just "natural" prices and "natural" distributions of revenue, we can describe laws that govern these, but to do that we must abstract away from the "accidental" and "temporary" events that disturb the natural functioning of the market:

> Having fully acknowledged the temporary effects which, in particular employments of capital, may be produced on the prices of commodities, as well as on the wages of labour, and the profits of stock, by accidental causes...we will leave them entirely out of our consideration, whilst we are treating of the laws which regulate natural prices, natural wages and natural profits, effects totally independent of these accidental causes.[26]

The idea here is that if we hold constant at their average level variable conditions such as weather, people's health, demands for various products, and so on, then the market economy will be subject only to the decisions of participants each trying to better their purchasing power within that market and competing against one another. Given this abstraction, it is then possible to predict how revenues will flow among the three classes of participants—landlords, labourers, and capitalists—and how the economy will evolve until it reaches some static equilibrium. Although this basic idea had already been put forward by Smith, Ricardo dressed it up as analogous to a physical science in which the fundamental abstractions, such as mass, acceleration, and force, obey certain laws, although when the science is applied to a concrete physical system external forces can always cause the system to depart from what the science predicts. No actual physical system is entirely isolated from the rest of the world. Similarly, no real economy is entirely divorced from the vagaries of myriad factors that are not themselves dependent on the economic system, that is, on the market.

Ricardo's pessimism about an economy's natural tendency was not shared by Smith, even though his ideas do basically derive from Smith's; but the spirit in which Ricardo presents his is entirely other. Smith's great book is titled *Inquiry*, a term that avoids any implication that the treatise is definitive; Ricardo's is titled *Principles*, echoing the title of Newton's renowned work, *The Mathematical Principles of Natural Philosophy*. Smith's book is filled with the results of observations of how economic life is actually being carried on as well as with what he knows (or thinks he knows) about economic life in past societies. He constantly tests his theoretical generalizations against these supposed empirical facts. He frequently reminds his reader that the pure, free market rarely exists in the real world, so one should not expect the kinds of results that the dynamic of such a market, if left alone, will tend toward. Ricardo's *Principles* is almost exclusively devoted to demonstrating *a priori* what the inevitable results of that dynamic are going to be. In his introduction to the Pelican edition of the *Principles*, R.M. Hartwell sums up Ricardo's achievement, accurately I think, as follows:

> It was Ricardo who made economics a positive science, "a method of thinking rather than a body of concrete results," a science

capable of tackling problems by the logical method of deduction. This is Ricardo's abiding achievement. He was, as Bagehot proclaimed, "the true founder of abstract Political Economy."[27]

With Ricardo's work we have a heady brew: the exposition of a putative science akin to physics that instructs us on the measures necessary to avoid an otherwise inevitable economic stagnation with its accompanying misery for the labouring masses. The measures recommended are freeing up international trade and introducing machines and technology generally into both agriculture and manufacturing. These will maintain a sufficient rate of profit to keep more and more capital deployed and thereby increase the demand for labour even while cheapening the goods on which labourers depend for their subsistence. The way forward out of the economic crisis of post-Napoleonic Europe to a world of plenty and an end to poverty is set forth with all the backing of scientific rigour. But the solution to the problem is not simply to grow until the economic "pie" is large enough to make everyone reasonably happy. No, for once the growth stops, then the "dismal" scenario sets in. Rather, growth must keep going forever if the masses are to be kept from falling into destitution or, worse yet, rebellion.[28]

The introduction of machinery into manufacturing and transportation became much more rapid in Europe after the Napoleonic wars were over than it had been in Smith's day, and was augmented by the development of the steam engine, which provided an additional source of power in addition to the ancient ones of water, wind, animals, and, of course, human muscle. Maxine Berg has described the controversy that developed in Britain in this period over the introduction of machinery and the unemployment, particularly among artisans, that was often its immediate consequence. Robert Owen led a popular protest against it, claiming that deploying machinery in a market economy led to the degrading of the worker and general misery for the labouring class.[29] He was severely criticized by the majority of political economists, who brandished the conclusions of their new science.

The work of the political economists of this period had an important effect on popular culture and usually favoured the causes Ricardo had championed, although his analysis came in for considerable criticism. Berg notes how these economic doctrines were often taught in the Mechanics Institutes that were founded at the time and that advocated both for machinery and for increasing the skills of the labouring force.[30] Familiarity with political economy was thought to be an important part of a working person's education. But, as one might expect, the doctrines of the economists were most adopted as a creed by the more affluent middle class, who in fact most profited both from free trade and from the cheapening of consumer goods as a result of machine production. Berg draws this conclusion:

> Political economy had become the peculiar creed of the middle classes; it justified claims to middle-class superiority and offered a millennial picture. The great work of popularisation began in the 1820s: political economy was presented as a science which would explain the triumph of British industry and British economic supremacy. Popularisations displayed the natural laws by which the economy and society operated, explained all social problems in terms of the violation of these laws, and encouraged the view that submission to the laws led to infinite progress.[31]

What emerged, then, in Britain of the first half of the nineteenth century was a revitalization of the millennial dreams we have documented in earlier chapters of this work, but now those dreams were buttressed by a supposed science of the economic world complementing the already well-developed sciences of the physical world and their practical application by engineers. The stage was now set for a scientifically directed ascent to the promised world of material plenty. But before this could be fully realized, a way had to be found to open up virtually the whole of human life—not just the strictly economic side of it—to the rational direction of science. We proceed now to see how such a way was in fact invented.

The Hedonist Turn: Bentham and Jevons

In the previous chapter we saw how in the letters of Sophie de Grouchy a hedonist psychology of human behaviour found a basis in human nature for the acceptance of something close to utilitarianism, that is, the ethic which demands that we seek not just our own well-being but that of all around us. In England hedonist psychology of a radical sort had earlier been championed by one of the most influential of all modern philosophers from the British Isles, Jeremy Bentham (1748–1832), who in *An Introduction to The Principles of Morals and Legislation*[32] (PML), published in 1789, had made this the opening line: "Nature has placed mankind under the governance of two sovereign masters, *pain* and *pleasure*." From this psychology Bentham thought he could deduce his "principle of utility," which he explained as follows:

> By the principle of utility is meant that principle which approves or disapproves of every action whatsoever, according to the tendency which it appears to have to augment or diminish the happiness of the party whose interest is in question: or, what is the same thing in other words, to promote or to oppose that happiness, I say of every action whatsoever; and therefore not only of every action of a private individual, but of every measure of government.[33]

By the "party whose interest is in question" Bentham means either the "community in general" or "a particular individual," depending on the circumstances. By promoting that party's "interest" when it is an individual, he means:

> A thing is said to promote the interest, or to be *for* the interest, of an individual, when it tends to add to the sum total of his pleasures: or, what comes to the same thing, to diminish the sum total of his pains.[34]

The interest of a community is, then, just the sum of the interests of the individuals making it up.[35] And "utility" itself he defines as follows:

> By utility is meant that property in any object, whereby it tends to produce benefit, advantage, pleasure, good, or happiness, (all this in the present case comes to the same thing) or (what comes again to the same thing) to prevent the happening of mischief, pain, evil, or unhappiness to the party whose interest is considered.[36]

The logical connection, however, between the hedonist psychology and the principle of utility thus understood is not at all clear in this work. The psychology, after all, is egoistic (each person seeks the increase of *their own* pleasure and the diminishing of *their own* pain), while the principle demands that one be motivated to promote benefits to others. To uncover how one is supposed to infer the latter from the former we have to go to works that Bentham wrote much later, in fact around the time that Ricardo was formulating his doctrines in political economy. In *A Table of the Springs of Action* (hereafter simply *Springs*) written between 1813 and 1815 but not published until 1817, Bentham made clear that any person's motives for action arise out of pleasures and pains:

> True it is that, when the question is, "What, in the case in question, are the *springs of action*, by which, on the occasion in question, the mind in question has been operated upon, or to the operation which it has been exposed?," the species of *psychological entity* to be looked out for in the first place is the *motive*. But, of the sort of *motive* which has thus been in operation, no clear idea can be entertained otherwise than by reference to the sort of *pleasure* or *pain* which such *motive* has for its *basis*: viz. the pleasure or pain, the idea, and eventual expectation of which is considered as having been operating in the character of a *motive*.[37]

Bentham, in fact, calls motives and desires "fictitious" entities, whereas pleasures and pains are "real," but he does not mean that the former are to be dismissed from any genuine science of human behaviour. Rather he explicitly says they are indispensable.[38] What he does mean is that they are reducible back to real entities, in other words, that their existence is explained by the existence of the real entities, in this case, pleasures and pains.[39] It is crucial, then, to know what he includes under the categories of *pleasure* and *pain*. He claims that all pleasures and pains are observable "sensations," although there are other sensations that are "neutral," that is, do not provide the impetus behind motives for action. In *PML* (chapter 5) and *Springs* (79–88) he provides elaborate classifications of these, and we find that they go far beyond what would ordinarily be called sensations. There is the pleasure that comes when one recognizes that one is wealthy or that one is becoming wealthy, and the pain that comes when one realizes one is in poverty or descending into poverty. There is the pleasure that comes with recognition that one has power over others and the pain in recognizing that one is dominated by another. There is pleasure in recognizing that one has the goodwill of others, and pain in recognizing the opposite. There is pleasure in noting the success of another, something that leads to benevolence, and pleasure in noting the failure or ill fortune of another, something that leads to malevolence. Likewise, there is the pain of noting another's failure or ill fortune, which also leads to benevolence, and the pain of observing the other person's success, which leads again to malevolence.

It seems from the breadth of the lists Bentham gives us that wherever there is a desire for anything there is either some pleasure the agent takes in the object of the desire or some pain attendant on a thing the agent wishes to avoid or eliminate. Indeed, it is clearly Bentham's thesis that behind any desire or motive lies some pleasure or pain. Of course, some things we desire only because we see that they are needed to attain something pleasurable in itself or to avoid something painful in itself, and in that case the thing desired as a means may be in itself not pleasurable or even in itself painful.

It is axiomatic for Bentham that each person pursues as their primary goal their own happiness, that is, the maximizing of pleasure and the minimizing of pain in their own life, and they never, save for mistakes in judgment, direct their actions in any other direction:

> Well-being, composed as hath been seen, of the maximum of pleasure minus the minimum of pain—the pleasure it will be seen is man's own pleasure, the pain is man's own pain—will upon a strict and close enquiry be seen to be actually the intrinsic and the ultimate object of pursuit to every man at all times.[40]

Immediately following the above passage Bentham imagines the objection that any reader might well raise:

> "Nay!", cries an Objector, "But if this be so then where is sympathy? Where is benevolence?"

And Bentham has his riposte prepared:

> Answer: exactly where they were.
> To deny the existence of this social affection would be to talk in the teeth of all experience...
> But the pleasure I feel at the prospect of bestowing pleasure on my friend, whose pleasure is it but mine? The pain which I feel at the sight or under the apprehension of seeing my friend oppressed with pain, whose pain is it but mine?

In other words, what is moving me forward to an act of altruism here is the pleasant prospect of the pleasure of performing that act, or should it be that I am intent on relieving the other's pain, I am moved by my own pain at the sight of the other's to relieve not only his but my own.[41]

This analysis of motivation leads Bentham elsewhere to say that strictly speaking no act is "disinterested." He defines "interest" as follows:

> A man is said *to have an interest in any subject* in so far as that *subject* is considered as more or less likely to be to him a source of pleasure or exemption.[42]

By "exemption" he means avoidance or release from pain. Bentham then holds that any motive (and all acts must have a motive) is associated with an interest in the above sense.

> In regard to *interest*, in the most extended, which is the original and only strictly proper sense of the word "disinterested," no human act ever has been or ever can be *disinterested*. For there exists not ever any voluntary action, which is not the result of the operation of some *motive* or *motives*, nor any motive, which has not for its accompaniment a corresponding *interest*, real or imagined.[43]

He goes on to allow that "disinterested" is commonly applied only to acts that do not have any interest of the "self-regarding" sort, that is, where the pleasure or "exemption" sought is solely the agent's own. The motivation of "sympathy" is not self-regarding in this sense, since it seeks pleasure or exemption for someone other than the agent.[44] It must not be thought that Bentham downplays the role of this other-regarding motivation in human life; rather he recommends indulging it to the full. In 1830 he penned the following touching advice to the oldest daughter of his friend and collaborator John Bowring:

> Create all the happiness you are able to create; remove all the misery you are able to remove. Every day will allow you,—will invite you to add something to the pleasures of others,—or to diminish something of their pains. And for every grain of enjoyment you sow in the bosom of another, you shall find a harvest in your own bosom, while every sorrow which you pluck out from the thoughts and feelings of a fellow creature shall be replaced by beautiful flowers of peace and joy in the sanctuary of your soul.[45]

The passage beautifully illustrates what Bentham had in mind when he wrote the texts from *Deontology* and *Springs* cited earlier.

This side of Bentham's thought comes very close to the sort of hedonist psychology we found in Sophie de Grouchy's letters, but her thinking, as we noted, did not end up claiming that the only benefit for a person is an increase in their pleasure or a decrease in their pain, and thus in a hedonist utilitarianism, while Bentham's does. We must see how that comes to be. In the following text we find Bentham seeming to promote what one would think is the doctrine of *egoistic* hedonism rather than hedonistic utilitarianism:[46]

> For its ultimate and practical result, this work has for its object the pointing out to each man on each occasion what course of conduct promises to be in the highest degree conducive to his happiness: to his own happiness, first and last; to the happiness of others, no farther than in so far as his happiness is promoted by promoting theirs, than his interest coincides with theirs. For that in the case

of man in general regard should any further be had to the happiness of others will be shewn to be neither possible nor upon the whole desirable: though on the other hand, what will also be shewn is in how many different ways, more than is very generally understood, each man's happiness is ultimately promoted by an intermediate regard shewn in practice for the happiness of others.[47]

On this account the happiness (i.e., pleasure[48]) of others should be an individual's aim only because they see that it promotes their own happiness, and in fact people in general are not capable of anything else. At this point, however, it is crucial to see how Bentham understands the meaning of a judgment that someone *ought* or *ought not* to do something. He says the following as regards what "ought" means:

> What by myself is meant by it is altogether clear to me…As often as, speaking of any man, I say he ought to do so and so or he ought not to do so and so, what accordingly I know and acknowledge myself to be doing is neither more nor less than endeavour[ing] to bring to view the state of my own mind, of my own opinion, of my own affections in relation to the line of conduct which on the occasion in question is stated as pursued by him—this much and nothing more.[49]

In other places Bentham speaks of these judgments as expressing the speaker's approval or disapproval of some line of conduct, intention, or motive.[50] And now, immediately after the above text, he anticipates a hostile query:

> If it can not ever cease to be, then what can ever be the use of this or that or any other discourse on any part of the field of ethics?

In other words, if all the *ought*-judgment is doing is showing the audience what the attitude of the speaker is toward the object under judgment, what good is it? Bentham's reply is quite prolix and falls into three parts, of which the first follows:

> Answer: use the 1st.
> To shew him that, however conducive to his well being according to his then present view of it the conduct which otherwise he might be disposed to pursue might present itself to him as being, it will not, on a cool and comprehensive view, be seen to be so at the upshot, inasmuch as the present or other nearer good, by the prospect of which he could be determined so to do, would be outweighed by a mass of evil preponderant in value.[51]

It seems Bentham has in mind an *ought-not* judgment passed upon someone's intention to act in a certain way, and that by showing the speaker's disapproval of it that prospective agent is made to realize that they may incur a "mass of evil" that outweighs the good which they thought they might obtain by the action. In other words, the judger's disapproval itself may entail unwelcome consequences for the agent.

The second use that Bentham describes (in his incredibly convoluted way) is the following:

> Answer: use the 2nd.
> If so it be that by the line of conduct in question the effect is more or less likely to prove prejudicial to the interests of this or that portion of the society in which he lives—that while they sustain evil in this shape, the source from whence and the person from whom it comes will be visible to their eyes—and that accordingly, were it only by the principle of self-preservation, they will stand engaged in some shape or other to wreak their vengeance upon the author for the injury which they regard themselves as having sustained.[52]

Here Bentham seems to move to a situation in which the agent whose intended conduct is being judged faces not the disapproval of just one person but of the whole society in which they live, a disapproval which threatens "vengeance" should they proceed with the action in question, since it will be clearly visible who is responsible for something damaging to the interests of that society. Finally, there is still a third use:

Answer: use the 3rd.

If so it be that with or without reason, the species of conduct in question is in the breasts of a portion more or less considerable of the community productive of displeasure, and thus of damage in some shape or other determinate or indeterminate to the man himself, to bring before his view by way of warning the tendency of this practice to become productive of this effect.[53]

This use seems to differ from the preceding one only in that the mere displeasure itself of the community threatens some sort of damaging results for the agent, perhaps nothing more than a certain unfriendliness or disrespect in the way the people of the community deal with him or her.

Bentham's point is that an ethical judgment, whether by an individual or by a community, is meant to have an effect on what prospective agents deem to be in their interests, since the approval and disapproval of one's associates and fellow citizens can hardly be of no consequence to the agent when deciding what to do or not do. Now it is Bentham's contention that it is in any person's interest to see other members of their community adopt an interest in promoting the happiness of all the members and to steer clear of doing what detracts from that happiness. Hence everybody who thinks for a moment will subscribe to the general ethical judgment that one ought to do what promotes the greatest happiness of the greatest number, that is, the principle of utility. In other words, each will show to one another what approval they have for people who promote general utility and what disapproval they have for people who do the opposite, and hope that realizing these are their attitudes will make people see how much it is in their own interest to accede to those attitudes. Bentham makes much the same point in *Springs*:

> Principle of Utility: In its *censorial* sense, it holds up the greatest happiness of the greatest number as the only universally *desirable* end.
>
> In its *enuntiative* sense, each man's own happiness, his only *actual* end.
>
> Thence, for the influencing his conduct, influencing his happiness the only means.

> Utilitarianism states as the only proper *end* in view of the moralist and legislator the greatest happiness of the greatest number.
>
> And as the only *means* by which any individual can be engaged to operate toward it, the happiness of that individual: viz; either by indicating or creating an *interest* operating upon him as a motive and engaging him to operate towards that end.[54]

By the "censorial" sense of the principle Bentham means its sense as expressing the approval of the community for conduct in accord with that principle. By the "enuntiative"[55] sense he means the sense in which it states that something is the case in objective reality. In other words, it functions both as a prescriptive ethical judgment and as a descriptive statement of psychological fact. Bentham then goes on to claim that an individual can only be influenced to follow the ethical principle by "creating an interest operating on him as a motive," that is, by convincing him that it is actually in his interest to follow the principle. This is exactly what the aforementioned three "uses" describe in detail. It is summed up in what he calls the "moralist's rule": "Moralist's rule: what you would have done, shew that it is a man's interest to do it."[56] It is Bentham's view, then, that proclaiming the principle of utility in its "censorial" sense "shews" exactly that to those who hear it, and that engaging in such "shewing" is in in each individual's own interest. Such is Bentham's way of defending the general principle of utility on the basis of egoistic hedonism taken as a descriptive truth about human motivation.

Bentham proceeds in *Springs* to list the "eulogistic" and "dyslogistic" terms which are applied to the various motives people have for acting and that express the general approval or disapproval of people for them. (A "eulogistic" term is one implying praise, e.g., "thrift," "integrity"; a "dyslogistic" one implies condemnation, e.g., "impertinence," "vanity").[57] In introducing this topic Bentham speaks of the force of "public opinion":

> Of the declared opinions, of such of the several members of the community, by whom respectively in relation to the subject in question, an opinion or judgement of *approbation* or *disapprobation* is expressed, is that quantity of *the force of public opinion*, otherwise

termed "the force of the popular or moral sanction," which is thus brought to bear upon that subject, composed and constituted. In and by any act by which intimation is given of such his judgement, in quality of member of the tribunal by which that judgement is considered as pronounced, a man may be considered as delivering his *vote*. On the present occasion, the subject matter of this judgement will be seen to be the several *springs of action*, by which, on the several occasions in question, human *conduct*—human *action*—is liable to be influenced and determined.

Of course, Bentham will approve of the specific ways in which popular opinion pins these labels on human motives according as the practice accords with the ethical principle of utility. An individual by partaking in a labelling of this sort is said to deliver his or her "vote." Such is the way in which a morality is established in a community, and Bentham is not about to condemn this general practice no matter how much he might disagree with certain particular judgments of that morality.

It is useful, I think, to compare Bentham's conception of morality with Smith's in his *TMS*. Both base morals on the feelings people have that move them to approve or disapprove of the particular actions or feelings of others. Smith's basic idea is that everyone has a desire to know that their feelings and attitudes are shared by others, and is moved to disapprove of feelings in others that they cannot by an exercise of empathy come to share. This develops in the end into a person's taking a distance from themself[58] and imagining what an "impartial spectator" would feel about their actions and feelings. The more a person feels uncomfortable with an adverse judgment on themself by this disinterested observer and tries to fall into line with that judgment, the more they are following the "voice of conscience" and being genuinely a moral person.

Now Bentham might well acknowledge that there is pain involved both in recognizing that others cannot by empathizing find themselves sharing in one's own feelings and attitudes and also in recognizing that someone whose own self-regarding interests are not involved would view one as out of line, so to speak, and thus Bentham would recognize that there is a motive for adapting one's feelings and actions to what others can approve and to what this impartial spectator would find fitting. In following that motive one would make progress both toward one's own happiness and toward the happiness of others who would have been pained by one's behaviour and would rejoice in its reform. It seems then to conform totally to the principle of utility.

A problem arises for Bentham, however, when we encounter feelings of approval people naturally have for motives that often lead to results counter to utility. Smith gives the following example:

> When we see one man oppressed or injured by another, the sympathy which we feel with the distress of the sufferer seems to serve only to animate our fellow-feeling with his resentment against the offender. We are rejoiced to see him attack his adversary in his turn, and are eager and ready to assist him whenever he exerts himself for defense, or even for vengeance, within a certain degree. If the injured should perish in the quarrel, we not only sympathize with the real resentment of his friends and relations, but with the imaginary resentment which in fancy we lend to the dead...And with regard, at least, to this most dreadful of all crimes, nature, *antecedent to all reflections upon the utility of punishment,* has in this manner stamped upon the human heart, in the strongest and most indelible characters, an immediate and instinctive approbation of the sacred and necessary law of retaliation.[59] (my emphasis)

Here I think we can assume that the injured party finds both their peers and the "impartial spectator" or disinterested observer in accord with their desire for revenge, without any consideration whatsoever of the utility, in Bentham's sense, of the consequences of that vengeance. Indeed, they may well still approve even after it is pointed out that the likely result will be more pain and less pleasure for the community than if the injured party had exercised self-restraint. The only consequence being considered is the damage to the interests of the oppressor, which is the opposite of "useful" but only strengthens the approval of the onlookers. If Smith's description of how humans in fact react is accurate, it seems to establish what Bentham would have to admit is a moral judgment but one that does not accord with the principle of utility.

To this Bentham's reply is simply that apart from an appeal to utility no individual has any way of justifying their attitudes and actions, and no government any way of justifying its laws. Bentham will not allow actions and intentions to be judged good or bad except by examining their consequences and determining whether they conduce to happiness or not.[60] On his view it is the height of irrationality to suppose that the desire for revenge, for example, is good unless in particular circumstances one can see that actions in accord with it will lead to more pleasure or less pain for more people than would restraining oneself from such actions. Nor can the desire be judged bad unless we see the opposite. Smith's position he would call "sentimentalism," and his verdict on it is uncompromising:

> Utilitarianism, working by calculation, is consistent and solicitous beneficence. Sentimentalism, in so far as independent of utilitarianism, is in effect a mask for selfishness or malignity, or both for despotism, intolerance, tyranny.[61]

But this is simply name-calling. In the end, although Bentham fully acknowledges that we feel pleasure and pain in our reactions to all sorts of things, he will not allow that the intrinsic character of these things can be a *reason* for approving or disapproving them and not just the *cause*, for that would mean that something other than utility should serve as our end.[62] When confronted with an example of something we feel indignant about apart from any consideration of whether it involves pain or diminution of pleasure, Bentham treats us as irrational "ipsedixitists," that is, people who think something is wrong just because they say it is. But a position such as Bentham's that relies so much on what humans in fact feel cannot ignore what in fact those feelings urge us nearly universally to take as our ends.

Questions about the philosophical tenability of Bentham's views aside, one thing is certain: his proposals once adopted remove any obstacles to our full approval of those desires, habits, and practices that Bernard Mandeville touted as conducive to the affluence of society despite their being judged disgraceful or even criminal. The reader will recall his "Fable of the Bees," discussed in chapter 7, where we found that lust, pride, vanity, cheating, luxury, prodigality, envy, and so on were all "ministers to industry" and turned the wheels of trade that made the hive so prosperous. Bentham would have no trouble dismissing those feelings of disapproval and disgust that seem to arise so naturally in us when we view those traits Mandeville mentions and that the hive depends on. If indeed the members of the community are happier with those traits in place than they would be if they were not—and Mandeville makes clear that this is certainly so—then the principle of utility decrees that they must be allowed to flourish at least to the extent required. Bentham would have no sympathy with the moralists whom Mandeville describes as trying to reform the ways of the hive. They would be exactly the sort of killjoys Bentham continually rails against.

This spirit comes to infect the new science of economics once the view of human motivation that Bentham advocated is taken as the basis of that science. This had already occurred among some French thinkers in the eighteenth century to the extent that they thought of themselves as forwarding a science of wealth accumulation, but in the anglophone world it was William Stanley Jevons (1835–1882) who introduced it.[63] Jevons is clearly inspired by his reading of Bentham. He cites not only *PML* but *Springs* as well, calling the latter "remarkable."[64] He announces his accord with Bentham's hedonist psychology thus:

> The words of Bentham on this subject may require some explanation and qualification, but they are too grand and too full of truth to be omitted.[65]

He then immediately quotes the opening lines of Bentham's *PML*. On the same page he affirms Bentham as his guide:

> Jeremy Bentham put forward the utilitarian theory in the most uncompromising manner. According to him, whatever is of interest or importance to us must be the cause of pleasure or of pain; and when the terms are used with a sufficiently wide meaning, pleasure and pain include all the forces which drive us to action. They are explicitly or implicitly the matter of all our calculations, and form the ultimate quantities to be treated in all the moral sciences.[66]

We see from this passage that Jevons rightly reads Bentham to be treating as pleasures and pains all "the forces which drive us to action," and it is as a total theory of motivation in the human individual that Jevons adopts this hedonist line.[67] It is important to Jevons that pleasures and pains be quantifiable in both their intensity and duration. As for intensity, he accepts an individual's own mind as making the judgment as to which of its feelings is more or less intense than others, but it is actions that reliably reveal this comparison:

> Now the mind of an individual is the balance which makes its own comparisons, and is the final judge of quantities of feeling. As Mr Bain says, "It is only an identical proposition to affirm that the greatest of two pleasures, or what appears as such, sways the resulting action; for it is this resulting action that alone determines which is the greater."
>
> Pleasures, in short, are, for the time being, as the mind estimates them; so that we cannot make a choice, or manifest the will in any way, without indicating thereby an excess of pleasure in some direction.[68]

To sum up in Jevons's own words, "it is from the quantitative effects of the feelings that we must estimate their comparative amounts."[69]

The *utility* of something is, again in accord with Bentham, the sum of the pleasures and pains (where pains are treated as negative quantities) that a given individual derives from the thing in question. But given that all motivations are pleasures or pains, this really means that any object of desire and effort will be useful for that person:

> It will be well to...employ the term *utility* to denote the abstract quality whereby an object serves our purposes, and becomes entitled to rank as a commodity. Whatever can produce pleasure or ward off pain *may* possess utility...but we must beware of restricting the meaning of the word by any moral considerations. Anything which an individual is found to desire and to labour for must be assumed to possess for him utility.[70]

It is well to remember this broad conception of utility when we come to the following passage:

> The theory which follows is entirely based on a calculus of pleasure and pain; and the object of economics is to maximize happiness by purchasing pleasure, as it were at the lowest cost of pain...I have no hesitation in accepting the utilitarian theory of morals which does uphold the effect upon the happiness of mankind as the criterion of what is right and wrong.[71]

When you put these remarks together, you see that Jevons has adopted Bentham's principle of utility in its ethical or prescriptive sense, and that has to mean, according to the immediately preceding passage, that the object of economics must be to maximize people's success in obtaining what they most desire and labour for, for this is what has utility for them, and hence that success simply is their happiness. Bentham's philosophy, then, has given to economics not just a descriptive theory of human motivation but an ethical purpose. It is part of the human effort to produce the greatest happiness for the greatest number, and that happiness comes from fulfilling as much as possible the desires of that number.

It should be noted, however, that Jevons does not think that economics is a science for the whole of that utilitarian effort. He believes that human feelings come in different grades, higher and lower:

> As it seems to me, the feelings of which a man is capable are of various grades. He is always subject to mere physical pleasure or pain, necessarily arising from his bodily wants and susceptibilities. He is capable also of mental and moral feelings of several degrees of elevation.[72]

Then he goes on to assign to economics the lower range of feelings and hence the fulfilment of the lower grade of desires.

> My present purpose is accomplished in pointing out this hierarchy of feeling, and assigning a proper place to the pleasures with which the economist deals. It is the lowest rank of feelings which we here

treat. The calculus of utility aims at supplying the ordinary wants of man at the least cost of labour. Each labourer, in the absence of other motives, is supposed to devote his energy to the accumulation of wealth. A higher calculus of moral right and wrong would be needed to show how he may best employ that wealth for the good of others as well as himself. But when the higher calculus gives no prohibition, we need the lower calculus to gain us the utmost good in matters of moral indifference...And we may certainly say, with Francis Bacon, "while philosophers are disputing whether virtue or pleasure be the proper aim of life, do you provide yourself with the instruments of either."[73]

In other words, humans have their "ordinary wants," and they also have the more elevated desires that moralists are concerned with, for example philanthropic motivations, what Bentham would have called "extra-regarding" feelings. The former are what Jevons himself is concerned with; the latter require some "higher calculus," which he leaves others to develop. The assumption seems to be that the world of economic activity is almost entirely carried on in the area of "moral indifference"; otherwise a treatise such as Jevons's would seem to be of little practical value. The citing of Francis Bacon is certainly most appropriate here, since, as we saw in a previous chapter, he was a vigorous proponent of the separating of science from morality.

It has to be said that this manoeuvre on Jevons's part is not at all consistent with his acceptance of Bentham's utilitarianism, for that theory is a theory of what is morally right and morally wrong, and any area in which it is deployed cannot be an area of "moral indifference." If in our economic life we are concerned to maximize pleasure and minimize pain, we are *ipso facto* in an area where actions are morally right if they obey the principle of utility and morally wrong if they do not. Nor on Bentham's theory is there any ground for thinking that the satisfaction of our "extra-regarding" sentiments is subject to some sort of "higher calculus." Whatever calculus it is that applies to "self-regarding" desires is going to apply to the extra-regarding ones as well, for in fact it is Bentham's view that the latter ones have no hold on us independent of the former. Jevons cannot consistently adopt Bentham's psychology and ethics and not think that the theory he develops on that basis is applicable to the whole of human interactions. It is hard to believe that he himself did not see this; it is such an obvious inference to make. But perhaps the very radicalness of the conclusion was so repulsive to him that he was blinded to the fact that it resulted from what he had already committed himself to.

That objection aside, although the "market" for its own existence and maintenance requires the enforcement of certain moral rules, once functioning, on Jevons's account, it becomes a realm where the activities carried on are morally indifferent. Jevons has his own "myth of origin" for how the market works, and it is here that the most distinctive of his views are expounded. He is still thinking of barter exchange, where each party brings a commodity to the market to exchange for the commodities that other parties are bringing. He is careful to say exactly what he thinks of as a market and in effect defines an ideal that can only be more or less approximated in reality:

> By a market I shall mean two or more persons dealing in two or more commodities, whose stocks of those commodities and intentions of exchanging are known to all. It is also essential that the ratio of exchange between any two persons should be known to all the others. It is only so far as this community of knowledge extends that the market extends...Every individual must be considered as exchanging from a pure regard to his own requirements or private interests, and there must be perfectly free competition, so that anyone will exchange with anyone else for the slightest apparent advantage. There must be no conspiracies for absorbing and holding supplies to produce unnatural ratios of exchange.[74]

Besides the ideal market, Jevons describes above the ideal buyer/seller or what he calls a "trading body." This person must be solely concerned to forward their own interests, that is, to increase utility to themselves, must be willing to trade with anyone where the trade would be advantageous to them, and must know what the ratios of exchanges between commodities in the market are. Given that the market is ideal, what Jevons calls the "law of indifference" will hold, that is, *in the same open market, at any one moment, there cannot be two* *prices for the same kind of article.*⁷⁵ In other words, if one unit of commodity A is sold by seller α to a buyer β for 3 units of commodity B, it will be sold at that same ratio by all sellers of A to all buyers who are selling B in exchange. The law holds because any disparity in the ratios would result in the totally self-interested, omniscient sellers and buyers of A doing business with the similarly characterized sellers and buyers of B that offered the best deal, and that would immediately cause an adjustment equalizing the ratios of exchange between the different traders in A and B.

Jevons bases his theory of exchange value simply on the utility that traders expect to gain by the exchanges they make in the market. Here he consciously sets himself against the labour theories of value advanced by Smith and Ricardo, and regards any factor that constitutes a cost in the production of a commodity, whether it be rent, expense of equipment and raw materials, or labour, as contributing to the negative utility suffered by the trader bringing it to market and that must be outweighed by the positive utility that trader gains by the exchange.⁷⁶ The direct cause of exchange values' being what they are on the ideal market is simply the varying desires and interests of the traders and how much given trades serve to satisfy them. In the background, of course, are all the costs of production affecting those desires and interests, but there is no reason to give to any one such cost, such as labour, a prominence over the others.

Another way in which Jevons differs from his British predecessors in political economy is that he emphasizes the law of diminishing returns. When a trader has acquired through exchange a certain amount of a commodity, the usefulness of further amounts to him begins to decline, and consequently he begins to lower the price he is willing to pay. Eventually, the utility of additional quantities of that commodity is to him so small that he will choose to purchase instead other commodities additional quantities of which will add more to his utility, that is, satisfy his interests to a greater extent. So it is not the *total* utility some purchased commodity provides the buyer that determines how high a price he is willing to pay for it, but rather the additional utility provided by an additional purchase. Jevons calls this the "final degree of utility,"⁷⁷ but in the vocabulary that came to be used, it is the utility being added at the *margin* that matters.

Now we must imagine all the traders in the market being motivated to purchase each of the variety of commodities on the market with an intensity equal to what the *marginal utility* of each commodity is for them. This will, of course, vary from trader to trader, but once the market has a large number of traders we can lump together, on the one side, buyers of X, and on the other side, sellers of Y, and so on, and treat of the average marginal utilities for each of these.[78] On the ideal market we will see in the end that the ratio in which X and Y will exchange will be the inverse of the ratio of the marginal utility of X to buyers of X and the marginal utility of Y to buyers of Y. For example, if an additional unit of X gives 3 additional utiles to its buyers while an additional unit of Y gives only 1 additional utile to its buyers, then 1 unit of X will purchase 3 units of Y.[79] What marginal utilities for traders will be for various commodities will of course vary over time as a function of conditions external to the market such as changes in population levels, changes in tastes, changes in availability of raw materials, and so on, but an ideal market will adjust itself so that this sort of ratio is reached for all commodities, or, at least, we can say that of itself it will always be tending in that direction, that is, toward what economists call an "equilibrium."

Although I do not find Jevons explicitly saying so, I believe he thinks that when labour, land, machinery, and other things necessary for production are included as commodities, a market of the sort he describes will produce more overall utility of the sort economics deals with than any other arrangement for exchange.[80] He does not depart from his classical forebearers so far as esteem for the market is concerned.

Jevons thought that his main contribution to political economy was to mathematize it and by so doing strengthen its claims to being a science.[81] He attained this goal by bringing to bear the differential and integral calculus that had proved so useful in mechanics and other areas of the physical sciences. Indeed, he contended that economics should be developed in the way that mechanics is:

> But as all the physical sciences have their basis more or less obviously in the general principles of mechanics, so all branches and divisions of economic science must be pervaded by certain general principles. It is to the investigation of such principles—to the

tracing out of the mechanics of self-interest and utility, that this essay has been devoted. The establishment of such a theory is a necessary preliminary to any definite drafting of the superstructure of the aggregate science.[82]

The idea of marginal utility lends itself quite naturally to treatment by the calculus, because it can be viewed as the rate at which utility is being added by additional acquisitions of some commodity. If we imagine a graph on which the vertical axis measures total utility and the horizontal axis measures quantity of the commodity acquired, then according to the law of diminishing returns the curve that shows the increase in utility with increases in acquired quantity of the commodity will rise quite steeply as it leaves the origin, but farther along its steepness will decline until at some point it may become totally flat or even turn downward, indicating a decrease in utility. At any point on the curve the steepness of the angle can be expressed as du/dq in the language of the calculus, where u is the total utility at that point and q is the total quantity of the commodity at that same point. It is then, in ordinary language, the rate at which u is changing with infinitesimal additions of the commodity q. Jevons generalizes the point as follows:

> It is clear that economics, if it is to be a science at all, must be a mathematical science...My theory of economics, however, is purely mathematical in character. Nay, believing that the quantities with which we deal must be subject to continuous variation, I do not hesitate to use the appropriate branch of mathematical science, involving though it does the fearless consideration of infinitely small quantities. The theory consists in applying the differential calculus to the familiar notions of wealth, utility, value, demand, supply, capital, interest, labour and all the other quantitative notions belonging to the daily operations of industry.[83]

Jevons's mathematical emphasis no doubt arose in part from his training in the physical sciences, particularly chemistry and meteorology, during the earlier half of his life, but he might well have been influenced here as well by

Bentham, whose own advocacy of "calculating" utility and disutility was well-known. Bentham could become quite vitriolic in his condemnation of those who thought calculation was out of place in ethics:

> He who, on whatever subject or occasion, discards *calculation*, i.e. reason, to follow the dissocial passion is an enemy to mankind, no less than the Savage whom he takes for his model.[84] (Bentham's emphasis)

The assumption, of course, is that pleasures and pains, in their dimensions of intensity and duration, at least, admit of being given some sort of numerical values. Though Jevons claims that he avoids measuring the total pleasure (or pain) a person may experience through acquiring a commodity (or through a period of labour), he has to give some value to the intensity of a pleasure (or pain) for that person at a given moment, since that is just the "final degree of utility," or marginal utility, which is the key quantity in his whole theory of exchange.

In Jevons's work the theory of economics has become the description of a machine, the ideal market, whose motors are the ideal "trading bodies," and that machine operates according to laws that hold because of the way those ideal entities are defined. It becomes, in fact, a branch of mathematics, and Jevons himself said he was willing to turn it over to the mathematicians should they be ready to take it on:

> In short, I do not write for mathematicians, nor as a mathematician, but as an economist wishing to convince other economists that their science can only be satisfactorily treated on an explicitly mathematical basis. When mathematicians recognize the subject as one with which they may usefully deal, I shall gladly resign it into their hands.[85]

Presumably real markets motivated by real traders approximate in significant degree the way in which the ideal market performs, and thus we can achieve some degree of accuracy in predicting how real markets will react to changes in circumstances by calculating how the ideal one would react.

This means we have a science with mathematical tools that can tell us how to manipulate the real economy so as to secure the maximum amount of material well-being possible in the circumstances for all whose livelihoods are tied to that economy. But material well-being means nothing more than the satisfaction of the "lower" or "ordinary" desires for sustenance, health, and comfort; and we should probably include as well (particularly if we are loyal disciples of Bentham) those for luxury and prestige, that is, the kind of desires that Mandeville said moralists held in low repute but that nevertheless turned the wheels of commerce and made a society prosperous.

The question of what distinguishes science from mere inquiries into some aspect of the world we observe about us does not admit of any precise answer, but certainly the more an inquiry results in ways of reliably predicting how things will develop and how things will react to various stimuli the more it can be said to merit the status of a science. To achieve that capacity the right abstractions and the right precise laws relating those abstractions have to be found. The modern science of mechanics achieved this *par excellence* beginning in the eighteenth century. Its laws (i.e., those of Newtonian mechanics) were formulated mathematically and thus attained a level of precision beyond that of any other physical science. This opened up ways for engineers to manipulate the world that were hitherto unavailable to them, and the results were evident everywhere in the Western world of the nineteenth century. But the promised millennium had not been achieved, and this could only be, people thought, because of the perversity of human behaviour. If there were some science of that, then society itself could be "engineered" into what all people longed for. The neoclassical economics developed by Jevons, Walras, and others promised just such a science.

But how much did it really merit that honorific title? This revised form of political economy relied heavily on modelling, that is, describing an ideal, or idealized entities, and then deducing laws governing those entities in precise mathematical terms. Robert Skidelsky, an economist of our own day, has written the following:

> In modelling economies, New Classical economists were not fazed
> by the unrealism of their assumptions; indeed, they regarded this

as a strength of their models. The important thing was that their models should be logically coherent.[86]

Any inquiry that achieves predictive and manipulative success has to idealize to some extent by assuming that the abstract realities it finds explanatory are operating apart from the welter of extraneous factors that are present in any real situation. Otherwise, no precise laws could be formulated. The question is whether in real situations the "extraneous" factors are just as significant to understanding what is happening (if not more so) as the abstract ones the model describes. When Skidelsky speaks of the "unrealism" of the neoclassical models, he is saying that this question is in fact answered in the affirmative so far as that approach is concerned. In other words, the model of self-interested, omniscient traders operating in an ideal market isolates factors that in the real economies of the modern world are only a few of the ones that must be considered if we are to understand how those economies operate. Hence, they fail to yield the predictive and manipulative virtues we expect of a genuine science.[87]

Skidelsky has an explanation for why the neoclassical theory as well as the classical ones that preceded it have had such a hold on some people's minds. It is, according to him, in part because they have provided an ideological cover for the promotion of certain class interests.[88] In recent times the revival of ideas from classical economics has, he notes, coincided with the rise of neoliberalism as a political platform, and it is well known that neoliberalism has been promoted by wealthy interest groups that view themselves as gaining from the policies it advocates.[89] No doubt there is considerable truth in what Skidelsky says here, but it has been my intent in this work to place these theories in a broader historical context that points to a web of ideas at work that have been resonating in Western Europe for a couple of centuries.

Skidelsky also notes how neoclassical economics brought a conception of human psychology to the fore in intellectual circles, a conception he calls the idea of the "optimizing agent," by which he means the person who aims to maximize benefits to themselves, essentially the conception Bentham promoted. David Graeber, in his review of Skidelsky's book, is explicit about the academic results of this innovation that we have found so prominent in the thought of Bentham and Jevons:

This allowed *Homo economicus* to invade the rest of the academy, so that by the 1950s and 1960s almost every scholarly discipline in the business of preparing young people for positions of power (political science, international relations, etc.) had adopted some variant of "rational choice theory" culled, ultimately, from microeconomics.[90]

As an academic myself, I can add to Graeber's list philosophy as a field in which "rational choice theory" has had a profound effect. There can be no doubt, then, that the ideas Jevons was championing in the 1870s were to have a broader influence on how thinking men and women were in the twentieth and on into twenty-first century to conceive both of society and humans generally than it seems Jevons himself did. Those ideas helped make intellectually respectable a view of humans that placed their happiness entirely in the satisfaction of whatever desires and preferences they might have. In addition, Jevons and the other neoclassical economists offered up something that appeared to be a science of just how to understand a market economy as maximally achieving that end. The millennium, on this reasoning, would be one of mass consumption.

CONCLUSION

Unleashing the Western *Gesellschaft*

> It would not be better if things happened
> to people just as they wish.
> —Heraclitus (c.500 BCE)

With the establishment of a science of economics promoting utilitarian goals of the sort advocated by Bentham and Jevons (not to mention J.S. Mill and a host of his followers), the ideological equipment for justifying and directing the explosive expansion of industry and affluence in the Western world (and later throughout the planet) was completely in place.[1] As I said at the beginning of this work, an ideology works not just through those who sincerely believe in it but also, and perhaps more effectively, through those who use it to make actions appear glamourous that are in fact motivated by personal gain and ego satisfaction. But no matter how and how much ideology has been operative, we now see that the West's expansion has created an eco-catastrophe of monumental proportions that will devastate human civilization and send to extinction a great percentage of the life forms on this planet. I assume that the readers of this book are aware not just of the disasters of climate change, water shortages, soil erosion, plastic pollution, depletion of fish stocks, reduction in wildlife habitat, and so on, but also realize that these have arisen from the demands of exponential human population growth coupled with the recent adoption of the goal for nearly all people of a standard of comfort and convenience once reserved for the very rich. None of the thinkers who played a role in entrancing the minds of many Europeans and Americans with the possibility and desirability of such expansion had any but the dimmest awareness of this particular dire consequence of the developments their ideas were buttressing, and just about all would have been appalled had they learned of it. It was left mainly to a few thinkers and activists not enamoured of the millenarian ideology of endless expansion to sound warnings of what was to come.

Urban-centred civilizations in general were from the start ways of organizing human life with short shelf lives. They inevitably led to devastating wars, terrible oppression of the masses by a small power elite, slavery, and environmental degradation on a large scale. Imperialism was the political remedy tried everywhere, from Central America to the Mediterranean Basin, to the Middle East, to India, to China, and it continued to be practised right through the nineteenth century. The great wars of the twentieth were its denouement. We saw in chapter 3 that reflective people in the ancient civilizations of the Mediterranean, India, and China had reacted to this in ways designed both to salvage individuals from the wreckage around them and to put forward concepts of what a good human life amounts to, ones that, if generally adopted, would have placed constraints on the self-destructive ways of the surrounding society. In that respect they were only moderately successful: the ills endemic to urban-centred societies were ameliorated only a little if at all. Some individuals, usually members of a literate elite, did manage, on the basis of the new ideas about the good life, to lead lives worth living despite the surrounding chaos, but those ideas had little effect on the illiterate masses, who often found their solace in various phantastic religious cults. But inadvertently those ideas did help direct society away from the kind of massive expansion that would lead to planetary eco-catastrophe.

What those ideas had in common was the recommendation to give up on thinking that satisfaction would be found by seeking fulfilment in the ordinary activities of the world around one, and instead to look for satisfaction in one's inner life. In other words, detachment from the successes and pleasures of the world and conscientious cultivation of one's inner life were the common elements in what sages as different as Indian ascetics, Confucian civil servants, and Stoic intellectuals prescribed. Despite the differences in these culturally diverse systems of thought, the actual practical ethical results were, nevertheless, remarkably similar. Generally speaking, the wise practitioner of these ideas led a life in which egocentric desires were put aside and actions were directed toward goals set by what were perceived as objective rather than personal demands. In fact, what was demanded was conduct of the kind required for harmonious life in the earlier *Gemeinschaft* communities. In China and in the Greco-Roman world this led to the erection of ideals of moral character that the wise person strove to achieve in his or her own life. In India there developed the ideal of the person totally lacking in any ego-centricity. These were all efforts to construct a new sort of human being, one suited to survival in advanced civilization, for it was abundantly apparent that the old type of human was not so suited and the result was recurrent disaster, both individual and social. What was *not* proposed was changing civilization itself in order to make it more compatible with what humans in fact already were and more or less had been for millennia. In reality, a future a lot different from the present was not something people in those cultures at all hoped for. Their concern was mostly to maintain some sort of balance and order in what already existed. Consequently, these ancient prescriptions seem to us modern Westerners balefully complacent in the face of gross inequalities of wealth and power, of cruel oppression, and of frequent bouts of destitution among the masses. They also tend to create in their devotees a certain pride in their supposed moral superiority to the "unenlightened," much like that of the Pharisees whom Jesus lashes out against in the gospels.

These ideas emanated from persons steeped in urban civilization and used to the *Kürwille* mentality that had created the dominating *Gesellschaft* of urban life. The conceptions such persons adopted were the result of deep conscious reflection on people's ways of thinking about their lives and how they related to the surrounding world, and ended in a thorough critique of those ways, including of the *Kürwille* mentality itself, which was the root of *Gesellschaft* association. They were, then, the reactions of some members of an intellectually sophisticated elite who had become profoundly self-critical.

All this contrasts with the other reaction to the trauma of urban-centred civilization we explored, the one that originated apparently among a pastoral people in Central Asia dependent on raising cattle and subject to vicious raids by some domineering foreign power. Their own powerless resentment found expression in the phantastic cosmological story put together, so far as we know, by a prophetic figure going by the name of "Zarathustra." His story takes the age-old myth of cosmic conflict between the gods and turns it into a moral tale in which the forces of "the Lie" and falsehood are arraigned against those of truth and light. Humans are urged to take the side of the truth-telling deity in this conflict; they must *freely choose* to do this, and to choose otherwise is to fail morally and be deserving of severe punishment. In this story we can see the transposition of *Gemeinschaft* moral standards onto the whole cosmos, so that a person's own free choices determine that person's position within this cosmic drama of moral good against moral evil. Along with this goes the development of an idea that at the end of history, when the good divinities have conquered their lying adversaries, there will be a divine judgment on a person's life, leading to their consequent assignment either to a beautiful new world or to a place of torture and punishment.

It is important to notice in Zarathustra's phantasy how complete is the transformation of the world after the final victory over the evil deities, for it was the influence of the chief of those evil deities that had corrupted the world to begin with; this deity had made the world we in fact inhabit have those features of it that are inhospitable to human life, and in the end, in the "Frashegird" (the Making Wonderful), all these would be eliminated and human life in our world would become entirely enjoyable and effortless. We have here the dream of the *Wesenwille* mentality, emerging from an oppressed and endangered *Gemeinschaft* projecting its values and deepest longings onto the whole of cosmic history. Now we find that a future in which everything is vastly changed and made totally accommodating for human existence is something people not only long for but expect, even if getting to that destination will be fraught with violence and destruction.

Chapter 4 of this book traced the transmission of this sort of phantasy through late ancient Judaism into earliest Christianity, finding its way into John's *Apocalypse* with its potentially revolutionary idea of the millennium; but this new faith, upon becoming the dominant one of the Greco-Roman world, had to submerge that radical vision under the values inherited from Stoicism and Platonism in order to make itself palatable to a literate and educated elite. The end result was medieval Europe with its ideal of the *viator* (wayfarer), who looked forward to his or her eventual acceptance, probably after death, into the Kingdom of Heaven, the wayfarer's *patria* (true homeland), while maintaining a certain emotional and mental detachment from the actual world of ordinary life. A culture built around that ideal could not, in its main stream at least, develop an impetus toward radical social and economic change and development. The emphasis was always still on inner progress toward the moral ideal represented by Christ's life on Earth and reinforced by the teachings of the ancient pagan sages. Although medieval Europe gradually became more urbanized, the domination of *Gesellschaft* over *Gemeinschaft* was never so complete as it had been in the ancient empires, and consequently *Kürwille* thinking had to pay attention to the *Wesenwille* values of the mass of the population.

The emergence of modern Europe out of the slow disintegration of this medieval order saw the step-by-step dismantling of the ideology of the Christian *viator* and its replacement with something that did open up the conceptual space for ideas that would justify the kind of economic expansion that if carried to an extreme could lead to planetary eco-catastrophe. The old dream of the Frashegird refashioned by the *Apocalypse* of Saint John into the millennium and all its accompanying cosmic drama had re-emerged in the European late middle ages among various radical reformers and their followers; moreover, the idea that not just individual souls might be transformed but that the whole of society could be reformed so as to better accord with certain ideals took an increasing grip on the minds of reflective people as well as many ordinary folk, a grip it retains in the West to our own day. As time went on, that thought came more and more to be a form of millennialism, that is, it became associated with a story about the inevitable direction of human history leading to some perfect world. In one way or another the phantasy of the Frashegird, the "Making Wonderful," in its various metamorphoses provided the psychic energy that propelled Western civilization in the glorious but tragically destructive direction that it took.

The first step, then, was the devaluation of the medieval *viator*'s psychological detachment from the activities of this world. The Church with its endorsement of a life of "poverty" as the superior way to imitate Christ in this life and its consequent approval of both monasticism and of mendicant orders, like the Franciscans and the Dominicans, had established an ideal that it readily admitted was one only a minority could attain. But it was not necessary to lead a life of such perfection in self-denial and detachment from the world in order to be saved. Our ordinary *viator* by avoiding the more serious sins and practising a good measure of Christian charity in the world could rest assured of a favourable judgment on that Last Day. The Protestant Reformers would have none of this. There were not two forms of Christian life, one more perfect than the other, and the monkish, mendicant life was not superior at all. The Christian was called to take part in the world of ordinary activity and to conscientiously try to succeed in this "calling." If this meant that he or she became wealthy, that was laudable as long as a direct craving for wealth and status, and the luxury that often accompanied these, was not the motivation for the worldly effort. Rather, the Christian undertook his calling in order to benefit all around him, in terms of both their physical comfort and their spiritual edification. Indeed, success in a worldly calling was a sign of divine favour, particularly desirable if you were convinced that God had already decided whom to save and whom to send to the lake of fire!

Other than the hopeful orientation toward the future that was part of the mainstream Christian outlook, this was perhaps the most fundamental step away from the ideological constraints the ancient world views had placed on the expansion of urban civilization. But it left in place much of that ideological heritage, in particular an overriding concern with the moral health of the souls and minds of individuals. Protestants now were concerned to do their best in their worldly vocations, but their chief preoccupation was not with improving the world but with the improvement of their own souls. In fact, improvement of the surrounding society was thought contingent on the creation of people who embodied Christian virtues and values. The Protestant utopias we examined, Christianopolis and Nova Solyma, both put the emphasis on education in Christian values infused with much wisdom from the ancient pagan philosophers. The development of the intellect and reason was encouraged, and in Christianopolis there was the full incorporation into education of the new empirically based physical sciences, which had arisen in opposition to the medieval scholastic approach to the study of nature. Protestant reformers in England in the seventeenth century led in promoting this sort of program.

It was Lord Verulam, Lord Chancellor for a time under James I, and better known to us as Francis Bacon, who more than anyone else initiated a second necessary step in the ideological release of Western Europe's high culture from the ancient bonds. He placed natural science in the service of humanity, saw its expansion and development as fulfilling humanity's destiny to recover the knowledge of nature it had lost in the Fall, and argued for its marriage to technology. Before Bacon the value of natural science to Protestant thinkers lay in its uncovering the magnificent designs of the Divine Architect and thus inspiring a deeper adoration of Him. For Bacon, in contrast, the value mainly lay in its ability to aid in the "relief of man's estate," that is, in the amelioration of hardship and in remedying the scarcity of the necessities of life. In pursuing knowledge of the natural world humans were only recovering what they had originally been endowed with but had lost as a result of trying to grasp rationally what is really good and evil rather than simply relying on the Creator's revealed instructions in that regard. Christian ethics, on Bacon's view, was basically God's demand that we love our neighbour, and all virtue was simply charity. By serving the welfare of mankind, the "common-weal," science was fulfilling that demand and exercising that virtue.

The theme of uniting science with the mechanical arts, that is, with technology, went along with Bacon's picture of scientific research being carried out cooperatively by large numbers of inquirers and experimenters, many using equipment invented by artisans and alchemists. He foresaw science as an industry with elaborate division of labour and requiring state financial support. In this he was well ahead of his time, for it would take another two centuries before this dream would be realized. According to Bacon, science should acknowledge no restrictions, no limits to its goals, other than those imposed by the requirement that whatever it accomplish be for the good of humanity. Among the purposes of Salomon's House, the scientific brain trust of Bacon's utopian society, is the "effecting of all things possible." It was Bacon's achievement to have made the new natural science already under development in Europe, along with the mechanical arts, the keystone of a millennial dream of material prosperity. Without the extraordinary advances in the physical sciences and technologies that eventually occurred the West would never have had the sheer power to effect the catastrophic environmental destruction that it inadvertently brought on.

But in the seventeenth century the Christian religion's emphasis on spiritual development still played a crucial role in people's conception of the good life and of where humanity should be headed, and this was a serious brake on any attempt to see the goal as simply unlimited material affluence such as might be produced by Baconian scientists working for humanity's welfare. The eighteenth century saw the dissolution of the traditional Christian aspect of this constraint. This was the next step in the process of ideological release.

Protestant divines promoted both the mission to improve the world materially through rational effort including science and the arts, and the emphasis on spiritual improvement that would rid the soul of desires for luxury, status, and power while concentrating people's thoughts on doing God's work of helping one's fellow human beings. Consequently they were prone to inveigh against many of the "sinful" practices of people who still indulged in the pleasures of the "flesh." This kind of mindset was, of course, constantly teetering on, if not in fact drowned in, hypocrisy. It is against such moralists that Mandeville wrote his famous poem, which points directly at the contradiction between the two goals such people had: first, the goal of a prosperous society in which the poor have full employment and "lived better than the Rich before," and which "was counted the great Nursery of Sciences and Industry"; and, second, the goal of a society in which their moral harangues against self-indulgence, licentiousness, and dishonesty had become so successful that they no longer had anything to inveigh against. Prosperity, in the sense in which all Western Europeans of the day understood it, required a goodly measure of the sins the moralists decried. This was the uncomfortable truth that Mandeville sprung upon his Protestant milieu.

On the other hand, if one found the sophisticated culture of eighteenth-century Western Europe with all its affluence (for a minority, of course) merely a breeding ground for pretence, phoniness, and hypocrisy, and hence not worth preserving, then rather than go back to the traditional Christian values of the *viator* one might take to heart Rousseau's claim that basic human nature, untutored in the ways of civilization, possessed innately the wherewithal for a morally honourable life in which the person honestly avowed the passions that naturally arose in his or her breast. Here was another way to break entirely with the Christian tradition, and particularly with its Protestant form: deny the doctrine of original sin. That dogma had always justified a certain skepticism as regards large-scale human efforts to change things. Somewhere lurking behind the veil of good intentions must lie devilish desires for personal power, wealth, and status. According to Rousseau these despicable motives arose not from the inner, innate nature of human beings, but from their acculturation into a society in which individuals had to warp their nature into some hypocritical, status-hungry distortion of itself in order to survive. Abolish all these mores and institutions of sophisticated civilization and human nature could reassert itself in its pristine original form. We would not then have Mandeville's prosperous society, but we would have excellent human beings. Needless to say, few would adopt as jaundiced a view of civilization as Rousseau's, but the idea of a human nature that was good in the beginning and then later hamstrung by artificial institutions was one that would become immensely popular and a foundation stone for the Romantic movement.

We can see it emerge in Adam Smith's basing ethics in "moral sentiments," which he posited humans were created with in order to make possible social life, the only life in which humans could prosper. Building on ideas broached earlier by his friend David Hume, Smith developed a theory in which our access to moral guidance comes not from reading scriptures or the advice of ancient sages, but from our feelings, and especially our ability for "sympathy," that is, to feel in our imagination the feelings of others. In fact, apart from those feelings there is no morality in the world. The "Author of Nature" has simply created in humans the feelings that make them adopt attitudes and principles we call moral and abhor attitudes and conduct we call immoral. The beneficent Author's purpose in this was just to make social life possible, and even enjoyable, for us. But then why should we not forget about this morality and simply adopt the goal of the Creator, viz., the happiness of the human race, as the goal of all our deliberate behaviour? Smith's answer is that following the dictates of our innate feelings will be a much more effective way of arriving at that goal in the long run than using our rather weak minds to figure out and calculate what sort of behaviour will most improve social life and thereby human happiness.

Again we fall back on a nature perfectly created to lead the sort of life that will be most satisfying to its owner. No cloud of original sin dims its innate moral capacities.

Even more Rousseauian in spirit is the way in which Sophie de Grouchy, patroness of salons of radical thinking in France before and during the revolution, reworked Smith's theory of sentiments into an Epicurean, hedonistic psychology. Humans by nature feel pain at the sight of another human suffering and are spontaneously moved to relieve that suffering. Likewise, although not so intensely, they feel pleasure at the sight of another human being happy and are spontaneously moved to perpetuate that happiness. Out of such immediate altruistic motivations arises the desire to increase happiness and reduce suffering generally. All this will come naturally to a person if it is encouraged as he or she is growing up and the surrounding culture does not through institutions and education based in ignorance and inequality warp that person's personality in some egotistical direction. De Grouchy did not think civilization *per se* necessarily distorted people's attitudes, but she did think the ignorance and oppression perpetrated by the Church and the whole *ancient régime* forced people away from their natural altruistic impulses. Whereas Smith used the psychology of "sentiments" to establish a basically Stoic morality, de Grouchy in effect put the Christian virtue of charity on the same totally secular basis.

All the above, however, is hardly sufficient to inspire a mammoth effort to establish a worldwide utopia of affluence and cultural perfection. What it lacks is the essence of millennialism, the conviction that there is a historical process ineluctably working itself out toward its inevitable utopian finale, and that people enlightened enough to be aware of this course of history can play a role in its unfolding. Out of the Enlightenment of the French *philosophes* came at least two ways of filling that gap. Anne Robert-Jacques Turgot saw the chaotic and often cruel course of human history as providing the "violent fermentation" required to allow persons of genius to invent and enact improvements in science, the arts, and human institutions generally, which over time, and with many reverses, would lead to a better and better life for humanity. It was periods in which there was stability in human affairs that saw stagnation. As painful as the demolition of such stability always was, it nevertheless provided an opportunity for geniuses to enlist support for their ideas. In difficult times people would be passionately stirred to desire change, and it was these passions, not Reason, that motivated their acceptance of new ideas. If in human history Reason and its practical twin, Justice, had always dominated, the result would have been total mediocrity, not the kind of improvement that had already appeared in the history of Europe since the Renaissance, although it was still far from complete.

Turgot still believed in a divine Author of Nature, and his conception of human history provided him with a modern, naturalistic theodicy. All those evils that so dominate the story of human civilization—the wars, the oppression, the hardships of the masses, not to mention all the moral failings, such as vainglory—can be seen as serving to slowly push humanity toward its cultural perfection. This was and is the divine plan, but it is fulfilled not by direct divine intervention, as in the Frashegird and the Christian Parousia, but by the nature that the Author bestowed on humans from the beginning. Their natural passions propel them, when faced with disaster, to follow the suggestions of the geniuses, who, though few in number, always arise in any human culture. As in Smith, it is again human nature and its natural impulses that are best relied on.

A second way of envisioning human history as an inevitable progress toward human perfection was put forward by the mathematician and political activist Antoine Nicolas de Condorcet. In his view, laws of nature governed human activity as much as they had been shown by Newton to govern the world of matter in motion, and those laws dictated that humanity, admittedly with fits and starts, progress *indefinitely* toward perfection. There is no final utopia for Condorcet, just a progress that will end only with the end of the planet itself.

The engine of progress in Condorcet's vision is the improvement of knowledge and the gradual extirpation of ignorance and superstition. This improvement arises from the natural growth of the human mind, and because that growth is perfectly natural there can be a fully natural science of that development just as there are sciences of the physical world. A constant war has been and still is being waged between the forces of enlightenment and those promoting ignorance. In Europe of the modern era this has pitted the physical scientists against the Church, and inevitably the former will win out. This new knowledge must not be restricted to a learned elite; it must be made available to the people generally, for then individuals will know how best to promote their own interests, and in doing so they will improve society as a whole. Condorcet sees the growth of knowledge as the dominating theme in human history, for progress in all other fields depends on growth in that one. The improvements that accompany that growth are certainly not limited to technological developments; more importantly, they lead to an increase in equality among people and to the recognition of the natural rights of individuals. Along with all this goes a heightening of moral sensibility, following the lines his wife and widow Sophie de Grouchy proposed.

Condorcet's vision was for all of humanity. He thought that enlightened Europeans should take the knowledge they had won to the rest of the globe and thereby improve the lives of all the less advanced peoples. Europe had what would later be called a "civilizing mission." We have here a fully secularized vision of the millennium equipped both with a cosmic drama of truth and light inevitably conquering falsity and ignorance and with a mission to spread the former to all the peoples of the earth. No ideology could have provided a more inspiring justification for the further penetration of enlightened Western culture and the material advances made possible by Western science into the rest of the world.

Still, neither Turgot nor Condorcet had tried to diminish the importance of moral advances in the coming great improvement in human civilization. Nor had they given physical science and the mechanical arts quite the central role that had been envisioned by Bacon. A concern with spiritual development and living a good moral life could conceivably have distracted people from the task of advancing in material affluence through ever more sophisticated ways of dominating nature, and thus perhaps have avoided placing too crushing a burden on the planetary ecosystem in the rush to bring the whole of humanity into the ways of Enlightenment. The nineteenth century saw the development of ideas that would eventually undermine this constraint as well. This would be the next step in the unleashing process.

Henri de Saint-Simon with his millenarian ideas elevated what he called "positive" science and its practitioners to a position hitherto reserved for philosopher-kings. It was not simply that they provided the knowledge that would improve technology; there could also be a science for how to run society.

What, after all, was the main business of society? It was to facilitate and encourage economic production and employment. That would address in one blow the need for greater availability of the goods people needed as well as for moral improvement, since in expanding industry it would abolish idleness, which was the main source of moral decay and criminality, in Saint-Simon's opinion. Industry was to be organized by the leading *industriels*, that is, people with experience in managing industrial enterprises and their financing, but they were to be guided by a science. And what science is that? According to Saint-Simon, it was just being born under the name "political economy." Here he cited J.B. Say as the leading protagonist, though soon criticizing him for claiming a distinction between political economy and politics. Society was now to be scientifically administered, and people who did not understand the science of that administration were to be excluded from influence. With scientific direction, society would ramp up industrial production and put people to work with an efficiency never before attained. To improve morality would require only that people be educated to honour productivity and esteem those who were especially productive, for being productive is the best way to fulfil the basic commandment to love one's brothers. How could one love them better than by improving the material conditions of their lives? But for Saint-Simon this improvement depended not as it had for Smith and Turgot on the natural impulses of human beings but rather on the rational organization of social life and individual lives. The tension between faith, on the one hand, in unreflective but natural human impulses, so eulogized by Rousseau, and, on the other hand, in the belief in the need to resort to the critical gaze of self-conscious reason, such as had been lauded by the Christian Stoic Justus Lipsius, has remained a fundamental contradiction in Western ideology right up to the present day.[2]

After breaking off his collaboration with Saint-Simon, Auguste Comte advocated for a system of thought he called "positivism," which went far beyond that of his earlier mentor into a systematic science of society. Much in the spirit of Condorcet, he saw human history as being governed by the natural development of the human mental capacities through positive science, its discovery of nature's laws being the apogee of this development. He was much more insistent on the moral side of the improvement of human life than Saint-Simon had been, but his prescription for attaining this was not all that different. First of all, the ample provision of the necessities of life would free the human spirit to become more altruistic, since a person would no longer need to focus so much on obtaining what they personally needed. But besides this, the development of a science of society would show that the unalterable laws of nature made life in society necessary to human survival and the perpetuation of altruism a requirement for social life. When people realized the existence of these inescapable laws, they would be completely motivated to adopt the altruistic attitude. So, as with Saint-Simon, it was the increased knowledge of science that accounted for both sides of human progress: for the technological improvement that ended scarcity of necessities, and for the subordination of self-seeking to interest in the welfare of all. Moreover, Comte situated this vision of progress within an *inevitable* historical process leading through three epochs and ending in one in which the positivist philosophy he promoted would dominate human thought. In this construction the millenarian character of his ideas becomes totally obvious.

The conviction that science, and particularly applied science, could lead the way not just to material affluence but to social stability and moral improvement became the inspiration for the creation of the engineering profession in France, through the establishment of the École Polytechnique and later the École Centrale. The founding of the former was very much under the direction of Freemasons, who were to play a leading role in putting engineering and engineers at the forefront of progressivist thinking and projects in both Britain and America during the nineteenth century. The Masons had a highly optimistic view of human nature and little sympathy with Christian doctrines of the Fall and original sin, but they had inherited the millenarian spirit of Protestant reformers in seventeenth-century Britain. This combination meant that the vision they promoted for the engineering profession was very much in line with what Saint-Simon and Comte would have desired. By the latter half of the nineteenth century, then, an ideology existed, and had been adopted by many leading citizens of the West, that saw the symbiosis of theoretical and applied science as leading the way to a "promised land" of material plenty, social peace, and moral perfection. The Masons and many other enthusiasts of engineering set themselves the task of realizing the original Baconian vision for reform of the world through science and technology.

There was, however, one important feature of the coming world order envisioned by Saint-Simon that needed to be put in place. This related to his call for a science for administering the entire economic realm so as most efficiently to increase production of goods and services and satisfy the wants of the populace. In fact, the faith in what humans find natural, as opposed to artificially contrived plans and regulations—so much a part of eighteenth-century thought—stood in the way of that demand. Saint-Simon saw, as we noted, the replacement of government in most of its functions by this administration of the economy. Science could replace politics, and scientists would replace politicians with all their ignorant "twaddle." The "budget" was to be the crucial product of this administrative order, and a science was needed to properly construct it. Presciently, he believed that political economy was in his own day becoming just such a science. The near fulfilment of this dream was realized later in the nineteenth century, not so much in France, where the foundations had largely been laid, but in Britain, by thinkers who used Adam Smith's WN as their point of departure. This was the next step in the ideological liberation of the West's expansive drive.

Smith, in accord with his faith in allowing free rein to certain natural impulses, believed that the material progress of human society arose basically from the impulse to "truck and barter," which led to the establishment of markets that facilitated this trucking and bartering and thus promoted increase in material affluence. He argued that what we would call a rise in the "standard of living" would be achieved mainly by an increase in the division of the labour required to produce things, and that an expansion of trade (i.e., of the market) was the chief way of enabling greater division of labour, although the introduction of machinery, something itself made possible by more division of labour, also cheapened goods and thus made them more available to the masses, thereby increasing their access to comforts and conveniences. In fact, he argued, the prosperity of the labouring class could only be improved if the economy of the country were growing rather than remaining static. Smith's analysis provided, then, a strong ethical motivation for opening up international trade and mechanizing the factories. Such were the policies that would advance affluence among the masses, what we now call mass consumption. In fact, in accord with Smith's analysis, economic growth now came to be seen as a social necessity.

David Ricardo later argued that if left to its "natural" course a nation's market economy would slide toward a static state of general misery for the labouring class. Hence again we see the need to expand international trade, for this would rectify that "natural" tendency toward misery. Free trade, he argued, would be beneficial to all concerned, since each country would be able to sell what it could produce at less cost than other nations could and import what cost it more to produce on its own. Here, however, Ricardo noted that importing only luxury goods would not have the desired amelioration of the lives of the workers; rather, what was needed was importing the basic goods on which the labourers survived so as to lower their prices. Even more than Smith, Ricardo welcomed machinery, although he warned that in the short run it could cause unemployment. But both Smith and Ricardo held that economic growth had to be maintained indefinitely in order for the labouring class not to descend into near destitution once again. Here began the West's obsession with endless growth that continues to the present day.

Ricardo's analysis of how a market economy works was much more abstract than Smith's and consequently much more explicable through simple mathematical reasoning. In his hands political economy was looking much more like what anyone trained in the physical sciences expected a science to look like, and indeed the subject was increasingly popularized as a science as the nineteenth century went on. Politicians, as well, had to pay more and more attention to the advice of its practitioners when planning government finances.

Up to this point probably the main motivation for studying political economy at all was something akin to Christian charity, that is, a genuine wish to see the living standards of the labouring masses improved. This is quite obvious in both Smith and Ricardo. But there now occurs a twist to the subject arising from a revolution in philosophical ethics, one that provided a new way of envisioning the benefits that might be derived from proper administration of the economic realm. Adam Smith in his *TMS* had followed the lead of David Hume in basing morality in natural human feelings rather than in Reason, although Reason played a subsidiary role. This approach aligned with ideas germinating in France that emphasized pleasures and pains as motivating forces in human psychology. Earlier, we saw this become a full-fledged ethical theory in the letters written by Sophie de Grouchy. The full restoration of this

Epicurean psychology, however, was the work of Jeremy Bentham, who founded the British philosophy of hedonistic utilitarianism, which wholeheartedly espoused the view that individual actions as well as government policies should be directed toward achieving maximum satisfaction of the various desires of the people in one's community—that is, maximum happiness. Furthermore, Bentham thought that this was the philosophy that persons in a community would naturally be led to by their efforts to satisfy *their own* desires. His psychology was both hedonist and egoist, but a rational egoist, he thought, would come to assert the principle of utility—in short, the imperative to seek the greatest happiness for the greatest number. Not only that, but happiness was quantifiable, so individuals and governments should take seriously the *calculation* of how much happiness their actions and policies were engendering.

It was William Stanley Jevons's genius to see that Bentham's psychology and ethics could be used to put political economy—now to be called simply "economics"—on a quite different basis than its classical founders had envisioned. To understand how the market operated one needed only to see each of the traders coming to the market with the intention of satisfying as much as possible their own desires, that is, maximizing their utility. In an ideal market in which every participant has full knowledge of the prices of all commodities being traded, the motivation for any given purchase will be the rate at which the acquisition of additional quantities of the commodity adds to the purchaser's utility. This conception leads quickly to the application of the infinitesimal calculus to the whole proceedings of the market, thus enabling the calculation of what prices will be at an equilibrium.

With this stroke Jevons had accomplished two things. First, he put economics on a mathematical basis so that its similarity to physical science was totally evident. This, of course, in an age that worshipped Newton's mechanics, greatly enhanced the prestige of the subject and its practitioners. But second, and perhaps more significantly, he made economics a science of how society could maximize desire satisfaction among the populace without any moralizing about what desires were and were not worth satisfying. Now Mandeville's observation about how affluence relied on people acting on desires the Christian moralists decried could be completely accommodated. At last an ideology existed that disposed of the last remnants of traditional religious and philosophical urgings that we stand back from ourselves and let Reason (the Stoics) or biblical Revelation (the Puritans) pass judgments on our desires. No desire on Bentham's account was bad in itself; a desire should be restrained only when it would get in the way of satisfying other desires to such an extent as to make maximizing the satisfaction of the totality of one's desires impossible. Reason here enters only as a calculating device. The last remaining ethical restraints on mass consumption had been lifted.

It should by now be clear how this complex of ideas that arose in the West could justify at every turn the further and further expansion of the economic engine the West constructed, expansion both in the overall quantity of goods and services produced and in the area of the world in which it took hold as well. We now know that this has meant not only a huge increase in affluence but also a great increase in population, for Western medical science has reduced infant mortality and prolonged life spans in all the parts of the world to which it has been introduced. I assume the reader is more than familiar with the "hockey-stick" graphs of both world population increase and per capita energy use since 1800. Humanity's artificial home has both expanded and intensified, but this has come at great cost to its inherited home. *Eco*-nomy has largely destroyed *eco*-logy.

We now realize that our inherited home is not so dispensable as most people have long thought. Those humans who existed before civilization, of course, recognized their dependence on that home. With civilization came the realization that that dependence could be diminished to a degree, and with the city came a disregard for that home as humans adopted a certain hubris that they could master nature as needed. But urban-centred civilization has never been something humans have easily adapted to. This is not to deny all the technological advances, all the achievements in science and the arts, all the comforts and conveniences it provided for some; it is only to take full note of the wars, the slavery, the oppression, and the huge inequalities in wealth and power that have always accompanied it.

To its great credit, Western civilization in the modern period has taken laudable strides toward moderating these pathological features. In the West it is now generally accepted among most citizens that government should have as its aim the welfare of *all* citizens, that education should be made available to *all*, that war is a horror to be avoided, that slavery is not to be allowed, that women should have the same rights as men, that racial differences are not marks of innate inferiority or superiority. These are all great achievements. Most of us Westerners would mourn their reversal.

What this book has tried to show, however, is that some of the leading ideas of the West, when combined and motivated by the ancient millenarian dream of a future, radically improved world, form a justification for the very practices that threaten to bring down civilization around the world and much of the current natural order with it. Note how, when we take each of these ideas by themselves, they often constitute elements of received wisdom and possess a compelling force. Would you want to deny that humans ought to view the world around us as our true home in which we should take a full and constructive part, and instead affirm the medieval *viator* picture? Do you have any doubt that the collaboration of theoretical science with technology can produce immense benefits for humanity (the Baconian vision)? Are you going to cast doubt on the basic goodness of human beings enabling them to manage their own lives and that of their societies in a reasonably beneficial way (the gospel of Rousseau and Smith)? Would you refuse to grant that the advances in science and technology made in the West should be gifted to the rest of the world (Condorcet's plea)? Are you ready to deny that the augmenting of the pleasures of life and the diminishing of its pains should be the ultimate aim of society for its citizens (Bentham's proclamation)? If you at least feel the pull of these ideas—and note that they are still among the most defining of modern Western civilization—then you will understand why the ideology that combines them into a millenarian utopianism continues to have a grip on us Westerners today.

But now we see that the extraordinary power of urban civilization to change things was something humans were not suited to. The doctrine of original sin needs to be removed from its mythical, moral origins and recast as humans' natural tendency to delight in power and use it as much as they can.[3] They even define their goals in terms of what the power they have available can accomplish. The *Kürwille* side to our mentality has shown a marked tendency to take advantage of power to escape the bonds of *Gemeinschaft* and remodel society more and more along *Gesellschaft* lines. The Greeks called this *hubris*, and it was evident from the very beginnings of urban civilization in the ancient Middle East, as was also the potential for disastrous results in the form of highly organized warfare with technologically advanced equipment,[4] of enslavement of foreign peoples, of ecologically destructive agricultural practices, of monstrous projects of civil engineering, of granting unlimited political power to one person, of enormous class divisions and oppression of the poor. The examination of ancient history shows how that mentality, when equipped with the powers that came with urban civilization, was a deadly combination. The modern West, however, developed an ideology that exalted in power. It provided a rationale for releasing the West's *Kürwille* mentality from virtually all of the restraints formerly in place.

That ideology now, I judge, has less of a hold on us Westerners than it did in the recent past. We can get some psychological distance from it now and see its weaknesses, but that is not to say we can save ourselves from eco-catastrophe by consciously rejecting it and adopting something else. Changes in basic ideologies come only with radical changes in the way people live, and they do not occur that fast; the "we" here does not have a single mind that can reverse its direction like a driver who realizes he is on the wrong road. Besides, we find ourselves in one of those "progress traps" that Ronald Wright speaks of.[5] Our present trap has a particularly strong grip on us because to do the things that are required to break out of it in the very limited time left to save ourselves would mean such suffering and devastation as to make the cure utterly unacceptable to just about everybody. It would require, for starts, such a huge cutback in energy use as would cripple industry as we know it and cause widespread destitution and social unrest. Eco-catastrophe is inevitable, and perhaps the human race can survive it, particularly if some of us, at least, don't try to restore the old economy after each descending step. We'll need innovations that build community solidarity while accepting a life of comparative material poverty. Perhaps this can be aided by taking some lessons from the Confucians and Stoics and placing a lot more value on virtues of character than on physical comfort. We can hope, I think, that the catastrophe will be one that only slowly worsens so that some humans at least will have the time to make step-by-step adaptations to an increasingly hostile world. Or perhaps some of the few remaining people who have never been incorporated into the global economy will be able to survive and perpetuate their ways.[6] As for the home we inherited in the Holocene, as humans become fewer and less intrusive and the global climate shifts, its remnants will on their own become something else, with much less of the marvellous biological diversity some of us have learned to appreciate. That, to say the least, will be a great shame, something to be much grieved, but there is no cure for it.

I can think of no better way of ending this essay than to let Ferdinand Tönnies, whose concepts have formed the basic framework for what I have had to say here, have the last say. Writing in 1913, before the world wars and before any planet-wide eco-catastrophe was foreseen, and having just acknowledged the scientific achievements of European civilization, he said:

> However, modern civilization is caught in an irresistible process of disintegration. Its very progress dooms it. This is hard for us to conceive, and harder still to acquiesce in it, to admit it and yet to cooperate with it willingly and even cheerfully. We must bring ourselves to look upon tragedy, wrestling with both fear and hope so as to rid ourselves of them, and to enjoy the cleansing effect of the dramatic course of events. Scientific analysis can do this if it has matured and transformed itself into philosophy, that is, into wisdom.[7]

NOTES

PREFACE

1. My definition is in line with one of those given in *Webster's Ninth New Collegiate Dictionary* of 1984, viz., "the integrated assertions, theories, and aims that constitute a sociopolitical program."

INTRODUCTION

1. Elizabeth Kolbert, *The Sixth Extinction: An Unnatural History* (Henry Holt, 2014).
2. "But, soon or late, it is ideas, not vested interests, which are dangerous for good or evil." John Maynard Keynes, *The General Theory of Employment, Interest, and Money* (Cambridge University Press for the Royal Economic Society, 1973), 383–84.
3. Likewise, please allow me to make the same distinction between "phantastic" and "fantastic," "phantasize" and "fantasize." The distinction I am making here is nicely caught by this quote from the Italian philologist Fausto Cercignani, which I found in a bridge column by Bobby Wolff: "Do not confuse fantasy with imagination. The former consumes itself in daydreaming; the latter stimulates creativity in the arts and in the sciences."

1 Human Life before There Were Cities

1. In what follows I shall be using the term "civilization" in two senses: first as an abstract noun embracing any of the ways people lived when they had permanent settlements with domesticated plants and animals; and, second, as a count noun to refer to groups of settled people who share a common culture or are politically unified (e.g., the Greco-Roman civilization, or the Harappan civilization). I shall not use at all the terms "civilized" and "uncivilized," as the laudatory connotations of the former and the pejorative ones of the latter imply judgments I have no intention of making. Instead I shall just refer to "settled" and "non-settled" life, and to people as "settled" or "non-settled."
2. Besides the instances discussed above, this kind of civilization also arose in the third millennium BCE on the coast of Peru and in the Andes, late in the first millennium BCE in the African Sahel, and in the first millennium CE in Central America. The first two were largely independent of earlier cases and the third perhaps dependent on the first. I have not had the time to research these civilizations, and in any event the evidence for judging what dynamic was at work in any of them is much scarcer.
3. Recent discoveries in North Africa, however, seem to show that modern humans were living there 300,000 years ago. See Ashley Strickland, "Oldest Homo Sapiens Fossils Discovered," *CNN Health*, June 8, 2017, https://www.cnn.com/2017/06/07/health/oldest-homo-sapiens-fossils-found/index.html. Obviously, the science here is changing rapidly.
4. A detailed review of the evidence on this can be found in Pamela R. Willoughby, *The Evolution of Modern Humans in Africa* (Altamira Press, 2007), 140–44, and elsewhere.
5. See William James Burroughs, *Climate Change in Prehistory: The End of the Reign of Chaos* (Cambridge University Press, 2005), 83, 131.
6. This is not to deny that Paleolithic humans could and did modify the natural environment so as to increase its capacity to provision them. Fire was often used for this purpose. James C. Scott discusses this in *Against the Grain: A Deep History of the Earliest States* (Yale University Press, 2017), 38–40. He plausibly credits people with using fire to "landscape" their habitat.
7. Richard Leakey and Roger Lewin agree. See their *The Sixth Extinction*, 82. There may well be some connection between human tool-making and language development. See "Origin of Language," *Wikipedia*, https://en.wikipedia.org/wiki/Origin_of_language.
8. Max Weber was very conscious of this wide gap in the way people think. In his 1917 lecture *The Scholar's Work*, he remarked: "Increasing rationalization and intellectualization...means the disenchanting of the world. Unlike the savage for whom such mysterious forces existed, we no longer need to adopt magical means to control or pray to the spirits—we make use, instead of technology and calculation. This above all is what intellectualization means" in *Charisma and Disenchantment: The Vocation Lecture*, ed. Paul Reitter and Chad Wellmon, trans. Damion Searle (New York Review of Books, 2020), 18.
9. There is also the possible use of psychotropic substances for such purposes.

10. Clive Ponting makes this point in *A New Green History of the World: The Environment and the Collapse of Great Civilizations*, rev. ed. (Penguin Books, 2007), 19.
11. The scientist E.O. Wilson coined the term "biophilia" in recognition of this innate desire for contact with the natural world. Richard Louv in his *Our Wild Calling* (Algonquin Books, 2019) writes and talks about "nature deficit disorder" as a pervasive ailment among those of us who live almost entirely within the artificial ambience we have created for ourselves.
12. Scott, *Against the Grain*, 47–55.
13. See "Ceramic History," https://depts.washington.edu/matseed/mse_resources/Webpage/Ceramics/ceramichistory.htm.
14. Villages in India right up to the present day sometimes exhibit a high degree of specialization in the division of labour and consequently achieve a large degree of self-sufficiency. See "Peasant Societies," *Britannica*, https://www.britannica.com/topic/primitive-culture/Peasant-societies.
15. For a sparse population, foraging in a well-stocked natural environment would have provided an intake of calories far in excess of the calories expended in the foraging effort. In other words, the energy returned on energy invested (EROEI) was high compared to subsistence farming. Perhaps it was only when and where the actual EROEI of foraging had fallen to the point that it was roughly equal to that of farming that the shift was made. (Thanks to Professor Charles Schweger for pointing this out to me.)
16. See Andrew Curry, "Who Were the First Europeans?" *National Geographic*, August 2019, 100–13.
17. See Burroughs, *Climate Change in Prehistory*, 248.
18. Scott devotes an entire chapter to these perils. See *Against the Grain*, 93–115. He nicely catches the precariousness of the "domus," as he calls these communities, in this passage: "An illness—of crops, livestock, or people—a drought, excessive rains, a plague of locusts, rats, or birds, could bring the whole edifice down in the blink of an eye" (112–13).
19. This is one of the themes of Norman Cohn's *Cosmos, Chaos, and the World to Come: The Ancient Roots of Apocalyptic Faith*, 2nd ed. (Yale University Press, 2001).
20. Mircea Eliade remarks: "'Primitive' man lived in constant terror of finding that the forces around him which he found so useful were worn out. For thousands of years men were tortured by the fear that the sun would disappear forever at the winter solstice, that the moon would not rise again, that plants would die forever, and so on" (*Patterns in Comparative Religion*, trans. Rosemary Sheed [University of Nebraska Press, 1996], 346). My view is that such paranoia would have developed only after life became settled.
21. Eliade, *Patterns in Comparative Religion*: "Agriculture taught man the fundamental oneness of organic life: and from that revelation sprang the simpler analogies between woman and field, between the sexual act and sowing, as well as the most advanced intellectual syntheses: life as rhythmic, death as a return, and so on" (361).
22. Water in fact was often considered the formless origin of all the world. Cleansing with water could thus be considered a return to the beginning, a "new start," as we say. See Eliade again:

> In cosmogony, in myth, ritual and iconography, water fills the same function in whatever type of cultural pattern we find it; it *precedes* all forms and *upholds* all creation. Immersion in water symbolizes a return to the pre-formal, a total regeneration, a new birth, for immersion means a dissolution of forms, a reintegration into the formlessness of pre-existence; and emerging from the water is a repetition of the act of creation in which form was first expressed. (*Patterns in Comparative Religion*, 188)

2 The Trauma of Urban-Dominated Civilization

1. See "Jericho," *Britannica*, https://www.britannica.com/place/Jericho-West-Bank.
2. See "Ancient Anatolia," *Britannica*, https://www.britannica.com/place/Anatolia.
3. See "Sumer," *Wikipedia*, https://en.wikipedia.org/wiki/Sumer.
4. Lewis Mumford imaginatively pictured this transition: "The local chieftain turned into the towering king, and became likewise the chief priestly guardian of the shrine, now endowed with divine or almost divine attributes. The village neighbours would now be kept at a distance: no longer familiars and equals, they were reduced to subjects, whose lives were supervised and directed by military and civil officers, governors, viziers, tax-gatherers, soldiers, directly accountable to the king" (*The City in History: Its Origins, Its Transformations, and Its Prospects* [Penguin, 1966], 41). I presume something like this to have taken place not only in Sumer but in many other places where cities first arose.
5. Again Mumford, in *The City in History*, described the sort of process I am suggesting: "In a society confronting numerous social changes brought on by its own mechanical and agricultural improvements, which provoked serious crises that called for prompt action, under unified command, the hoarded folk wisdom born solely of past experience in long-familiar situations was impotent" (43). Notice his reference to the impotence of "folkways"—that is, in Ferdinand Tönnies's terms, which we shall come to shortly, in *Gemeinschaft und Gesellschaft*, in *Gesmtausgabe*, eds. Bettina Clausen and Dieter Haselbach, vol. 2, 1880–1935 (De Gruyter, 2019).
6. See "Sumer/Military," *Wikipedia*, https://en.wikipedia.org/wiki/Sumer.
7. I have relied on the critical edition published in 2019 in Volume 2 of the *Gesamtausgabe*. See Tönnies, *Gemeinschaft und Gesellschaft*. All the excerpted texts that follow have been translated by myself from that edition. The first German edition appeared in 1887, the eighth and last in 1935. I have also consulted the translation of the work by Charles P. Loomis (Tönnies, *Community and Association* [*Gemeinschaft und Gesellschaft*], trans. Charles P. Loomis [Routledge and Kegan Paul, 1955]), and in what follows I cite page references to that work under "Loomis." My rendition of Tönnies's concepts does not stick closely to his own exposition, and the applications I have made of them are my own and not necessarily any that Tönnies would have endorsed, although I do think they are totally consonant with those concepts.
8. Loomis translates it as "natural will."
9. Loomis translates it as "rational will."

10. "The sharpest contrast, then, arises if affirmation of a social entity for its own sake is distinguished from an affirmation of such an entity because of an end, or purpose, which is extraneous to it. I call a will of the first kind *essential will* [= *Wesenwille*] and a will of the second kind *arbitrary will* [= *Kürwille*]." Tönnies, "The Concept of Gemeinschaft," in *On Sociology: Pure, Applied, and Empirical*, ed. W.J. Cahneman and R. Heberle (University of Chicago Press, 1971), 65.

11. Ellul, in *The Technological Society*, trans. John Wilkenson (Vintage Books, 1964), notes much the same distinction as we have drawn from Tönnies:

>Today we are witnessing a kind of technical reconstitution of the scattered fragments of society; communities and associations flourish everywhere... If we examine these new sociological forms in detail, we find them all organized as functions of techniques. We hardly need to examine industrial associations, but the same applies to all other twentieth century associations. They may be associations for sport or for culture, the goal of which is clearly recognizable...The social morphology of these societies indeed differs radically from that of traditional societies. Traditional societies were centered upon human needs and instincts (for example, in family, clan, seignory). Modern societies, on the other hand, are centered on technical necessity and derivatively, of course, on human adherence. Man, in modern societies, is not situated in relation to other men, but in relation to technique; for this reason the sociological structure of these societies is completely altered. (305)

Ellul's notion of "technique" is a close relative of Tönnies's *Kürwille*.

12. Loomis translates *Gefallen* as "liking."

13. Tönnies, *Gemeinschaft und Gesellschaft*: "The innate pleasure in certain things and in certain activities that occurs in the human way of being I call its form of the general animal instinct, or its *delight*" (232; Loomis, 124–25).

14. Tönnies, *Gemeinschaft und Gesellschaft*: "For what one knows how to do and can do is what one does easily, and consequently willingly, and is ready and willing to do; on the other hand the more unfamiliar something is the more it is undertaken painfully or with effort, and the less willingly" (236; Loomis, 128).

15. Tönnies, *Gemeinschaft und Gesellschaft*: "Learning is partly one's own experience, partly imitation, but especially the receiving of instruction and teaching as to how something must be done in order to be right and good, and which things and ways of being are healthy and worthwhile. This is, then, the real value of Memory: to know the Right and the Good in order to love and to do them" (239; Loomis, 130).

16. Tönnies, *Gemeinschaft und Gesellschaft*, 249 (Loomis, 138).

17. Tönnies, *Gemeinschaft und Gesellschaft*, 251 (Loomis, 140).

18. Tönnies, *Gemeinschaft und Gesellschaft*: "Thus it deals only with a similar and indifferent quantity of possibilities which are for him present and to be decided, and in each case determined to be realized just to the extent that it seems necessary for bringing about a previously imagined effect" (252; Loomis, 141).

19. Tönnies, *Gemeinschaft und Gesellschaft*: "To understand deliberation one has to inquire into the purpose or aim; to understand discrimination, where the aim is laid

out in advance, one must inquire after the basis; to understand concept one must inquire into the rules for constructing it" (253; Loomis, 141-42).
20. Tönnies, *Gemeinschaft und Gesellschaft*:
>It is the unmediated, friendly, well-intentioned tendency of the will, considerateness ("flower of the noblest soul," as a poet says), a ready willingness to share joy and sorrow, the clinging to and recollection of friendly companions in life. So we may define the purity and beauty of "character" as sincerity and truthfulness, the deep, as we say, and the nobility of the "soul" generally as kindness; but the goodness and morality of the "conscience," the tender, perhaps anxious, conscientiousness, as loyalty. From these three all natural moral values can be derived. (247; Loomis, 137)

21. Tönnies, *Gemeinschaft und Gesellschaft*: "Such consciousness must, for a calculation to be correct, be the basis for all estimates and evaluations. Here is the knowledge that is accessible and suitable for fully planned applications; the theory and method for ruling over nature and humans. The conscious individual scorns all dark feelings, premonitions, prejudices as of negligible or dubious value in this regard" (255; Loomis, 143).
22. Tönnies, *Gemeinschaft und Gesellschaft*: "…and he wants to set up his plans, his direction in life and his outlook on the world in accord only with his clearly and distinctly grasped concepts" (255; Loomis, 143). Tönnies obviously has the archetypical nineteenth-century businessman in mind, and it is clear that he thinks the moral dangers of leaning too far to the *Kürwille* pole are much greater than those of leaning too far toward *Wesenwille*.
23. Tönnies, *Gemeinschaft und Gesellschaft*: "This is why consciousness leads to self-criticism with its condemnation just as much against one's own (practical) stupidity as conscience is directed against one's own supposed badness. The former is the highest expression of *Kürwille*, while the latter is the highest or most spiritual expression of *Wesenwille*" (255-56; Loomis, 143).
24. Tönnies, *Gemeinschaft und Gesellschaft*:
>If, then, *Kürwille* wants to order and define everything toward ends or utility, it has to drive out the given, traditional, deep-rooted rules to the extent that they do not adapt themselves to such ends, i.e., submit as much as this may occur. Therefore, it not only has to be the case that the more definitely *Kürwille* develops or thought about ends gets involved with and concentrates on knowledge, attainment, and application of means, the more the feeling and intellectual complex which makes up the particular or individual instance of a *Wesenwille* is by not being used in danger of atrophy; but there exists also a more direct opposition in which this complex tries to hold *Kürwille* back and resist its freedom and domination, while *Kürwille* tries first to break loose from *Wesenwille* and then to dissolve, to destroy or to dominate it. (282-83; Loomis, 162-63).

25. Tönnies, *Gemeinschaft und Gesellschaft*, 320-23 (Loomis, 192-94).
26. Tönnies, *Gemeinschaft und Gesellschaft*, 413 (Loomis, 265).
27. Tönnies, *Gemeinschaft und Gesellschaft*, 413 (Loomis, 265).
28. See "Sumer/Military," *Wikipedia*, https://en.wikipedia.org/wiki/Sumer.

NOTES

29. Tönnies emphasizes the inherent opposition between the trader and the peasant:
> Trade is for any pure, indigenous, settled culture an alien and easily detested phenomenon. And the merchant is a typical member of the educated class. He is homeless, a traveler, knowledgeable in foreign customs and art, with no love or respect for any particular country, fluent in several languages, glib and two-faced, skilled at adapting himself, and above all one who keeps his eye on his end goal...In this he is the exact opposite of the farmer clinging to his soil, and also of the respectable town-dweller plying his handicraft. (*Gemeinschaft und Gesellschaft*, 321; Loomis, 193).

I suggest that this sort of conflict would have been present from the very beginnings of settled communities.

30. Tönnies mentions mathematics as archetypical of *Kürwille* thinking. See Tönnies, *Gemeinschaft und Gesellschaft*, 286 (Loomis, 165). It is part of *Kürwille*'s passion for mechanical precision in calculating efficiency.

31. Hipparchus of Nicacea (second century BCE) is credited with its discovery, and he may have had access to earlier Babylonian records. See G.E.R. Lloyd, *Greek Science after Aristotle* (W.W. Norton, 1973), 69–71. The order and regularity of the motions of the heavenly bodies had been noted, admired, and wondered about even in Paleolithic times. It must have played an important role in the association of the sky gods with the maintenance of order in the world.

32. See article by Joshua J. Mark, "Sargon of Akkad," *World History Encyclopedia*, https://ancient.eu/Sargon_of_Akkad.

33. Mumford, in *The City in History*, suggests part of the process I have in mind: "The cycle of indefinite expansion from city to empire is easy to follow. As a city's population grew, it was necessary either to extend the area of immediate food production or to extend the supply lines, and draw by cooperation, barter, and trade, or by forced tribute, expropriation, and extermination, upon another community" (67). To this I add the need to protect what was already secured from foreign threats.

34. I am aware that *The Book of Isaiah* was not written by a single author but rather by at least three persons working decades apart. This is not the place, however, to delve into the intricacies of biblical scholarship. All passages from the Bible are from the Revised Standard Version.

35. David Graeber and David Wengrow, *The Dawn of Everything: A New History of Humanity* (Penguin Random House, 2021) 304–05.

36. Graeber and Wengrow, *Dawn of Everything*, 307.

37. Graeber and Wengrow, *Dawn of Everything*, 307.

3   Designers of the Inner Self

1. This was part of the eleventh-century BCE Bronze Age collapse, which affected the Fertile Crescent civilizations as well.
2. But unlike in most of today's democracies, full citizenship did not extend beyond adult, native-born, unenslaved males, so that of the total adult population of Athens,

far fewer than half—probably more like a quarter—were entitled to participate in government.
3. Plato, *Apology*, 29–30 (Jowett, vol. 1, 412–13). In all of Plato's dialogues I follow with some modifications of B. Jowett's translation as found in his *The Dialogues of Plato* (2 vols., Random House, 1937). The numbers refer to pages in the standard edition of the Greek text (given in the margins of Jowett's translation), not to pages in the translation itself.
4. Plato, *Apology*, 30 (Jowett, vol. 1, 413).
5. Plato, *Apology*, 37–38 (Jowett, vol. 1, 419–20).
6. Plato, *Crito*, 48 (Jowett, vol. 1, 432).
7. Plato, *Crito*, 49 (Jowett, vol. 1, 433).
8. These men were Socrates's chief accusers at his trial.
9. Plato, *Apology*, 30 (Jowett, vol. 1, 413).
10. Plato, *Gorgias*, 469 (Jowett, vol. 1, 527–28).
11. Plato, *Gorgias*, 471 (Jowett, vol. 1, 529).
12. Plato, *Protagoras*, 352 (Jowett vol. 1, 121). Protagoras is, of course, bound to agree, since he makes his living by offering to instil knowledge that will make the student successful in life.
13. Sue Hamilton notes this as a feature of Yogic perception that is very strange to Western readers. See her *Indian Philosophy: A Very Short Introduction* (Oxford University Press, 2001), 9–10.
14. Plato was heavily influenced by Pythagoreans with whom he had personal contact. His sharp division between the physical body and a spiritual soul owes much to the Pythagorean conception.
15. Athens's most important leader during its rise to power after the Persian wars. Born 495, died 425.
16. Another Athenian statesman and general who was important in Athens's rise after the defeat of the Persians. Born 510, died 450.
17. The general who devised the strategy that defeated a Persian invasion at the Battle of Marathon in 490. He was the father of Cimon, mentioned earlier. Born 555, died 489.
18. The Athenian general and statesman most responsible for the construction of the fleet that defeated the Persians at the Battle of Salamis in 480. He was a populist in the Athenian democracy and an object of scorn by the aristocrats, of whom Plato was one. He eventually left Athens and ended up in the employ of the Persian king. Born 524, died 459.
19. Plato, *Gorgias*, 515 (Jowett, vol. 1, 576).
20. Plato, *Gorgias*, 517 (Jowett, vol. 1, 578).
21. Plato, *Republic* IV, 443 (Jowett, vol. 1, 707).
22. Plato, *Theaetetus*, 176 (Jowett, vol.2, 179).
23. All passages cited here from this work come from the translation by Raphael Woolf, titled *On Moral Ends*, ed. Julia Annas (Cambridge University Press, 2001). Cicero composed the work in 45 BCE. This was after the civil war that saw Julius Caesar seize power and militarily defeat his chief rival, Pompey. Caesar proceeded to dismantle the republican constitution of Rome, which Cicero had defended. After Caesar was assassinated in March of 44, in the ensuing chaos a triumvirate

of Mark Antony, Lepidus, and Octavian Caesar came to power. At Mark Antony's insistence, Cicero was killed in 43. In his youth Cicero had spent time in Athens listening to philosophers of different sects. He obviously had great sympathy for the Stoics, although he never fully aligned himself with them, preferring the skepticism championed by the school of Philo of Larissa, whom Cicero heard lecture when he came to Rome.

24. Cato sided with Pompey in the civil war between him and Caesar, and when Pompey lost in 46 he committed suicide. Hence he had been dead only a little over a year when Cicero wrote *De finibus*.
25. Cicero, *On Moral Ends*, bk. 3, sect. 10, 68.
26. Cicero, *On Moral Ends*, bk. 3, sect. 14, 69.
27. Cicero, *On Moral Ends*, bk. 3, sect. 20, 71.
28. Cicero, *On Moral Ends*, bk. 3, sect. 22, 72.
29. I have used the translation of *The Bhagavadgītā* by Kees W. Bolle (University of California Press, 1979). The *Gītā* is divided into books and verses, and the numbers after each text indicate these. Bolle's book gives the Sanskrit and English on facing pages.
30. Bolle, *The Bhagavadgītā*, 55, 57.
31. From the *Tao-te ching* as translated in Wing-Tsit Chan, *A Source Book in Chinese Philosophy* (Princeton University Press, 1963), 158.
32. Wing-Tsit Chan, *A Source Book in Chinese Philosophy*, 158.
33. Wing-Tsit Chan, *A Source Book in Chinese Philosophy*, 140.
34. Cicero, *On Moral Ends*, bk. 3, sect. 62, 85.
35. Morality is here understood as a quality of character, viz. moral integrity.
36. Cicero, *On Moral Ends*, bk. 3, sect. 21, 71–72.
37. The idea that the whole of physical creation aside from humans was made to serve humans was taken over by medieval Western Christianity and continued on through the Reformation into modern times. In the thirteenth century, Saint Bonaventure wrote in his *Breviloquium*: "Hence it is indubitably true that we human beings are the end of all existing things. All material things are made to serve man, and to enkindle in him the fire of love and praise for the Maker of the universe through whose providence all is governed." Cited in James Schaefer and Tobias Winright, *Environmental Justice and Climate Change: Assessing Pope Benedict XIV's Ecological Vision for the Catholic Church in the United States* (Lexington Books, 2013), 11.
38. The Stoics accept a kind of dualism of what is active, "fire," versus what is merely passive, matter. The fire is on its own physical in the sense of having extension in space, but it is not material. The Stoics are, I believe, the first thinkers in the West to have the idea of physical but immaterial entities, now a commonplace in modern physics.
39. Epictetus, *Discourses*, trans. Robert F. Dobbin (Clarendon Press, 1998), bk. 1, chap. 1.
40. Q. Paconius Agrippinus was a senator and Stoic philosopher of the first century CE, who was exiled after being accused of conspiring against the emperor Tiberius.
41. Where his estate was.
42. Epictetus, *Discourses*, bk. 1, chap. 1.
43. Epictetus, *Discourses*, bk. 1, chap. 18.

44. Epictetus, *Discourses*, bk. 1, chap. 29.
45. Bolle, *The Bhagavadgītā*, 33.
46. Quotes are from Śāntideva, *The Bodhicaryāvatāra*.
47. Śāntideva, *The Bodhicaryāvatāra*, 34.
48. Śāntideva, *The Bodhicaryāvatāra*, 88.
49. Epictetus, "Handbook," in *Epictetus's* Handbook *and the* Tablet of Cebes: *Guides to Stoic Living* (Routledge, 2005), chap. 29, 110–11.
50. The work has been wonderfully translated, with notes, by Wing-Tsit Chan and titled *Reflections on Things at Hand: The Neo-Confucian Anthology*, ed. Chu Hsi and Lu Tsu-Ch'ien (Columbia University Press, 1967). All page references are to this translation.
51. Wing-Tsit Chan, *Reflections*, 40.
52. Wing-Tsit Chan, *Reflections*, 40.
53. Wing-Tsit Chan, *Reflections*, 46.
54. Wing-Tsit Chan, *Reflections*, 153.
55. For Marcus Aurelius's *Meditations*, I rely on the translation by George Long in *Marcus Aurelius and His Times* (Walter J. Black, 1945). This passage is from bk. 6, sect. 50, 66.
56. Marcus Aurelius, *Meditations*, bk. 4, sect. 4, 34.
57. Marcus Aurelius, *Meditations*, bk. 4, sect. 3, 33.
58. Marcus Aurelius, *Meditations*, bk. 12, sect. 12, 128.
59. Marcus Aurelius, *Meditations*, bk. 7, sect. 9, 69.
60. Marcus Aurelius, *Meditations*, bk. 5, sect. 8, 47.
61. Marcus Aurelius, *Meditations*, bk. 2, sect. 3, 20.
62. Marcus Aurelius, *Meditations*, bk. 6, sect. 42, 64.
63. Marcus Aurelius, *Meditations*, bk. 11, sect. 1, 114.
64. Marcus Aurelius, *Meditations*, bk. 9, sect. 35, 99.
65. Marcus Aurelius, *Meditations*, bk. 8, sect. 6, 80.
66. The youngest of the three Fates in Greek mythology.
67. Marcus Aurelius, *Meditations*, bk. 4, sect. 34, 40.
68. Marcus Aurelius, *Meditations*, bk. 10, sect. 5, 103.
69. The quote is from a short selection from *Plutarch's Lives*, translated by Bernadotte Perrin (William Heinemann, 1917), printed in *Lapham's Quarterly*, vol. 14, no. 1, 46–48.
70. Lloyd, *Greek Science after Aristotle*, 112.
71. Something similar may have stymied China's economic expansion. The historians John King Fairbank and Merle Goldman (*China: A New History*, 2nd ed. [Harvard University Press, 2006]) suggest that "Neo-Confucian throttling" may have been part of the cause of the withdrawal of Ming China in the fifteenth century from intercourse with the wider world as well as a disinterest in technological and economic progress. They then go on to make the following comment, with which I fully concur:

> This disparaging judgment comes out of the context of the late twentieth century, when technology and growth have created innumerable disorders in all aspects of life all over the world without disclosing as yet the principles of order that may postpone the destruction of human

> civilization. In time the self-contained growth of Ming China with its comparative peace and well-being may be admired by historians, who may see a sort of success where today we see failure. (139)

The early twenty-first century has amply reinforced this reappraisal, especially now that China itself has adopted the expansionist aspirations of the West and begun contributing mightily to augmenting the probability of eco-catastrophe.

China's own lead over the rest of the world in technology and economic development—a lead that it held until the West's Industrial Revolution in the early nineteenth century—may in ironic fashion have also contributed to the pause in its development that many historians think set in in the early modern period. Mark Elvin, in *The Retreat of the Elephants: An Environmental History of China* (Yale University Press, 2004), an environmental history of China from ancient times to the present day, attributes this pause to China's unparalleled expansion in the ancient and medieval periods of projects involving its sophisticated expertise in hydraulic engineering. These works included massive canals, dams, and irrigation systems, on which the Chinese economy became very dependent, but which came to require constant, expensive maintenance. Elvin writes:

> Hydraulic enterprise moved from a mix of impressive early successes and some massive failures, along a curve of steadily improving technology, toward an eventual form of environmentally constrained premodern technological lock-in. That is, once a large system had been established, it became the foundation of a local optimum that could not be easily abandoned because of the threat to livelihood and even lives. (xvii)

In other words, its earlier commitment to hydraulic projects could not be abandoned even though they now consumed the resources that would have been needed for further economic advances. (Thanks to one of the peer reviewers of an earlier draft of my book for drawing my attention to Elvin's work.)

4 From Zarathustra to Revolutionary Millennialism

1. Cohn, *Cosmos*, 77ff.
2. Cohn, *Cosmos*, 82.
3. Cohn, *Cosmos*, 88.
4. Cohn, *Cosmos*, 96–98.
5. Cohn, *Cosmos*, 98–99.
6. A "Yasna" is a piece of poetry to be recited or sung in an act of worship.
7. As translated by Boyce in *Textual Sources for the Study of Zoroastrianism* (University of Chicago Press, 1990), 35.
8. As translated by Jacques Duchesne-Guillemin and retranslated into English by Mrs. M. Henning in *The Hymns of Zarathushtra: Being a Translation of the Gathas together with Introduction and Commentary* (C.E. Tuttle, 1992), 103.
9. One of the Holy Immortals, that is, the divine assistants to Ahura Mazda.
10. The Lie.
11. A king whom Zarathustra converted to the faith.

12. Two early followers of Zarathustra.
13. A Saoshyant was a kind of saviour. These were thought to have appeared several times through history.
14. In Boyce, *Textual Sources*, 57.
15. Duchesne-Guillemin, *The Hymns of Zarathustra*, 101.
16. Duchesne-Guillemin, *The Hymns of Zarathustra*, 145.
17. Boyce, *Textual Sources*, 82–83.
18. Boyce, *Textual Sources*, 83.
19. Boyce, *Textual Sources*, 85.
20. Boyce, *Textual Sources*, 88.
21. Boyce, *Textual Sources*, 88.
22. Enrico G. Raffaelli, *The Sīh-rōzag in Zoroastrianism: A Textual and Historico-Religious Analysis* (Routledge, 2014), 106.
23. In Boyce, *Textual Sources*, 86.
24. All quotes from this text are from Boyce, *Textual Sources*, 46–53.
25. Boyce, *Textual Sources*, 48.
26. In Duchesne-Guillemin, *The Hymns of Zarathustra*, 71.
27. Boyce, *Textual Sources*, 52.
28. Boyce, *Textual Sources*, 52.
29. See Cohn, *Cosmos*, 94.
30. The reference is likely to the Sons of God mentioned in *Genesis* 6:2–4, who before the Flood had sex with the fair daughters of men, the fruits of which unions were mighty men of old. The term "watcher" emerges more significantly in *The Book of Enoch*, to be discussed shortly.
31. All texts of *Enoch* come from *The Ethiopic Book of Enoch*, edited, translated, and commented on by Michael A. Knibb (Clarendon Press, 1978). This text is found on 88.
32. Knibb, *The Ethiopic Book of Enoch* 10.12 (89).
33. Knibb, *The Ethiopic Book of Enoch* 11.1–2 (91–92).
34. Knibb, *The Ethiopic Book of Enoch* 14.17–20 (99).
35. Knibb, *The Ethiopic Book of Enoch* 15.4–7 (100–01).
36. Knibb, *The Ethiopic Book of Enoch* 25.3–6 (113–14).
37. Knibb, *The Ethiopic Book of Enoch* 68.9–11 (161).
38. Andrei A. Orlov, *Heavenly Priesthood in the Apocalypse of Abraham* (Cambridge University Press, 2013), 74.
39. All texts from *The Apocrypha of the Old Testament*, edited by Bruce M. Metzger (Oxford University Press, 1957). This excerpt found on page 31.
40. Metzger, *The Apocrypha*, 35.
41. Metzger, *The Apocrypha*, 37–38.
42. Metzger, *The Apocrypha*, 37–38.
43. Metzger, *The Apocrypha*, 45.
44. Metzger, *The Apocrypha*, 51.
45. *Matthew* 5:38–39.
46. Page 167 in the translation by Dennis D. Buchholz in his *Your Eyes Will Be Opened: A Study of the Greek (Ethiopic) Apocalypse of Peter* (Scholars Press, 1988). All quotes from this apocalypse are from that work.

47. Buchholz, *Your Eyes Will Be Opened*, 183.
48. Buchholz, *Your Eyes Will Be Opened*, 189.
49. Buchholz, *Your Eyes Will Be Opened*, 199.
50. Buchholz, *Your Eyes Will Be Opened*, 199.
51. Buchholz, *Your Eyes Will Be Opened*, 228. Plato recounts a version in his *Phaedo*, 113a.
52. Buchholz, *Your Eyes Will Be Opened*, 228.
53. All references to this work are to J.L. Lightfoot, *The Sibylline Oracles* (Oxford University Press, 2007).
54. Lightfoot, *The Sibylline Oracles*, 317.
55. Lightfoot, *The Sibylline Oracles*, 318.
56. Lightfoot, *The Sibylline Oracles*, 318–19.
57. Lightfoot, *The Sibylline Oracles*, 319.
58. Lightfoot, *The Sibylline Oracles*, 319.
59. James H. Cone, *God of the Oppressed*, 50.
60. Cone, *God of the Oppressed* (Orbis Books, 1997), 72.
61. Cone, *God of the Oppressed*, 72.
62. Cone, *God of the Oppressed*, 119.
63. Cone, *God of the Oppressed*, 121.

5 Apocalyptic Thought in the Medieval West

1. Saint Augustine, *The City of God*, in *Basic Writings of Saint Augustine*, trans. M. Dods, ed. Whitney J. Oates (Random House, 1948), xx.9, 2:523.
2. Augustine, *The City of God*, xx.8, 521.
3. Augustine, *The City of God*, xx.9, 524.
4. Augustine, *The City of God*, xx.7, 519.
5. The term "Antichrist" does not figure much in the canonical New Testament. It is used only in John's first and second letters. But later the term refers to some powerful human who will wage war on Christendom before Christ's Second Coming. The very indefiniteness of the reference allowed for all sorts of identifications both with persons mentioned in the apocalyptic works and with people currently existing.
6. Augustine, *The City of God*, xx.8, 521.
7. Augustine, *The City of God*, xx.16, 533.
8. Thanks to Sean Hannan for drawing this passage to my attention and producing a translation, which I have modified slightly.
9. Much of what I say in the above paragraph draws on the work of Robert E. Lerner in his "The Medieval Return to the Thousand-Year Sabbath," found as chapter 4 in *The Apocalypse in the Middle Ages*, edited by Richard K. Emerson and Bernard McGinn (Cornell University Press, 1992).
10. I draw here on the discussion by Paul J. Alexander in his "The Diffusion of Byzantine Apocalypses in the Medieval West and the Beginnings of Joachimism," found in *Prophecy and Millenarianism : Essays in Honour of Marjorie Reeves*, ed. Ann Williams (Longman Group, 1980).
11. Alexander, "The Diffusion of Byzantine Apocalypses," 57.

12. Alexander, "The Diffusion of Byzantine Apocalypses," 57.
13. Also discussed by Alexander in "The Diffusion of Byzantine Apocalypses," 62–65.
14. See Norman Cohn, *The Pursuit of the Millennium: Revolutionary Millenarians and Mystical Anarchists of the Middle Ages* (Pimlico, 2004), 71.
15. Marjorie Reeves, *Joachim of Fiore and the Prophetic Future* (SPCK, 1976), 57.
16. Quoted in Bernard McGinn, *Visions of the End: Apocalyptic Traditions in the Middle Ages* (Columbia University Press, 1979), 136–37.
17. On this aspect of Joachim's thought, see F. Seibt, "*Liber Figurarum XII* and the Classical Ideal of Utopia," in Williams, *Prophecy and Millenarianism*, 257–66.
18. Gordon Leff, "The Franciscan Concept of Man," in Williams, *Prophecy and Millenarianism*, 217–37.
19. Leff, "The Franciscan Concept of Man," 222.
20. Leff, "The Franciscan Concept of Man," 223.
21. Leff, "The Franciscan Concept of Man," 227.
22. Leff, "The Franciscan Concept of Man," 228.
23. McGinn, *Visions of the End*, 204.
24. McGinn, *Visions of the End*, 205.
25. McGinn, *Visions of the End*, 228.
26. McGinn, *Visions of the End*, 231.
27. McGinn, *Visions of the End*, 237.
28. McGinn, *Visions of the End*, 237.
29. It should be noted too that Wyclif was sympathetic to the "Peasants' Revolt" in Britain in 1381, during which millenarian beliefs were tied to the demands for social reforms. All this would have been known to Hus and his followers.
30. See Thomas A. Fudge, *Jerome of Prague and the Foundations of the Hussite Movement* (Oxford University Press, 2016), especially chapter 2.
31. Howard Kaminsky, *A History of the Hussite Revolution* (University of California Press, 1967). See especially chapter 7.
32. Kaminsky, *A History of the Hussite Revolution*, 311.
33. Kaminsky, *A History of the Hussite Revolution*, 312.
34. Kaminsky, *A History of the Hussite Revolution*, 331.
35. Kaminsky, *A History of the Hussite Revolution*, 330.
36. Kaminsky, *A History of the Hussite Revolution*, 350.
37. Norman Cohn discussed these movements in *The Pursuit of the Millennium*, 159–77. Their most distinguishing belief was in the perfectibility of humans so that they became equal to the Divine.
38. Kaminsky, *A History of the Hussite Revolution*, 355, gives a helpful summary of the doctrines that the Council of Vienne in 1311 found to be taught by this group.
39. Cohn, *The Pursuit of the Millennium*, 236.
40. On this and other aspects of Müntzer's theology, see Frank E. Manuel and Fritzie P. Manuel, *Utopian Thought in the Western World* (Harvard University Press, 1979), 181–202, especially 194.
41. Cohn discusses the events at Münster in detail in *The Pursuit of the Millennium*, 257–80.

6 Reformation and Utopia

1. Max Weber, *The Protestant Ethic and the "Spirit" of Capitalism*, trans. and ed. with introduction Peter Baehr and Gordon Wells (Penguin, 2002), 82.
2. Charles Taylor, *A Secular Age*, (Belknap Press of Harvard University Press, 2007), especially 82.
3. Taylor, *A Secular Age*, 45ff.
4. An English translation by Ralph Robinson first appeared in 1551. All citations are from Mildred Campbell's modernized version of this, published in 1947.
5. "Commonwealth" is the term used by Ralph Robinson in his translation of 1551 to render *res publicae*. The Latin phrase is derived from Cicero and was usually translated as "republic." The phrase "common weal" was familiar in medieval English and meant the welfare of the whole society, but Robinson was among the first to use "commonwealth" to mean a state. Its appropriateness for referring to More's Utopia will be apparent as we proceed.
6. Thomas More, *The Utopia of Sir Thomas More*, trans. Ralph Robinson, with notes and introduction by Mildred Campbell (D. Van Nostrand, 1947), 29.
7. More, *The Utopia*, 85-86.
8. More, *The Utopia*, 28-29.
9. More, *The Utopia*, 171.
10. More, *The Utopia*, 107.
11. More, *The Utopia*, 107.
12. More, *The Utopia*, 109-10.
13. More, *The Utopia*, 111.
14. More, *The Utopia*, 110.
15. More, *The Utopia*, 155.
16. More, *The Utopia*, 111-12.
17. See statement by Master Chang Tsai quoted above, chapter 3, 67.
18. Whether he did later as chancellor under Henry can be doubted. His persecutions of Protestants at that time were unrelenting and cruel.
19. More, *The Utopia*, 123.
20. More, *The Utopia*, 169.
21. More, *The Utopia*, 174.
22. More, *The Utopia*, 59-60.
23. More, *The Utopia*, 61.
24. More, *The Utopia*, 61-62.
25. In the early sixteenth century, Flanders, with its very wealthy trading center of Antwerp, came under the rule of the Spanish king, Charles V (also Holy Roman Emperor). When Protestantism spread there, Charles and, later, his son Philip II, tried to suppress it. In the latter half of the century there were successive insurgencies and brutal repressions by the Spanish military. Many Flemish people became refugees, some fleeing to England and Scotland.
26. Justus Lipsius, *On Constancy (De Constantia)*, trans. Sir John Stradling, ed. with introduction John Sellars (Phoenix Press, 2006), 50.
27. Justus Lipsius, *On Constancy*, 50.

28. Justus Lipsius, *A Guide to Stoic Philosophy* [Selections]," trans. Robert V. Young, in *Cambridge Translations of Renaissance Philosophical Texts*, ed. Jill Kraye, vol. 1, *Moral Philosophy* (Cambridge University Press, 1997), 200-09.
29. Justus Lipsius, *On Constancy*, 46.
30. Justus Lipsius, *On Constancy*, 53.
31. Justus Lipsius, *On Constancy*, 51.
32. Johannes Valentin Andreae, *Christianopolis* trans. Felix Emil Held (Oxford University Press, 1916), 238.
33. Andreae, *Christianopolis*, 148.
34. Andreae's connection with Campanella is discussed by Manuel and Manuel, *Utopian Thought*, 290.
35. Andreae, *Christianopolis*, 209.
36. Andreae, *Christianopolis*, 216.
37. Andreae, *Christianopolis*, 221-22.
38. Andreae, *Christianopolis*, 223.
39. Andreae, *Christianopolis*, 223.
40. Andreae, *Christianopolis*, 231.
41. Cf. the reference to Saint Bonaventure in chapter 3 of the work before you, 58n37.
42. Andreae, *Christianopolis*, 233.
43. Andreae, *Christianopolis*, 196-97.
44. Andreae, *Christianopolis*, 196-97.
45. A similar observation is made by Manuel and Manuel, *Utopian Thought*, 304-05.
46. Andreae, *Christianopolis*, 198.
47. Andreae, *Christianopolis*, 198.
48. We should not forget that among the Puritans of the time were those who carried on revolutionary forms of millennialism akin to those mentioned in the previous chapter. Notable among these were the "Ranters" and the "Fifth Monarchy Men." These are discussed by David Katz and Richard Popkin in *Messianic Revolution: Radical Religious Politics to the End of the Second Millennium* (Allen Lane, 1999). See also John Gray, *Black Mass: Apocalyptic Religion and the Death of Utopia* (Farrar, Straus and Giroux, 2007), 23.
49. Samuel Gott, *Nova Solyma, the Ideal City; or Jerusalem Regained* (*Novae Solymae Libri Sex*, Joannis Legatus, London, 1648). Though attributed to John Milton, the book itself mentions no author. Rev. Begley, the translator, was convinced that John Milton wrote it, but some years after his translation appeared a list was found of books printed for Thomas Underhill, and in it *Nova Solyma* was attributed to Samuel Gott. This information comes from the introduction to the translation of Andreae's *Christianopolis* (78) by Felix Held, cited earlier.
50. Gott, *Nova Solyma*, vol. 1, 237-38.
51. Gott, *Nova Solyma*, vol. 1, 128-29.
52. Gott, *Nova Solyma*, vol. 1, 235-36.
53. Gott, *Nova Solyma*, vol. 1, 240-41.
54. Gott, *Nova Solyma*, vol. 1, 242.
55. Gott, *Nova Solyma*, vol. 1, 254.
56. Gott, *Nova Solyma*, vol. 1, 168.

57. Gott, *Nova Solyma*, vol. 1, 171-2.
58. Gott, *Nova Solyma*, vol. 2, 132.
59. Gott, *Nova Solyma*, vol. 2, 36.
60. Gott, *Nova Solyma*, vol. 2, 120-21.
61. Gott, *Nova Solyma*, vol. 2, 125.
62. Gott, *Nova Solyma*, vol. 2, 125.
63. Taylor, *A Secular Age*, 82.
64. Francis Bacon, *The Major Works of Francis Bacon*, ed. with introduction and notes Brian Vickers (InteLex Corp, c. 2009), bk. 1, 172.
65. "The Advancement of Learning," in Bacon, *The Major Works of Francis Bacon*, bk. 1, 147-48.
66. Quoted in Manuel and Manuel, *Utopian Thought*, 260, and drawn from Benjamin Farrington, *The Philosophy of Francis Bacon: An Essay on Its Development from 1603, with New Translations of Fundamental Texts* (Liverpool University Press, 1964), 7.
67. Bacon, *The Major Works*, 471.
68. Bacon, *The Major Works*, 471.
69. Bacon, *The Major Works*, 479.
70. Bacon, *The Major Works*, 481.
71. Bacon, *The Major Works*, 482.
72. Bacon, *The Major Works*, 483-84.
73. Bacon, *The Major Works*, 486.
74. Bacon, *The Major Works*, 486.
75. Bacon, *The Major Works*, 487.
76. Bacon, *Valerius Terminus*, in *The Works of Francis Bacon*, ed. James Spedding, Robert Leslie Ellis, and Douglas Denon Heath (Longmans, 1876) vol. 3, 219.
77. Bacon, *Valerius Terminus*, 219.
78. Bacon, *Valerius Terminus*, 218.
79. Bacon, *Valerius Terminus*, 221.
80. David F. Noble gives a good account of Eriugena's advocacy of the "mechanical arts" in *The Religion of Technology : The Divinity of Man and the Spirit of Invention* (Alfred A. Knopf, 1997), 15-17.
81. Bacon, *Valerius Terminus*, 222.
82. *Novum Organum*, in Bacon, *Works*, ed. Spedding, Ellis, and Heath, vol. 1, xxxviii. Quoted in Anthony J. Funari, *Francis Bacon and the Seventeenth-Century Intellectual Discourse* (Palgrave Macmillan, 2011), 19-20.
83. Bacon, *Valerius Terminus*, 221. The passage in Daniel was quoted in chapter 4 of the work before you, 103-04.
84. Bacon, *Valerius Terminus*, 221.
85. Quoted in Charles Webster, *The Great Instauration: Science, Medicine, and Reform 1626-1660* (Holmes and Meier, 1975), 1.
86. The following account of millennial-inspired thought among Puritan intellectuals depends heavily on the work of Charles Webster in *Samuel Hartlib and the Advancement of Learning* (Cambridge University Press, 1976), and Noble in *The Religion of Technology*.
87. See Webster, *Samuel Hartlib*, 30.

88. See Webster, *Samuel Hartlib*, 83–84.
89. See Webster, *Samuel Hartlib*, 36–37.
90. Quoted in Webster, *The Great Instauration*, 50.
91. What immediately follows is a short summary of Webster's account in *The Great Instauration*, 68–77.
92. Webster, *The Great Instauration*, 69.
93. Webster, *The Great Instauration*, 74.
94. How much Bacon inspired the formation of the Royal Society can be gauged from this poetic passage in Thomas Sprat's *History of the Royal Society* (1667), qtd in Roddam Narasimha: "Culture Views Nature: Bacon and Sāṁkhya Compared," in Roddam Narasimha and Sangeetha Menon, eds., *Nature and Culture*, vol. 15, pt. 1, *of History of Science, Philosophy, and Culture in Indian Civilization*, ed. D.P. Chattopadhyaya (Centre for Studies in Civilization, 2011), 324.

> Bacon, like Moses, led us forth at last,
> The barren Wilderness he past,
> Did on the very border stand
> Of the blest promised land,
> And from the Mountain top of his Exalted Wit,
> Saw it himself, and shewed us it.

95. Manuel and Manuel, *Utopian Thought*, 110.

7 Secularizing the Millennium

1. Bernard Mandeville, *The Fable of the Bees: Or Present Vices, Publick Benefits*, ed. with introduction Irwin Primer (Capricorn Books, 1962), 27, ll. 1–6.
2. Mandeville, *The Fable of the Bees*, 28, ll. 33–40.
3. Mandeville, *The Fable of the Bees*, 28, ll. 57–58.
4. Mandeville, *The Fable of the Bees*, 29, ll. 85–90.
5. Mandeville, *The Fable of the Bees*, 31, ll. 154–68.
6. Mandeville, *The Fable of the Bees*, 31–32, ll. 177–87.
7. Mandeville, *The Fable of the Bees*, 32, ll. 197–203.
8. Mandeville, *The Fable of the Bees*, 38, ll. 411–14, 425–33.
9. Mandeville, *The Fable of the Bees*, 22.
10. Mandeville, *The Fable of the Bees*, 24.
11. Mandeville, *The Fable of the Bees*, 45.
12. Mandeville, *The Fable of the Bees*, 46.
13. Mandeville, *The Fable of the Bees*, 90–91.
14. Mandeville, *The Fable of the Bees*, 143.
15. Jean-Jacques Rousseau, *Basic Political Writings*, trans. and ed. Donald A. Cress (Hackett, 1987), 3.
16. Rousseau, *Basic Political Writings*, 4.
17. Rousseau, *Basic Political Writings*, 10.
18. Rousseau, *Basic Political Writings*, 13.
19. Rousseau, *Basic Political Writings*, 15.

20. Rousseau, *Basic Political Writings*, 17.
21. Rousseau, *Basic Political Writings*, 21.
22. Rousseau, *Basic Political Writings*, 33. The inscription said: "Know thyself."
23. Rousseau, *Basic Political Writings*, 33.
24. Rousseau, *Basic Political Writings*, 43.
25. Rousseau, *Basic Political Writings*, 52.
26. Rousseau, *Basic Political Writings*, 69.
27. Rousseau, *Basic Political Writings*, 70.
28. Adam Smith, *The Theory of Moral Sentiments* (Prometheus Books, 2000), 234.
29. Smith, *The Theory of Moral Sentiments*, 161, 164.
30. Smith, *The Theory of Moral Sentiments*, 166–67.
31. Smith, *The Theory of Moral Sentiments*, 235.
32. Smith, *The Theory of Moral Sentiments*, 109–10n.
33. Smith, *The Theory of Moral Sentiments*, 193–94.
34. On Smith's view the natural level of the prices of products for sale in the market would be proportional to the amount of labour required for their production and thus reflect their real value, since, Smith thinks, the real exchange value of a marketable product is proportional to just that amount of labour.
35. Further discussion of these matters will come in chapter 9.
36. I rely here on Sophie de Grouchy, *Letters on Sympathy: A Critical Edition*, trans. and ed. Karin Brown and James E. McClellan III (American Philosophical Society, 2008). See xiii.
37. De Grouchy, *Letters on Sympathy*, 113.
38. De Grouchy, *Letters on Sympathy*, 115–16.
39. De Grouchy, *Letters on Sympathy*, 148.
40. De Grouchy, *Letters on Sympathy*, 132.
41. De Grouchy, *Letters on Sympathy*, 157–58.
42. De Grouchy, *Letters on Sympathy*, 171.
43. De Grouchy, *Letters on Sympathy*, 112.
44. Some theorists apply the term "utilitarianism" only to what I think of as its hedonist variant, but I prefer to see any ethical theory as utilitarian that takes the supreme end of human action to be benefit to humans generally, where what constitutes a benefit is left to be determined.
45. As found in Anne Robert-Jacques Turgot, *Turgot on Progress, Sociology and Economics*, trans. and ed. with introduction by Ronald L. Meek (Cambridge University Press, 1973), 41.
46. Turgot, *Turgot on Progress*, 69.
47. Turgot, *Turgot on Progress*, 47.
48. Turgot, *Turgot on Progress*, 72. Note the repetition of the words found in the text above from the *Philosophical Review*.
49. Turgot, *Turgot on Progress*, 111.
50. Turgot, *Turgot on Progress*, 112.
51. Turgot, *Turgot on Progress*, 83.
52. Turgot, *Turgot on Progress*, 83
53. Manuel and Manuel, *Utopian Thought*, 467–68.

54. From "On Universal History" in Turgot, *Turgot on Progress*, 94.
55. Turgot, *Turgot on Progress*, 94–95.
56. Turgot, *Turgot on Progress*, 46.
57. Turgot, *Turgot on Progress*, 64
58. Turgot, *Turgot on Progress*, 70
59. Turgot, *Turgot on Progress*, 70.
60. Turgot, *Turgot on Progress*, 64.
61. Turgot, *Turgot on Progress*, 71.
62. Turgot, *Turgot on Progress*, 70.
63. Turgot, *Turgot on Progress*, 57.
64. Manuel and Manuel, in *Utopian Thought*, write: "The *Esquisse* [de Condorcet's last work] was the form in which the eighteenth-century idea of progress was generally assimilated by Western thought. Condorcet wrote his manifesto with full awareness of its world revolutionary significance" (491).
65. Nicolas de Condorcet, *Sketch for a Historical Picture of the Progress of the Human Mind*, trans. June Barraclough with introduction Stuart Hampshire (Weidenfeld and Nicolson, 1955), 173.
66. Turgot, *Turgot on Progress*, 41.
67. This is evident in Turgot's much later work, *Reflections on the Formation and the Distribution of Wealth*, which is included in Turgot, *Turgot on Progress*, 119–82.
68. De Condorcet, *Sketch*, 3–4.
69. De Condorcet, *Sketch*, 4.
70. De Condorcet, *Sketch*, 184.
71. De Condorcet, *Sketch*, 128.
72. De Condorcet, *Sketch*, 128–29.
73. De Condorcet, *Sketch*, 130–31.
74. De Condorcet, *Sketch*, 130–31. One suspects that the law is just this: if each individual gains some benefit, then the group formed by their association will be benefited. But in that case, it is an instance of the fallacy of composition.
75. De Condorcet, *Sketch*, 120.
76. De Condorcet, *Sketch*, 162–63.
77. Manuel and Manuel, *Utopian Thought*, 496–97.
78. De Condorcet, *Sketch*, 24.
79. De Condorcet, *Sketch*, 64.
80. De Condorcet, *Sketch*, 105.
81. De Condorcet, *Sketch*, 177.

8 The Cult of Science

1. From *Lettres à un Amèricain*, translated by me from *Oeuvres de Claude-Henri de Saint-Simon* (hereafter *Oeuvres*), vol. 1, pt. 2, 148. An English translation of portions of this and other works can be found in *Henri Saint-Simon (1760–1825): Selected Writings on Science, Industry, and Social Organisation*, translated and edited by Keith Taylor (hereafter Taylor) (Croom Helm, 1975), 162. All translations of passages

from Saint-Simon's works are by me unless otherwise noted, but I also indicate the corresponding texts in Taylor.
2. From *De la réorganisation de la société européenne*, in Saint-Simon, *Oeuvres*, vol. 1, pt .1, 247–48 (Taylor, 136).
3. From Saint-Simon, *Lettres d'un habitant de Genève*, first letter, 31 (Taylor, 73).
4. Saint-Simon, *Lettres d'un habitant d'un Genève*, 34 (Taylor, 74).
5. Saint-Simon, *Lettres d'un habitant d'un Genève*, 67–68 (Taylor, 81–82).
6. Quoted material from the second letter as translated by Taylor, 81–82.
7. From *Introduction aux travaux scientifiques du XIXe siècle*, 2 vols. 1807–08, in *Oeuvres*, vol. 6, 27 (Taylor, 88).
8. From the same work, in *Oeuvres*, vol. 6, 101 (Taylor, 94).
9. From *Mémoire sur la science de l'homme* (1813), in *Oeuvres*, vol. 5, 144–45 (Taylor, 121).
10. From the same work, in *Oeuvres*, vol. 5, 173 (Taylor, 123).
11. From "Travail sur la gravitation universelle," as translated by Taylor, 125.
12. Taylor (24) suggests that this shift may have been due to the influence of Jean Baptiste Say.
13. *Oeuvres*, vol. 1, pt. 2, 165–66 (Taylor, 164–65).
14. *Oeuvres*, vol. 1, pt. 2, 129–30 (Taylor, 158).
15. *Oeuvres*, vol. 1, pt. 2, 130–32 (Taylor, 158–59).
16. *Oeuvres*, vol. 3, pt. 1, 48 (Taylor, 212–13).
17. *Oeuvres*, vol. 5, pt. 1, 203–04 (Taylor, 279–80).
18. *Oeuvres*, vol. 2, pt. 2, 193–94. (Taylor, 208).
19. *Oeuvres*, vol. 2, pt. 2, 188–89. (Taylor 209).
20. From "Des intérèts politiques de l'industrie," as translated by Taylor, 181.
21. From *Du système industriel*, pt. 1, in *Oeuvres*, vol. 3, pt. 1, 17n (Taylor, 230).
22. Say was the most influential of the political economists to come out of the French *Idéologue* movement. He rejected the labour theory of value ascribed to by Smith and was aware of the importance of technological innovation for improving production. See Richard G. Olson, *Science and Scientism in Nineteenth-Century Europe* (University of Illinois Press, 2008), 21–34.
23. *Oeuvres*, vol .1, pt. 2, 185 (Taylor, 166).
24. *Oeuvres*, vol .1, pt. 2, 186n (Taylor, 167).
25. *Oeuvres*, vol .1, pt. 2, 186 (Taylor, 166–67).
26. *Oeuvres*, vol .1, pt. 2, 186–87 (Taylor, 166–67).
27. *Oeuvres*, vol .1, pt. 2, 188 (Taylor, 167–68).
28. *Oeuvres*, vol .1, pt. 2, 187 (Taylor, 167).
29. *Oeuvres*, vol. 3, pt. 3, 108–09 (Taylor, 289).
30. The other long work is his *Système de Politique Positive* (1851–1854).
31. All page references to the texts from Comte's works are to the selections from those in English translations compiled by Gertrud Lenzer in her *Auguste Comte and Positivism: The Essential Writings* (Transaction, 1998). This quote appears on page 83.
32. Lenzer, *Auguste Comte*, 72.
33. Lenzer, *Auguste Comte*, 72.
34. Lenzer, *Auguste Comte*, 72.
35. Lenzer, *Auguste Comte*, 83.

36. Lenzer, *Auguste Comte*, 37.
37. Lenzer, *Auguste Comte*, 38.
38. Lenzer, *Auguste Comte*, 34.
39. Lenzer, *Auguste Comte*, 71.
40. Lenzer, *Auguste Comte*, 31.
41. Lenzer, *Auguste Comte*, 403–04.
42. Lenzer, *Auguste Comte*, 233.
43. Lenzer, *Auguste Comte*, 233.
44. Lenzer, *Auguste Comte*, 234.
45. Lenzer, *Auguste Comte*, 342.
46. Lenzer, *Auguste Comte*, 279.
47. Lenzer, *Auguste Comte*, 284.
48. Lenzer, *Auguste Comte*, 301.
49. Lenzer, *Auguste Comte*, 400.
50. Lenzer, *Auguste Comte*, 400–01.
51. Lenzer, *Auguste Comte*, 402.
52. Lenzer, *Auguste Comte*, 325.
53. Lenzer, *Auguste Comte*, 325.
54. Lenzer, *Auguste Comte*, 325–26.
55. Lenzer, *Auguste Comte*, 395–96.
56. Lenzer, *Auguste Comte*, 410.
57. The kinship between Comte and Joachim has been noted by Noble in *The Religion of Technology*, 83.
58. Gaspard Monge (1746–1818) was a brilliant scientist and mathematician who invented descriptive geometry, a technique important in the development of engineering. He supported the Revolution and was active in its military defence. Later he was honoured by Napoleon, but fell into disfavour after Bonaparte's fall.
59. Lenzer, *Auguste Comte*, 90.
60. Noble, *The Religion of Technology*, 81. What follows about Freemasonry is very much inspired and informed by Noble's work.
61. Noble, *The Religion of Technology*, 78ff.
62. The connection of Masonry with Francis Bacon was suggested by the historian of Masonry, William James Hougham, writing in the introduction to H.L. Stillson and William James Houghan, *History of the Ancient and Honorable Fraternity of Free and Accepted Masons, and Concordant Orders*, published in 1898 by the Fraternity Publishing Company. Hougham writes: "I have ventured so far as to declare that the *New Atlantis* seems to be, and probably is, the key to the modern rituals of Freemasonry" (xxxvi).
63. Margaret Jacob, *Living the Enlightenment: Freemasonry and Politics in Eighteenth Century Europe* (Oxford University Press, 1995), 10.
64. Jacob, *Living the Enlightenment*, 47.
65. Jacob, *Living the Enlightenment*, 57.
66. Stillson and Houghan, *History*, 167–73, contains a facsimile of the portion of the manuscript with the poem and a translation.
67. Stillson and Houghan, *History*, 168, ll. 19–25.

68. Stillson and Houghan, *History*, 169, ll. 35–42.
69. Stillson and Houghan, *History*, 170, ll. 53–56.
70. Stillson and Houghan, *History*, 178–79.
71. Born into a Presbyterian family in Scotland, he moved to Vermont in the United States, where he was active in politics. Later he took up the principalship of a school in Quebec and led a fight against the dominance of Catholic education in that province.
72. Stillson and Houghan, *History*, 693.
73. That is, a stone to be hewn and squared.
74. Stillson and Houghan, *History*, 693
75. Stillson and Houghan, *History*, 693–94.
76. Stillson and Houghan, *History*, 695.
77. That is, the items Graham thinks comprise the "mission" of Freemasonry. Stillson and Houghan, *History*, 696.
78. John H. Weiss, *The Making of Technological Man: The Social Origins of French Engineering Education* (MIT Press, 1982).
79. Weiss, *The Making of Technological Man*, 226–27.
80. Olivier studied at the École Polytechnique and went on to be a critic of educational practices in France. He eventually became a professor of geometry and mechanics at the École Centrale.
81. Theodore Olivier, *Mémoires de géométrie descriptive, théorique, et appliquée* (Paris, 1851), iv. Quoted in Weiss, *The Making of Technological Man*, 158.
82. Weiss, *The Making of Technological Man*, 162–63.
83. Weiss, *The Making of Technological Man*, 174.
84. De Comerousse wrote with E. Roché a very popular textbook on mathematics. At the École he taught courses on cinema and mechanics.
85. Weiss, *The Making of Technological Man*, 225–26.
86. Weiss, *The Making of Technological Man*, 234.
87. Weiss, *The Making of Technological Man*, 237.
88. Weiss, *The Making of Technological Man*, 237.
89. Olson, in *Science and Scientism in Nineteenth-Century Europe*, makes this assessment: "It was the mentality of the engineering student and medical student, largely ignorant of traditional learning, but hungering for more than mere technical facility and open to rational and radical social experimentation, that allowed the scientistic and idiosyncratic visions of men like Henri Saint-Simon and Auguste Comte to generate significant and enthusiastic followings" (21).
90. The story of the rise of the engineers in late nineteenth- and early twentieth-century America to prominence in the corporate world as well as in higher education, and their promotion of "scientific management" of the workforce, has been told by David F. Noble in *America by Design: Science, Technology, and the Rise of Corporate Capitalism* (Oxford University Press, 1979); see especially chapter 3. That the dominance of engineering in American culture has continued into the twenty-first century is obvious to all, although now their chief field of innovation is digital telecommunications and all forms of AI.

9 The Vulgarization of the Millennium

1. First published in London in 1776, but four more editions followed in 1778, 1784, 1786, and 1789. All references given here are to the edition of the first three (of five) books by Penguin Books, with an introduction by Andrew Skinner, titled simply *The Wealth of Nations* (Penguin Books, 1970).
2. Smith, *Wealth of Nations,* bk. 1, chap. 8, 172: "It is not the actual greatness of national wealth, but its continual increase, which occasions a rise in the wages of labour."
3. Smith, *Wealth of Nations,* bk. 1, 176. His reference, of course, is to the East India Company and the dreadful famine that afflicted Bengal in Smith's lifetime.
4. Smith, *Wealth of Nations,* bk. 1, 181.
5. "When this real wealth of the society becomes stationary, his wages are soon reduced to what is barely enough to enable him to bring up a family, or to continue the race of labourers." Smith, *Wealth of Nations,* bk. 1, 357.
6. Smith, *Wealth of Nations,* bk. 1, 453–54.
7. Smith, *Wealth of Nations,* bk. 1, 358.
8. Smith, *Wealth of Nations,* bk. 1, 358.
9. Smith, *Wealth of Nations,* bk. 1, 117.
10. Smith, *Wealth of Nations,* bk. 1, 115.
11. Smith, *Wealth of Nations,* bk. 1, 112.
12. Smith, *Wealth of Nations,* bk. 1, 114:
    > I shall only observe...that the invention of all those machines by which labour is so much facilitated and abridged seems to have been originally owing to the division of labour...A great part of the machines made use of in those manufactures in which labour is most subdivided, were originally the inventions of common workmen, who, being each of them employed in some very simple operation, naturally turned their thoughts towards finding out easier and readier methods of performing it.
13. Smith, *Wealth of Nations,* bk. 1, 443.
14. Speaking of Ricardo after his marriage in 1793, R.M. Hartwell, in his introduction to the Pelican edition of Ricardo's *Principles,* says: "Indeed he was, in belief and habit, as near to being an atheist as was then socially and intellectually respectable." Ricardo, *On the Principles of Political Economy and Taxation* (Penguin Books, 1971), 36.
15. Ricardo, *On the Principles,* 121.
16. Smith, *Wealth of Nations,* bk. 1, 133: "The value of any commodity...to the person who possesses it, and who means not to use or consume it himself, but to exchange it for other commodities, is equal to the quantity of labour which it enables him to purchase or command."
17. Ricardo, *On the Principles,* 67.
18. Ricardo, *On the Principles,* 115.
19. "Corn" is used here in the British sense where it refers to wheat grain.
20. Ricardo, *On the Principles,* 101n.
21. Ricardo, *On the Principles,* 134–35.
22. Ricardo, *On the Principles,* 281: "There cannot, then, be accumulated in a country any amount of capital which cannot be employed productively, until wages rise so high

in consequence of the rise of necessaries, and so little consequently remains for the profits of stock, the motive for accumulation ceases."

23. Maxine Berg, *The Machinery Question and the Making of Political Economy, 1815–1848* (Cambridge University Press, 1980), 47.
24. Ricardo, *On the Principles*, 140: "This tendency, this gravitation as it were of profits, is happily checked at repeated intervals by the improvements in machinery, connected with the production of necessaries, as well as by discoveries in the science of agriculture which enable us to relinquish a portion of labour before required, and therefore to lower the price of the prime necessary of the labourer."
25. Ricardo, *On the Principles*, 151.
26. Ricardo, *On the Principles*, 114.
27. Ricardo, *On the Principles*, 31.
28. Berg, *The Machinery Question*, 65: "Ricardo's *Principles* put forward a new ideology of economic and technological improvement—if not of limitless growth, then of growth to which an empirical limit could not yet be set."
29. Berg, *The Machinery Question*, 98. Ricardo himself, however, became less sanguine about technological advances. In the third edition of *Principles* (1821) he announced a change of mind and that he now thought the introduction of machinery could in some instances be against the interest of the labourers. *Vide* Ricardo, *On the Principles*, 380.
30. Berg, *The Machinery Question*, 162–63. Berg remarks: "Most of this work was middle-class propaganda of the crudest kind…Thomas Chalmers said he 'was not aware of a likelier instrument than a judicious course of economical doctrine for tranquilizing the popular mind and removing from it all those delusions which are the main cause of popular disaffection.'"
31. Berg, *The Machinery Question*, 161.
32. All references to passages in this work are from the edition published by Hafner in New York in 1948, which includes an introduction by Laurence J. Lafleur.
33. Jeremy Bentham, *An Introduction to the Principles of Morals and Legislation*, with introduction by Laurence J. Lafleur (Hafner, 1948), 2.
34. Bentham, *The Principles of Morals*, 3. In this and all quotes from Bentham the emphasis is his.
35. Bentham, *The Principles of Morals*, 3
36. Bentham, *The Principles of Morals*, 2.
37. *Deontology* together with *A Table of the Springs of Action* and *Article on Utilitarianism*, in Bentham, *The Collected Works* (hereafter Goldworth), edited by Amnon Goldworth (Clarendon Press, 1983), 98.
38. Goldworth, 75.
39. Note how in *The Principles of Morals*, 3, Bentham says the community is a "fictitious body" since it is composed of its individual members.
40. *Deontology*, in Goldworth, 147–48.
41. "Pursuing another's, it follows not that he pursues not his own. His own is the breast in which the pain and pleasure of sympathy are seated." *Springs*, in Goldworth, 36.
42. *Springs*, in Goldworth, 91.
43. *Springs*, in Goldworth, 99–100.

44. Bentham calls it "extra-regarding." "Of the above list there are certain pleasures and pains which suppose the existence of some pleasure or pain of some other person, to which the pleasure or pain of the person in question has regard: such pleasures and pains may be termed *extra-regarding*. Others do not suppose any such thing: these may be termed *self-regarding*" (*The Principles of Morals*, 41).
45. Quoted by Goldworth in his introduction, xix.
46. It may be useful here to explain the distinction just made. Egoistic hedonism, as an ethical doctrine, claims that one ought to aim in all one's deliberate actions at the increase of *one's own* pleasure and the decrease of *one's own* pain. Hedonistic utilitarianism, by contrast, says that one ought to aim at the increase in the sum of all the pleasures *of those affected by one's action* and the decrease in the sum of all their pains.
47. *Deontology*, in Goldworth, 122–23.
48. "What happiness is has also been seen: any pleasure or combination of contemporary pleasures, considered as existing at an elevated point, though without the possibility of marking it in the scale of intensity." *Deontology*, in Goldworth, 135.
49. *Deontology*, in Goldworth, 149.
50. In this Bentham is, I believe, very close to the mid-twentieth-century doctrine among some Anglo-American philosophers called "emotivism." The crucial move is to cease thinking of ethical judgments as doing the job of describing some fact about the world. What they do is express and reveal the attitudes of the one making the judgment.
51. *Deontology*, in Goldworth, 149.
52. *Deontology*, in Goldworth, 149–50.
53. *Deontology*, in Goldworth, 149–50.
54. *Springs*, in Goldworth, 59–60.
55. In the Latin of the scholastics an *enuntiatio* was simply a declarative sentence purporting to state some fact.
56. *Springs*, in Goldworth, 66.
57. These are taken from the copious tables that Bentham constructed and that are given in *Springs*, in Goldworth, 79–86.
58. I trust the reader will not take offence at this extension of the singular and gender-neutral "they" to the reflexive pronoun. See note at end of the preface to this work.
59. Smith, *The Theory of Moral Sentiments*, 98–99.
60. "Conclusion: unless consequences be taken into account, 'bad' and 'good motives' can not be said without teaching error." *Springs*, in Goldworth, 17.
61. *Springs*, in Goldworth, 35.
62. In *The Principles of Morals*, 22–23, Bentham does distinguish between a cause and a reason and then rules out any reason other than utility:

> There are two things which are very apt to be confounded, but which it imports us carefully to distinguish: —the motive or cause, which, by operating on the mind of an individual, is productive of any act: and the ground or reason which warrants a legislator, or other by-stander, in regarding that act with an eye of approbation...

> The only right ground of action, that can possibly subsist, is, after all, the consideration of utility, which, if it is a right principle of action, and of approbation, in any one case, is so in every other. Other principles in abundance, that is, other motives, may be the reasons why such an act *has* been done: that is the reasons or causes of its being done: but it is this alone that can be the reason why it might or ought to have been done.

He does not seem to make this distinction in either *Springs* or *Deontology*.

63. William Stanley Jevons, *The Theory of Political Economy* (1871, 1879). Between the work's first edition and its second Jevons became aware that most of his theory had been anticipated by several thinkers. In the preface to the second edition he lists Destutt de Tracy, Condillac, Dupuit, and Cournot. He particularly lauds an almost totally overlooked work in German by Hermann Heinrich Gossen published in 1854. *Vide* Jevons, *The Theory of Political Economy*, ed. with introduction R.D. Collison Black (Penguin Books, 1970), 56-62. What Jevons seems unaware of is the work of the Austrian economist Carl Menger, who developed marginal utility theory in his *Principles of Economics*, published in 1871. A whole Austrian school developed out of his work and included such influential later figures as Friedrich Hayek, Ludwig von Mises, and Joseph Schumpeter.
64. Jevons, *The Theory*, 56, 82.
65. Jevons, *The Theory*, 91.
66. Jevons, *The Theory*, 91.
67. Thorstein Veblen noted this hedonist line in the theory of marginal utility and criticized it in his "The Limitations of Marginal Utility" published in the *Journal of Political Economy* 9, no. 9 (November 1909), which can be found in Veblen, *The Place of Science in Modern Civilization and Other Essays* (Russell and Russell, 1961), 234.
68. Jevons, *The Theory*, 84.
69. Jevons, *The Theory*, 83. Jevons places special emphasis on these words.
70. Jevons, *The Theory*, 101-02.
71. Jevons, *The Theory*, 91.
72. Jevons, *The Theory*, 92.
73. Jevons, *The Theory*, 93.
74. Jevons, *The Theory*, 133.
75. Jevons, *The Theory*, 137.
76. Jevons's disagreement with Ricardo, Smith, and J.S. Mill is most clearly expressed in the preface to the second edition of Jevons, *The Theory*, 69-72.
77. Jevons, *The Theory*, 110-11.
78. Jevons, *The Theory*, 86.
79. This I think is the meaning of the following statement on p. 139 of Jevon's treatise: "The keystone of the whole theory of exchange, and of the principal problems of economics, lies in this proposition—*The ratio of exchange of any two commodities will be the reciprocal of the ratio of the final degrees of utility of the quantities of commodity available for consumption after the exchange is completed.*"
80. Otherwise why would he say: "the object of economics is to maximize happiness by purchasing pleasure, as it were at the lowest cost of pain" (91).

81. Jevons says in the preface to the first edition: "I have long thought that as it deals throughout with quantities, it must be a mathematical science in matter if not in language" (44).
82. Jevons, *The Theory* (in the preface to the 2nd ed.), 50.
83. Jevons, *The Theory*, 78.
84. *Springs*, in Goldworth, 35.
85. Jevons, *The Theory* (in the preface to the 2nd ed.), 47.
86. Robert Skidelsky, *Money and Government: The Past and Future of Economics* (Yale University Press, 2018), 200.
87. In reviewing Skidelsky's book the late anthropologist David Graeber nicely made the point:
    > Surely there's nothing wrong with creating simplified models. Arguably this is how any science of human affairs has to proceed. But an empirical science then goes on to test those models against what people actually do, and adjust them accordingly. This is precisely what economists did *not* do. Instead, they discovered that, if one encased those models in mathematical formulae completely impenetrable to the noninitiate, it would be possible to create a universe in which those premises could never be refuted…The mathematical equations allowed economists to plausibly claim theirs was the only branch of social theory that had advanced to anything like a predictive science. (*New York Review of Books*, 5 December 2019, 57)
88. Skidelsky, *Money and Government*, 13 et passim.
89. Skidelsky, *Money and Government*, 6.
90. Graeber, *New York Review of Books*, 57.

Conclusion

1. I do not believe that the twentieth century added anything substantial to this complex of ideas, but it certainly carried on the millenarian ideology. On this, see David W. Noble, *Debating the End of History: The Marketplace, Utopia, and the Fragmentation of Intellectual Life* (University of Minnesota Press, 2012). Note in particular his account on pages 70 and 71 of the millenarian style of thinking exemplified by the MIT economist Walt Rostow in *The Stages of Economic Growth: A Non-Communist Manifesto* (Cambridge University Press, 1960). Rostow envisions the ultimate stage in societal development as one of "high mass-consumption." The United States has already achieved this, he judges, and Western Europe is not far behind, while the rest of the world is in various stages of progress toward it. He does not, however, see this progress as inevitably reaching what the Americans already have.
2. In an ideology, in contrast to a philosophical system, an internal contradiction is not necessarily a weakness. Often it enables the ideologue to manoeuvre adroitly against very different opponents, who are effectively countered only by proposals that are themselves at odds with one another.

3. Richard Heinberg has rightly diagnosed power as the Achilles's Heel of our civilization and has written a book on it, titled *Power: Limits and Prospects for Human Survival*, recently published by New Society Press (2021).
4. I write this as we mark the seventy-fifth anniversary of the atomic bombing of Hiroshima, the most monstrous demonstration so far of how military technology bursts through all moral limitations.
5. In Ronald Wright, *A Short History of Progress* (House of Anansi Press, 2004).
6. "Curiously, if we do see a collapse, it will be the citizens of many cultures disconnected to the global political economy who will be best placed to survive, as they are comparatively self-sufficient and the least dependent on the technologies and interconnected markets and institutions of the industrial world." From Jules Pretty and Sarah Pilgrim: "Nature and Culture: Looking to the Future for Human-Environment Systems," in Sarah Pilgrim and Jules Pretty, ed., *Nature and Culture: Rebuilding Lost Connections*, (Earthscan, 2010), 258.
7. Tönnies, "The Individual and the Modern Age" (1913), in *On Sociology*, 316–17.

WORKS CITED

Andreae, Johannes Valentin. *Christianopolis*. Translated by Felix Emil Held. Oxford University Press, 1916.

Augustine, Saint. *The City of God*. In *Basic Writings of Saint Augustine*. Edited with an introduction and notes by Whitney J. Oates. 2 vols. Random House, 1948.

Aurelius, Marcus. "Meditations." Translated by George Long. In *Marcus Aurelius and His Times*. Walter J. Black, 1945.

Bacon, Francis. *The Major Works of Francis Bacon*. Edited with an introduction and notes by Brian Vickers. InteLex Corp, c. 2009.

Bacon, Francis. *The Works of Francis Bacon*. Edited by James Spedding, Robert Leslie Ellis, and Douglas Denon Heath. Longmans, 1876.

Bentham, Jeremy. *An Introduction to the Principles of Morals and Legislation*, with an introduction by Laurence J. Lafleur. Hafner, 1948.

Bentham, Jeremy. *The Collected Works of Jeremy Bentham: Deontology together with A Table of the Springs of Action and Article on Utilitarianism*. Edited by Amnon Goldworth. Clarendon Press, 1983.

Berg, Maxine. *The Machinery Question and the Making of Political Economy, 1815–1848*. Cambridge University Press, 1980.

Bolle, Kees W. *The Bhagavadgītā: A New Translation*. University of California Press, 1979.

Boyce, Mary, ed. and trans. *Textual Sources for the Study of Zoroastrianism*. University of Chicago Press, 1990.

Buchholz, Dennis D. *Your Eyes Will Be Opened: A Study of the Greek (Ethiopic) Apocalypse of Peter*. Scholars Press, 1988.

Burroughs, William James. *Climate Change in Prehistory: The End of the Reign of Chaos*. Cambridge University Press, 2005.

Cicero, Marcus Tullius. *On Moral Ends*. Translated by Raphael Woolf, edited by Julia Annas. Cambridge University Press, 2001.

Cohn, Norman. *Cosmos, Chaos, and the World to Come: The Ancient Roots of Apocalyptic Faith*, 2nd ed. Yale University Press, 2001.

Cohn, Norman. *The Pursuit of the Millennium: Revolutionary Millenarians and Mystical Anarchists of the Middle Ages*. Pimlico, 2004.

Chu Hsi and Lu Tsu-Ch'ien, eds. *Reflections on Things at Hand: The Neo-Confucian Anthology*. Translated by Wing-Tsit Chan. Columbia University Press, 1967.

Cone, James H. *God of the Oppressed*. Orbis Books, 1997.

de Condorcet, Nicolas. *Sketch for a Historical Picture of the Progress of the Human Mind*. Translated by June Barraclough with an introduction by Stuart Hampshire. Weidenfeld and Nicolson, 1955.

de Grouchy, Sophie. *Letters on Sympathy: A Critical Edition*. Translated and edited by Karin Brown and James E. McClellan III. American Philosophical Society, 2008.

Duchesne-Guillemin, Jacques. *The Hymns of Zarathustra: Being a Translation of the Gathas together with Introduction and Commentary*. Translated by Mrs. M. Henning. C.E. Tuttle, 1992.

Eliade, Mircea. *Patterns in Comparative Religion*. Translated by Rosemary Sheed. University of Nebraska Press, 1996.

Ellul, Jacques. *The Technological Society*. Translated by John Wilkenson. Vintage Books, 1964.

Elvin, Mark. *The Retreat of the Elephants: An Environmental History of China*. Yale University Press, 2004.

Emmerson, Richard K., and Bernard McGinn, editors. *The Apocalypse in the Middle Ages*. Cornell University Press, 1992.

Epictetus. *Discourses*. Translated by Robert F. Dobbin. Clarendon Press, 1998.

Epictetus. "Handbook." In *Epictetus's* Handbook *and the* Tablet of Cebes: *Guides to Stoic Living*. Routledge, 2005.

Fairbank, John King, and Merle Goldman. *China: A New History*, 2nd ed. Harvard University Press, 2006.

Farrington, Benjamin. *The Philosophy of Francis Bacon: An Essay on Its Development from 1603, with New Translations of Fundamental Texts*. Liverpool University Press, 1964.

Fudge, Thomas A. *Jerome of Prague and the Foundations of the Hussite Movement*. Oxford University Press, 2016.

Funari, Anthony J. *Francis Bacon and the Seventeenth-Century Intellectual Discourse*. Palgrave Macmillan, 2011.

Gott, Samuel. *Nova Solyma, the Ideal City; or Jerusalem Regained*. 2 vols. Translated and introduction by Rev. Walter Begley. John Murray, 1902.

Graeber, David. "Against Economics." *New York Review of Books*, 5 December 2019, 52–57.

Graeber, David and David Wengrow. *The Dawn of Everything: A New History of Humanity*, Penguin Random House Canada, 2021.
Gray, John. *Black Mass: Apocalyptic Religion and the Death of Utopia*. Farrar, Straus and Giroux, 2007.
Hamilton, Sue. *Indian Philosophy: A Very Short Introduction*. Oxford University Press, 2001.
Jacob, Margaret. *Living the Enlightenment: Freemasonry and Politics in Eighteenth-Century Europe*. Oxford University Press, 1995.
Jevons, William Stanley. *The Theory of Political Economy*. Edited with an introduction by R.D. Collison Black. Penguin Books, 1970.
Kaminsky, Howard. *A History of the Hussite Revolution*. University of California Press, 1967.
Katz, David, and Richard H. Popkin. *Messianic Revolution: Radical Religious Politics to the End of the Second Millennium*. Allen Lane, 1999.
Keynes, John Maynard. *The General Theory of Employment, Interest, and Money*. Cambridge University Press for the Royal Economic Society, 1973.
Knibb, Michael A., ed. and trans. *The Ethiopic Book of Enoch*. Clarendon Press, 1978.
Kolbert, Elizabeth. *The Sixth Extinction: An Unnatural History*. Henry Holt, 2014.
Leakey, Richard, and Roger Lewin. *The Sixth Extinction: Biodiversity and Its Survival*. Weidenfield and Nicolson, 1996.
Lenzer, Gertude, ed. *Auguste Comte and Positivism: The Essential Writings*. Transaction, 1998.
Lightfoot, J.L. *The Sibylline Oracles*. Oxford University Press, 2007.
Lipsius, Justus. "A Guide to Stoic Philosophy [Selections]." Translated by Robert V. Young. In *Cambridge Translations of Renaissance Philosophical Texts*, vol. 1: *Moral Philosophy*. Edited by Jill Kraye. Cambridge University Press, 1997.
Lipsius, Justus. *On Constancy (De Constantia)*. Translated by Sir John Stradling. Edited with an introduction by John Sellars. Phoenix Press, 2006.
Lloyd, G.E.R. *Greek Science after Aristotle*. W.W. Norton, 1973.
Louv, Richard. *Our Wild Calling*. Algonquin Books, 2019.
Mandeville, Bernard. *The Fable of the Bees: Or Present Vices, Publick Benefits*. Edited with an introduction by Irwin Primer. Capricorn Books, 1962.
Manuel, Frank E., and Fritzie P. Manuel. *Utopian Thought in the Western World*. Harvard University Press, 1979.
McGinn, Bernard. *Visions of the End: Apocalyptic Traditions in the Middle Ages*. Columbia University Press, 1979.
Metzger, Bruce M., ed. *The Apocrypha of the Old Testament*. Oxford University Press, 1957.
More, Thomas. *The Utopia of Sir Thomas More*. Translated by Ralph Robinson with notes and introduction by Mildred Campbell. D. Van Nostrand, 1947.
Mumford, Lewis. *The City in History: Its Origins, Its Transformations, and Its Prospects*. Penguin, 1966.
Narasimha, Roddam, and Sangeetha Menon, eds. *Nature and Culture*. Vol. 15, pt. 1, of *History of Science, Philosophy, and Culture in Indian Civilization*, D.P. Chattopadhyaya, general editor. Centre for Studies in Civilization, 2011.
Noble, David F. *America by Design: Science, Technology, and the Rise of Corporate Capitalism*. Oxford University Press, 1979.
Noble, David F. *The Religion of Technology: The Divinity of Man and the Spirit of Invention*. Alfred A. Knopf, 1997.

Noble, David W. *Debating the End of History: The Marketplace, Utopia, and the Fragmentation of Intellectual Life*. University of Minnesota Press, 2012.

Olson, Richard G. *Science and Scientism in Nineteenth-Century Europe*. University of Illinois Press, 2008.

Orlov, Andrei A. *Heavenly Priesthood in the* Apocalypse of Abraham. Cambridge University Press, 2013.

Pilgrim, Sarah, and Jules Pretty, eds. *Nature and Culture: Rebuilding Lost Connections*. Earthscan, 2010.

Plato. *The Dialogues of Plato*. 2 vols. Translated by B. Jowett. Random House, 1937.

Ponting, Clive. *A New Green History of the World: The Environment and the Collapse of Great Civilizations*, rev. ed. Penguin Books, 2007.

Raffaelli, Enrico G. *The Sīh-rōzag in Zoroastrianism: A Textual and Historico-Religious Analysis*. Routledge, 2014.

Reeves, Marjorie. *Joachim of Fiore and the Prophetic Future*. SPCK, 1976.

Ricardo, David. *On the Principles of Political Economy and Taxation*. Penguin Books, 1971.

Rostow, Walt. *The Stages of Economic Growth: A Non-Communist Manifesto*. Cambridge University Press, 1960.

Rousseau, Jean-Jacques. *Basic Political Writings*. Translated and edited by Donald A. Cress. Hackett, 1987.

Saint-Simon, Henri. *Henri Saint-Simon (1760–1825): Selected Writings on Science, Industry, and Social Organisation*. Translated and edited by Keith Taylor. Croom Helm, 1975.

Saint-Simon, Henri. *Lettres d'un habitant de Genève a ses contemporains*. Introduction by Alfred Pereire. F. Alcan, 1925

Saint-Simon, Henri. *Oeuvres*, 6 vols. Editions Anthropos, 1966.

Śāntideva. *The Bodhicaryāvatāra*. Translated with an introduction by Kate Crosby and Andrew Skilton. Oxford University Press, 1995.

Schaefer, James, and Tobias Winright, eds. *Environmental Justice and Climate Change: Assessing Pope Benedict XIV's Ecological Vision for the Catholic Church in the United States*. Lexington Books, 2013.

Scott, James C. *Against the Grain: A Deep History of the Earliest States*. Yale University Press, 2017.

Skidelsky, Robert. *Money and Government: The Past and Future of Economics*. Yale University Press, 2018.

Smith, Adam. *The Theory of Moral Sentiments*. Prometheus Books, 2000.

Smith, Adam. *The Wealth of Nations, Books 1–3*, with an introduction by Andrew Skinner. Penguin Books, 1970.

Stillson, Henry L., and William J. Houghan, eds. *History of the Ancient and Honorable Fraternity of Free and Accepted Masons, and Concordant Orders*. The Fraternity Publishing Company, 1898.

Taylor, Charles. *A Secular Age*. Belknap Press of Harvard University Press, 2007.

Tönnies, Ferdinand. *Community and Association (Gemeinschaft und Gesellschaft)*. Translated by Charles P. Loomis. Routledge and Kegan Paul, 1955.

Tönnies, Ferdinand. *Gemeinschaft und Gesellschaft*. In *Gesmtausgabe*, Vol. 2: 1880–1935. Edited by Bettina Clausen and Dieter Haselbach. De Gruyter, 2019.

Tönnies, Ferdinand. *On Sociology: Pure, Applied, and Empirical.* Edited by W.J. Cahneman and R. Heberle. University of Chicago Press, 1971.

Turgot, Anne Robert-Jacques. *Turgot on Progress, Sociology, and Economics.* Translated and edited with an introduction by Ronald L. Meek. Cambridge University Press, 1973.

Veblen, Thorstein. *The Place of Science in Modern Civilization and Other Essays.* Russell and Russell, 1961.

Weber, Max. *The Protestant Ethic and the "Spirit" of Capitalism.* Translated and edited with an introduction by Peter Baehr and Gordon Wells. Penguin, 2002.

Weber, Max. *The Scholar's Work.* Translated by Damion Searle. In *Charisma and Disenchantment: The Vocation Lecture.* Edited by Paul Reitter and Chad Wellmon. New York Review of Books, 2020.

Webster, Charles. *The Great Instauration: Science, Medicine, and Reform 1626–1660.* Holmes and Meier, 1975.

Webster, Charles. *Samuel Hartlib and the Advancement of Learning.* Cambridge University Press, 1976.

Weiss, John H. *The Making of Technological Man: The Social Origins of French Engineering Education.* MIT Press, 1982.

Williams, Ann, ed. *Prophecy and Millenarianism: Essays in Honour of Marjorie Reeves.* Longman Group, 1980.

Willoughby, Pamela R. *The Evolution of Modern Humans in Africa.* Altamira Press, 2007.

Wing-Tsit Chan. *A Source Book in Chinese Philosophy.* Princeton University Press, 1963.

Wright, Ronald. *A Short History of Progress.* House of Anansi Press, 2004.

INDEX

accumulation of wealth
    A. Smith's theory of, 319–25, 373
    in Comte's development of civilization, 295–96, 303
    D. Ricardo on, 404n22
    and inequality, 16–17
    Jevons on, 346, 348
    Protestant view of, 169
    and utilitarianism, 349
administration, 285–89, 371
The Advancement of Learning (Bacon), 203, 215
affluence
    and A. Smith's theory of wealth creation, 319–25, 373
    explosive expansion in 19th century, 359–60
    in More's *Utopia*, 174
    Rousseau's view of, 236–37
    spiritual development as distraction from, 370
    in Western European civilization, 241
African Americans, 134–37
agricultural communities
    beginnings of, 6–8, 9
    coping strategies of, 10–14
    and development of religion, 12–14
    and development of war/class division, 15–16
    management of difficulties in, 17
    and oneness of organic life, 383n21
    precariousness of, 9–10
Akkadian empire, 30–31
Alembert, Jean le Rond d', 281
Alexander the Great, 78, 103
alienation of self from world, 186–87
Alsted, Johann Heinrich, 216
altruism, 67, 177, 299–302, 337, 372
amelioration of life, 290, 296–98, 309, 365, 374
Amos, 34–35, 116
Amos, The Book of, 93
Anabaptists, 164–65
Andreae, Johann Valentin, 187–92, 202, 217
Anthropocene, xviii
Antichrist
    Augustine and, 142
    expected arrival of in medieval times, 157
    indefiniteness of term, 393n5
    Joachim of Fiore and, 148, 149
    Olivi and, 154, 155
    and *Sibylline Oracles*, 145–46
    St. Jerome and, 145
Antiochus IV Epiphanes, 101, 102–03
The Apocalypse of Abraham, 109–10
The Apocalypse of Peter, 125–27
apocalyptic prophecy
    The Apocalypse of Abraham, 109–10
    and belief in coming of new world, 165
    of Black Americans, 134–36

INDEX

The Book of Daniel, 101–04
The Book of Enoch, 104–09
  common features of, 124–25
  and destruction of society, 163
  of early Christianity, 108, 124–34
  importance to Hussite reform movement, 158, 159
  in Jewish literature, 112–13
  popularity of in medieval times, 157–58
  The Second Book of Esdras, 110–12
  and Taborites, 160–64
  and T. Müntzer, 164
  two English works of, 216
Apology (Plato), 43–44, 46–47, 49
applied science
  ability to predict of, 355
  development of in France, 311–14, 372, 403n89
  and freemasonry, 307
  messianic view of, 314–15
  and rise of engineering, 304
Archimedes, 73
Aristotle, xxii, 159, 171, 204
arithmetic, 29. *See also* mathematics
Arrian, 61
art, 5–6
arts, 236, 237
art *versus* nature, 197–98
asceticism, 151–52, 168–69
Assyrian empire, 32–35, 95
astronomy, 13, 29, 190, 387n31
Athens, 41–42
Augustine of Hippo, 139–44
Aurelius, Marcus, 67–72
Averroes (Ibn Rushd), 204
Avesta, 78, 83
Avicenna (Ibn Sina), 204
Azazel, 105, 109

Babylonian Empire, 94, 95, 101
Bacon, Francis
  belief that knowledge serves human prosperity, 205–06
  connection to freemasonry, 402n62
  and creation of Royal Society, 219, 221, 398n94
  defends advancement of knowledge to Christian divines, 212–14
  and development of science in *New Atlantis*, 207–12, 220
  engineering as part of his vision, 315
  his vision of utopia compared to T. More's, 220–23
  how he allies religion with science, 214–16
  how his idea of progress differs from Condorcet's, 272
  influence on Commenius, 218
  influence on works of educational reform, 216, 217
  Jevons' reference to, 349
  legacy of, 365–66
  and meaning of The Fall, 225
  and progress, 254
  in Saint-Simon's work, 283
  Turgot's view of, 259
  views of foreshadowed in *Christianopolis*, 191
  views of science that brought on economic expansion, xxv, 277
  views on learning, 203–04
Ball, John, 173
banks, 289
Beethoven, Ludwig van, 275
Beghards, 163
Behemoth, 108, 132
Belshazzar, 101
Benedict XI, Pope, 155
beneficial results without conscious design, 70
Bentham, Jeremy
  conception of utilitarianism, 338–46, 375, 406n62
  influence on Jevons, 346–48
  Jevons' departure from on moral indifference, 349–50
  and neoclassical economics, 356
  on pain and pleasure, 334–38, 374–75, 376, 406n44

view of calculation in ethics, 354
Bernardone, Giovanni di Pietro di, 151. *See also* Francis of Assisi, St.
Bhagavadgītā, 56–57
Bockelson, Jan (John of Leyden), 165
Bonaventure, St., 389n37
Boniface VIII, Pope, 155
The Book of Dreams, 109
The Book of Parables, 108–09
The Book of Watchers, 105–8
Bowring, John, 338
Boyle, Robert, 219
Bridge of the Separator, 84–85
brigands, 10, 15
British Parliament, 219
Buddhism, 39, 64–65
Bundahishn, 88, 89

Cabanis, P.J.G., 249
Calvin, John, 168–69
Calvinism, 170, 201
Campanella, Tommaso, 188
carnal pleasures, 169, 170
Çatal Hüyük, 19–20
catastrophe, coming, 127–28, 131–33, 158, 161. *See also* eco-catastrophe
Catholic Church, 164
Cato the Younger, 54–56, 59–60, 62–63, 389n24
change/inconstancy *versus* changeless/permanent, 116
Chang Tsai, 67
Charles II, King, 219
Ch'eng Hao, 66
Ch'eng I, 66
China
　advances in technology in, xxi, 202, 390n71
　and A. Smith on conditions of workers in, 318
　civilizational unrest in, 39, 40
　and halt to economic expansion, 390n71
　and tradition which constrained modern forces, xix
　and Turgot's view of, 256–57, 261

Chinvat Bridge. *See* Bridge of the Separator
choice of morality, 82–84, 111, 120
chosen one
　African-Americans belief in Jesus as, 135–37
　in *The Apocalypse of Peter*, 125–26
　in Book of Parables, 108
　Hebrew prophets view of, 98–99
　in New Testament, 121, 122
　in *The Second Book of Esdras*, 110–11, 112
Christian Church
　attacks on popes in medieval times, 157–58
　Augustine's view of, 141–42
　dealing with heretics, 158–59
　dismantling of ideology of, 363–64
　dispute with Franciscans on poverty, 154–56
　and Great Schism, 158
　medieval reform of, 150
　and Roman Empire, 139, 141–42
　view of apostolic life by, 150–51
Christianity
　apocalyptic prophecy of, 108, 124–34
　and Bacon's thought, 206
　in *Christianopolis*, 187–88, 192
　Condorcet's view of, 270
　dissolution of its impact, 366
　familiarity with *The Book of Enoch*, 104
　as favoured religion of Roman Empire, 139
　how Bacon allies science with, 214–16
　idea that physical creation serves human ends, 389n37
　impact of stoicism on, 72
　importance of Paul's writing to, 114
　influence of Hebrew prophets on, 93
　meaning of The Fall, 199, 212–14, 225–26, 235–36
　and modification of *The Revelation to John*, 130
　in *Nova Solyma*, 193, 199–200
　in Saint-Simon's view of society, 290–91
　and *The Second Book of Esdras*, 110

writings of New Testament apostles,
  120–24
Christianopolis (Andreae), 187–92, 364
Chrysippus, 54
Chu Hsi, 65–66
Cicero, 54–55, 388n23
Città del Sole (Campanella), 188
civilization
  ancient philosophies' failure to advocate
    change in, 361
  Comte's idea of three stage development
    of, 291–96, 303
  Condorcet's view of, 271
  effect on morality, 16
  and F. Bacon's ideas, 222
  meaning of, 382n1
  Rousseau's view of, 235–41, 242, 366–67
  Saint-Simon's plan to perfect, 278–83
  S. De Grouchy's antipathy towards, 252
  and unrest in China and India, 39, 40.
    See also Greek civilization; Sumerian
    civilization; urban-dominated
    civilization; Western civilization
class division, 10, 15–16, 35–36
Clavis Apocalyptica (Mede), 216
Cleanthes, 54
colonialism, 272–74, 275
Comberousse, Charles de, 313
Commenius, 194, 217, 218
commodity value, 326–32
communism
  of Anabaptists, 165
  in Bacon's *New Atlantis*, 209
  in *Christianopolis*, 187
  in More's *Utopia*, 178–80
  and *Nova Solyma*, 193
  of Taborites, 161
  of *Utopia*, 220
Companion in Tribulation (John of Rupecissa),
  156
Comte, Auguste, 291–304, 311, 317, 371–72,
  403n89
Condorcet, Marquis de
  and French Revolution, 252
  on rights and politics, 267–72

and view of Europe's treatment of
  colonies, 272–74
view of science, 277
views on progress, 263–67, 275, 369–70
Cone, James H., 135–37
Confucianism, 65–67, 177, 202, 230
conscience, 243, 245–46
Constantine, 139
Copernicus, 202
cosmic determinism, 60–61
critical attitude/criticism, 196–97
Crito (Plato), 45–46
Crusades, 147
Cyrus the Great, 78, 96

Daniel, The Book of, 101–04, 105, 214–15
Da Vinci, Leonardo, 202
The Dawn of Everything (Graeber and
  Wengrow), 36
De finibus bonorum et malorum (Cicero),
  54–55, 388n23
De Grouchy, Sophie, 248–54, 263, 338, 368
democracy, 267–69
Descartes, Rene, 202, 259, 281
detachment
  of Bhagavadgītā, 63–64
  in Buddhism, 64–65
  and discipline for, 65–67
  M. Aurelius' view of, 71–72
  in Middle Ages, 144–45
  as part of Stoicism, 61–63
  and St. Francis, 152
determinism/inevitability
  and science's laws, 280–81, 294–96
  Stoic acceptance of, 61, 71
  in theories of progress, 254–55, 261, 264,
    266, 270, 275, 301–02, 303
devil/satan, 132, 133, 139, 140–42
dialectic, 204–05
Diderot, Denis, 281
Discourse on the Origin of Inequality
  (Rousseau), 238–40
Discourses on the Sciences and the Arts
  (Rousseau), 235–38
disease in farming communities, 9–10

divine law, 69–70
division of labour, 322–23
Dolcino, Fra, 155–56
Dury, John, 194, 216, 217, 218–19

eco-catastrophe
    and ancient traditions which might have prevented, xix, xx
    Comte's impact on, 303–04
    facets of, 359–60
    and F. Bacon's ideas as setting potential for, 221
    inevitability of, xviii, 378
    planetary scope of, xviii
    role of humanities in explaining, xxii–xxiii
    what its likely effects will be, 378–79, 409n6
École Centrale des Arts et Manufactures, 312–14, 372
ecology, xvii
economic development
    and A. Smith's ideas on wealth creation, 319–25
    and A. Smith's view of open markets, 247–48
    and Comte's three phases of, 295–96
    Condorcet's view of laws governing, 265
    constraints on, 317
    D. Ricardo's theory of, 325–32, 374
    halt to in China, 390n71
    ideas which spurred on, xxv–xxvi
    impact of Protestantism on, 248, 364
    importance of Bacon's views to, xxv, 277
    and importance of vice in, 233–35
    and neoclassical economics, 356–57
    in Protestant utopias, 202
    and reduction of protest against inequality, 314
    and Saint-Simon's views on production, 283–91. *See also* material progress; progress
economics
    application of utilitarianism to, 348–50
    Jevons' belief in scientific basis of, 352–54, 375
    meaning of, xvii
    and moral indifference, 349–50
education
    in Andreae's *Christianopolis*, 188–92
    changes to before Reformation, 171
    and dialectic, 204–05
    in early farming communities, 16
    F. Bacon's views on, 203–04
    and Gemeinschaft of settled life, 24
    in More's *Utopia*, 174–75
    in *Nova Solyma*, 194–98, 201
    Plato's plan of, 51
    in Protestant utopias, 202
    and Socrates' idea of wisdom, 49
    and Stoicism, 67
    works on English reform of, 216–18
egalitarian community, 129–30
egoistic hedonism, 338–39, 406n46
Egyptian Empire, 94, 95
elenchus, 49
Eliade, M., 383–84n21–23
elites, 35, 72, 77, 222–23
Ellul, Jacques, 385n11
Elvin, M., 391n71
emotivism, 406n50
end of days
    in *The Book of Daniel*, 103, 104
    in Christian apocalyptic prophecy, 125
    in Jewish apocalyptic literature, 113
    in New Testament, 120, 121–22
    in Paul, 117–19
    in *The Second Book of Esdras*, 110
    in *The Sibylline Oracles*, 128–29, 130
    and T. Müntzer, 164
engineers/engineering
    and ability to predict of, 355
    development of in France, 311–14
    dominance in US of, 403n90
    and freemasonry, 304–05, 311, 372
    and messianic view of science, 314–15
    rise of, 304
English Civil War, 218
English peasants' revolt, 173

INDEX

Enlightenment, 201, 226, 247, 309, 368
Enoch, The Book of, 104–09, 115
Epictetus, 61–62, 65, 67, 200
Epicurus, xxii, 271, 272
Eriugena, John Scotus, 213
ethics, 54–55, 215–16, 341–43, 354
Euclid, 307, 308
eudaimōn, 48
evildoers
    in *The Apocalypse of Peter*, 126–27
    attacks on as part of Zorastrianism, 83–84
    in Book of Parables, 108–09
    in Jewish apocalyptic literature, 113
    in New Testament, 120, 124
    in Paul, 116, 118
    in *The Second Book of Esdras*, 111
    Stoic view of, 69
Ezekiel, The Book of, 95, 96, 97–98, 99–101, 102, 120

The Fable of the Bees (Mandeville), 226–31
Fairbank, J.K., 390–91n71
faith, 119
Fall, the
    and Christianized Platonism, 199
    F. Bacon's view of, 213, 214, 365
    and freemasonry, 308, 373
    Joachim de Fiore and, 148
    Mandeville's view of, 235
    Rousseau's view of, 235, 236
    various interpretations of, 225–26
fantasy, xxii, 91, 162, 381n3
farming
    class division in, 15–16
    development of, 8, 9
    and government, 11–12
    and religion, 12–14
    and urban-dominated civilizations, 20
Fénelon, François, 219
Flanders, 395n25
folk psychology, 4
foreign trade, 329–30
forgiveness, 153
Four Horseman of the Apocalypse, 131

Franciscans, 153–54
Francis of Assisi, St. (Giovanni Bernardone), 151–52, 153, 155
Frashegird (making wonderful)
    conception of, 90–91, 362–63
    fuels enthusiasm for expansion, 134
    idea taken up by Hebrew prophets, 101, 113
    in *The Revelation to John*, 134
fraternal harmony, 306
Fratticelli (Franciscan group), 157
freemasonry, 304–11, 317, 372
free trade, 323–24, 329, 374
French Revolution
    as disaster, 280
    impact on western culture, 278
    and Marquis de Condorcet, 252, 263–64, 274, 275
    and Saint-Simon, 279

Galileo Galilei, 202, 259
Gemeinschaft
    appeal of New Testament to, 124
    context of More's *Utopia*, 181
    described, 21
    Kürwille's place in, 25
    Lipsius' view pulling away from, 184
    and non-millennarian philosophy, 361
    St. Paul's accordance with, 114–15
    in Sumeria, 29
    and superstition, 24
    view of Middle Eastern civilization taken by, 32–35
    and Zoroastrianism, 91, 362. *See also* Wesenwille
Gemeinschaft und Gesellschaft (Tonnies), 21–28
Genesis, 105, 108
genius, 255–56, 261, 279–80
German Peasant Rebellion, 164
gerontocracy, 11
Gesellschaft
    and close fit with F. Bacon's ideas, 223
    described, 21–22
    dominance in ancient Israel, 35
    Hebrew prophets rage against, 93, 101

INDEX

in Sumeria, 27
taking over modern society, 25–26. *See also* Kürwille
Giles, Peter, 171
Gog of the land of Magog, 100–01, 133, 146
Goldman, M., 390–91n71
good and evil
    in *The Apocalypse of Abraham*, 109–10
    and Bacon's views on the Fall, 212–14
    in *The Book of Enoch*, 106–07
    and S. De Grouchy on, 250–51
    Zoroastrianism's view of, 88–91, 362
Gorgias (Plato), 47–48, 51–53
Gossen, Hermann H., 407n63
Gott, Samuel, 193–201
government
    A. Smith's view of, 324–25
    and Condorcet's view of democracy, 267–69
    dominated by Gesellschaft views in Sumeria, 27
    in early farming communities, 11–12
    effect of tyranny on progress, 257–58
    and freemasonry, 305
    J. Lipsius' views of, 182–83, 186
    and need for defense from raiders, 15
    in *Nova Solyma*, 194
    Plato's view of in *Gorgias*, 52–53
    and Roman investment in infrastructure, 74
    Saint-Simon's views on, 283, 284–85, 286, 287–89
    and urban-dominated civilizations, 20
Graham, John H., 309–11, 403n71
Great Schism, 158
Greco-Roman world, xxiv, 72–75, 130, 201. *See also* Greek civilization; Roman Empire
Greek civilization
    and humanist education, 171
    major wars of, 40–42
    in More's *Utopia*, 175
    and religion, 42
    technological advances of, 72–73
    and Turgot on, 257

Greek Science after Aristotle (Lloyd), 73–74
Gui, Bernard, 156

Han empire, 32
happiness
    and Bentham's conception of utilitarianism, 338–46, 375
    B. Mandeville's view of, 230–31
    Comte on, 296
    Condorcet on, 267
    and J. Bentham's pain and pleasure theory, 334–38
    and Jevons' application to economics, 348–50
    Saint-Simon on, 289–90
    S. De Grouchy on, 250, 368
    in Smith's *Theory of Moral Sentiments*, 244–47
    Turgot on, 262
Hartlib, Samuel, 194, 216, 217, 218–19
Hartwell, R.M., 331–32
Harvey, William, 202
heaven and hell
    and Hebrew prophets' view of, 98
    and J. Lipsius, 185–86
    in *The Second Book of Esdras*, 111
    in *The Sibylline Oracles*, 129
    as Zoroastrian idea, 84–88
Hebrew Bible, 92–104
Hebrew prophets
    from the Bible, 92–101
    and Jewish apocalyptic literature, 112–13
    poetry of, 32–35
hedonistic utilitarianism, 406n46
hedonist psychology
    and Condorcet, 271–72
    and economics, xxvi
    of J. Bentham, 334–38, 375
    of S. De Grouchy, 249–51, 253–54, 368
    W.S. Jevons on, 346
Hermeticism, 309
Hero of Alexandria, 73
Hipparchus of Nicaea, 387n31
history, study of, 190
Hittite nation, 77

homeland, 143–44, 167
human action, 150, 168, 171, 181
human development, 296–98, 299–302, 371–72
humanism, 171, 203
humanities, xxii–xxiii
humanity
    Augustine on, 143
    Condorcet on predicting future of, 264
    Joachim of Fiore's view of, 149–50.
    See also virtue of humanity
human perfection
    Comte's view of, 297–98, 300
    Condorcet's view of, 264, 266–67, 271
    Saint-Simon's view of, 278–83
    Turgot's view of, 263
human rights, 267–69
Hume, David, 242, 246
Hus, John, 158, 159
Hussite reform movement, 158–60, 164

idleness, 284, 288, 290
immortality, 214
imperialism
    allegory of in *The Second Book of Esdras*, 112
    European, 272–74, 275
    of urban-dominated civilization, 30–31, 92, 101, 360
India
    advanced tradition of science in, xxi
    and A. Smith on conditions of workers in, 318, 404n3
    civilizational unrest in, 39, 40
    ideas of borrowed by Greece, 42
    influence of *Bhagavadgītā* in, 56–57
    and sages' conception of knowledge, 205
    and tradition which constrained modern forces, xix
    way to enlightenment in, 50
Indigenous Peoples, 275
industry
    and applied science, 311
    and A. Smith, 319–25, 375
    and avoiding eco-catastrophe, 378
    explosive expansion of, 359
    in *The Fable of the Bees*, 226, 228, 229
    and Jevons, 350–54
    Saint-Simon's views on, 278, 283–91, 370–71
inequality
    in agricultural settlements, 10
    in ancient Israel, 35
    of civilization, 252
    and development of government, 11
    and development of war, 15
    inadequacy of ancient philosophies and, 361
    increased productivity as hedge against protest about, 314
    in medieval life, 151
    of Middle Eastern civilization, 33–35
    in More's *Utopia*, 172–74
    Rousseau's view of, 238–40
    as theme of Protestant utopias, 202
    and wealth accumulation, 16–17
    in Western European civilization, 241
innovation, 255–56, 259
Instauratio Magna (Bacon), 214
intention, 48
An Introduction to the The Principles of Morals and Legislation (Bentham), 334, 335, 346
Irish War, 219
Isaiah, 32, 33, 92, 96–97, 116
Islam, 146, 147, 258
Israel, ancient
    in Book of Dreams, 109
    class division in, 35–36
    Hebrew prophets on, 93–101
Italian Renaissance, 257

Jeremiah, 34
Jeremiah, The Book of, 94–95
Jericho, 19
Jerome, St., 145
Jerome of Prague, 158, 159
Jerusalem, 93–94, 96, 97, 133
Jesus Christ
    and African-Americans, 135–37

Augustine's view of, 140–41
portrayal in New Testament, 120–21
in *The Revelation to John*, 130, 131
role in judgement in New Testament, 123–24
in *The Sibylline Oracles*, 129
St. Francis uses example of, 153, 155. *See also* chosen one; Second Coming of Christ

Jevons, William Stanley
as Bentham acolyte, 346–50
contribution to political economy, 352–54
later influence of his ideas, 357
view of how markets work, 350–52
work which anticipated his, 407n63

Jewish apocalyptic tradition, 124–34
Jewish mysticism, 110
Joachim of Fiore
Franciscans' use of his work, 154
as interpreter of scripture, 147–50, 162
leaves Cistercian order, 151
and progress, 254
similarity of his ideas to Comte's, 303
and Taborites, 162
John of Rupescissa, 156
John XXII, Pope, 157
Judah (state), 94, 95
judgement day
Augustine's view of, 142–43
in *The Book of Daniel*, 104
in *The Book of Enoch*, 106, 107
and Calvinism, 170
in Jewish apocalyptic literature, 113
in New Testament, 122–24
in Paul, 116–17
in *The Revelation to John*, 133
in *The Second Book of Esdras*, 111
in *The Sibylline Oracles*, 128–29
and Taborites, 161
in Zoroastrianism, 85–86. *See also* end of days
Julius Caesar, 388n23
justice
belief in millennium of, 133, 135–37, 156
conception of in Plato's *Crito*, 45–46

and S. De Grouchy, 251
in Smith's *Theory of Moral Sentiments*, 245
and Turgot's view of its impact on progress, 260–61, 262–63

Kepler, Johan, 259
knowledge
Bacon defends advancement of, 212–16
Bacon on abuse of, 215
Bacon's belief it serves prosperity, 205–06
and Comte's three phases of development, 294
Condorcet's belief in spread of, 269–70, 271, 272, 370
in More's *Utopia*, 220–21
Plato's view of, 51
and Socrates' view of wisdom, 48–50
Komensky, Jan Amos, 217
Kürwille
in ancient Israel, 35
appeal of F. Bacon's ideas to, 222
approach to warfare, 28
character of people ruled by, 23–24
described, 21–22
and development of writing, 29–30
disparagement of in Greco-Roman philosophy, 74–75
dissatisfaction with in first millennium BC, 39–40
dominance in urban-dominated civilization, 25–27, 377–78
engineers share mentality of, 313, 315
its place in Gemeinschaft, 25
and J. Lipsius' turn to, 187
mentality of More's *Utopia*, 181
in modern society, 25, 378
and natural affinity for domination, 37
non-millenarian thinkers antipathy toward, 361
in opposition to Wesenwille, 24
Plato's refashioning of, 53
religions using to react, 91
and sexagesimal numerical system, 36–37
Socrates' turning it back on itself, 45

and Taoism, 59
three forms of, 22-23
trauma caused by shift to, 27, 37
view of goals, 23, 57. *See also* Gesellschaft

language, 3-4, 29-30
Lao-tzu, 58-59
last emperor, 145-47, 148, 155-56
Laurence of Březová, 160
law of diminishing returns, 351, 353
Leff, Gordon, 151-52
Leibniz, Gottfried Wilhelm von, 219
Leviathan, 108, 132
libertarianism, 269
liberty, 267
Lipsius, Justus, 181-87, 202, 244
Lloyd, G.E.R., 73-74
London, 231
Lucretius, xxii, 272
Luther, Martin, 164, 168-69

Macaria (Plattes), 217-18
magic, 14
Mandeville, Bernard, 226-31, 240, 345-46, 366
man's dominance over nature, 214, 216, 222, 223
Manuel, F.E. and F.P. Manuel, 219, 258, 270
marginal utility, 352
market economy, 247-48, 321-24, 326-27, 329, 350-52
Martin V, Pope, 158
Marx, Karl, 288
Masculine Birth of Time (Bacon), 206-07, 208
mass consumption, xix, 234-35, 317, 357, 373
material progress
in Bacon's *New Atlantis*, 220
and B. Mandeville's view of vice in, 226-35
Comte's view of, 296, 297-98, 303
impact of the Enlightenment on, 226
and Joachim of Fiore, 150
and Rousseau's view of natural and artificial, 241
view of in Greco-Roman world, 74-75. *See also* economic development

mathematics
advances from Greco-Roman world, 73
in Andreae's *Christianopolis*, 189
and freemasonry, 306-08, 310-11
and Greek civilization, 42
and Jevons' belief in as basis of economics, 354
as key to Plato's idea of knowledge, 51
"Matthew Cooke" ms., 307-08
Matthys, Jan, 165
Mauryan empire, 32
Mede, Joseph, 216
Meditations (Aurelius), 67-72
Menger, Carl, 407n63
Meno (Plato), 68
metaphysical approach, 292
Methodius, 146
Micah, The Book of, 93-94
Michael of Cesena, 155
middle classes, 333
military virtues, 237
Mille Annis Apocalypticis Diatribe (Alsted), 216
millennialism/millenarian ideology
of 20th century, 408n1
and A. Comte, 291
of Anabaptists, 165
Augustine's view of, 140-44
belief in the agency of human action in, 150
boosted by doctrines of political economy, 333
and Calvinism, 170-71
and Comte, 303
Condorcet's vision of, 274
of the Enlightenment, 368
and F. Bacon, 215, 220, 222-23
and freemasonry, 304-05
grip of on people today, 377
J. Lipsius' opening to, 187
medieval views of, 145-46, 165
and neoclassical economics, 357
and Saint-Simon's perfection of civilization, 278-79
and St. Paul, 114
of Taborites, 163

INDEX

thinkers who opposed, 360-61
and T. More's *Utopia*, 172
of two English works, 216
Milton, John, 194, 216, 396n49
Ming Dynasty, 390n71
Minoan civilization, 40
Monge, Gaspard, 304, 402n58
morality
  in Andreae's *Christianopolis*, 188, 189-90
  and applied science, 314
  B. Mandeville's theory of, 231-33
  and Comte's view of human development, 296-98, 299-302, 371-72
  and Condorcet, 271-72
  and De Grouchy's view of pain and pleasure in, 249-51, 253
  development in farming communities, 16, 17
  and freemasonry's tie to mathematics, 310-11
  in Gemeinschaft, 24
  J. Bentham's conception of, 343-45
  in More's *Utopia*, 175, 177
  in Paul, 120
  Plato's view of, 46, 53
  and Rousseau's view of how civilization has affected, 235-40
  Saint-Simon on, 289-90
  in *Second Book of Esdras*, 111
  in Smith's *Theory of Moral Sentiments*, 242-47, 367-68
  in writing of Joachim of Fiore, 148-49
  Zoroastrian view of, 80, 81-84
moral reform, 225-26
More, Henry, 216
More, Thomas
  his vision of utopia compared to F. Bacon's, 220-23
  similarities to in *Christianopolis*, 187
  and *Utopia*, 171-81
  and view of wealth inequality, 202
Mount Toba, eruption of, 2
Mumford, Lewis, 384n4, 384n5, 387n33
Müntzer, Thomas, 164

music, 189-90
Mycenaean civilization, 40
myths, 51

Nahum, 32-33
Napoleon Buonaparte, 275, 278, 279, 332, 402n58
Naram-Sin, 31
natural home/artificial home
  and adoption of farming, 8, 9
  of ecology and economics, xvii-xviii
  and settled village life, 11-12, 17
  and Western expansion, xxiv, 376
natural law, 68-69
nature
  versus art, 197-98
  and Cato, 59-60
  farmers' view of, 12
  man's dominance over, 214, 216, 222, 223
  Stoic belief in, 59-60
nature deficit disorder, 383n11
Nebuchadnezzar, 101, 102
neoclassical economics, 355-57, 408n87
neoliberalism, 356
Neolithic era, 6-8, 9
Neoplatonism, 144, 217
New Atlantis (Bacon), 203, 207-12, 215-16, 220-23
Newton, Isaac, 265, 281
nomadic pastoralism, 8, 9
Nova Solyma (Gott), 193-201, 396n49
Novum Organum (Bacon), 214
numerology, 132, 147-48, 189

Olivi, Peter John, 154-55
Olivier, Theodore, 312-13, 403n80
On Christian Doctrine (Augustine), 143-44
On Constancy (Lipsius), 182-83
On Universal History (Turgot), 254, 255-58, 260-62
oppression, 134-37, 156-58, 172-74
optimizing agent, 356
original sin
  denying doctrine of, 367, 368
  F. Bacon's view of, 214

427

and freemasonry, 311
in *Nova Solyma*, 199–200
resetting of, 377
Owen, Robert, 332

Paleolithic era
    art forms of, 5–6
    and belief in spirits, 4–5
    and human adaptation, 2–3
    and language development, 3–4
    and morality, 16
    and use of fire, 382n6
pansophia, 217, 218
paradise
    in *The Apocalypse of Peter*, 127
    Augustine's view of, 142, 143
    in New Testament, 120
    in *The Sibylline Oracles*, 129
    and Taborites, 162
Parallel Lives (Plutarch), 73
passions, 234–35, 260, 261, 298, 369
Paul, St., 114–20
Persian empire, 41, 78–79
phantasy
    in *The Book of Daniel*, 102–03
    in *The Book of Ezekiel*, 97–98
    distinguished from fantasy, xxii, 381n3
    of Hebrew prophets, 35
    in Paleolithic times, 5
    as part of thought-systems, xxii
    and *The Revelation to John*, 134
    role of religion in, 14
    of Taborites, 160–64
    and Zoroastrian view, 80, 84–91
physical creation serves human ends, 308, 389n37
Plato
    background, 43
    in *Christianopolis*, 189
    and dialectic, 204–05
    importance of to modern western thought, 42
    influence on *Nova Solyma*, 199
    J. Lipsius' use of, 185–86
    medieval thinkers and, 159
    reflected in Paul, 114, 116
    and Socrates in his dialogues, 43–47, 68
    on Socrates' view of wisdom, 48–50
    theory of the soul, 50–51
    view of what people should be aiming at in life, 51–53
Platonism, xxii, 171, 230
Plattes, Gabriele, 217–18
pleasure
    Bentham's attack on moralizing objections to, 345–46
    carnal, 169, 170
    and J. Bentham's pain and pleasure theory, 334–38, 374–75, 376, 406n44
    and Jevons' application to economics, 348–50
    Jevons' approval of Bentham's views on, 346–47
    in More's *Utopia*, 175–76
    in *Nova Solyma*, 194
    S. De Grouchy's view of, 249–51, 253
Plutarch, 73
political economy
    D. Ricardo's influence on making a science, 328, 329, 331–32, 374
    effect on popular culture of, 332–33, 374
    Jevons' contribution to, 352–54
    Saint-Simon's views on, 287–89, 373
politics
    Condorcet on, 267–72
    Plato's view of in *Gorgias*, 52–53
    replaced by science, 373
    Saint-Simon's view it should be science based, 287–89
    of virtue, 232–33, 234–35
population explosion, xix, 376
positivism, 291, 293–94
predestination, 120, 170
Příbram, John, 161, 162
pride, 231–33, 240
progress
    Bacon on, 254
    belief in applied science's role in, 314–15
    Condorcet's views of, 264–70, 271–74, 275, 369–70

effect of tyranny on, 257–58
ideas which boosted idea of, xxv–xxvi
influenced by doctrines of political economy, 333
role of passion in, 260, 261, 369
Turgot on, 254–63, 264–65, 275, 368–69
views of early European thinkers on, 254. *See also* economic development; material progress
progressivist activism, 303
progress traps, 378
property, institution of, 239–40
Protagoras (Plato), 48–49
Protestantism
    and economic development, 248, 364
    and freemasonry, 305
    and utopia, 187–201, 202, 366
    and vocation, 169, 170
Protestant Reformation, 168–69
Pseudo-Methodius, 146–47
public opinion, 342–43
Puritanism, 225, 230, 396n48
Pythagoreans, 42, 388n14

rational choice theory, 357
rational egoism, 49
rationality, 68
rational planning, 27, 31, 181, 222, 260
reason
    and Comte's view of regarding passions, 298
    and Gott's *Nova Solyma*, 201
    J. Lipsius' view of, 183–87
    as part of Plato's soul, 51
    and restraining of human appetite, 231–35
    and Socrates, 48
    Stoic view as hegemonic, 61
    and Turgot's view of impact on progress, 260–61, 262–63
religion
    of A. Smith, 325
    in *Christianopolis*, 192, 203
    Comte's view of, 300–01, 302
    Condorcet's view of, 269–71, 272
    development in early farming communities, 12–14
    and D. Ricardo, 404n14
    F. Bacon on, 214–16
    and freemasonry, 214–16, 308–09, 311
    as Gesellschaft's veil of sacredness, 27
    of Greek civilization, 42
    and Kürwille, 91
    of the masses in Greco-Roman world, 75
    mixed with science in freemasonry, 306
    in More's *Utopia*, 176
    plea for unity of in *Macaria*, 218
    replaced by science, 282
    Saint-Simon's view of, 281
    in Smith's *Theory of Moral Sentiments*, 244–47
    and spiritual development as distraction to affluence, 370
    and taboos in settled life, 15–16
    in Turgot's view of progress, 261–62
    and urban-dominated civilization, 20. *See also* Christian Church; Christianity; Islam
Rensselaer, Stephen van, 304–05
Republic (Plato), 51, 53
resurrection of the dead
    in *The Apocalypse of Peter*, 127
    Augustine's view of, 142
    in *The Book of Daniel*, 103–04
    in Hebrew Bible, 99–100
    in New Testament, 122–23
    in Paul, 116, 118–19
    in *The Revelation to John*, 133
    in Zoroastrianism, 80, 90
The Revelation to John (*Apocalypse*)
    described, 130–34
    impact on Augustine of, 139–44
    influence on Joachim of Fiore, 149
    medieval commentary on, 145
    and Taborites, 161–62
    use of by African Americans, 134–37
revenge, 344–45
Ricardo, David
    on economic growth, 325–32, 374
    religion of, 404n14

on technology, 329–30, 374, 405n29, 405n33
Roman Empire
  advances of, 74
  Christianity's accommodation to, 139, 141–42
  and economic improvement, 72
  extent of, 40–41
  and *The Revelation to John*, 130, 132
  in *The Second Book of Esdras*, 112
  Tiburtine Sibyl's view of, 146
Rosicrucians, 309
Rostow, Walt, 408n1
Rousseau, Jean Jacques, 235–40, 242, 366–67
Royal Society, 219, 221, 398n94

Sabbath, 145
Saint-Ange, Walter de, 314
Saint-Simon, Henri de
  on essence of Christianity, 290–91
  ideas of inspired applied science, 312, 403n89
  interest in perfecting civilization, 278–83
  on politics and political economy, 286–89, 370–71
  views on industrial production, 283–91, 370–71, 373
Śāntideva, 64–65
Saoshyants, 83, 392n13
Sargon the Great, 30–31
Say, Jean Baptiste, 287, 401n22
science/scientific knowledge
  and ability to predict with, 280, 354–55
  advances during 15th-16th centuries, 201–02
  advances of insufficient for expansion, xxi
  in Andreae's *Christianopolis*, 190, 191, 192
  Bacon's conception of and tie to economic expansion, 277
  and Bacon's ideas for research, 210–11
  and Bacon's *New Atlantis*, 207–12, 220
  and Bacon's uniting with technology, 365–66
  as basis for economics, 287, 289, 375
  and Comte's civilizational development, 293–94
  and Comte's full development of humans, 299–302
  Condorcet's belief in spread of, 269–70, 271
  and Condorcet's view on human affairs, 264–67
  and creation of Royal Society, 219
  F. Bacon's view it serves human prosperity, 206–07, 222
  and freemasonry, 306, 309–11, 372
  how Bacon allies religion with, 214–16
  and idea for clearing house of information, 218–19
  in India and China, xxi
  Jevons' belief in economics as, 352–54, 375
  messianic view of, 314–15
  in More's *Utopia*, 177–78, 220
  and *Nova Solyma*, 200
  and Platte's view of in *Macaria*, 217–18
  of political economy, 287–89, 328, 329, 331–32, 374
  replacing politics with, 287, 373
  replacing religion, xxv, 282
  role in Saint-Simon's perfection of civilization, 278–83
  Rousseau's view of, 236
  and Saint-Simon's ideas for administration of economy, 286–89, 371
  of scholastics, 204–05
  Turgot's views on, 255–58, 259–61, 277
  in works of English educational reform, 217. *See also* applied science; technology
scripture interpretation, 147–48
The Second Book of Esdras, 110–12
Second Coming of Christ
  in *The Apocalypse of Peter*, 125–26
  Augustine's view of, 142–43
  in Black Christian thinking, 135–36
  and Joachim of Fiore, 148
  in Pseudo-Methodius, 146–47

and Taborites, 160, 161
self-cultivation, 64, 65–67
self-discipline, 170, 200
Seneca, 182, 183
sensibility, 249–51, 252–53, 271–72
sentimentalism, 345
settled life, 6–8, 9, 383n20
sexagesimal numerical system, 36–37
The Sibylline Oracles, 125, 127–30
Sigismund, King, 163
sixth great extinction, xviii
Sketch for a Historical Picture of the Progress of the Human Mind (Condorcet), 264–70, 281
slavery, 28, 31, 41
Smith, Adam
    compared to Turgot, 262
    how he differs from D. Ricardo, 331
    how his view of morality differs from Bentham's, 343–44
    influence on D. Ricardo, 326
    interest in working class, 317–19
    and the "invisible hand," 247
    on technology, 248, 322–23, 404n12
    and *Theory of Moral Sentiments*, 241–47, 367–68
    and theory of wealth creation, 319–25, 373
    and *Wealth of Nations*, 247–48, 317–25
society, 163, 289, 290–91, 296–98
sociology, 294
Socrates
    on doing wrong and suffering it, 45–48
    in Plato's dialogues, 43–47, 51–53, 68
    Saint-Simon's view of, 282
    view of citizenship, 184
    view of wisdom, 48–50
soul
    in Book of Dreams, 109
    in Jewish apocalyptic literature, 113
    Plato's theory of, 50–51
    in *The Second Book of Esdras*, 111
    Socrates' idea of improving, 44–45
    Zoroastrian view of, 84–88, 90
Sparta, 42
spirits, 4–5, 14

The Spirituals, 153–56
spirit *versus* flesh, 107, 113, 114–16
state, the, 182–83, 186, 194. See also government
Stoicism
    and accordance with nature, 59–60
    in Andreae's *Christianopolis*, 190
    and B. Mandeville, 230, 235
    Cicero's tie to, 389n23
    cosmology of, 60–61, 389n38
    and critical judgement, 61
    and detachment, 61–63
    of Epictetus, 61–63, 65
    impact on Christianity of, 72
    importance of performance over goals in, 55–56, 68
    influence on medieval thinkers, 144
    and J. Lipsius, 182, 184–85
    of Marcus Aurelius, 67–72
    and moral virtue, 53–56
    in *Nova Solyma*, 198–99, 200
    in Smith's *Theory of Moral Sentiments*, 241, 244
Sumerian civilization, 20, 27, 29–30
sympathy, 241–42, 249, 336–37, 338, 367

A Table of the Springs of Action (Bentham), 335, 341–42, 346
Taborites, 160–64
Taoism, 58–59
Tao-te ching, 58
technology
    advances in 15th–16th centuries, 202
    advances in Greco-Roman world of, 72–74
    advances of insufficient for expansion, xxi
    A. Smith on, 248, 322–23, 404n12
    in Bacon's *New Atlantis*, 210, 211, 220
    and Bacon's uniting of science with, 365–66
    in *The Book of Enoch*, 105–06
    D. Ricardo's view of importance to economy, 329–30, 374, 405n29, 405n33

of earliest settled life, 7
effect on Europe in 19th century, 332
in India and China, xxi, 202, 390n71
in *Nova Solyma*, 198
Rousseau on, 239
in *The Sibylline Oracles*, 127
Turgot on, 263
united with science in *Christianopolis*, 191
in works of English educational reform, 217
theological approach, 292, 294
Theory of Moral Sentiments (Smith), 241–47, 262, 322
Thierry, Augustin, 279
thought-systems, xxi, xxii
Tiburtine Sibyl, 145–46
Tonnies, Ferdinand, 21–28, 379. *See also Gemeinschaft und Gesellschaft.*
trade
and disease, 10
D. Ricardo on, 329–30, 374
in Jevons' view of markets, 350–52
in Neolithic era, 8
as part of A. Smith's view of wealth creation, 321–25
of Persian empire, 78
traditional constraints on expansion, xix–xx, xxiv, xxvi, 39–40, 74, 201, 360–61
transhumance, 8–9
trauma, 27, 37
Turgot, Anne Robert-Jacques
on Descartes, 259
Manuels' view of, 258
role of religion in his view of progress, 260–61
view of science, 277
views on progress of, 254–65, 275, 368–69
tyranny, 257–58

Ubertino of Casale, 155
unintended but beneficial consequences, 70, 234, 247, 255, 262
universal love, 309–11
urban-dominated civilization
beginnings of, 19–21
cultural features of, 1
and development of commerce, 29
dissatisfaction with their world, 39–40
examples of, 2
the Gesellschaft character of, 25–27, 377–78
impacts of, 360, 376, 377–78
and imperialism, 30–31, 92, 101, 360
L. Mumford on, 384n4, 385n5
Rousseau's view of impact of property on, 239–40
and slavery, 28
thought-systems which arose in, xx–xxi
and war, 21, 28
utilitarianism
application to economics by Jevons, 348–50
Bentham's conception of, 338–46, 375, 406n62
described, 399n44
Jevons' approval of Bentham's, 346–47
and Jevons' view of how markets work, 350–52
of S. De Grouchy, 253–54
Utopia (More), 171–81, 220–23
utopia/utopian writing
and Bacon's *New Atlantis*, 207–12
B. Mandeville's view of, 229–30, 235
comparison of More's *Utopia* with Bacon's *New Atlantis*, 220–23
dark side of regarding colonialism, 274–75
of Hebrew prophets, 97, 101
impact of the Enlightenment on, 226
importance of in bringing on eco-catastrophe, xxiv
inspired by turmultuous times, 192–93
in Jewish apocalyptic literature, 113
J. Lipsius' opens door to view of, 186, 187
Joachim Fiore's view of human design of, 150
of late 17th to early 18th centuries, 219
and *Macaria*, 217–18
and More's *Utopia*, 171–81
Protestant views of, 187–201, 202, 366

of S. De Grouchy, 252
of S. Gott and *Nova Solyma*, 193
of Taborites, 163
and Zoroastrianism, 80
Utraquism, 159

Venerable Bede, 145
Via Lucis (Commenius), 218
via moderna, 159
vices, 226–35, 240
virtue/excellence
    J. Lipsius' views on, 183
    military, 237
    political origin of, 232–33, 234–35
    in Smith's *Theory of Moral Sentiments*, 244
    in Socratic dialogue, 44–46, 48, 53
    and Stoicism, 53–56
virtue of humanity, 66, 177
vocation, 169, 170

Waldensians, 161
war
    and agriculture, 10
    in *The Book of Enoch*, 106
    development of, 15
    in England, 218, 219
    feature of civilization, 1
    and Greek civilization, 41, 42
    in India, 57
    and Middle Eastern civilizations, 31, 32, 35
    of religion in Europe, 192, 203
    and Roman Empire, 72
    in Sumeria, 28
    and technology, 210
    and urban-dominated civilization, 21, 28
    and Zoroastrianism, 91–92
Watchers, the, 104–07, 108–09, 115, 116, 127
water, 20–21, 383n22
wayfarers (viator)
    in Augustine, 143–44
    Calvinist rejection of, 171
    J. Lipsius' view of, 186
    medieval view of humans as, 144–45, 167, 168, 363
Wealth of Nations (Smith), 247–48, 317–25, 326

Weber, Max, 169, 382n8
Webster, Charles, 217
Wenceslaus IV, King, 158
Wesenwille
    and Bhagavadgītā, 57
    character of people ruled by, 23
    described, 21
    how they view goals, 23
    Jewish apocalyptic writing as, 113
    in modern society, 25
    opposition to Kürwille, 24
    theme in *On Constancy*, 182
    three forms, 22
    trauma as result of shift from, 27, 37
    in urban-dominated civilization, 26–27
    and use of language, 30
    and Zoroastrianism's source, 80, 91. *See also* Gemeinschaft
West, modern
    attractiveness of ideology, xxvi, 377
    dominance of the technical in, 385n11
    and explosion of economic development, xxiv, 359–60, 376
    Gesellschaft taking over, 25–26
    impact of French Revolution on, 278
    importance of Plato on, 42
    Kürwille in, 25, 378
    and population increase, xix, 376
    Wesenwille in, 25
Western civilization
    in 18th century, 241
    advances of, 376–77
    as cause of eco-catastrophe, xix, xxiv–xxv, 359
    as destroyer of moderating traditions, xx
    Rousseau on, 240
    and treatment of colonial peoples, 272–74, 275
    Turgot's opinion of, 263
William of Ockham, 155
wisdom, 48–50
women, 14, 234
Wright, Ronald, 378
writing, 29–30, 36–37, 109
Wycliffe, John, 158, 159, 394n29

xenophobia, 24

Zarathustra (Zoroaster), 77–78, 89, 362
Zeno, 54
Žižka, John, 163–64
Zoroastrianism
    and battle between good and evil, 88–91, 362
    conception of heaven and hell from, 84–88
    cosmology of, 79–81
    and Frashegird (Making Wonderful), 90
    and free choice, 82–84
    and Gemeinschaft, 91, 362
    influence on Hebrew prophets, 97, 98, 99, 101
    influence on Jewish apocalyptic writing, 103, 113
    influence on *The Book of Enoch*, 105, 106
    and morality, 80, 81–84
    realm of flesh in, 115
    spread of, 77–79

Other Titles from University of Alberta Press

NUMINOUS SEDITIONS
Interiority and Climate Change
TIM LILBURN
Explores how poetry and the West's contemplative tradition can help us bear the sorrows of climate change.

THE LARGER CONVERSATION
Contemplation and Place
TIM LILBURN
Philosophical commentaries on the difficult task of forming a deep, respectful relationship with the land.

UNSUSTAINABLE OIL
Facts, Counterfacts and Fictions
JON GORDON
Groundbreaking study of theoretical, political, and environmental issues around the culture and ethics of petroculture.

More information at uap.ualberta.ca